ALEXANDER CAMPBELL

Adventurer in Freedom

A Literary Biography

VOLUME TWO

Portrait of Alexander Campbell
in middle age
Painted by James Bogle.
Collection of D.Duane Cummins.

ALEXANDER

Adventurer in Freedom

CAMPBELL

A Literary Biography

VOLUME TWO

Eva Jean Wrather

Edited by D. Duane Cummins

A *project of*
TCU Press
and the
Disciples of Christ Historical Society
Fort Worth, *Texas*

Library of Congress Cataloging-in-Publication Data

Wrather, Eva Jean.
Alexander Campbell: adventurer in freedom: a literary biography / Eva
Jean Wrather; edited by D. Duane Cummins. — 1st ed.
p.cm.
Includes bibliographical references and index.
ISBN 13: 978-0-87565-343-3 (alk. paper)
ISBN 10: 0-87565-343-X
1. Campbell, Alexander, 1788-1866. I. Cummins, D. Duane. II.
Title.
BX7343.C2W69 2007
286.6'092-dc22
2004011034

TCU Press
P. O. Box 298300
Fort Worth, TX 76129
817-257-7822 / fax: 817-257-5075
email: tcupress@tcu.edu
web: http://www.prs.tcu.edu/
to order books: 800-826-8911

Designed by Barbara M. Whitehead

CONTENTS

VOLUME TWO

Acknowledgments vii

Preface ix

BOOK THREE:

The Temple is Destroyed (1823-1830)

ACKNOWLEDGMENTS

Several versions of the Campbell manuscript written by Eva Jean Wrather are housed in a filing cabinet at the Disciples of Christ Historical Society. Since her death in 2001, an enormous addition of private papers has been added to the society's Wrather collection. For the privilege of studying the early draft of her work and for access to her private correspondence as well as selected essays from among her collection, I express enormous gratitude to the historical society. Their extreme patience in photocopying a huge quantity of material for my use is genuinely appreciated. Particular words of appreciation are due David McWhirter and Sara Harwell for their helpful research support, and Peter and Lynne Morgan for their gracious presence during sessions with Eva Jean, and, along with Doug Foster, for pressing this work toward final publication.

James and Dudley Seale stand tall among those who should receive acknowledgment. Jim, former president of the historical society, first approached me about the possibility of becoming involved in this project and then helped arrange my early conversations with Eva Jean. Jim and Dudley then provided the needed funds through the James and Dudley Seale Publications Fund to support the publication of the manuscript—a philanthropic act for which the entire church is grateful.

My trusted colleague in historical research, Jeanne Cobb, archivist at Bethany College, deserves special commendation for her invaluable assistance in accumulating illustrations for all three volumes and providing appropriate captions. Among her sources were Ian S. Davidson's excellent personal Campbell Heritage Collection; the Bethany archives at Bethany College; the Upper Ohio Valley History Collection at Bethany College; the library and archives of the Disciples of Christ Historical Society; and the personal collection of Eva Jean Wrather. Her thoughtful reading of the manuscript was extremely helpful to me.

Lester McAllister offered steady and insightful guidance along the way, having read all of volumes I and II. And most especially I acknowledge my wife Suzi, who typed two drafts of the rewritten manuscript for volumes I and II, and more importantly, gave happy encouragement and abiding good cheer across the whole sixteen-year labor. Finally, I express appreciation to TCU Press for its faith and confidence in this work, and the helpful influence it can bring to the life of the Christian Church (Disciples of Christ).

D. Duane Cummins
June 4, 2006

PREFACE

Volume one of this literary biography of Alexander Campbell contains a twenty five-page preface detailing the seventy-year chronicle of the research, writing, methods, and sources used by Eva Jean Wrather. My own involvement as editor of this manuscript has reached sixteen years with the publication of this second volume. The third and final volume remains to be edited and published.

This volume covers *The Christian Baptist* years, 1823–1830. Eva Jean believed this was a crucial period in Campbell's life and that what he wrote during those years in The Christian Baptist was misunderstood by later historians and contributed to devaluation of Campbell's place in American religious history and of his role as a reformer. She referred to these chapters as the "hinge" of the book and she wanted to set the record straight on the consistency of Campbell's thought from the days of *The Christian Baptist* through the end of his career. The final chapter in this volume, Chapter XIII—The Charms of the Political Life, Eva Jean regarded "in some ways my favorite chapter" of the entire biography.

The narrative of this volume begins with the development of

the prospectus for *The Christian Baptist,* continues with the response—both hostile and supportive—of Baptists and Presbyterians to the new periodical, public debates with W. L. MacCalla and Robert Owen, and concludes with his election and service as a delegate to the Virginia Constitutional Convention in 1829. The long series of articles on "The Restoration of the Ancient Order of Things," another series on the "Holy Spirit," the famous "Third Epistle of Peter," and the parable of the "Iron Bedstead" are all here. And throughout the decade a number of glimpses of his home life also appear—the death of Margaret, his marriage to Selina, management challenges on his farm, and the birth of his daughter, Margaret.

Eva Jean's facile pen and inimitable style are apparent throughout the manuscript. The editing of Volume I eliminated the equivalent of approximately two chapters of material; and Volume II eliminated about the same quantity. In both volumes this was done to reduce repetition without doing injury to the flow of the narrative or to the writing style. Other editing included polishing a passage here and there, checking punctuation and grammar, and updating language usage where it may have been offensive. I have done my best to preserve the integrity of Eva Jean's literary purpose—as well as her historic purpose in regaining for Campbell his rightful place among America's and the world's religious reformers. Eva Jean has succeeded in revealing Alexander Campbell's humanity, his learnedness, and his effectiveness as a public communicator. I hope you will find much pleasure in reading this part of the story of her beloved Mr. Campbell.

BOOK THREE

The Temple is Destroyed
1823–1830

"I call no man master upon the earth …
I have been so long disciplined
in the school of free inquiry,
that, if I know my own mind,
there is not a man upon the earth
whose authority can influence me,
any farther than he comes with
the authority of evidence,
reason and truth."

Alexander Campbell

PROSPECTUS

OF THE

CHRISTIAN BAPTIST,

A Monthly Paper,

To be Published on BUFFALOE CREEK, Brooke County, Va.

EDITED BY ALEXANDER CAMPBELL, AND PUBLISHED BY SOLOMON SALA.

THE "CHRISTIAN BAPTIST" shall espouse the cause of no religious sect, excepting that Ancient Sect, called "CHRISTIANS FIRST AT ANTIOCH." Its sole object shall be the eviction of truth, and the exposure of error in doctrine and practice. The Editor acknowledging no standard of religious faith or works other than the Old and New Testaments, and the latter as the only standard of the religion of Jesus Christ will, intentionally at least, oppose nothing which it contains, and recommend nothing which it does not enjoin. Having no worldly interest at stake from the adoption or reprobation of any article of faith or religious practice—having no gift nor religious office of any worldly emolument to blind his eyes or to pervert his judgment—he hopes to manifest that he is an impartial advocate of truth.

This work shall embrace the following items in the prosecution of its object.

    I. Animadversions on the morals of the Christian religion.
    II. Strictures on the religious systems of the present day, and the leading measures of the religious sects of our country.
    III. Essays on man's primitive state, and on the Patriarchal, Jewish, and Christian dispensations.
    IV. Religious News, or a record of the passing events of our time, accompanied with such remarks as they may naturally excite.
    V. Historical Sketches, or retrospective views of the origin and progress of the most reputable opinions and practices of modern times.
    VI. Biographical notices, and religious anecdotes.
    VII. General Views of the religious and political state of nations not professing the Christian religion.

Such are the contemplated outlines of the "Christian Baptist," for the accomplishment of which he must appeal to the professing community. Having obtained a few Christian friends, of general information, to co-operate with him, who are devoted to the pure and undefiled religion of the Gospel of Christ, the Editor flatters himself that this publication will be highly interesting and useful to those into whose hands it may fall.

CONDITIONS.

For a year or two until this work shall have established its own character, each number shall contain 24 pages duodecimo, published on the first Monday of every month, at ONE DOLLAR per annum, exclusive of postage; to be paid on the delivery of the first number.

No subcription will be taken for a less term than one year, nor will a paper be discontinued until all arrearages are paid.

A failure at the expiration of a year to notify a discontinuance, will be considered a new engagement.

Those obtaining ten subscribers, and guaranteeing the payment, shall have one copy gratis.

All communications to the Editor must be post paid.

BUFFALOE, March, 12, 1823.

N. B. As it is intended to issue the first number in June or July next, those holding subscription papers will please return them in April or May, or an account of the names of subscribers and their place of residence.

SUBSCRIBERS' NAMES.	RESIDENCE.	NO. OF COPIES

"Ecrasez L'Infame"

WHEN Alexander Campbell decided to become an editor he laid his plans with customary thoroughness. He purchased a printing press and installed it in a one-story frame building constructed at the foot of Cemetery Hill, near the ford in Buffaloe Creek. It was a convenient location for a press, as the plates could be washed in the waters of the creek. Cautious Scot that he was, Alexander did not plan to launch the publication on an ambitious scale. His magazine would be small, about four by six and three-eighths inches, running eighteen pages to the number, and issued monthly. Printed on inexpensive paper, in appearance it would not be prepossessing.

The name Campbell selected, *The Christian Baptist,* was not one to excite attention. He had preferred a different title—perhaps just *The Christian*—but his friend, Walter Scott, prevailed upon him to add the name *Baptist,* thinking their supporters in the Baptist church might be better pleased. Whatever the title of the new publication those who knew its editor knew its pages would not be dull.

In the spring of 1823 Campbell published the Prospectus for his magazine. It proclaimed that:

> *The Christian Baptist* shall espouse the cause of no religious sect, excepting that ancient sect "called Christians first at Antioch." Its sole object shall be the eviction of truth and the exposing of error in doctrine and practice. The editor, acknowledging no standard of religious faith or works other than the Old and New Testament, and the latter as the only standard of the religion of Jesus Christ, will, intentionally at least, oppose nothing which it contains and recommend nothing which it does not enjoin. Having no worldly interest at stake from the adoption or reprobation of any articles of faith or religious practice, having no gift nor religious emolument to blind his eyes or to pervert his judgment, he hopes to manifest that he is an impartial advocate of truth.

Campbell warned that *The Christian Baptist* would embrace a range of subjects and pursue a course not precisely similar to those of any other periodical of the day. Then he added,

> We have learned one lesson of great importance in the pursuit of truth: one that acts as a pioneer to prepare the way of knowledge—one that cannot be adopted and acted upon, but the result must be salutary. It is this: never

"In this out-of-the-way place he had fitted up a printing office, in a little frame of a house, just sixteen feet square. . . .I found the office on the bank of the creek, so near the water's edge that the pressman wet the paper for the presswork by dipping directly into the stream, selecting a big stone to lay the paper board upon and another for the dry paper, while he stood half leg-deep in water, which gently played over his bare feet . . . .The printing office, as I have said, was a single room, about sixteen feet square, unconnected with any other building, and it had in it two double composing stands, a bank and a hand press. This made it pretty close quarters; and in the latter part of the summer when I was there, when Mr. Campbell printed his debate with Owen, the little office overflowed, and they put up stands for three or four printers to set type out of doors under sheds. . . .The printing office at Buffaloe Creek was in the corner of a field, some distance from Campbell's own house, but near to one occupied by a tenant, where any transient printers boarded . . . .I boarded with Mr. Young while I was there."

Top: *It is believed that the shed described by William Howells later evolved into this building and lean-to where The Christian Baptist was printed during its final years.*
Above: *The original print shop, built in 1823 was described by William Cooper Howells, an itinerant printer who, during the 1820s, worked for Alexander Campbell.*

to hold any sentiment or proposition as more certain than the evidence on which it rests… All beyond this we esteem enthusiasm—all short of it incredulity.

He concluded with the promise to his readers "that we shall neither approve nor censure any thing without the clearest and most satisfactory evidence from reason and revelation."

Doubtless his method of seeking truth and his promise sounded strange to the ears of a large part of his frontier audience. Was this talk of evidence and reason not more befitting the scientist than the theologian? He was a seeker after truth, and truth, whether religious or scientific, was best discovered through the empirical psychology that John Locke had formed by applying the inductive, scientific method of Francis Bacon. From his first reading of the *An Essay Concerning Human Understanding*, coupled with his first serious studies in philosophy, Campbell believed that Locke's theory of knowledge and Bacon's inductive method, along with the principles of Sir Isaac Newton, subject to some restrictions by the teaching of Thomas Reid, opened the door to the only reasonable process of philosophical thought. Campbell had no intention of abandoning these tools of knowledge as he took up his pen to become a religion editor.

He opposed the theory of reason as a source of knowledge in itself, superior to and independent of sense perceptions. Undiluted empiricism, he realized, would lead to sheer muddle-headedness and futility; it must be corrected by clear, cogent thinking. The human mind was not so simple that any clear absolute line could be drawn between sensationalism and intellectualism. Locke himself admitted both sensation and reflection. Both Bacon and Locke talked much of reason. Yet there was no danger of their tending back toward "the rationalistic orgy of the

Middle Ages," toward the sterile speculation, the endless elaboration of theories untested by experience, which Alexander so much despised.

His respect for reason, like that of the humanists, was a "respect for rational judgment, emancipated from custom and dogma." Like the humanists, his was a belief in reason "in its richest sense of belief in an intelligible universe and a humanity capable of direction by reason." He would lay stress "on what has been happily called the quality of being 'judgmatical' [*sic*] as the fine quality of reason…" He would place his trust in experiment, compromise, and judgment rather than abstract rationalism.

Influenced by Bacon and Locke, Campbell adopted an attitude toward "pure reason" and "absolute truths" which, three-quarters of a century later, placed him in the company of pragmatists. In answer to the rationalists, presuming in their minds a picture of reality "ready made and complete for all eternity," the pragmatists replied that however fixed certain elements of reality may be, humanity still has freedom to deal with them, for reality is "still in the making" and awaiting "part of its complexion from the future." Bacon had written, "we [could not] hope to succeed, if we arrogantly searched for the sciences in the narrow cells of the human understanding, and not submissively in the wider world." Campbell would apply the same canon to complex religious doctrines, about which he felt no person had the right or the power by sheer reason to presuppose some final "truth-for-all-time."

Locke spoke in the characteristic voice of the eighteenth century—"a belief in Reason happily espoused to Common-Sense." It was the voice most likely to be harkened to by the practical young farmer-editor on the Buffaloe. In the Scottish school of philosophy, in fact, he had found that the term "common sense" was used, according to Reid's own words, "as only another name for one branch or degree of reason." In the first book of his Essay, Locke made his appeal to "common reason" which he, too, called "common sense."

This emphasis on reason served another purpose in Campbell's philosophy—to put a rein on emotionalism and enthusiasm. Here again he followed the lodestar of John Locke. In his chapter "Enthusiasm" Locke wrote, "Government of our Passions is the right Improvement of Liberty." Locke would always travel, as would Campbell after him, the good Confucian, Aristotelian route of the middle way. Locke made the bold claim that "the passions of man may be controlled by his reason, tacking from side to side in its long progress through a universe of experience, calculating like a scientist or navigator the probabilities as it goes," though he would make the reservation somewhat sadly that in religion, "men make a greater allowance to raving, though indeed it be a more dangerous madness; but men are apt to think in religion they may, and ought to quit their reason." To follow "the guidance of reason ascending upon the stairway of experience" was Locke's creed. It was a creed fundamentally hostile to fanaticism.

Steering the way between raving enthusiasm and cold reason, such was the course Campbell attempted to set for himself. And he could find some light along the way in his esteemed Samuel Johnson, the pragmatic doctor. In his *History of Rasselas* Johnson had written: "Of the uncertainties of our present state, the most dreadful and alarming is the uncertain continuance of reason...All power of fancy over reason is a degree of insanity."

But it was in Locke that Campbell found his surest touchstone. He thought Locke especially convincing in his attitude toward reason and emotion, where he placed the accent on liberty. Locke would insist that reason, "furnished by new individual experience...is able to control the natural inclinations," and in this power of control lies the freedom of human beings. He believed that humans are, "of [their] own quality, thinking being[s] gifted with reason," and their natural liberty is a consequence of that quality. He was quite ready to positively affirm: "We are born free, as we are born rational." It was an affirmation Campbell found peculiarly satisfying.

Nor did Alexander have any fears that embracing rationalism would lead to a denial or even a weakening of his religious faith. It might have done so in David Hume and Thomas Paine. But Campbell stood secure on the ground of his intellectual forbears. What better disclaimer of unbelief could he want than the words from Bacon's essay *Of Atheism?*

> I had rather believe all the fables in the Legend, and the Talmud and the [Koran], than that this universal frame is without a mind …A little philosophy inclineth a man's mind to atheism; but depth in philosophy bringeth men's minds about to religion.

"Man would be at a great loss," Locke wrote, "if he had nothing to direct him but what has the certainty of true knowledge." Human beings have their reason, their practical judgment, which operates in "the twilight of probability" and which, Locke did not doubt, would attest to the "reasonableness" of belief in the ultimate mysteries. By maintaining his "more sober theory of the limits of human knowledge," Locke steered his middle way between the dogmatic knower who proclaims his absolute truth and the dogmatic skeptic who proclaims there is no truth. The title of his work, *The Reasonableness of Christianity*, was significant. Revelation in the Bible might not be attested by pure rationalism, but it was in harmony with man's best judgment. It appeared "reasonable" in the light of man's sense experience, together with his memory, imagination, and judgment.

Alexander accepted the efficacy of reason and the scientific method, but in his acceptance he would always keep a wary eye on the scientist to see that he did not usurp the place of Deity. He realized that, as the person of experiment is more mature than the person of dogma, so the person of faith may be more mature than the person of science; for when the scientist turns materialist he is reducing life to simple certainties and dogmatically denying the existence of truths that cannot be reduced to exact formula and tested in a laboratory. Campbell had not yet worked out in detail his philosophic position on the vexing problems of faith and reason—at least, no considered statement of his views would come for several years from the press on the Buffaloe. Although he was accepting the Lockian theory that knowledge of natural and material things comes from sensation and reflection; knowledge of spiritual things comes from Divine Revelation. Because this Revelation has to operate through the senses, it opens to the senses a world which natural reason could never perceive. Alexander assured his public that he would prove all things to them by "evidence from reason and revelation."

Campbell's opening essay was entitled "The Christian Religion." It contained his concept of the ideal church, the Apostolic Church, and the sad plight into which it had fallen in the nineteenth century. Those who subscribed to the magazine in the hope of finding lively controversial reading, well seasoned with satire, were not disappointed. This essay alone furnished material for a hundred discussions. Its opening sentence contained a challenge to the ideology of all orthodox Calvinists: "Christianity is the perfection of that divine philanthropy which was gradually developing itself for four thousand years." Since Calvin in matters of religion, had been so completely lacking in the historic sense that he denied any possibility of the idea of "development" in God's relation to humanity, this statement by itself was enough to make Campbell suspect in the eyes of Calvin's followers. Covenant Theologians, revolting against Calvinism, protested that God could and did change methods of dealing with human beings as the needs of humanity evolved. Though Campbell had already advanced this theory in his "Sermon on the Law," he did not emphasize it in his essay on "The Christian Religion." This time he was using the idea of "development" to prove that God had finally reached the consummation of His plan in the perfect revelation—vouchsafed in Jesus Christ. The glory and power of Christ was always at the center of his thinking, and Campbell now wrote eloquently in his attempt to describe the "person, character, and reign of the Messiah, the Prince" that exhausts "all the beauties of language, all the grandeur and resplendencies of creation, to give some faint resemblances of them."

Passing to the nature of "the societies called churches" first established by Christ's apostles, Campbell declared:

> The ONLY BOND OF UNION among them was faith in him and submission to his will …Their meeting on the first day of the week was at all times alike solemn, joyful and interesting …their piety did not at one time rise to paroxysms, and their zeal to effervescence, and, by and by, languish into frigid ceremony and lifeless form. It was the pure, clear, and swelling current of love to God, of love to man, expressed in all the variety of doing good.

Among historic advocates for restoration of the primitive church, the motive of union was virtually non-existent. They were intent on restoring the "true Apostolic Church," not on solidifying Christendom. "Their object was not to be united with other Christians, but to be right." And the actual result of their efforts was, on the whole, divisive.

Campbell had come to the conclusion this was true because they tried to restore primitive Christianity on too many points; they talked about following "simple" apostolic Christianity, but did not reduce to simple enough terms their requirement for church communion. His vision was to fuse the two ideals of restoring primitive Christianity and of unifying the church. He did not doubt that unity could be achieved by reducing terms of admission to a unified church to the simplest essentials and granting liberty of opinion on all non-essentials. Influenced by his theological and philosophical background and predilections, Campbell naturally held his own theories about the interpretation of the Scriptures; but insofar as it was possible to hold such an ideal, he never intended to allow his own theology, however true he might consider it, to become a test for church membership. Here he was to make another significant contribution. Approaching the problem of reformation from the stand-point of promoting the unity of the church, he observed that there was far less room for difference of opinion about what the apostles had required as conditions of entrance into the church than about the doctrines, the organization, and the forms of worship of the early church. On this basis he decided to approach the problem of formulating a plan for union.

The plan, however, was not to be immediately presented in detail to the readers of *The Christian Baptist*. The statement in his opening essay—"The ONLY BOND OF UNION among them [the churches established by the Apostles] was faith in him and submission to his will"—could scarcely be called specific. Alexander's first objective was the seeking out and exposing of abuses in the current religious systems. To his task, his readers were assured, he brought enthusiasm, vitality, a talent for satire, and a personality that compelled attention whether or not it won approval.

Alexander contended that the early Christians not only enjoyed unity of spirit through personal loyalty to Christ but also that: "The order of their assemblies was uniformly the same." And this uniformity was possible, he believed, because of the "glorious simplicity" of their faith and practice:

No subscription to abstract propositions framed by synods; no decrees of councils sanctioned by kings; no rules of practice commanded by ecclesiastical courts were imposed on them as terms of admission into, or of continuance in this holy brotherhood ...In their church capacity alone they moved ...They dare not ...exalt the inventions of men above the wisdom of God.

Comparing this simplicity with the complexity of the religious machinery of his day, Campbell exclaimed:

But alas! 'how is the fine gold become dim!' Instead of the apostles' doctrine, simply and plainly exhibited in the New Testament, we have got the sublime science of theology, subdivided into scholastic, polemic, dogmatic and practical divinity. We have countless creeds, composed of terms and phrases, dogmas and speculations...Instead of the divinely established order of bishops and deacons...we have popes, cardinals, archbishops...presiding elders, circuit preachers, ...licentiates... monks, friars, &c, &c....

Campbell thus declared that creeds and metaphysical speculation were worthless because they were concerned not with the facts of religion, but with theories about the facts. These speculations, in his view, were worse than worthless. They were a positive evil, when they were exalted into terms of communion and thus prevented union on the simple basis of faith in, and obedience to, Christ. There was a further evil; by so complicating the terms of salvation, the freedom of the individual was destroyed. Christianity, at least that part of it that was essential to salvation, was supposed to be so simple a way-faring child could comprehend it. However, in Campbell's view, a tyrannous ecclesiastical system had come into existence when its teachings were distorted "into a mystery fit to employ linguists, philosophers, doctors of divinity, all their leisure hours, at a handsome per annum, in studying and then giving publicity to their own discoveries, or in retailing those of others."

In his opening essay, Campbell stated his case and it was thought to be a strong case by the audience for which it was intended—the independent, self-sufficient empire builders of the western waters. The French Revolution had founded a republic with a stirring motto: Liberty, Equality, Fraternity. Now an ecclesiastical revolution marshaled its forces behind the triune phrase: Liberty, Unity, Simplicity.

Readers of *The Christian Baptist*, especially later generations of religious historians, did not always perceive the fine distinctions so apparent to its editor. And quite ironically, the very qualities that made his little magazine so widely read, also helped contribute to its misunderstanding.

Having conceived the magazine as a means of broadcasting the seeds of reformation as far as the long arm of the press could reach, he gave free rein to his talents for wit and satire, employing every rhetorical device of exaggeration and paradox in order to attract the widest possible audience. There was a deeper intent, of course. The young editor viewed his paramount role as that of prophet, called to sweep away the "rubbish of the ages" and restore the temple of God to its pristine beauty and purity. With equal pride he also wore a second hat, that of "the adventurer in freedom;" and it was no accident that in 1823 he had timed the first issue of *The Christian Baptist* so that his Preface might bear the date, July 4.

For both Campbells the question of the nature of the church was answered in *The Declaration and Address*. The church is the mystical body of Christ, and therefore the rending of his visible body on earth is sin. Here was the high doctrine of the church.

As the Campbells read history, the long descent of the church into error had begun when Roman Catholicism transferred this authority from the whole church to a priestly hierarchy within the church; and Protestantism, in overreaction, made its stand on the "bible alone" doctrine, and so reduced the church to the status of a "moral society," with its emphasis on the direct intervention of the Holy Spirit operating on the individual conscience. When *The Christian Baptist* took issue with the "enthusiasm" of frontier camp meetings and proposed a scriptural concept of faith as belief in testimony, its editor provoked the outcry that he was denying the action of the Holy Spirit—an ultimate heresy. In truth, he was again affirming a high doctrine: That the Holy Spirit, having descended on the church at Pentecost, henceforth remained operative on earth through the actions of this mystical body of Christ. Both *The Declaration and Address* and *The Christian Baptist* argued for right government the church looks to two seats of authority: first, to the New Testament; and second, to "right reason," the consensus of the enlightened judgment of the church itself.

Luther had restored the New Testament emphasis on the "priesthood of all believers," but Protestantism had then immediately set off in two directions. On the one hand, it had reverted to old error with its own power structure of clerical orders and its own unholy alliances of church and state; on the other hand it had subverted the priesthood of all believers into the "priesthood of every believer" and so issued in the plague of small, jangling sects, each convinced of its own infallible interpretation of Holy Scripture.

One of the sharpest paragraphs in *The Christian Baptist* was directed to those Populists in politics and Independents in religion, who frequently, the editor warned, are "the greatest tyrants in the world," each one wishing to reign as king or pope in his own little domain. The real challenge was to safeguard both liberty and order by steering a true course between "clerical despotism" and "licentious equality."

The significance of Campbell's contribution here lay in his interpretation of the relationship between the church and its overseers, and of the nature of the authority vested in those overseers. From the first issue of his magazine he had proudly flaunted his allegiance to the philosophy of the Enlightenment in assault on the twin engines of tyranny: priest craft and kingcraft. A clear conception of his views on the Christian ministry emerged only through realization that his attacks were not so much anticlerical as non-sacerdotal, attacking the methods and systems of priest craft.

In later years he would sometimes baffle critics, friendly or hostile, by asserting that he had not changed his views on church government from the days of *The Christian Baptist*. In this he spoke a profound truth. Throughout a fifty-year ministry, he held constant to his high doctrine of the nature of the church. And this constancy was one element of his strength. Even while voicing his strongest sentiment on congregational independency—"An individual church ... is the only ecclesiastical body recognized in the New Testament"—he was also writing, "All the churches on earth ... are so many communities constituting one kingdom." Moreover, in one of the most eloquent passages of *The Christian Baptist*, he reminded his readers of the divine imperative cementing this union: "In Christ's kingdom a single monosyllable represents the active principle ... That monosyllable is LOVE. Love is the fulfilling of the whole law."

From first to last, the Bethany editor would free both the individual conscience and the individual congregation from fear of excommunication by some higher court, but never from their obligations as members of the one body of Christ, forever bonded together by his love. In Campbell's vision the autonomy of the local congregations and their union in the one body were complementary—not contradictory. He was to employ many fonts of type in the next decade before the Reformers generally would grow into such understanding, and so begin to define a structure of the church in harmony with the genius of their own movement.

Alexander Campbell was not likely to be disturbed by anything the established clergy might say against him. Rather, he expected and even courted their disfavor. One of the early subjects he undertook as editor was a series of satiric articles on "The Clergy."

Had he disliked ecclesiasticism less, Campbell would have been a poor Lockian disciple. The whole philosophy of the Enlightenment was a revolt against absolutism in government, against supernaturalism and ecclesiasticism in religion, and against tradition in both; for from these things came tyranny— tyranny over both body and mind. Turning his attention to the history of ecclesiasticism, Campbell could see it always following an inevitable progression, from power to tyranny, and from tyranny to corruption. Only when Christian sects were weak and unorganized had they pleaded for toleration and liberty. The Puritans had pleaded eloquently for toleration when under the oppression of the Stuarts; having won freedom and power in the new world, they, in turn, became ruthless oppressors of the Quakers. Alexander did not need to turn to written pages of history to find grounds for his fear of a systematized priesthood. Among his mother's people—the little band of exiled Huguenots on the shores of Lough Neagh—he had listened to the tales handed down from their ancestors of the days of heartbreak and terror when they had fled their homes in France to escape the vengeance of the Catholic hierarchy. He had grown to manhood in a country where a Protestant hierarchy in its turn waxed powerful and oppressed the Catholics to a position of ignorant serf-

dom. His childhood had been passed in a condition of near poverty because his own father, though a Protestant, was a Dissenter
who refused "to worship God according to act of Parliament."

So his youth in Ireland had bred in him a natural distrust and
fear of ecclesiastical power; and his experience in America had
not entirely allayed these fears. Some said the attacks of the
Presbyterian Synod on his father left an indelible imprint on
young Alexander. The makers of the Republic, haunted by these
same fears, had fought for a constitutional guarantee against religious oppression. But in his encounter with the "Moral Societies"
of western Pennsylvania, Campbell had seen how quickly any
ecclesiastical body, when holding numerical power, would
assume the prerogative of dictating the conduct of its neighbors in
accordance with its own religious beliefs. The Scots-Irish
Presbyterians of Washington County, Campbell was convinced,
would, if left to themselves, have set up in western Pennsylvania
an inquisition over the morals and habits of its citizens no less
oppressive than those instituted by the Puritans in colonial New
England. That such days might never again return to the country
of his adoption, Alexander was prepared to cast his first blows
against the power of the clergy. Others before him had engaged in
the warfare; and if his foray was to arouse a fiercer counter-attack,
it was because Campbell brought to the fight a magazine controlled by no other will than his own and a natural skill for satiric
attack.

From the start Alexander made it clear that it was the systems
and methods of organized ecclesiasticism he was attacking, not
the individual preacher of independent churches. After all, both
he and his father were ordained ministers! In his first article on the
clergy, he carefully specified at the beginning of his piece:

> Nota Bene.—In our remarks upon the 'Christian
> Clergy,' we never include the Elders or Deacons of a
> Christian Assembly, or those in the New Testament called

the overseers and servants of the Christian Church. These we consider as very different offices.

Nor, of course, in contending that the "kingdom of the clergy" was actuated by an ambition for power and opulence, did Campbell wish to include all clergymen in the charge: "There have been good and pious kings, and there are good and pious clergy."

Nevertheless, the analogy he believed, between "kingship" and "priestcraft" appeared perfect in every instance; "the allied monarchs and the allied clergy resemble a monstrous production of nature which we once saw, two bodies united, and but one soul."

Since the principle on which both rested was inimical to liberty and individual responsibility, both must be subdued. Though Campbell deplored the French Encyclopedists for allowing disgust with corruption in the church to drive them to skepticism, he nevertheless would agree with Diderot that: "Men will never be free till the last king is strangled with the entrails of the last priest."

The "kingdom of the clergy" had acquired their dominion over the people, argued Campbell, by "the use of two grand means." The first of these was "that of an alleged special call of God to what is commonly called the work of the ministry." In Roman Catholicism and Episcopacy this amounted to the lordly doctrine of apostolic succession, to the belief in a class of men divinely set aside as the sole dispensers of God's grace on this earth. Campbell knew that every preacher in the established churches, even to the lowliest and most ignorant circuit rider in the backwoods, believed that God had chosen him by a special effusion of His Spirit. In attacking so cherished a principle, Campbell moved with some reluctance. His own father, Thomas, devoutly believed that God had spoken to his troubled heart one day in County Down and brought him peace. Alexander observed:

I cheerfully admit that there are now, and there were formally, many good men who have advocated the necessity, and expiated on the importance, of a special call of the Holy Spirit to the work of teaching the Christian religion ...But shall we be deterred from examining any principle because good and great men have espoused it? Nay, verily! Should we adopt this course, examination of principles is at an end.

If God actually spoke to humans through the Holy Spirit as he did to the apostles, then, argued Campbell, the pronouncements of a person so chosen would have to be infallible—since the Holy Spirit could not err—and it would hence be "criminal in any to neglect or despise his instructions." Furthermore, if a person claimed to be moved by the Holy Spirit to preach, that person must confirm "his testimony by divine attestations, or by the working of miracles," just as the Twelve had been able to do. Since the clergy could produce no such evidence, reasoned Campbell: "It is then in vain to say they are so moved. Who is called to believe anything without evidence? Does God command any man to believe without evidence? No, most assuredly."

Campbell by no means took the extreme position that a person could not feel a "call" to preach. For he himself was building his whole life on the conviction that the special providence of God had set him aside for a special mission. His conviction, he felt sure, had its origin in reason, not in emotions. He had calmly considered God's special favors to him and by a process of rationalization reached his conclusion to be ordained. Hence, he explained, among "those who believe and understand the Christian religion, there are individuals called, in the subordinate sense of the phrase, to sundry good works ..." To claim anything more in the nature of a "special call" was "a scheme unwarranted by God, founded on pride, ignorance, ambition, and impiety."

The second of the "grand means" employed by the clergy to

secure dominion was, said Campbell, "the confederation of themselves into associated bodies, called councils, synods, associations or conferences." Through assuming this ecclesiastical authority:

> The modern clergy have often placed themselves upon this throne which was given to the apostles only; and they have, if possible, in some instances, been still more impious—they have placed themselves upon the throne of God, and dealt damnation with a liberal hand to all their foes, judging, as they thought, correctly, that whosoever opposed them, opposed God.

He therefore concluded, the "confederated priesthood appears in its naked deformity, unsupported by the most distant allusion to any scriptural warrant." All the "angry contests whether an episcopacy similar to a monarchy, whether a presbytery similar to an aristocracy, or an independency similar to a democracy, be the government instituted by God" appeared alike to Campbell "a mere 'vox et preterea nihil'—a sound and nothing else." For it was his opinion:

> The government of the church is an absolute monarchy, and the Lord Jesus Christ is the absolute monarch, on whose shoulders is the government and in whose hands are the reins. That his will, published in the New Testament, is the sole law of the church; no judicatory, court or tribunal, other than the judgment seat of Christ that every such society, with its bishops and deacons, is the highest tribunal on earth to which an individual Christian can appeal.

Campbell described the church as a society of disciples professing to believe the one grand fact, the Messiah-ship of Jesus, voluntarily submitting to his authority and guidance, having all of them in their Baptism expressed their faith in him and allegiance to him, and expressly meeting together in one place to walk in all his commandments and ordinances. This society, with its bishop or bishops, and its deacon or deacons, as the case may require, is perfectly independent of any tribunal on earth called ecclesiastical. It knows nothing of superior or inferior church judicatories, and acknowledges no laws, no canons or government other than that of the Monarch of the Universe and His laws.

Making use of the two "grand means," the clergy in Campbell's view, had gradually widened the distinction between clergy and laity.

> Behold the mighty difference! And in it see the arrogance of the clergy and the abject servility of the laity.
> ... No class or order of men that ever appeared on earth have obtained so much influence, or acquired so complete an ascendancy over the human mind, as the clergy.
> ... The scheme of a learned priesthood chiefly composed of beneficiaries, has long since proved itself to be a grand device to keep men in ignorance and bondage; a scheme, by means of which the people have been shrewdly taught to put out their own eyes, to fetter their own feet, and to bind the yoke upon their own necks.

Campbell's chief accusation against the clergy was that having converted the Christian religion into an obscure and complex theology. The clergy had set themselves up as the sole interpreters of this religion, and thus, had virtually usurped the authority of the Bible. Under their hands the Bible too often became merely an "armory of proof-text," unrelated sentences being lifted from their context to make an array of proof for some metaphysical theory. Scarcely a word was allowed its full meaning; all must be interpreted allegorically, and often a single clause was elaborated into misty speculation.

Thomas Campbell had once raised the question:

> What is the great difference between withholding the Scriptures from the laity, as the Romanists do, and rendering them unintelligible by arbitrary interpretation, forced criticisms and fanciful explanations, as many Protestants do? ...

Now in his essays on the clergy, Alexander was saying:

> Behold the arrogance of their claims! ... They have said, and of them many still say, they have an exclusive right, an official right to affix the proper interpretation to the scriptures.

Campbell assured his readers that to change this oppressive condition was his chief aim:

> We wish, we cordially wish, to take the New Testament out of the abuses of the clergy, and put it into the hands of the people. And to do this is no easy task, as the clergy have formed the opinions of nine-tenths of Christendom before they could form an opinion of their own. They have ... taught them in creeds, in sermons, in catechisms, in tracts, in pamphlets, in primers ...

Luther had given the people the opportunity of reading the Bible; Campbell would teach them to comprehend it. So "in a subserviency to our grand design," he suggested to his readers "a plan of reading the blessed volume which reason, common sense, and the experience of all who have tried it, recommend and enforce."

First of all, Campbell asserted that the Holy Spirit used language. A revelation in words not understood through common sense, is no revelation at all. With this in mind, the Bible should then be studied by the common-sense "course that we would take to understand any book." It was not a series of proof-texts, but a continuous history and revelation and was to be studied as such. He suggested they first read the gospels—the biographies of Christ—then the Acts of the Apostles, keeping in mind the history of each congregation as they read the Epistles to these churches. During this study, he cautioned: "Not until people studied the Bible, not "until they cast to the moles and to the bats the Platonic speculations, the Pythagorean dreams they have written in their creeds," would simple Christianity be rediscovered, and the people freed from dependence on their priests.

The clergy were angered most by Campbell's comments on the "hireling clergy." From his remarks on the influence over men's minds wielded by the clergy, Campbell continued:

> From this dominion over the feelings and consciences of mankind, it was not difficult to slide the hand into the purse of the superstitious. The most artful, and, indeed, the most effectual way to get hold of the purse, is to get a hold of the conscience. The deeper the impression is made on the one, the deeper the draft on the other. Thus it came to pass that the clergy obtained worldly establishments, enriched themselves, and became an order as powerful in the state as in the church.

Secure in a livelihood on a fertile farm, gifted with the energy and talent to turn his hand to many tasks and make them prosper, Alexander could afford to hurl his blasts at the "hireling clergy." But he offered that his condition was still far from affluent, and that his resolve to preach without pay had been reached when he was a boy, penniless and without prospects.

Nevertheless, wanting it clear that he did not object to support for independent ministers where it was necessary, he affirmed:

> I did not censure, nor do I censure, any Christian bishop who receives such earthly things as he needs, from those to whose edification and comfort he contributes by his labors … I know there are extremes on every side—I wish to avoid them.

But he did object—and object violently—to the taking of pennies from the poor to support an elaborate ecclesiastic machine, to pay salaries to men who should be giving to rather than receiving from their "poor brethren."

The two closing essays in his series entitled "The Clergy" presented a picture, in biting caricature, of the education of a clergyman. He then pictured a young clergyman, as a licentiate, visiting the "vacant churches" and paying "court to the most charming, i.e. the most opulent and honorable," until he finally accepts a "call" and is duly installed with ceremony as a priest for life, " … then he sets about building up his cause and interest, which is ever afterwards represented and viewed as the cause and interest of Christ.

It would not have been incongruous if Campbell had signed these essays on the clergy with the motto *Ecrasez l'infame*— "Crush the infamy." So Voltaire, "like another Cato," had begun signing all his letters when—after the Protestant Jean Calas was put to death by torture and the victim's family had fled to him for refuge—he was aroused from his attitude of ironic urbanity into a bitter determination to wage relentless warfare on the abuses in the church, to "crush the infamy" of ecclesiastical power in which intolerance and persecution had their root. Many of Campbell's sallies in his essays on the clergy sounded like restatements from, and were scarcely less caustic in their anti-clericalism than Voltaire's Treatise on Toleration:

Subtleties of which not a trace can be found in the
Gospels are the source of the bloody quarrels of Christian
history. The man who says to me, 'Believe as I do, or God
will damn you,' will presently say, 'believe as I do, or I
shall assassinate you.' By what right could a being created
free force another to think like himself? A fanaticism composed of superstition and ignorance has been the sickness
of all the centuries. Christianity must be divine, since it
has lasted 1,700 years despite the fact that it is so full of vil-
lainy and nonsense.

It was not strange that there should be some similarity
between the editor of a little magazine among the remote hills of
western Virginia and the great writer in a villa at Ferney. If on his
father's side he was Scottish, perhaps with some admixture of Irish
blood during his ancestors' long sojourn in Ireland, on his mother's side Alexander was French; and he inherited not only the
French leaning toward order and logic, but also the French gift for
cutting satire, albeit his French wit was made a little ponderous by
the infusion of Scottish metaphysics. Voltaire, writing for the
court of Louis XV, annihilated with a keen thrust of the rapier.
Campbell, writing for the American frontier, laid about him with
the broad sword. But both were effective weapons. Furthermore,
Voltaire and Campbell were both children of the Enlightenment.
Bacon, Descartes, and Locke had taught them the value of starting "with doubt and a clean slate," the importance of subjecting
all creeds to the test of sense experience and reason. "I have taken
as my patron saint," said Voltaire, "Saint Thomas of Didymus,
who always insisted on an examination with his own hands." "The
voice of God," said Campbell, "is the voice of reason."
Nevertheless, since Voltaire stood at the juncture where the philosophy of the Enlightenment started down the road from deism
to skepticism, Campbell himself would scorn the comparison. His

opponents, in the years to come, would not be slow to see and make capital of the affinity between the philosopher of Ferney and the theologian on the Buffaloe.

While Campbell was issuing his Prospectus and preparing the first number of *The Christian Baptist* for press, he was also making plans to enter the debating arena a second time. At the close of his debate with the Reverend Walker at Mount Pleasant he declared his readiness to meet any minister of any denomination in debate on the subject of infant sprinkling.

On May 17, 1823, the Reverend W. L. MacCalla a Presbyterian minister of Augusta, Bracken County, Kentucky, wrote Alexander accepting the challenge. Campbell answered, declaring himself "pleased with the style and spirit of your epistle" and having ascertained that he was of "'high standing' in the Presbyterian denomination," he "most cheerfully" consented to meet him in debate.

The correspondence continued throughout the summer, unfortunately not with the same courtesy that marked its beginning. They had trouble agreeing on the conditions for the debate; MacCalla insisted that since Campbell had not claimed the privilege of naming any terms in his challenge he had forfeited his right to do so. When it was intimated that perhaps MacCalla wished to retreat from the discussion, he retorted sarcastically that although he may not have "talents and preparation to be desired in such a controversy, he was willing to trust in the Lord, and encounter even the hero of Mount Pleasant."

Finally, in exasperation, Alexander wrote MacCalla: "you shall have the privilege of both opening and closing the discussion, and of speaking twice for my once"—if only he would come to the point and agree on the date and place for the debate. At length MacCalla named Washington, Mason County, Kentucky, and October 15th; but his final letter left no doubt of his attitude toward his opponent.

> ... I am inclined to meet you; not from any favorable opinion of your piety or sincerity, but [because] you are [reputed] (and I suppose justly) to be the greatest champion of Anabaptism in America.

Campbell agreed to the time and place of meeting and retorted to MacCalla's charges:

> As to my piety, I know I have nothing to boast of, God alone is my judge. As to my external deportment, men may judge ... You have told me that you are to meet me as 'an adversary ... Well, I hope you remember, that when Michael the archangel, disputed with the adversary, about the body of Moses, he durst not bring against him a railing accusation. As you are celebrated for piety and orthodoxy, and I, for the want of them, a great deal will be expected from you, and a very little from your Humble serv't A. Campbell.

Reverend MacCalla had not formed his poor opinion of Campbell's orthodoxy and piety merely from Presbyterian sources. During the years when Alexander had, as he said, "been engaged in teaching and presiding over a classical and scientific seminary of learning at my present residence" and consequently "did not itinerate so extensively as before," the group opposing the reformers in the Redstone Baptist Association "was annually strengthening itself." The publication of the prospectus and first issue of The Christian Baptist only served to increase their suspicion. But Campbell felt he still held the confidence of a majority in the Association, though the minority "was full of expedients ...

to thrust myself and friends out of it." Then in August, 1823, he learned that a "bill of heresies" had been made out of his printed "Sermon on the Law," and from his oral sermons and lectures and that "special brethren" traversed the district and "very ingeniously contrived" to have their friends elected as messengers to the next Association meeting, which was to be held in September, and "by this means had obtained what is usually called a 'packed jury,' sure to decide against us." "The terror of [being] solemnly excommunicated from the Baptist Church," said Alexander, "was to me, indeed, not very formidable." But since his proposed debate with MacCalla was scheduled for October, one month after the time fixed for his excommunication," Alexander feared that the debate would be frustrated by the sentence of excommunication, if carried out.

Campbell had been repeatedly urged by friends to leave the Redstone and become a member of the Mahoning Association in Ohio, and he decided the time had now come to accept the offer. Calling a meeting of the Brush Run Church, he explained "that a crises of great importance had arrived ..." and requested that letters of dismissal for himself and thirty-one other members be drawn up in regular Baptist style for the purpose of establishing a church in Wellsburg, Virginia. "The brethren ... granted my request."

Three messengers from the "newborn" Wellsburg church were immediately dispatched to the Mahoning Association to solicit admission and were "cordially received." The church enrolled as a member.

Having been long harassed by his opponents in the Redstone Association, Alexander did not intend to miss seeing their dismay, so he attended the September meeting as a spectator. Both his friends and foes were puzzled by his presence without being named a messenger from the Brush Run Church. The recent developments had been "so rapid and so private as to be wholly unknown to a single church in the Redstone Association." One of the brethren proposed that Campbell, along with several visiting ministers from a distance, be invited to a seat. Another immediately objected. Campbell's friends "advocated the motion with much zeal and assiduity," while his opponents objected "with at least equal power." Much time was spent on the matter until someone suggested "if brother Campbell would state the reason why he was not as usual elected as a representative of the church at Brush Run, it might enable the Association to decide the matter at once." Then, and not until then, Campbell proceeded to "relieve them from all further trouble" by explaining that his church now belonged to the Mahoning Regular Baptist Association of Ohio. "Never," said Alexander,

> did hunters, on seeing the game unexpectedly escape from their toils at the moment when its capture was sure, glare upon each other a more mortifying disappointment than that indicated by my pursuers at that instant on learning that I was out of their bailiwick, and consequently beyond their jurisdiction.

He was now free to hold his debate with MacCalla "without the brand of excommunication upon [him]."

Since the Ohio River in October was too low for steamboat navigation, Alexander set out for Kentucky on horseback. He was therefore able to take to the debate only such books as he could carry in his portmanteau. Sidney Rigdon accompanied him; and Alexander, whose health had suffered during the summer from overwork in establishing his printing-offices, felt his strength renewed as they traveled the three hundred miles through the rich valley of the Scioto and other districts of Ohio, which he had not before visited. The last one hundred miles of their journey was overcast with gloom; from New Lancaster to Wilmington, in Clinton County, a fatal form of autumnal fever was raging, and in town and country, many were dying. At length, after a ride of eight days, they arrived at Washington, Kentucky, and Alexander wrote home:

> My dear Margaret: ...we have arrived in safety and in health at the ground of debate ... This is a healthy and fine country, and everything is cheerful and animating ... Great expectations on all sides, and much zeal.

Washington, a village of about a thousand in population, and the seat of justice for Mason County, was located in one of the most fertile, and, some travelers said, the best-improved section west of the Alleghenies. It was laid out on an ambitious plan, in three parallel streets, and with a stone courthouse boasting a small belfry; but not being on a navigable river, it was not so thriving as some of its neighbors.

After resting a few days at the home of his host, Major Davis, Alexander held an interview with his opponent the evening before the debate. Neither of the controversialists being in the best of humor, they were unable to decide on any very satisfactory rules for debate. MacCalla still insisted that, since Campbell had attached no rules to his challenge, he could not demand any, and that to do so was tantamount to a withdrawal of the challenge. Still, they named their moderators; MacCalla chose the Reverend James K. Birch, Campbell chose the confident and popular Baptist Bishop Jeremiah Vardeman; and these two selected Major William Roper as president of the board of moderators.

When the morning of the fifteenth arrived, too great a crowd had collected for the debate to be held in the church, so the discussion was opened beneath the spreading trees of a near-by Methodist camp-meeting ground. MacCalla enjoyed high reputation among the Presbyterians of Kentucky. Though more slender and lower in stature than Campbell, he was still tall and com-

manding in person, with black hair, piercing eyes, and a "character for pugnacity, ability, and power of sarcasm," and a clarion
voice. He had been a lawyer, then an army chaplain under
General Jackson, and was now a popular pulpit orator. "But," said
his followers, "In polemics he was a master . . ."

The subject announced for debate was a popular one, and the
people of Kentucky were not likely to miss a debate on any subject. Living in isolated communities, or on farms many miles separated from neighbors and dependent for religious teaching on
itinerant evangelists who brought them discourses highly colored
by doctrinal bias, the frontier settlers were highly receptive to theological controversy. To the pious the debate offered the opportunity to hear their particular brand of theology defended; to the
non-religious it brought the attraction of a good fight and a social
gathering. So it was little wonder that no church in Washington
would hold the crowd assembled on the morning of October 15,
1823, to hear the Baptist-Presbyterian contest.

Campbell concluded his introductory remarks with the explanation:

> It is not our own reputation, nor sectarian victory we
> have in view; it is the triumph of truth, it is the union of
> Christians on a proper basis. We ardently desire the union
> of all Christians on the one foundation; we believe infant
> sprinkling to be a barrier, a stumbling block ... and there-
> fore we wish to see it removed, that those who believe and
> love the truth may walk in the fellowship of it. But I give
> way to Mr. M. that he may point out the use of this rite —
> if there be no use in the thing, why contend for it? And if
> there be, God forbid, that I should oppose it.

MacCalla, as Walker had done, based his argument for infant
Baptism on the continuity of the Jewish and Christian covenants,
and the analogy of Baptism with circumcision.

... when circumcision was done away, Baptism was substituted in its stead, from the similarity of their import and design. It was attached to the same covenant, and is now a sign and a seal of the covenant with Abraham.... a command of God by Moses, and a command by Paul, are equally the commands of God and entitled to obedience.

On one thing Campbell and MacCalla were agreed: An appeal to apostolic practice was necessary to carry their point. Within itself, Campbell's argument for the restoration of apostolic Christianity found no opposition. MacCalla was willing, he said—especially "as nothing will suit my opponent but what comes from the New Testament"—to rest his case on such an appeal:

If, indeed, we do not produce positive evidence of the Apostles baptizing infants we will give up our case. In producing this sort of evidence, we will have only to advert to the families, baptized by the Apostles of which there are four on record.

Here was the second of the two favorite arguments usually advanced in support of infant Baptism. MacCalla proceeded to elaborate on this line of reasoning, which he bolstered with the contention that "the word oikos, translated 'house,' necessarily implies infants as a part of the family." In presenting his proof for the antiquity of the rite of infant Baptism, MacCalla quoted learnedly from the church fathers of the first four or five centuries—Gregory, Cyprian, Origen, Pelagius, and others.

Campbell replied that MacCalla "could not produce probable evidence, much less positive evidence" that there were infants in the households baptized by the Apostles. He insisted that MacCalla's remarks on the word oikos were "erroneous criticism"—and worse Greek. "I have," he said, "corrected school boys for blunders less egregious." And he was ready to "pledge my erudition, my critical acumen, my respectability as a scholar," that MacCalla could not present the promised evidence. Campbell had no intention of denying the antiquity of infant Baptism, but he contended that the rite could not be proven of sufficient antiquity to sustain MacCalla's thesis. On the contrary, he insisted as he had done in the Walker debate, no writer had mentioned infant Baptism until Tertullian in the third century; and, never hesitant about making a strong statement to emphasize a point, Campbell continued:

> We have searched all the large and voluminous histories now extant, and many, if not all the abbreviated ones, we have examined all the writings of those called the apostles' successors, and many of the writings of their successors, both orthodox and heterodox, and fearlessly affirm, that there lives not the man, who can produce one instance to disprove our affirmation.
>
> Campbell had no intention in this debate of arguing technicalities and legal terms. His mind liked to move in the realm of broad concepts. He had already satisfied himself as to the proper "mode" and "subject" of Baptism and had clarified his thoughts in the Walker debate. Now, he decided, it was time to announce his views on a far more important aspect of the question—the mystic design.

Campbell had not reached this decision without a struggle. Having studied and contemplated long in the three years since the Walker debate, he was quite assured of the truth of his belief that Baptism was the medium through which sins were remitted, nevertheless, as he later wrote, "it was with much hesitation that I presented this view at that time, because of its perfect novelty." It was no easy thing for Alexander Campbell to break so sharply with Protestant tradition and announce a position that he knew would bring down on his head the epithet, "papist." But he was prepared to show that if this was "papacy" it was also good New Testament doctrine. While it might be the doctrine of Catholic Christianity in general, it was so with a difference, for the Baptism as he was affirming it, was for the remission of sins of sincere penitent believers. At any rate, the mere fact that Rome had postulated a doctrine did not automatically make it invalid. Alexander did not bring up the issue at this time, because MacCalla did not bring up the charge of "papist." But he was quite convinced that at several points—especially on the subject of the design of Baptism—the Protestant Reformers had run so fast out of Rome, they had run past Jerusalem. Several years after the MacCalla debate Campbell wrote:

> In shunning one extreme, we are wont to run into the contrary. The Papists in former times made the mere act of immersion or of sprinkling, irrespective of the sentiments, faith, or feelings, of the subject, wash away all sins.... Protestants ran to an equal extreme on the other side of the equator of truth; and therefore gave to Baptism, however administered, no connexion [sic] with the remission of sins. So much did they hate the errors of popery, that they did scarcely name 'the forgiveness of sins' on the same day on which they 'administered Baptism.'
>
> We connect faith with immersion as essential to forgiveness—and therefore, as was said of old, 'According to your faith, so be it to you,' so say we of immersion ...

Having made up his mind to introduce the question of the design of Baptism in the MacCalla debate, Campbell broached the subject at the end of his very first speech when he challenged his opponent to show the use of the rite. MacCalla had immediately protested against applying any such pragmatic test to a sacred question: "Reason ought not to be appealed to on such matters ... Our duty is to obey, although we could see no propriety in the command." MacCalla reminded Campbell that he himself had said practically the same thing in the Walker debate and quoted his remarks. Campbell retorted that he did not appeal to reason for the use of Baptism, but to revelation. He found the design described in the words of Jesus, "He that believeth and is baptized shall be saved" and "Unless a man be born of water and of the Spirit he cannot enter into the kingdom of God;" in the words of Peter on the day of Pentecost, "Repent and be baptized, every one of you, for the remission of sins;" and in Paul's words to Titus, "God our Father saved us by the washing of regeneration and the renewing of the Holy Spirit." From these passages Campbell maintained that Jesus "placed Baptism on the right hand of faith"—and the purpose of the ordinance was for the remission of sins. Quite specifically, Campbell deplored the "low" view of Baptism held by some Baptists who would "reduce this significant ordinance to the level of a moral example, or a moral precept" by declaring that they were baptized merely "to follow the example of Christ," or out of "obedience to a divine command." In contrast, he asked the audience to "pause and admire" the deep and mystic import of a rite through which "Divine philanthropy" had decreed that man, when truly believing and truly repentant, might bury his old sin and enter the world "a second time, ... as innocent, as clean, as unspotted as an angel" to enjoy "peace with God" under "the priesthood of Jesus."

MacCalla vehemently denied the first part of Campbell's argument. "I maintain," he said, "that faith is not essential to Baptism." But he did not deny that the rite had some connection with regeneration; drawing on the Old Testament for his figure, he declared that Baptism like the Jewish circumcision, "as a sign ... imported the inward or spiritual circumcision of the heart, which is equivalent to ... regeneration." If infants were baptized, this regeneration, obviously, would apply to "original sin;" and Campbell, disavowing this Calvinistic conception, replied that the remission specified in the New Testament was not for "original sin" but for actual, personal sins in the plural. He added, "I know it will be said that I have affirmed that Baptism 'saves us,' that it 'washes away sins.' Well, Peter and Paul have said so before me. If it was not criminal in them to say so, it cannot be criminal in me." Even the Larger Catechism, he pointed out, "says that Baptism is a sign of the remission of sins." How, then, he argued, could the rite be administered to infants, who had committed no sin, if it was ordained to be to a believer a formal and personal remission of all his sins? "Faith in Christ," Campbell concluded, "is necessary to forgiveness of sins, therefore Baptism, without faith, is an unmeaning ceremony." Here he rested his case for believer's Baptism—the sacrament demanded personal choice, personal belief, personal responsibility.

In declaring that Baptism was designed for the remission of sins, Campbell made an important distinction:

> The Blood of Christ …really cleanses us who believe…. The water of Baptism … formally washes away our sins … Paul's sins were really pardoned when he believed, yet he had no solemn pledge of the fact, no formal acquittal, no formal purgation of his sins, until he washes them away in the water of Baptism.

Though he always believed that in Baptism one's sins were "washed away in some sense that they were not before," Campbell never doubted that through limitless mercy and understanding God would receive into the kingdom even those believers who did not have a proper conception of the design of the holy ordinance of Baptism.

But there was further mystery involved in the rite of Baptism—its symbolic meaning, the emblematic import of its "action." Having already "shown that the washing away of sins was the doctrinal import of this ordinance, viewed in relation to the subject of it," Campbell turned to his proof that "the design of Baptism and the action are analogous." The action symbolized the death, burial, and resurrection of Christ by which was obtained divine forgiveness for sins. He found his authority in the writings of Paul:

> Hence the Apostle, in his epistles, declares that the disciples are buried in Baptism, and also raised in the likeness of Christ's death and resurrection. Baptism is therefore analogous to a burial and resurrection, as far as respects the action, and in consequence of this with Christ, and to have died by sin, to have been buried with Christ, and to have risen with him …"The design requires that the action should bear a resemblance to a burial and resurrection. But sprinkling bears no such resemblance,—therefore sprinkling is not Baptism.

In support of this interpretation he quoted Martin Luther: "I would have those that are to be baptized to be wholly dipped into the water as the word imports, and the mystery doth signify."

MacCalla, on the other hand, argued that Baptism "alludes to the gracious influences of the Holy Ghost …Now as water Baptism is the appointed emblem of this pouring out and sprinkling of the Holy Spirit, the conclusion necessarily is … that Baptism is to be administered by pouring or sprinkling."

Campbell responded:

> This is passing strange … Upon the whole nothing could be more unscriptural than to affirm that Baptism is an emblem of the Spirit's influences, seeing the apostles declare Baptism to have reference to the washing away of sin by the death and resurrection of Christ, and that being born of the water and of the spirit are two distinct things, and not the one an emblem of the other.

And here Campbell would rest his case for immersion as the proper mode of Baptism.

Many years later he wrote that though, knowing the great popularity of the subject of Baptism with the people, he had during the debate "seemed to enter into the denominational spirit and feeling with all the zeal of a real Baptist," he nevertheless felt keenly his peculiar mission and wished to advance its cause.

> I sought to introduce my views of Christianity in general …The only point on that occasion to them a novelty, and to me an interest, was the design of Baptism; and a more rational method of reading, interpreting, and using the Bible. True, indeed, other matters of church polity, an evangelical ministry, and a more consistent mode of 'preaching and teaching Christ,' greatly pressed upon my attention, and was much more near my heart than the difference between an infant and an adult, sprinkling or dipping a person.

If MacCalla had objected to laughter from the audience earlier in the debate, his temper was due for a sore trial on the last day of discussion. One of his concluding arguments against immersion proved, for the dignity of his cause, to be a most unfortunate choice. He argued that immersion was dangerous and pernicious both to subject and administrator. The latter "were exposed to sickness, and it must unavoidably be injurious to them to be plunging into cold water at all seasons, and continuing in it so long as they often did." Under the circumstances, this argument offered a chance for an amusing rebuttal that Campbell would not be slow to turn. He solemnly related to the audience a story:

> Benjamin Franklin, when minister in Paris, dined with a number of French and American gentlemen. A learned French Abbé at dinner entertained the company with a very learned disquisition on the deteriorating influ-

ence of the American climate on the bodies of all animals. That the human body diminished in size and energy, and that even the mind itself shared in the general deterioration. Dr. Franklin made no reply; ... but after dinner told the company with what pleasure he had heard the learned disquisitions of the philosopher: He moved the company be divided, observing that the fairest way of testing the correctness of the learned Abbé's theory, was to place all the Americans on one side the room, and the French on the other. The motion was carried: and behold a company of little, swarthy, insignificant Frenchmen on the one side, and a row of little giants on the other. Aye, says the Dr. see here is a striking proof of the correctness of your theory!! Now let us take the philosopher's way of testing the correctness of the theory of my opponent. There sits on the bench a Baptist and a Paido-baptist teacher, both well advanced in years; ...the former has, we are told, immersed more persons than any other person of the same age in the State, or perhaps in the United States; the other, from his venerable age, may be supposed to have sprinkled a great many infants.... Now see the pernicious tendency of immersion on the Baptist, and the happy influence of sprinkling upon the Paido-baptist.

Now, the Reverend Birch, the Presbyterian moderator, was a small man of delicate constitution, while Elder Vardeman was a man of magnificent proportions, six feet tall, weighing three hundred pounds, and with a remarkably florid and healthy aspect. The ironical contrast sent the audience into gales of laughter, and, consequently, increased MacCalla's bad temper. He published his concluding challenge in the words: "That he would never discuss this question again until an opponent would come from the regions discovered by Captain Simms, and until a moderator would come from Holland, weighing 500 lbs."

His temper not improved, MacCalla proposed that he have the right of closing the debate. The presiding moderator declared that Campbell had the right to reply if he thought it necessary, but Campbell granted MacCalla's request for the last word, "provided there should be no misstatement of facts." MacCalla then used his time to warn the audience against his opponent whom he described as "an enemy to all morality." Under the circumstances, Campbell claimed his right to a few words in reply. Again, he turned MacCalla's attack into an advantage. He briefly denied that his remonstrance against "those little, persecuting, fining, confining, anti-republican confederations, called moral societies" made him an enemy to morality and expressed his hope that "the congregation would know how to appreciate the last accusations of Mr. M. who had now descended to that vile slander which was the dernier resort of those who neither possessed, nor could wield the sword of truth." Then he took the opportunity to inform his audience that those who wished to know his views on any subject "can be made fully acquainted with them by perusing a monthly publication, entitled The Christian Baptist, which I had lately commenced editing," and so ended the discussion.

The debate lasted seven days, and the Kentuckians were well pleased with the week's entertainment. MacCalla, at the close of the debate, may have shown himself a little disgusted with the proceedings, but his followers felt that he had sustained their cause in able fashion. He was given the degree of Doctor of Divinity and was called to the pastorate of Scots Church, Philadelphia. For his part, Campbell found that he was securing "the special favor and attention of the Baptist ministry, and of the uncommitted public." In fact, he had been a little disturbed at first by the enthusiastic and unqualified support given him by the Kentucky Baptists. He had withheld The Christian Baptist from Kentucky, it was true, in order that he might receive an unbiased hearing, but still Campbell was not a man to sail under false colors. So, on the evening of the fourth day of debate, finding "all the principal Baptist preachers in the State" gathered to see him at the home of his "kind host," Major Davis, Campbell decided it was time to disabuse his Kentucky friends of any false notions they might have about his orthodoxy. "Hearing them," he said, "speak in such favorable terms of my defense of their tenets during these four days," he suddenly astonished his visitors with the following remarks:

Brethren, I fear that if you knew me better, you would esteem and love me less. For, let me tell you, in all candor, that I have almost as much against you Baptists as I have against the Presbyterians. They err in one thing, and you in another; and probably you are each nearly equidistant from original apostolic Christianity. I will read you a few specimens of my heterodoxy. They all said, ' let us hear the worst error you have against us.' I went up stairs and unwrapped the first three numbers—[July, August, and September numbers] of *The Christian Baptist*, that ever saw the light in Kentucky. I had just ten copies of the three first numbers. I carried them into the parlor, and, sitting down, I read, as a sample, the first essay on the clergy—This was the first essay ever read from that work in Kentucky. After a sigh and a long silence, Elder Vardeman said, 'Is that your worst error—your chief heterodoxy? I don't care so much about that, as you admit that we may have a providential call, without a voice from heaven, or a special visit from some angel or spirit. If you have anything worse, for my part I wish to hear it.' The cry was, 'Let us hear something more.' On turning to and fro, I next read an article on Modern Missionaries. This, with the 'Capital Mistake of Modern Missionaries,' finished my readings for the evening.

On closing this essay, 'Well,' said Elder Vardeman, 'I am not so great a missionary man as to fall out with you on that subject. I must hear more before I condemn or approve.' I then distributed my ten copies amongst the ten most distinguished and advanced Elders in the room— requesting them to read those numbers during the recess of the debate, and to communicate freely to me their objections. We separated.

The perusal of *The Christian Baptist* did not disturb the Baptist elders any more than Campbell's remarks to MacCalla, so he found the debate "terminated with so much of the approbation of the whole denomination, that at its close, I was requested to furnish the Elders present with a liberal supply of the Proposals for publication of *The Christian Baptist*, and with the most pressing invitation to make an immediate tour through the State." This he was unable to do because of "domestic duties and engagements," but he compromised by agreeing "to speak at May's Lick, Bryant's Station, the vicinity of Elder Vardeman's residence, and Lexington; and, if possible, the next autumn to visit a considerable portion of the State." Campbell, when he arrived to deliver the promised sermon at one of Elder Vardeman's churches, was surprised at the large crowd gathered to hear him speak.

His audience was equally surprised by the nature of Campbell's preaching. The frontier ministers to whom they were accustomed were given to oratory and controversial sermons. They reveled in debate and carried their pugnacity into the pulpit. The Methodists were violently Arminian, the Baptists and Presbyterians fanatically Calvinistic; and their preachers were likely to interrupt their discourse at any time with a slashing attack upon the favorite "isms" of the rival denominations.

Therefore, those who had heard Campbell's debate against MacCalla came to his preaching appointment expecting to hear a display of theological fireworks. They heard instead a calm and reasoned discourse delivered without gestures or the arts of elocution. They had anticipated differently only because they understood very little the nature of the man's religion. Campbell, as well as any, knew the tactical advantage of a forceful onslaught; he knew the dramatic value of a slashing, satiric attack. On the debating platform and in the editor's chair he was ready to use every weapon for gaining and holding the attention of his audience, because he considered himself merely a man defending his opinions against the opinions of other men. But, when he mounted the pulpit, Campbell believed he became an ambassador of God and any reference to the petty controversy was beneath the dignity and reverence of the occasion. He had been reared with an old world sense of decorum and the fitness of things, and the Christocentric character of his personal religion vested his sermons and his prayers with an innate air of reverence. So in the pulpit Campbell was simply the expositor of Scripture, the extoller of the Deity.

Such was the nature of Campbell's exposition of Scripture that his hearers again found themselves surprised, this time by the novelty of his discourse. They were accustomed to sermons that were likely to alternate between two extremes. There were the emotional, inflammatory sermons often heard at the camp meetings, which dangled the sinners over the lurid pits of hell, and called the righteous to a golden glorious reward. Then there was the doctrinal discourse, in which the preacher was concerned with defending some abstract and arid point of doctrine, and used the Bible as an "arsenal of text-proofs," all parts alike magically inspired and valid, so that a quotation from Moses or Amos possessed authority with the words of Peter or Paul.

This new preacher from the banks of the Buffaloe scorned both these accepted models of sermonizing. Presenting his strange theory of the dispensations, he denied that the Bible was an arsenal from which text-proofs, all of equal validity, might be drawn at random. Under his hands it became one continuous and fascinating record of the progressive revelation of God's will to man. He presented this concept with the same effortless simplicity with which he had instructed his young scholars at Buffaloe Academy. Though his manner was artless and unaffected, the dramatic was not lacking from his discourse. For there was nothing detached about his artlessness, nothing phlegmatic about his simplicity. The magnetic vitality that always seemed to radiate from him, the intenseness of the expression burning from his eyes needed no help from studied gestures to keep the attention of his audience. Nor were his words lacking in rhetorical eloquence so dear to the oratory-loving people of Kentucky. Time pressed so fast upon him that he must ever speak extemporaneously as he must write hurriedly, but Campbell had sat long at the feet of the eighteenth-century writers and learned their lessons well in the days when he dreamed of joining their ranks as a literary figure. His study of Addison was reflected in the simple ease with which he phrased his passages of plain exposition. But when he rose to his favorite theme—the culmination of divine revelation in the perfection of Jesus the Christ—he abandoned simplicity for grandiloquent Johnsonian rhetoric. So those who had come to hear Campbell's first sermon in Kentucky went away surprised—but not disappointed.

Nor did they seem appalled at his heresy. Campbell was becoming aware of a significant fact: These citizens of states whose western borders were washed by the waters of the Mississippi were not to be so easily frightened by novel doctrines as were the citizens of the older settled regions. The Mahoning Association of Ohio had received him into its fold when the Redstone Association of Pennsylvania sought to cast him out. The Kentuckians seemed as ready to give a hearing to his theories as had the citizens of Ohio and the Northwest Territory.

After fulfilling his engagements at the smaller congregations, Campbell made his way to Lexington where he was to speak in the church that was under the pastorate of Dr. James Fishback. Dr. Fishback was not only a brilliant and talented man—he had published a "valuable contribution to mental science"—but he was remarkably handsome as well, being tall and slender with dark hair and regular features. His manners were as engaging as his appearance, and his "elegant mansion" was considered a center of "munificent hospitality." He had once been a successful lawyer, but had abandoned the profession for medicine, and later became a Presbyterian minister. Then, changing his views on Baptism, he had joined the Baptist church at Lexington. At that time it was a small and somewhat scorned congregation. Under his leadership, it had become one of the largest and most prosperous churches in the West. It would be a challenge to any man's ability to speak in the pulpit of such a preacher, and in the home community of Henry Clay. Campbell's over-burdened schedule had brought on another attack of dyspepsia. He entered the pulpit pale and unable to stand entirely erect. But he chose as text the first chapter of Hebrews, written in glory of the Christ—"God …hath in these late days spoken unto us by his son …"

It was a theme on which Campbell found it easy to be eloquent, and he spoke for two hours. He proved himself worthy of the pulpit he occupied, for it was reported that he "created a great sensation by his startling and powerful sermon," and one young man in the audience remembered the occasion so well that many years later when he was a physician in Louisville he wrote:

> I never heard anything that approached the power of that discourse, nor have I ever heard it equaled since. Under the training of my mother, one of the most thorough scholars in the Bible that I ever knew, and of Dr. Fishback… I was almost as familiar with the Bible as with my alphabet. But that speech on Hebrews lifted me into a

world of thought of which I had previously known nothing. It has been forty-five years since I heard that pulpit discourse, but it is as vivid in my memory, I think, as when I first heard it.

Campbell returned to his "mansion" on the Buffaloe warmed and encouraged by the praise of the hospitable Kentuckians. They in turn were pleased to have discovered this gentleman from Virginia who could entertain them so well as debater, preacher, and editor, and who brought to his task something of the wit of France, the canniness of Scotland, and the laughter of Ireland.

As soon as Campbell returned home, he plunged himself into the work of preparing the debate for the press. It was published in 1824 on his own Buffaloe press. Publishing an issue of *The Christian Baptist* every month, fulfilling preaching appointments, and managing his farm, "forbid much close thinking or close application to my pen. It moved in my fingers with very little regard for elegancies, I was more concerned about the *matter* than about the *manner* ..."

MacCalla obviously thought it better if Campbell did not trouble himself at all with the venture, for he wrote an article in the *Kentucky Gazette* before the debate was published warning the public that it could not possibly be a correct transcription of the discussion. Campbell had compiled the debate from the notes of three preachers present and from his own copious notes; he made a practice of transcribing whole volumes of discourses from notes he took while "listening to lectures on languages and sciences." The result, Campbell was sure, was well worth the public's attention: It occupies 420 pages, and, with the exception of the Bible, it is the cheapest religious work published in this country."

Campbell desired to present his opponents' arguments in their strongest form; to do otherwise would weaken the force of his own arguments, as well as endanger his reputation. MacCalla was busy, he was aware, preaching throughout Kentucky in order, as the article in the Gazette stated, "that the people of 'all denominations may have a specimen of the contrast which I know will be seen between my real argument and the spurious production now in the press.'" Campbell calmly retorted that: "If the whole of this work were a forgery, it combats every argument advanced by the Paido-baptists; and if the arguments impugned in this volume are refuted, [the reader] may rest assured that there are no others to exhibit."

This assurance of the invincibility of his cause was so freely expressed in his debates and his writings, that those who came to hear Campbell preach for the first time were, like the citizens of Kentucky, always surprised at his unassuming air and simple sincerity. In the pulpit he was devout without being sanctimonious, reverent without being unctuous. It was only before God that Alexander Campbell could humble himself, for he was not a humble man. He had an inner consciousness of power, and he had worked long to acquire knowledge. Nevertheless, he was not an arrogant man, for he felt within himself a deep and humbling conviction that was not easily apparent to others—his power was given him, his knowledge was entrusted to him, by God for a divinely appointed purpose. After centuries of strife and oppression, the day had finally dawned when unity and liberty should come to the church, and he was permitted to be one of the instruments for achieving this glorious end. Had he not twice been saved from what seemed an almost certain death at sea? Had he not been the object of many other evidences of providential favor, which he had so seriously pondered that evening in 1811 when he had decided that he must irrevocably be ordained to the ministry? Since that day, had he not spent every possible moment in study that he might know all that scholars had said, and God had revealed about God's holy design? When it came to the sacrament of Baptism, his study had been crowned with a conviction that amounted to divine certainty—he had been placed on "a new peak of the mountain of God;" and all must fail to carry their point who did not rightly understand the mystery of this holy ordinance, and see its place in the whole "landscape of Christianity" as he had beheld it from the mountain peak. Hence, in the preface to the MacCalla debate he wished to make it clear that all honor for the victory won was due the truth he advocated. However self-assured he might appear, Campbell always felt that his invincibility came not from his person, but from the cause it was granted him to espouse.

His enemies were not likely to concern themselves with these fine distinctions. In their view, Alexander Campbell was a proud man. Pride came from the devil. Hence, from the day when the moral societies of Western Pennsylvania dubbed him Pluto's "beloved missionary," he would be represented as the purveyor of diabolical heresies clothed in a vestment of satanic arrogance.

The effect of Campbell's editorial forays was immediate. This was not a magazine to which the orthodox would remain indifferent, and the editor took pleasure in publishing the extremes of opinion, both complimentary and derogatory, aroused by his paper.

Scarcely was the third issue in the hands of the subscribers when an indignant reader in Ohio wrote:

> Sir—I request you to send me the *Christian Baptist* no more. I will pay for the present year, but I do not care

if I never see another number of it. My conscience is wounded that I should have subscribed to such a work.

But "the first stone cast at the *Christian Baptist*," said Campbell, was an article appearing in the Wooster Spectator during his trip to Kentucky to hold the MacCalla debate. It was written by the Reverend Thomas G. Jones, once president of the famous Bank of Wooster. He informed his readers that the *Christian Baptist* was a paper "edited by A. Campbell, a sort of religious Ishmaelite, whose hand is against every man, opposing almost everything the Christian world has received as being the religion of Christ." The president of a western college was more laconic in his dismissal of the editor. Thinking himself an unnamed "eloquent orator" lampooned in the magazine, he said succinctly to a friend of Campbell who had asked his opinion: "He is the devil." Campbell retorted that even though Satan had actually appeared in human form, "His serene highness," the Reverend D. D., should remember that Jesus had "rebutted the Devil with 'It is written,' and not with saying 'You are the Devil.'"

But the most annoying of his detractors was the author of a pamphlet published in Pittsburgh called "Letters to Alexander Campbell, by a Regular Baptist." Though he was not prone to answer "anonymous abuse," "for who knows not that the ebullitions of anonymous foes carry their own condemnation in their preface." Campbell decided that some good might come from replying to the "Regular Baptist, believing that medicine may be deduced even from the carcass of a serpent that has poisoned itself." So in an "Address to the Public," Campbell informed his readers that the pamphleteer was the Reverend Lawrence Greatrake, "from the city of Baltimore, or somewhere thereabouts," who had recently moved to Pittsburgh and launched his attack on Campbell, and on the Baptist Church under the care of Walter Scott and Sidney Rigdon. The pamphlet offered to prove, said Campbell, "that I am an unregenerate man, that the Devil is my master." Though he found nothing to condemn in Campbell's "extrinsic character," Greatrake was ready to prove, from a series of conjectures "predicated either upon the most evident falsehoods, or upon a false view of the facts," that his "intrinsic character" was bad. His account of Campbell's life, of which he knew little, was so garbled that Campbell felt it necessary to give an outline of the real facts in his article, and Greatrake presented and condemned Campbell's doctrines without quoting a line from his writings to prove his assertions. He based his charges on three conjectures: that Campbell had begun his career because of some personal pique; that he now aimed at establishing himself as head of a sect; and that he acted from two "grand controlling principles," an "insatiate vanity" and "pecuniary interest." The last charge he substantiated with an array of figures, showing an imposing profit on the sale of the Walker and MacCalla debates, figures that Campbell charged originated entirely in his own mind. Anyway, remarked Campbell, it would be difficult to deduce evidence of ambition and avarice from the life of a man who had "refused, as I have done, offers of connexion [sic] with popular sects, and of places of public and conspicuous eminence in the cities of Philadelphia and New York, who could take his Bible and the plough and sit down among the hills of Western Virginia, and, from the age of twenty-one to thirty-one, move in the quiet vale of retirement, without seeking in one instance to make himself more conspicuous than his immediate duties and business required." Having learned the identity of the "Regular Baptist," Campbell, with Walter Scott and another member of the Pittsburgh Church, called on Greatrake, and demanded a "recantation of the whole pamphlet." He promised a partial retraction, but Campbell informed him "that no other than a full and unequivocal one would, on my part, be accepted." This Greatrake was not likely to give, since he had declared in the pamphlet: "Confident that you have an undue and deleterious influence in the Baptist Church, I would wish to see it destroyed."

Positive as were those alarmed or outraged by the magazine being published on the Buffaloe, those approving the movement were no less emphatic. Requests for extra copies, offers to give their time in extending subscription lists, began to come from readers in Kentucky, Pennsylvania, Virginia, and on the Western Reserve. From the Western Reserve came the letter: "I have read the Christian Baptist with pleasure, believing it to be founded on truth, and is calculated to expose the popular and prevailing errors of the present times. It has appeared; but has not brought peace, but a sword; and is setting the father against the son, and the daughter against the mother. Shall we condemn it on this account ...? No."

From Kentucky a reader wrote: "I have perused with much pleasure the *Christian Baptist*; and I take pleasure in assuring you that every exertion shall be made by me to enlarge the list of subscribers to that useful paper."

Another subscriber in the same state requested: "Sir—Please send me ten sets of the *Christian Baptist* to this office ... I trust the work will do great good. Many are beginning to see ... like the blind man coming to his sight."

From Pennsylvania came the encouragement: "Sir—Day is dawning in the minds of many. I hear a rattling among the dry bones ... Send us copies of the *Christian Baptist*, and be assured that no exertions shall be wanting on my part to disseminate the truth as far and as fast as possible."

While Virginia cautioned: "Your enemies, or rather the enemies of truth, are waiting for your falling. Your pamphlets are read with more anxiety by those differing from you, than by your friends. Avoid extremes as far as consistent with truth. Keep close to Paul, and the truth will not fail in your minds."

Kentucky had received him cordially during the MacCalla debate, and Campbell later noted: "So few and futile were the objections to the Christian Baptist, that Kentucky alone furnished, in less than a year, one thousand subscribers, and at least five times that many readers. The debate also with M'Calla, soon as it appeared from the press, ... was immediately scattered over the State in thousands; and so Kentucky was, in a few months, every where sown with the seeds of a great evangelical and moral reformation."

Affairs in Pittsburgh were also progressing in a pleasing fashion. After the Redstone Association attempted, in 1823, to exclude the members of the Pittsburgh Church who were favorable to reformation, "a greater degree of intimacy," said Campbell, was cultivated by his friends Walter Scott and Sidney Rigdon, and by "their respective friends and admirers." As a result, their two congregations united in 1824. A minority opposed to the reformation withdrew and were recognized as the "only legitimate Baptist Church in Pittsburgh" by the Redstone Association. "Each community henceforth," said Campbell, "was separate and distinct."

Among those who wrote the editor of the Christian Baptist, one urged him into ways of moderation. He signed himself "Robert Cautious" and implored:

> Sir: ... approving of the general spirit and tendency of your work, I take the liberty of suggesting to you the necessity of avoiding prevailing errors with considerable ability and commendable zeal, have defeated their own good efforts by out stepping the fixed boundaries of truth; and thus introducing schemes and opinions, ... as fraught with mischief, ... as the schemes, which they opposed. In hastening out of Babylon they ran past Jerusalem ...

Campbell's answer was emphatic — to cure violent ills, violent remedies were necessary:

> We are convinced, fully convinced, that the whole head is sick, and the whole heart faint of modern Christianity — that many of the schemes of the populars

resemble the delirium, the wild fancies of a subject of fever, in its highest paroxysms…. It is not the administration of stimulants, but a system of depletion, that will effect a cure. It is not the recommendation of the popular schemes … that will heal the diseases of the people; but it is an abandonment of every human scheme, and a submission to learn and study Christianity as developed in the Bible. This is the course, the only course, that will effect a cure and renovate the constitution. Every other course resembles the palliatives, and sedatives, and stimulants of quackery …

Assuredly no reader of *The Christian Baptist* could feel they were being administered a sedative. Its editor was convinced that health could come only from a strong cathartic that would purge the system clean. His attack on the clergy was followed by an attack on the whole ecclesiastical machinery and all its agencies. He condemned missionary societies, tract societies, Bible societies, and even Sunday schools — not because he lacked sympathy with their ideals, but because he did not approve of the means they employed.

At the base of Campbell's opposition to these agencies lay his concept of the Church as the divine society solely authorized to carry on God's work. The majority of the missionary and tract organizations, it was true, were instruments of the churches; but many were not. Hence, Campbell felt, the prestige of the Church was being undermined by rival agencies which were undertaking extensive social and religious programs, acting apart from the Church, and encroaching on its functions. Distressed by this invasion of the sovereignty of God and the sanctity of His divine society, the editor on the Buffaloe began a vigorous assault.

So sensitive was he to the preeminent position that Christ

must occupy in all Christian thought, he could but "lament," he wrote, to see any of the glory of His Church "transferred to a human corporation. The Church is robbed of its character by every institution, merely human, that would ape its excellence and substitute itself in its place." Campbell regretted, he continued, "I am constrained to differ from many whom I love and esteem, and will ever love and esteem if we should never agree upon this point... At the same time I am very sorry to think that any man should suppose that I am either oblivious to the deplorable condition of the heathen world, ...I do not oppose, intentionally at least, any scriptural plan of converting the world."

Campbell, on the contrary, deplored the fact that his opponents either could not or did not wish, he said, "to discriminate, in my case at least, between a person's opposing the abuses of a good cause, and the cause itself." And, he added: "I did contribute my mite and my efforts to the popular missionary cause, until my conscience forbade me from an acquaintance with the abuses of the principle." These abuses, Campbell was convinced, were the appropriation of the missionary societies as "mere sectarian speculations, for enlarging their sects," and the raising of large sums of money "squandered at home and abroad under the pretext of converting the world."

Not all comment was adverse. Several joined Campbell in his attitude toward the missionary schemes—groups in many churches had started this attack years before him—and he often printed notices from another anti-mission paper, called the Reformer. A letter from a subscriber to the Reformer informed its editor that many churches were withdrawing from various Baptist associations, and calling themselves the "Reformed Baptist Churches," due to their opposition to the "missionary and money-begging system:"

> Many of the churches have long been grieved and troubled by the vile arts and schemes which have been

resorted to for obtaining money, under pretense of spreading the gospel, and they are now fully determined to rid
themselves of the abominations by denying their pulpits
to all missionary beggars, and removing from among them
such members as continue their adherence to any of the
popular and anti-Christian projects of the day…. And so
far as I am a prophet, I venture to predict that the Baptist
denomination will be divided on the ground of these missionary and other schemes throughout the Union.

Talk of division was not pleasing to Campbell with his ideal of
union; nor did he wish in attacking one evil to erect another even
more devastating in its stead. He was opposing those who were
"enthusiastic and chimerical in all those projects"—in the "missionary schemes, education societies, tract societies, with their
endless retinue of offices and officers." He penned even harsher
words describing those who used opposition to these schemes as
an excuse to "fold their arms and sit down in perfect apathy …"

Campbell was a Scots pragmatist. He was attacking the abuses not the system. To curtail the power of the clergy, he thought,
it was necessary to be on guard against all their agencies. In the
final analysis, Campbell's attack on the unscriptural methods
employed in the "popular schemes" was really a rationalization of
the emotion that motivated his whole pattern of thought: his passion for liberty, his dislike of the ecclesiastical tyranny that had
made church history a chronicle of bloodshed and persecution.
When a circular issued by the National Tract Society at New York
came into his hands, he felt that his suspicions were justified, and
he published a scathing article entitled "Priestly Ambition." It
began: "We have long considered the various societies called
Missionary, Bible, Sunday School, and Tract Societies, as great
religious engines, fitted and designed for the predominance of the
leading sectaries who set them a-going, and ultimately tending to
a national creed and a religious establishment." They were,

"abstractly considered," he agreed, good and benevolent works. "But there are intentions besides pure benevolence, and appendages to those good works in the manner in which they are performed, which convert them into religious intrigues for predominance."

Campbell, in spite of all urging to moderation, continued his vitriolic attack on the clergy. He then vented his sarcasm on the custom among some of the western colleges of a wholesale appointment of Doctors of Divinity: "There is no country in Christendom, with which we are acquainted, which is more congenial to the growth of distinguished Divines, than the regions round about Cannonsburg and Washington. It is apprehended that ...in a short time all our Divines will grow up into Doctors of Divinity. It is fairly presumable that the Doctors themselves will take a second growth, and shoot up into Metropolitans and Cardinals."

The close of his first year as an editor found Campbell no less emphatic in his purpose. The United States, he said in his preface to the second volume, had proven the fallacy of the doctrine of the divine right of kings and nobles. He hoped that the laity, even though "completely preached out of their common sense," might be aroused to so explode the doctrine of the divine right of the clergy, since "either a learned or an unlearned clergy are now, and ever have been the cause of all division, superstition, enthusiasm, and ignorance of the people." His only regret was that they had not accepted his invitation to discussion.

> Our remarks, puny and insignificant as the clergy view them, are honest, well meant, and above board. Their efforts to defend themselves, strong, powerful, and valiant as they are—are in secret, by the fireside, or in the wooden box, where they think themselves protected from exposure and defeat. Two honest men, it is true, my friend, Thomas G. Jones, and the reverend editor of the

Pittsburgh Recorder, have once, but not twice, manfully lifted up their pen like a two-edged sword; but alas! for the honor of the cloth it soon sought its scabbard.

Campbell had no doubt of the enduring interest for his work. The very first issue of *The Christian Baptist* had urged its readers to preserve their numbers "from being sullied or worn" so that the twelve issues might be bound as a "handsome volume." While the other religious publications of the day filled their pages with such ephemeral and dry things as "long accounts of revivals, ordinations, baptisms, reports of Bible and missionary societies, the constitutions and proceedings of cent societies, the election of presidents, vice-presidents, and managers, secretaries, and treasurers of mite societies, and all such splendid and glorious things." He was convinced that his publication would have more permanent value, and, therefore, would print only "such things as will bear to be read a year or two hence as far as the subject matter is concerned." To give added spice and interest to his essays, Alexander varied his writings by presenting his arguments in the form of dialogues. By sometimes casting his ideas in the form of parables, and by often presenting criticism in the form of parodies, Alexander, in addition to variety was, perhaps, satisfying his own desire for literary composition, reminiscent of the days when he had dreamed of becoming a man of letters. To give a more personal aspect to some of his opinions, Alexander started a series of essays entitled "Extracts from my Sentimental Journal," which drew on both fact and fancy for personal background.

Though the clergy, excepting Greatrake and one or two others, refused to write their opinions to the editor of *The Christian Baptist,* the general public was not so reticent. After receiving a score of criticisms of his work, Campbell wrote a series under the title "Address to the Readers of the Christian Baptist" answering the orthodox who considered his writings "heretical and blasphemous." There were three major complaints, and these he covered in three essays.

The first was that he denied the moral law—a charge he heard repeatedly during the seven years since he preached his "Sermon on the Law." As in his reply to the charge of antinomianism made in his two debates, Campbell again denied that refusal to obey the law of Moses was a licentious doctrine denying the force of moral law as a rule of life. "Blessed Jesus!" he exclaimed,

> are you this insulted by pretended friends? Are your laws an inadequate rule of life? Guided by your statutes, will our lives be licentious, our morals loose, ourselves abandoned to all crime? Was Moses a more consummate lawgiver than you?

The second charge was that he denied the Christian Sabbath. This Campbell freely admitted. The very expression was a contradiction in terms. The Sabbath was the seventh day of the week "exclusively the property of the Jews as circumcision," and was to be observed by the most rigid abstinence and ceremonial form. Christians were commanded to observe the first day of the week "in breaking bread, in fellowship, and in prayers." In calling this day "the Sabbath" they were confusing two laws and really obeying neither. That the Sabbath had been changed from the seventh to the first day, he denied, for:

> No two days are more unlike in their import and design, than the Sabbath and the first day. The former commemorated the consummation of the old creation; the latter commemorates the beginning of the new creation. The former was to Israel, a memorial that they were once slaves in Egypt—the latter assures us that the year of release has come. The former looked back, with mournful aspect, to the toils and sorrows entailed upon the

human body, from an evil incident to the old creation—
the latter looks forward, with an eye beaming with hope,
to perpetual exemption from toil, and pain, and sorrow.
The Sabbath was a day of awful self-denial and profound
religious gloom—the resurrection day is a day of triumph
of holy joy, and religious festivity.

The third charge against Campbell's theology was one that
brought him in conflict with the most deep-rooted beliefs of frontier religion. The "men of the western waters" were not prone to
quarrel with his attack on the clergy. The leveling tendency of the
frontier had given them little patience with clerical or any other
class distinctions, and the very vigor with which he persecuted the
assault appealed to their love of a lusty fight. But when he intimated that he considered "warm preaching, and warm feelings,
and great revivals" as evidences of "enthusiasm," it was a different
matter. He was accused of denying "experimental religion." This
was a charge he could not very well evade. Campbell's simplicity,
his forthrightness, and his crusading democracy all made him feel
at home on the American frontier, and gave him valuable insight
into frontier psychology. But he was not a product of the frontier,
and some things in this new civilization he would never accept.

In this category came "experimental religion." It was a term as
foreign to his vocabulary as the thing it signified was foreign to his
experience. It was not something he had encountered in the
courts of the University of Glasgow. Indeed part of his essay in
answer to the charge described his search through the Bible, ency-
clopedias, and theological dictionaries to find the meaning of the
term. Finally, claimed Campbell, he inquired of a friend "who
had once been deeply initiated into the modern sublimities of the
refined popular doctrine;" and from him he learned that the
phrase "denotes ...a certain mental experience to becoming a
Christian, an exercise of mind, a process through which a person
must pass before he can esteem himself a true Christian; and until

we know from his recital of it that he has been the subject of it, we cannot esteem him a Christian." So expressed, "experimental religion" was nothing more than the "experience" which Calvinistic theology demanded as an evidence of conversion and which had caused Alexander, Calvinist reared, so much consternation in the days of his youth. But he had learned, in the fifteen years he spent on the American Frontier that this doctrine had been carried to an arid and paralyzing extreme undreamed of among the Seceders of Ireland.

Since it was "some invisible, indescribable energy exerted upon the minds of men in order to make them Christians; and that, too, independent of, or prior to, the word believed," regeneration was popularly conceived as coming before faith and even before a knowledge of the gospel. Such a belief, declared Campbell "is replete with mischief;" and he recounted an example of its operation:

> A devout preacher told me, not long since, that he was regenerated about three years before he believed in Christ. He considered himself 'as born again by a physical energy of the Holy Spirit, as a dead man would be raised to life by the mighty power of the Eternal Spirit.' Upon his own hypotheses, (metaphysical, it is true,) he was three years a 'godly unbeliever' …and if he had died during the three years, he would have been saved, though he believed not the gospel. Such is the effect of metaphysical theology.

If regeneration could come independent of belief in or knowledge of the Scriptures, the doctrine led to an appalling conclusion: "The popular preachers," said Campbell, "and the popular systems, alike render the word of God of no effect. Some of them are so awfully bold as to represent it as 'a dead letter.' According to them it ought never to have been translated; for the reading of it in an unknown tongue, if accompanied with some supernatural power, with some new revelation of the Spirit, would have been as suitable to the salvation of men, as though read in our own tongue."

The belief that man was absolutely helpless to do anything toward effecting his salvation until he had been the recipient of this supernatural regeneration was naturally repugnant to Campbell because of his sense of human freedom and responsibility. Many years before, Alexander had rejected the Augustinian and Calvinistic anthropology that made the Fall of Man the most important point in the history of salvation, and blamed all the woes of humankind on the blighting effects of original sin. When he worked out his theory of the covenants, Campbell had relegated the Fall to a subordinate and very unimportant place. His "fallen man" was not a poor sinner trembling in the agony of guilt and shame. He was simply the man defined by Lockian psychology, whose knowledge must come only through the avenue of his five senses. Before the Fall, humanity could perceive God by sight and by hearing, the senses acted upon directly by the Spirit; after the Fall, the knowledge received through the senses was limited to the natural world, and the revelation of the Scriptures then became necessary. "Original sin" became, in Campbell's mind, an inherited and perpetual limitation of man's power of perception, instead of an inherited and perpetual guilt!

He never doubted that humanity, limited by senses, was a free agent who could work out destiny and salvation through the use of will and intellect. Hence, Campbell reserved some of the sharpest satire in his essay for the type of "orthodox divine" who "tells the people that they are 'spiritually dead as a stone;' nor can they, 'in the state of nature,' do any thing that can contribute to their regeneration. 'It depends entirely upon the Spirit of God, which, as the wind blows where it lists, works when, and upon whom it pleases.'" The twelve apostles, declared Alexander, "in all their public addresses, on record, delivered not one sentence of this kind of preaching;" it was "the most insipid and useless thing in the world. Miserable comforters are such preachers! They have no glad tidings of great joy to all people. They resemble a physician, who, instead of administering a remedy to his patient, delivers him a lecture on the nature of his disease."

Such a doctrine not only insulted Campbell's philosophy of common sense; it was equally repugnant to his philosophy of happiness. The result of such a doctrine was wholly repellent to Campbell's analytical mind. It issued the belief that humanity must have some physical sign of pardon, and that the emotions are the guide in determining salvation.

The "thousands of modern divines" who preached "the regeneration of pagans without the word" were teaching not the Scriptures but the philosophy of Plato, and to Alexander this theory was not even "quite so rational as the dogmas of a regeneration after death in purgatory." In spite of the assurance with which he spoke against the popular enthusiastic religion, Campbell had no illusion that he was dealing with a simple and easily explained question. In a footnote to his article he whimsically remarked

> In spite of all our efforts, the vortex of metaphysical jargon will draw us in. I wrote this to prevent mistakes—perhaps it may create some …We doubt not, but in the above we speak a mixed dialect; perhaps half the language of Ashdod and half the language of Canaan.

Many of Campbell's readers were positive he was creating new mistakes. A man who spoke so highly of reason and so lightly of the operations of the Holy Spirit was suspect, if not wholly damned. Some of his readers dropped their subscriptions; some retained them only through curiosity to see what new strange blasphemous theory he was about to enunciate. Of far more importance to Alexander, was his father Thomas' concern over his rashness. From the beginning of the publication of The Christian

Baptist, in fact, Thomas Campbell, however much he might approve the matter of his son's essays, had been disturbed at their fiery, caustic tone. To try to alleviate this effect, he had contributed articles, over the initials "T. W.," written in a more conciliatory vein. Doubtless he counseled moderation many times in conversation with his son, but Alexander's essay on "experimental religion" brought Thomas' first published protest of the editor's style. He agreed with Alexander's exposure of the false and absurd extremes to which the theory had been carried, and he objected to the term "experimental religion" as an "unscriptural, indefinite, unmeaning phrase, which, at best, is only calculated to perplex, mislead, and deceive." But Thomas Campbell was, and always remained, a reasonably sound Calvinist. He had had a proper "experience" and a "call," and he feared that his son's slashing attack would make Alexander appear to deny more than he thought Alexander meant to deny. So, Thomas wrote his views on the operations of the Holy Spirit in a letter to the editor signed "T. W.," which began:

> Sir: …upon reading your animadversions on experimental religion, I was persuaded that it would likely give offense to many of your pious readers; and that, instead of obviating the charge brought against you and your associates, of 'denying experimental religion,' it would rather increase it. This I have since understood to be actually the case. I, therefore for my part, could have wished, that you had treated that very delicate and, at the same time, very important subject, in a different manner.

Great as was his respect and affection for his father, Alexander, at thirty-six, would be his own judge of what he considered right. At the end of his first year as an editor, he was gratified that the circulation of his paper "far surpassed my expectations;" but he made it clear to his readers that "Whenever I cannot obtain a circulation for what I believe to be the truth, I will cease to be an editor." Heir to a firm sense of self-reliance, he believed that he had within himself a touchstone to guide his actions. Hence, his calm assertion at the close of the first volume of his magazine: "My great object was to please myself."

A RESTORATION
Of the Ancient Order of Things.
NO. I.

Extract from the Minutes of the Baptist Missionary Association of Kentucky, began and held at the Town-Fork Meeting-House, in Fayette county, on Saturday, the 11th September, 1824.

"THE next meeting of this association will be in the First Baptist Meeting-House in Lexington, on the 30th of July next, which will be on the *fifth* Saturday of that month, at 11 o'clock, A. M.

"It is proposed also to have a meeting of all the Baptist preachers who can attend, on Friday, the day preceding the meeting of the association, at 11 o'clock, A. M. at the same place, for the purpose of *a general conference* on the state of religion, and on the subject of reform. All the ministers of the gospel in the Baptist denomination, favorable to these objects, are invited to attend, and, in the spirit of Christian love, by mutual counsel, influence, and exertion, according to the gospel, to aid in advancing the cause of piety in our state.

"*It is obvious to the most superficial observer, who is at all acquainted with the state of Christianity and of the church of the New Testament, that much, very much is wanting, to bring the Christianity and the church of the present day up to that standard—In what this deficiency consists, and how it is to be remedied, or whether it can be remedied at all, are the points to be discovered and determined.* In the deliberations intended, it is designed to take these subjects into serious consideration, and to report the result by way of suggestion and advisement to the Baptist Christian community, and to the churches to which the members of the meeting may particularly belong. We know very well that nothing can be done *right* which is not done according to the gospel, or done *effectually* which is not done by the authority, and accompanied by the blessing of God. While God must do the work, we desire to know, and to acquiesce in his manner of doing it, and submissively to concur and obediently to go along with it."

The sentences we have *italicised* in the preceding extract, are sentences of no ordinary import. The first of them declares a truth as evident as a sunbeam in a cell, to all who have eyes to see. The second presents a subject of enquiry of paramount importance to all who expect to stand before the Son of God in judgment. It affords us no common pleasure to see Christians awaking from their lethargic repose to the consideration of such subjects. That the fact should be acknowledged and lamented that VERY MUCH IS WANTING TO BRING THE CHRISTIANITY AND THE CHURCH OF THE PRESENT DAY UP TO THE NEW TESTAMENT STANDARD amongst a people so

On February 7, 1825, the first of the essays, "A Restoration of the Ancient Order of Things," appeared in The Christian Baptist.

Restoration of the
Ancient Order of Things

THE EDITOR of *The Christian Baptist* gave free reign to his talent for satirical attack on whatever he considered an abuse in the Christian system, while his own program offered inference more than explicit statement. By the beginning of 1825, Campbell believed the time had arrived to develop his view of a pure and undefiled religion, and to present his plan for Christian unity. The first of a series of essays entitled "A Restoration of the Ancient Order of Things" appeared in February 1825. The series ran thirty-two issues, the final essay appearing in September 1829. The key word was *order*. Almost every major idea concerning the nature of Christian organization Campbell would expound and expand for the next quarter century appeared in these essays.

Aware of the implications of his title, he shared with many predecessors and contemporaries, "his general presuppositions in regard to the authority of Scripture and the normative character of the Apostolic Churches," Campbell still realized that in some respects he did not stand in the long line of other Protestant reformers. The small group that had gathered about him and his father were often called "the Reformers," but he considered it a misnomer. They did not seek to reform, but to restore. The time for reformation was past; and he wished to make the matter clear in his initial essay.

> All the famous reformations in history have rather been reformations of creeds and clergy, than of religion. Since the New Testament was finished; it is fairly to be presumed that there cannot be any reformation of religion … Human system, whether of philosophy or of religion, are proper subjects of reformation; but Christianity cannot be reformed. Every attempt to reform Christianity is like an attempt to create a new sun, or to change the revolutions of the heavenly bodies … In a word we have had reformations enough. The very name has become as offensive, as the term "revolution" in France.

He was glad to admit his debt to his predecessors: "I do cheerfully acknowledge, that all they who have been reputed reformers, have been our benefactors, and that we are all indebted to them in our political and religious capacities for their labors." But their work had not been enough since the church remained divided and in conflict. Reformers might become so intent on perfecting a religious system they would not concern themselves with the problem of unity. They might sidestep the problem by the appeal to the unity of an invisible church known only to the mind of God. Not Alexander Campbell.

For him, no movement could really be vital or sufficient that did not have as its basic motive the union of all Christians. Not just a nominal union of the sects—"I have no idea of seeing, nor wish to see the sects unite in one grand army," he said—but a corporate union in one body, visible and invisible. In 1809, he had accepted his father's Catholic plea that the church was "essentially, intentionally, and constitutionally one," and the years had only increased his conviction of the necessity for this unity. The more he read his Bible, the more he was impressed with the fact that throughout the New Testament there was a perfect horror of division in the church, and that the church was constantly described as the *Body of Christ.* Thus, the church became in a sense an extension of the Incarnation; as did Christ during His earthly life was "incarnate in a fleshly body." Now he resided "in a real visible Body—His Church." There was a great mystery concealed in the relationship of Christ to his body, the church universal; and any division in that Church was a virtual rending of his body. Whatever the later position of the church, it seemed obvious that the unity for which Saint Paul and Saint John were striving was "a visible unity, *institutional* in its character." No mere federation of denominations, Campbell thought, really touched the heart of the question of division. The only solution was individual churches could be considered no more than local organic unity societies of the one body.

This "high" doctrine vested the church with great authority, which was as Campbell thought it should be. The Protestant tendency to disregard the authority of the church, to look upon it simply as "a moral society," found no response in his mind, for he believed the church divine. The Protestant contention that salvation was consummated outside the church did not correspond with his concept of the church as "God's revelation in history." In

Campbell's opinion, salvation was assured through participation "in this community of divine grace." In the first volume of his magazine, Campbell submitted to his readers the "grand proposition, 'that the association called the church of Jesus Christ is, *in propria forma*, the only institution of God left on earth to illuminate and reform the world."

Although the Protestant world might oppose his concept of the church, Campbell was convinced that his position was philosophically sound. He had no patience with the idea that religion was entirely a personal affair, operating directly between God and the soul, or that the church was an unnatural institution, imposed upon man from without and foreign to his nature. On the contrary, he taught repeatedly that "religion was made for man and not man for religion." Anticipating a good deal of what was later advanced by the Harvard professor of philosophy, Josiah Royce, Campbell insisted that humankind was primarily and essentially social, and needed a society or a divine fellowship, in which to realize and work out salvation. In the spiritual as in the natural realm, human beings seek fellowship; and the church is a medium for satisfying that inmost spiritual need. There could be "no salvation in solitariness—because there is not solitariness!" The theories of social psychology reinforced Campbell's effort "to extricate Christianity from Protestant obscurantism and individualism, and to anchor the Christian life firmly in objective reality, that is, in what God has done and has revealed in history" through His creation of the Christian community. A purely private devotion, apart from church worship, could "only lead to a pietism which is superior in its attitude to others," and which "is totally inadequate to the conception of Christian living." A purely personal quest for individual moral life was all too likely to end in "Lord, I thank Thee that I am not as other men." In this concept of religion Campbell found little to admire, and he reserved some of his sharpest satire for the "sobering anchorite" who spent his life shrouded in concern about his own soul. To the theologian on the

Buffaloe, intensely interested in the world about him, Christianity was a way of service to humankind; Jesus "who served mankind in His Body" had given to His disciples a body—the church—that they too might "serve the world, and so glorify Him." So conceived, the church became an institution which met the most fundamental need of humanity, and to fail to strive for its corporate unity was unthinkable.

Through the years Alexander Campbell came to the conviction that the consecrated disciple must take with an awful literalness, the high priestly intercessory prayer of Jesus: "Holy Father—now I do not pray for these only (for the unity and success of the apostles), but for those also who shall believe that you have sent me." For someone who would give himself utterly to an understanding of and submission to the will of Christ, Campbell was wholly convinced that these words would admit of only one interpretation. He wrote:

> It will be confessed, without argument … that the conversion of the world, and the unity, purity, and happiness of the disciples of the Messiah, were the sublime subjects of his humiliation to death. For this he prayed in language never heard on earth before, in words which not only expressed the ardency of his desires, but at the same time unfolded the *plan* in which his benevolence and philanthropy were to be triumphant … There are unalterable laws in the moral world, as in the natural … it is enough to say, on this topic, that the Savior made the *unity of the disciples* essential to the conviction of the world; and he that attempts it independent of this essential, sets himself against the wisdom and plans of heaven, and aims at overruling the dominion and government of the Great King. On this subject we have many things to say, and hard to be uttered, because the people are dull of hearing …

The title of the essays Campbell elected to discuss was "A Restoration of the Ancient Order of Things"—a title that stressed the ideas of the primitive church rather than the idea of unity. In these essays, as well as in other articles in *The Christian Baptist*, he gradually developed his plan. He talked far more about the early church than about the union of Christians but not because he wished to delegate the ideal of unity to second place. On the contrary, he was simply convinced, as all the earlier reformers had been, that the Apostolic Church presented the perfect model. If Christians could accept the essential qualities of this church, then union of the denominations would automatically follow.

Campbell did not feel that placing his model for Christianity back almost two thousand years in history was out of harmony with the adventurous spirit of his age. He was as interested as any person of enlightenment in the development of the full powers of human beings, and he would place no embargo on thought, whether in the field of science or philosophy or religion. He was satisfied that the model of religious perfection lay not in the future but in the past, in the life of Christ. All else, as the *Declaration and Address* had affirmed, belonged to the edification of the church, and might be changed from century to century to meet the changing needs of humanity without disturbing the essential body of the faith. So impressed was Campbell with the idea that a restoration of the Apostolic Church, which to him was synonymous with the regaining of a proper understanding of the mind of Christ, would usher in a golden age of unity and harmony in His body, that he closed his first essay in the series on the "Ancient Order" with the comment:

> ... Celebrated as the era of reformation is, we doubt not but that the era of restoration will as far transcend it in importance and fame, through the long and blissful Millennium, as the New Testament transcends in simplicity, beauty, excellency, and majesty, the dogmas and

notions of the creed of Westminster and the canons of the
Assembly's digest … For to the end of time, we shall have
no other revelation of the spirit, no other New Testament,
no other savior, and no other religion than we now have,
when we understand, believe, and practice the doctrine
of Christ delivered to us by his apostles.

He admitted he had not always felt this high conviction of the
necessity of a united church, founded on a restudy of the "Ancient
Order." So he interpolated a bit of his personal experience into
one of the essays:

> … Thus I went on purging my views, and returning to
> his institute until I became so speckled a bird that scarce
> one of my species would cordially consociate with me; but
> I gained ample remuneration in the pursuit, and got a use
> of my wings which I never before experienced. Thus too
> I was led into a secret, which as I received freely, I com-
> municate freely. It is this: There is an ancient and modern
> order of things in the Lord's house. Now I am sure that if
> all my brethren had only the half of the religious experi-
> ence I have had upon this subject, they would be doubly
> in the spirit of this ancient order, and their progress would
> be geometrically proportioned to what it is now. My
> *friends* will forgive me for so much egotism —*and my ene-*
> *mies will find fault with me at any rate;* so that it is little
> matter as respects them, what I say or do …

Egotism or not, Alexander could not escape the conviction
that he had been given some new vision and had been entrusted
with a peculiar mission. A review of the history of Christianity had
convinced him no further "attempt 'to reform the doctrine, discipline, and government of the church,' … can promise a better
result than those which have been attempted and languished to

death." Making their appeal to the theory and practice of the
Apostolic Church, Luther and Calvin had sought to formulate a
complete Biblical theology, Cartwright and Laud an authoritative
form of government, Glass and Haldane a *jure divino* program of
public worship. All failed to bring unity to the church because
they attempted too much. Campbell was ready to attack the problem from a different perspective, to suggest something simpler
and yet more inclusive.

Still, Campbell realized, Christian union, to be real and vital,
must be maintained by visible bonds—even though those bonds
must be as few as possible. Some external forms, and some real
symbols, were necessary for the unity of the church. He would
insist, with Saint Paul, that unity must be safeguarded by the
authority of a common faith; by the obligation of common sacraments; by the recognition of a common ministry; and it must be
expressed in some common mode of public worship. Nor, as he
had already indicated, would he have any patience with those who
insisted in regarding "*visible* unity as something lower than spiritual unity, or as a denial of *spiritual* unity." Visible unity, of course,
might be entirely artificial; and no one had ever deplored the cold
and lifeless formalities of a worship untouched by the true spirit of
holy communion with God more than did the crusading editor of
The Christian Baptist. But with his complex turn of mind,
Campbell was convinced there could be no real spiritual unity
unless it revealed itself in a visible way. A visible unity, properly
considered, was nothing less than the "true expression of spiritual
unity."

Barton W. Stone and Thomas Campbell had preceded
Alexander by several years with their plea for Christian unity, and
there were no more passionate apostles of the "One, Holy, and
Catholic Church" than these two consecrated men. But they were
too inclined to be content with "vague expressions of unity;" fearing old tyrannies, they emphasized a personal religion of the spirit, and treaded lightly on the question of authority. Alexander

Campbell loved unity, tolerance, and liberty no less than did his
father or his friend Stone. But he was more realistic. He acknowledged that absolute intellectual freedom could never produce
unity, and without authority humanity was "bound to wander in
lonely paths;" a religious experience confined entirely to the
realm of a person's own spirit in its contact with God might be
very satisfying for the individual, but it was destructive to the
organic union of the Divine Society which Campbell felt essential
for the well-being of the world. Such a union must rest on some
authority. The problem was "to limit the field of this authority"—
to achieve "the maximum of liberty with the minimum of authority." To protest the problem was too complex for solution, that it
would involve the relinquishing of too many cherished traditions,
was simply to surrender the ideal of Christian unity and the conviction of its necessity. And Alexander Campbell, no more than
his father or Barton Stone, was a man to surrender an ideal or a
conviction. Where they talked passionately and long of a unity
accomplished through Christian love and tolerance, Alexander
tried to formulate a definite plan on which all might agree.

The first great question in formulating a plan for unity was,
naturally, that of a common faith. Campbell refused to use the
term "creed." He wished to stress the fact that the church was
founded on a person, not a creed. Christianity was not a philosophy or a theology, but a religion. There was, indeed, high ground
for contending that the simple oath of loyalty to Christ was the
one permanently binding statement of belief for all the centuries,
nothing further was ordinarily necessary for the maintenance of
unity of faith. This allegiance, mystically conceived, would forever save this religion from degenerating into a mere ethical or
moral code. "There is something higher than the *Sermon on the
Mount*—something which defies reduction to formula or creed—
the life of Jesus."

The requirement of submission to only this simple confession
of faith would, Campbell was convinced, assure liberty of opinion

and allow room for the free development of thought within the church. Additions to the faith were unthinkable; the foundations for the belief were forever laid in the New Testament. The New Testament did not limit the possibility of development—though that development must be in harmony with its principles. Campbell insisted that there must be within the church "the fullest room for theological and philosophical advancement," and a Christian community. A community which would dare "to found itself on the principle of an instructed church membership rather than a dogmatically guided membership must, more than any other, give attention to scholarship." It was for this very reason that "the Church must not lend herself to, nor base her unity upon, the philosophy or theology of any one age. She must base it on something deeper and more abiding."

Thomas Campbell made it plain in the *Declaration and Address*, and Alexander had several times repeated, they did not object to creedal statements of belief, provided these creeds were not made terms of admission to the church or tests of fellowship binding on all future generations. They made a clear distinction "between 'dogma' as a fact of Christian experience, and 'theology' as an explanation of Christian facts in language suited to the thought of a single age." Creeds had not been the best safeguards of the church's unity, as the numerous creeds, existing among sorely divided Christendom, seemed sufficient proof. They had their definite limits. Language was the tool of ideas, and as the expressions of thought in different ages changed, the terms in which the church expressed its belief would need to change. Also, there was the possibility the "new learning" would find some article of theology outmoded or erroneous, and belief were permanently enshrined in a creed, orthodoxy would be made "synonymous with ignorance." It was in this train of thought that Campbell, in January 1828, answering a circular on creeds written by Dr. Noel, penned his most pertinent indictment of these stringently binding articles of belief:

Now I unfeignedly declare, that my chief and almost exclusive objections to a creed are the two following: 1st. That they do keep corruptions and heresies in the church; and 2dly, that they do lay unrighteous restraints upon the human mind. All the corruptions in the Romish church—all the corruptions in the Protestant or Episcopal church—all the corruptions in the Presbyterian church, are kept in them, locked up by the efficiency of their creeds from one generation to another. And in the second place, the minds of their youth are embargoed and restrained by the creed and her daughter, the catechism; so that the descendants of Papists and Protestants do not, and cannot keep pace with the advance and progress of light in the age in which we live. Thus I find the Catholic the same today as before Luther was born. Although the world has made great advances for four hundred years, the Catholic youth is, in religious views and apprehensions, just the same that Frederick Credulitas was who lived in Germany, A.D. 1400. And among the Episcopalians, John Simplex, who is not an admirer of the 39 Articles, Liturgy and Homilies, has not one new idea above William Nomind, who flourished under the reign of Queen Elizabeth. Thus I find my neighbor George Stedfast, who got his child christened last 'Sabbath Day,' has not advanced with the age one idea above Peter Bluesocks, who was nephew to John Knox, A.D. 1630. Now all this has been accomplished by a human creed, which has equally held fast the notions of a darker age, and shut out from the mind all the benefits and advances of this age in the knowledge of the Holy Scriptures. I say, then, that 'creeds' are in my judgment, to be denounced as masters over our faith—as rules or standards: For instead of keeping corruptions out, they lock it in, the church; and instead of helping the mind for-

ward in the study of that book, the meaning of which was
entirely lost two or three centuries ago, they do most
undeniably prevent its illumination and emancipation.

Finally, Campbell was assured that his plan for preserving the
unity of the faith not only safeguarded the right of freedom of
thought within the church, but also represented the true fusion of
liberty and authority. Also evident from the beginning of his editorial career, Campbell saw no conflict between the emphasis on
individual liberty in Paul's epistles to the Romans and Galatians,
and the emphasis on order realized in institutionalism in Paul's
later epistles to the Colossians and Ephesians. Hence, he was resting his whole case for unity on the Pauline basis of liberty and corporate loyalty.

Whatever his other defects of vision, this much of Saint Paul's
meaning Alexander Campbell had clearly perceived. He was
ready to stake his whole program on Paul's high view of the
church as a divine society, as "an organism—not a machine—a
body, capable of growth and development," as a *fellowship* society, "whose keynote is *corporate loyalty*, and not legalized discipline; whose bond is love and not authority in the usually accepted sense." But Saint Paul saw "a religion which *based itself on personality* for such was Christianity—the possibility of a Church
which transcended both," a church which should be "at once the
home of freedom and of loyalty." For the soul, he realized, needed "both freedom and loyalty for its highest development." In fact,
loyalty was the only atmosphere in which freedom could truly
work toward attainment. Perceiving these things, Alexander
Campbell would heartily subscribe to a dictum that Josiah Royce
later pronounced: "In loyalty, when loyalty is properly defined, is
the fulfillment of the whole moral law."

Thus, the theologian evolved the plan that, he was assured,
could work to the unification and purification of the faith. That,
he felt, might, paradoxical as it seemed, free the Church "from

legalistic and authoritarian institutionalism on the one hand, and from anarchical individualism on the other." In seeking "to secure a personal basis for love working itself out in loyalty to Jesus and to the corporate society which is His Body," in not agreeing that "loyalty is best preserved in the Body by legalized methods of setting up infallible standards in credalized forms," in stressing the fact "that to be a traitor to such a loyalty, based and founded in love, is a more heinous sin than to be a little muddle-headed on some theological explanation of a fact of experience," Alexander Campbell had no fears that he was opening the way to a dangerous looseness of doctrine within the Church. Placing confidence in the value of the distinction between "dogma" as a fact of Christian experience and "theology," as a metaphysical explanation of the Christian concepts, he believed that "the great Christian facts of the Fatherhood of God, the Deity, and perfect Humanity of Jesus Christ, His redeeming work for humankind, and the indwelling of the Holy Spirit" could be "tenaciously held by the disciples without theological creeds playing any part at all in conserving their unity." As in the early Church, the unity of such a Divine Society would be "a unity of life based upon a mystical experience of these great facts" of the common faith. The unity of this common faith, Campbell believed, was to be safeguarded and the concept of the one body implemented by the obligation of the common sacraments of Baptism and the Eucharist.

In the first place, were they not "the Church's first center of unity?" Did not the Apostles preach one Baptism and the Supper as the two visible symbols of the disciples' unity of faith? Symbols, in Campbell's opinion, were necessary to the disciples of the nineteenth century. The Church should see in these two rites what Saint Paul had seen: they were social ceremonies expressive of the

Unity within a common faith was to be safeguarded by an obligation to the sacraments of Baptism and the Eucharist, wrote Campbell. Oral tradition holds that this pewter communion set was used by Alexander Campbell in formal worship services.

koinonia, the fellowship. The disciples were to express their love corporately in the two great sacraments of unity. And thus the sacramental way became the way of Christianity fitted to the needs of all humanity. Mystical experiences, however great their value, could come to only a few; mysticism was distinctly individualistic. Therefore, the sacramental, and not the mystic, must be "the way of God's coming to the general mass of Christians." Whereby the sacraments became real channels of His grace—a

Catholic doctrine that Alexander Campbell would not hesitate to espouse. Furthermore, he did not overlook the value, which the sacraments have of preserving belief; he was fully aware of the value of their dramatic appeal. Yet, it might be reasoned, "dogma is best enshrined in dramatic form, better transmitted by art than by logical definition;" and it seemed the first three centuries the Christian doctrine of the Cross had been enshrined—not in creeds—but in the two redemptive rites of Baptism and the Lord's Supper. So Campbell thought it must always be, if the church was to preserve its potent vitality.

Many Protestant sects held the legalistic view that Baptism and the Lord's Supper were mere commands to be attended to, not having any sacramental value, or "rich provisions of grace." Such a view of God was detestable to Campbell and, he believed, without an atom of justification in the New Testament. If these sacraments were commanded, it was because they were vital to the spiritual life of the worshipper. Campbell interpreted the whole process of spiritual knowledge and enjoyment in the kingdom of God on the basis of Locke's theory of natural knowledge. As in the natural world the five senses were the five avenues to knowledge and pleasure, reasoned Campbell, so in the spiritual world faith opened the gateway to the blessings of the Kingdom, and the ordinances became the necessary means of this spiritual enjoyment. In a lengthy essay on "The Kingdom of Heaven," written several years after the close of his series on "The Ancient Order," Campbell explained:

> In the Kingdom of Heaven, faith is, the *principle*, and ordinances the *means* of enjoyment; because all the wisdom, power, love, mercy, compassion, or *grace of God* is in the ordinances of the Kingdom of Heaven; and if all grace be in them it can only be enjoyed through them. What, then, under the present administration of the Kingdom of Heaven, are the ordinances which contain

the grace of God? They are preaching the gospel—
immersion in the name of Jesus into the name of the
Father, and of the Son, and of the Holy Spirit—the reading and teaching of the Living Oracles—the Lord's day—
the Lord's supper—fasting—prayer—confession of sins—
and praise ... These primary and sacred ordinances of the
Kingdom of Heaven are the means of our individual
enjoyment of the present salvation of God.

Considering the sacraments, or the ordinances, Campbell by
no means limited their number to two—though Baptism and the
Eucharist naturally remained the central institutions. Campbell
would never change his belief that "the whole essence" of his reformation movement was found in this insistence on a proper
understanding of the spiritual and philosophical import of the
sacred ordinances. Many years later, writing an article in which he
even classed the Bible itself as one of the sacraments of the
church, and described an ordinance as "the mode in which the
grace of God acts on human nature," he declared: "The current
reformation, *if conspicuous now or hereafter* for anything, must be
so because of the conspicuity it gives the Bible and its ordinances
as the *indispensable moral means of spiritual life* and health ...
The distinguishing characteristic is a *restoration of the ordinances
of the new institution to their place and power.*"

Campbell did not specifically discuss the ordinance of
Baptism in his series on "The Ancient Order," which was concerned with affairs in the Church, and not with the means of
admission to the divine society. Rather in another series, entitled
the "Ancient Gospel," he addressed this question and devoted
some seven articles to his views on "Christian immersion." In the
Walker debate he had done little more than present the conventional Baptist arguments for "believer's Baptism." Now he was
beginning to see a full richness of beauty in the sacrament.

He was impressed with the power of both Baptism and the

Eucharist to enshrine belief, to present in simple symbolism the drama of the Cross and the Resurrection. He wrote:

> These two ordinances of the glorious and mighty Lord fully exhibit the gospel in the most appropriate symbols. The preaching of the Lord and his apostles, we all agree was the gospel in words. The historic books of the New Testament are the gospel in facts. Immersion is the gospel in water—the Lord's supper is the gospel in bread and wine—and a pure and a holy life is the gospel in its effects.

But far more important was the fact Campbell was sure it was a fact, and not just an opinion that through Baptism, man might be assured of the divine forgiveness of his sins. The realization of this position naturally led Campbell to the belief that Baptism was a most singular and wonderful institution; and so he now amplified his view:

> The laws of grace are as sure in their operation, and as certain in their effects, as the laws of nature. When I put my finger into the fire, by a law of nature, it is burned: and just as certainly am I forgiven of all my trespasses, by a law of grace, when in faith I am immersed in water into the name of the Lord Jesus.... Hence in the moral fitness of things in the evangelical economy, Baptism or immersion is made the first act of a Christian's life, or rather the regenerating act itself ...

Lest he again be accused of preaching a "water salvation," Campbell continued by emphasizing the position that there was no efficacy in the water—any more than in the bread and wine. The miracle was not magical but moral.

Campbell's mature views on the other great sacrament of the church—the Eucharist—was presented to his readers in four of the essays on "The Ancient Order" subtitled, "The Breaking of the Bread" and in a lengthy disquisition written some few years later called "The Breaking of the Loaf." Campbell preferred this specific term as used in Acts, because it linked the Communion so closely with the primitive church and with the fellowship meals of Jesus with His disciples; but he did not object to the designation "the Lord's Supper." "The communion of the saints," he thought too general; and he most emphatically did not like the Latin designation, "the Sacrament"—the sacramentum, the oath of loyalty—or Greek term, the Eucharist, the eucharistia, "giving of thanks." He considered them not in harmony with his announced principle of "the calling of Bible things by Bible names." Campbell wrote with even more than his usual vigor and enthusiasm; he felt that in the observance of this sacred ordinance the Protestant world had become especially heedless and neglectful. They had forgotten the full significance of its nature and design, Campbell insisted that the Apostolic Church had made "the Breaking of the Loaf" the central feature, the center of adoration, of its regular worship. The Lord's Supper was observed every Lord's Day when the saints assembled together, and, Campbell added, "apostolic example is justly esteemed of equal authority with an apostolic precept." To impress his idea that the ordinances of the early Church were elements of the ancient order binding to all eternity, he continued with one of his characteristic extreme remarks:

> There is not a proposition in Euclid susceptible of a clearer or fuller demonstration than this: *Every regenerated man must be devoted to the ancient order of things in the church of God*–provided it be granted as a postulatum, that *the ancient order of things was consonant to the will of the Most High*. A mind not devoted to the whole will of God, revealed in the New Book, is unregenerated. He that does not obey God in every thing, obeys him in nothing.

Applying this dictum to the body which he was holding rather uneasy communion, Campbell could not resist a few slyly tart thrusts for he felt that the Baptist, in general, observed the Lord's Supper in as infrequent and casual a fashion as any other Protestant sect:

> Some Baptists are extremely devoted to immersion. They have read all the Baptisms on record in the New Testament, and beginning at the Jordan they end at the city of Philippi, in the bath in the Roman prison. The *ancient* mode and nothing else will please their taste. Away with your sprinkling and pouring and babyism! ... But when the ancient mode of observing the Lord's day or of breaking of Bread is called to their *attention*, they fall asleep ... They have got a *Baptist conscience*, and not the conscience of the regenerate. A Baptist conscience hears the voice of God and regards his authority only where there is much water... Many, we fear, think they are pleasing and serving God, while they are pleasing and serving themselves. They think they are devout, but they are devoted to their own will.

Then, calling as usual on the testimony of history to support his point, "There is," he remarked, "a corroborating influence in authentic history, which, while it does not authorize any thing as of divine authority, it confirms the conviction of our duty in things divinely established, by observing how they were observed and how they were laid aside." Campbell presented his authorities among the apostolic fathers to prove that: "All antiquity concurs in evincing that for the first three centuries all the churches broke bread once a week." Though in the Greek Church, weekly communion was observed until the seventh century, and "by one of their canons, 'such as neglected three weeks together were excommunicated.'" In the Roman Church the practice started to decline in the fourth century "when all things began to be changed by baptized Pagans," and finally "the breaking of bread in simplicity and godly sincerity once a week, degenerated into a pompous sacrament once a year at Easter." At the reformation, continued Campbell, "this subject was but slightly investigated by the reformers." Nevertheless, Calvin had declared yearly communion "a most evident contrivance of the Devil" and added, "every week, at least, the table of the Lord should have been spread for Christian assemblies, and the promises declared, by which, in partaking of it, we might be spiritually fed." To corroborate his evidence Campbell presented extracts from the writings of John Mason, the eminent Presbyterian doctor, and other modern scholars. Then, for the benefit of the Methodists, he quoted from John Wesley's sermon on "The Duty of Constant Communion," and repeated a sentence from Wesley's letter to America in 1784: "I also advise the elders to administer the supper of the Lord on every Lord's day." In spite of this advice from the reformers, the situation had continued much as before until near the end of the eighteenth century. Alexander Campbell became aware of the existence of small independent groups, leaders among whom were the Glasites, and, later, the Mclean Baptists, which emphasized the return of the Lord's Supper to its primitive position as the center of the church's corporate worship. When he was a student at Glasgow, for the church of the Reverend Greville Ewing, he observed weekly communion. By the time he wrote his essays "On the Breaking of the Bread," he could report:

> Since the commencement of the present century, many congregations in England, Scotland, Ireland, and some in the United States and Canada, both Independents and Baptists, have attended upon the supper every Lord's day, and the practice is every day gaining ground.

The desire of the Glasites to restore the Eucharist to its place as the central act of worship was, in part, a reaction to the over-emphasis on preaching to which the Presbyterians had witnessed, and Campbell thoroughly shared this attitude of the Glasites, which by no means indicated that he undervalued preaching. On the contrary, he listed preaching among the sacred ordinances. He realized that to be vital, preaching must be sacramental. He agreed that, "It must be an act prolonging the Great Act, mediating it and conveying it." But he was concerned with the danger that the minister and the sermon usurp the place of God in worship. The insistence on the centrality of the Lord's Supper as the supreme point of communion between God and humanity was, in Campbell's opinion, the surest defense against this danger. The main theme of the worship was not dependent on a person or any message delivered. The Lord's Supper assured a permanent, accessible, silent witness to His presence.

It would not do so if the administration of the Supper were only in the hands of the ordained clergy. Thomas Campbell's first experience on the American frontier revealed to him that many churches must go months, sometimes years, without the communion of bread and wine simply because no regular preacher was there to administer them. Hence, Alexander was logically led to the assertion of another proposition in his essay, "The Breaking of the Loaf:"

> All Christians are members of the house or family of God, are called and constituted a holy and royal priesthood, and may, therefore, bless God for the Lord's Table, its loaf and cup—approach it without fear and partake of it with joy, as often as they please in remembrance of the death of their Lord and Savior.

Thus, his doctrine of "the priesthood of all believers," directly serving the high priest without need of a "human mediator," furnished him his argument that wherever a group of consecrated believers were gathered together there the Lord's Supper could be served. Therefore, he continued, "he that gives thanks for the loaf should break it, not as the representative of the Lord, but after his example." To support these views, Campbell quoted from "the great John Milton." But he was aware of a danger in giving the administration of the sacrament into the hands of the average member: it might lack the beautiful and simple solemnity the occasion demanded. So Campbell cautioned that:

> ...much depends upon the *manner* of celebrating the supper, as well as upon the *frequency* ...The bred Christian is like the well-bred gentleman—his manners are graceful, easy, artless, and simple. All stiffness and forced formality is as priceless in the Christian as in the gentleman. A courteous and polite family differs exceedingly from a soldier's mess mates, or a ship's crew, in all the ceremonies of the table. There is a Christian decency and a Christian order, as well as political courtesy and complaisance.

Though he might draw his first argument for weekly communion from apostolic precedent, it was, Campbell hastened to explain, by no means his strongest argument, which, he said, "will be drawn from the nature, import, and design of the breaking of bread." Those who made the Lord's supper "an *extraordinary* and not an *ordinary* act of Christian worship" could not, he felt, be fully comprehending. "Much darkness and superstition," he wrote,

> ...are found in the minds and exhibited in the practice of the devout annual, semi-annual and quarterly observance of the breaking of bread. They generally make a Passover of it ...With all the bitterness of sorrow, and

gloominess of superstition, they convert it into a religious penance, accompanied with a morose piety and an awful affliction of soul and body, expressed in fasting, long prayers, and sad countenances on sundry days of humiliation, fasting and preparation.

On the other hand, Campbell averred, "the intelligent Christian views it in quite another light." To him it was symbolic of many divine truths. It served many holy purposes. The Zwinglian view generally adopted by Methodism, that it was a pure memorial, and nothing more, would seem to Campbell a "low" view that missed much of the sacrament's deepest import.

It was a memorial, but not merely a memorial of the awful fact of the crucifixion, to be observed in sorrow and gloom. It was a symbol of the glorious promise of the resurrection; the bread was "the Bread of Life." "This institution commemorates," wrote Campbell,

> ...the love which reconciled us to God and always furnishes us with a new argument to live to him who dies for us. Him who feels not the eloquence and power of this argument, all other arguments assail in vain ...It is as well intended to crucify the world, as to quicken us to God, and to diffuse his love within us. The Lord's Supper became both the great emotional center of the Christian religion and its moral dynamic, for the bread and wine were the truest and most vivid possible symbols of the passionate love of Christ. The Supper became the "great dramatic act of Christianity community." It was a Proclamation, of the most solemn and holy fact of the Christian religion, setting for the mystery of redemption.

In the Holy Communion, Campbell believed the worshippers had communion both with His body and with one another. It was a fellowship meal, expressive of that passionate love of people, which was at the heart of Christ's teaching. Furthermore, in its broadest sense, this sacrament was symbolic of the one communion of the church universal. So intent was Campbell on impressing this idea of unity inherent in the ordinance, he insisted that on the Lord's table there must of necessity be, literally, but one loaf. The necessity, he hastened to explain, arose from no low legalistic view; it was "not that of a positive law enjoining one loaf and only one, as the ritual of Moses enjoined twelve loaves." Rather it arose from that deep mystic "meaning of the Institution" as explained by Saint Paul. "Because there is one loaf, we, the many, are one body; for we are all partakers of that one loaf." Hence, concluded Campbell: "As there is but one literal body and but one mystical or figurative body having many members; so there must be but one loaf." Surely, when all men came together with cleansed and contrite hearts to break the one loaf, symbolic of His one body, there would be no more bickering and strife in their holy fellowship.

Thinking on this varied import of the Eucharist, Campbell in one of his essays "On the Breaking of Bread," described the sacred ordinance:

> It is an institution full of wisdom and goodness, every Way adapted to the Christian mind. As bread and wine to the Body, so it strengthens his faith and cheers his heart with the love of God. It is a religious feast ... of joy and gladness; ... the sweetest ante past on earth of the society and entertainment of heaven ... If such be its nature and import, and such its design, say, ye saints, whether this act of Christian worship would be a privilege, or a pain, in all your meetings for edification and worship. If it be any proof of the kindness of the Savior it institute it at all, would it not be a greater proof to allow the saints in all their meetings to have this token of his love set before

them, and they called to partake? ... But ... convert it into
an awful and grievous penance, and then grace is exhibited in not enforcing it but seldom ... Just, then, as we
understand its nature and design, will its frequency
appear a favor or a frown. Man is a social animal. As the
thirsty hind pants for the brooks of water, so man pants for
society congenial to his mind. He feels a relish for the
social hearth and the social table; because the feast of sentimental and congenial minds is the feast of reason. Man,
alone and solitary, is but half blessed in any circumstances. Alone and solitary, he is like the owl in the desert,
and the pelican in the wilderness. The social feast is the
native offspring of social minds. Savage or civilized, man
has his social fire, and his social board. And shall the
Christian house and family be always the poorest and
emptiest under heaven? Is the Lord of Christians ... par-
simoniously poor and niggardly? Tell it not ... lest the
votaries of Ceres rejoice! Lest the sons of Bacchus triumph! ... The religion of Jesus Christ is a religion for
men; for rational, for social, for grateful beings. It has its
feasts, and its joys, and its ecstasies too. The Lord's house
is his banqueting place, and the Lord's day is his weekly
festival.

Holding this "high" view of its nature and import, Alexander
Campbell could not fail to consider the Lord's Supper the center
around which the Lord's Day service was formed. If the center was
missing, the rest was likely to seem like a hollow shell. Even so, he
did not mean to imply that only those who gave to the Eucharist
this central place were truly worshipping God or would receive
the grace of His salvation. Such an attitude toward those who disagreed with his interpretation of God's will would simply be a
revival of the bigotry and intolerance, which he was proposing to
combat. But Campbell did, and always would, insist that only

those comprehending the full richness of meaning in both the great sacraments of the Church—Baptism and Eucharist—could enjoy, in the most complete sense the blessing of the kingdom and the communion of the saints on earth. In introducing his essay, "The Breaking of the Loaf," he remarked:

> To come into the kingdom of Jesus Christ is one thing, and to live as a wise, a good, and a happy citizen is another. As every human kingdom has its constitution, laws, ordinances, manners, and customs; so has the kingdom of the Great King. He, then, who would be a good and happy citizen of it, must understand and submit to its constitution, laws, ordinances, manners, and customs. Thus, those Christians holding a "low" view of sacramental values might be citizens of His kingdom, but they were not enjoying the full benefits of their citizenship.

In Campbell's attitude toward the sacraments of the Church, more than at any other one point, was illustrated those complex and various trends of thought and temperament that were entering into the compilation of his religious system. As a child of English Enlightenment, he held a high concept of the dignity of persons and the worth of their natural powers, which rendered untenable the Calvinistic dogmas of total depravity and arbitrary election. But stern Scots Calvinism was irrevocably a part of his heritage, and it would always serve as a check on any tendency toward arrogance that might lurk in a too-exalted view of human dignity. Imperfect humanity ever stood in need of the divine grace—of a constant renewal of spiritual energy, which God, in His goodness, had provided through His holy ordinances. Rationalistic French and mystical Celt met in Campbell's concept of faith as the principle and the sacraments as the means of enjoyment of the grace of God.

✠

Having discussed the basis of the common faith and the obligation of the two common sacraments, which he felt necessary to bind the Church together in unity, Campbell turned his attention to the question of a common ministry. Reacting against an extreme professionalism in the ministry, he embraced the Lutheran doctrine, then current among small groups of Independents, of "the priesthood of all believers." Nevertheless, he recognized that there must be some special orders of ministry. The problem, addressed in some five of the essays on "The Ancient Order," was to make these orders as simple and democratic as possible.

Campbell said in beginning his discussion:

> 1st. That as the church, or congregation, or assembly, (as it is expressed by all these names), is repeatedly called a kingdom– the Kingdom of God, and the kingdom of heaven, it is fairly to be presumed, from the terms themselves, that the government under which the church is placed, is an *absolute monarchy* ... he [the Christ] claims absolute dominion in express and unequivocal terms, and lays all his disciples under the strictest injunctions of unreserved submission ... On this, as a first principle, I found all my views of what is commonly called *church government.* All the churches on earth that Christ has ever acknowledged as his, are so many communities constituting one kingdom, of which he is the head and sovereign ... as the different counties or corporations in the state of Virginia are all component parts of the state, and under the same government. In every congregation or community of Christians the persons that are appointed by the Great King to rule, act pretty much in the capacity of our civil magistrates; or in other words, they have only to see that the laws are obeyed, but have no power nor right to legislate in any one instance, or for any one purpose. The

constitution and laws of this kingdom are all of divine origin and authority, having emanated from the bosom, and
having been promulgated in the name of the Universal
Lord.

Since there was no human body with the right to originate
laws for the kingdom of God, Campbell was naturally led to the
conclusion that: "An individual church or congregation of Christ's
disciples is the only ecclesiastical body recognized in the New
Testament. Such a society is *the highest court of Christ*' on earth."
Within the congregation, of course, were those who were to "act
pretty much in the capacity of our civil magistrates ... to see that
the laws are obeyed." These persons were in the New Testament
termed bishops, or, sometimes, elders, "because they were generally aged persons, and always amongst the oldest converts in the
community in which they officiated." Campbell preferred the title
"bishop" as a designation for the office. The bishop was to be chosen carefully in accordance with stringent requirements both
intellectual and moral, for the duties were manifold: or must be
qualified to teach, and be able by sound teaching both to convince and exhort those who oppose the truth. He must feed the
flock of God with all those provisions that their exigencies require,
or with which God has furnished them in the Christian institution. He must *preside* well. He is from office the standing president of the congregation.

Hence they must have "the dignity of character which [their]
prominence in the Christian congregation behooves [them] to
possess." Basing their call upon these qualifications, the members
of the congregation were vested with the authority to choose their
own bishops.

Campbell gave the power of election and ceremony of ordination to the congregation itself—which was his priestly body and
the normal realm of the Holy Spirit's operations. Though the congregation needed representatives through whom to act, and the

Holy Spirit human agents through whom to work, the power of ordination did not reside in any particular individual or class. The ceremony of ordination was sacramental in the sense that grace was conveyed through it—just as in Baptism and the Eucharist. But here again was nothing magical or mechanical in the rite; its grace was entirely dependent on the intention of those ordaining, and on the faith of the ordained. Nevertheless, the symbol of ordination—the imposition of hands—was no less necessary than the water in Baptism, or the bread and wine in the Eucharist. Signifying they did not consider the ceremony in any way magical was the fact that among the early Christians prayer always accompanied it. God was the ordainer, and God granted the grace of ordination wherever there was the sanction of the church, pure heart in the recipient, and the valid form of prayer and the imposition of hands. Furthermore, Campbell insisted that the act of ordination not be performed by "a collection of elders from different congregations assembled; but those of one congregation." Nor did a bishop of one congregation have authority of any kind in another congregation. Not just because of apostolic precedent, Campbell reasoned, but because intellectual endowments might fit a person "to teach, and to preside over one flock, who would not be qualified to teach or preside over another."

If a bishop had many duties to his flock, Campbell also wished to emphasize that the flock had a duty to its bishop. Since he had written so unsparingly of the evil of the giving of money, which might be used to build despotic ecclesiastical machinery, Campbell realized the necessity of special emphasis on the obligation of the church to support decently those overseers who gave their life to its service:

> The bishop of a Christian congregation will find much to do that never enters into the idea of a modern preacher or "minister." The duties he is to discharge to Christ's flock in the capacity of teacher and president, will

engross much of his time and attention. Therefore the idea of remuneration for his services was attached to the office from its first institution. This is indisputably plain, not only from the positive commands delivered to the congregations but from the hints uttered with a reference to the office itself. Why should it be so much as hinted that the bishops were not to take the oversight of the flock *"for the sake of sordid gain,"* if no emolument or remuneration was attached to the office? The abuses of the principle have led to oppose even the principle itself. We have said much against the hireling system, and see no ground as yet to refrain; so long as the salvation of the gospel, the conversion of the world, and heaven itself, are articles of traffic, and in the market, like other commodities, accessible to the highest bidder ... But to discriminate on this subject, and to exhibit where, and then, the hireling system begins: to graphically define, bound, and limit, beyond the power of cavil, on the one hand, and abuse on the other, has appeared to be a desideratum ...the bishop who thus labors in the word and teaching is ... *justly entitled* to the supply of his wants, whether of food, raiment, or money, or all. Paul himself declares, and reason itself teaches; and those Christian deserve not the name, who would suffer such a bishop to be in need of any necessary good thing which they had in their power to bestow. If he waive his right to receive it, he is the more worth; but the right exists whether he used or waives it, whether it is or is not recognized by others. So says the Christian institution, so says reason, and so say I.

While the spiritual welfare of the church was the concern of the bishops, its temporal matters were in the hands of a second group of officers—the deacons. These were the stewards, who "attended to all pecuniary matters, and out of the same fund three sets of tables were furnished. These were the Lord's table, the bishops' table, and the poor's table." Wishing to emphasize the social duty of the church, Campbell devoted one essay in the series to the question of "fellowship," a term frequently used, he pointed out, in the specific sense of contribution and distribution. Campbell enforced a view of the congregation as primarily a fellowship of service, to protest any narrow individualism, and to resist that attitude of other-worldliness, which had been too characteristic of some other forms of evangelical Christianity. Though his concept of the supreme position of the church had made him averse to setting up other societies outside the church, he did not mean that members of the divine society should neglect their duties to social reform. Rather, he stressed just the opposite. In his essay on "Fellowship," he insisted that in the day of judgment "the works particularized as of highest eminence, and most conspicuous virtue" would not be "You have built meeting-houses—you have founded colleges, and endowed professorships—you have educated poor and pious youths, and made them priests—you gave your parsons good livings." Nor have you have shown a "zeal for sound doctrine;" "but, You visited the sick, you waited on the prisoner, you fed the hungry, you clothed the naked Christian," not just attending to the wants of their own poor but also to those in the most remote communities "in times of general scarcity or pecuniary difficulties." For, in truth, said Campbell, "God never did institute a religion on earth that did not look with the kindest aspects towards the poor—which did not embrace, as its best good works, acts of humanity and compassion."

These two offices—that of bishop and that of deacon—encompassed all that was necessary and even all that was desirable, Campbell believed, to the government of the church. He was well aware that most of Christendom would not agree with him; so Campbell complained that: "The term *reverend* … is become such common property, that the preacher of the dreams of Swendenborg, or the leader of the dance of a Shaker meeting is fully entitled to all its privileges and emoluments."

But if the work of the kingdom was to be carried throughout the world, Campbell realized that a third order was necessary. These might be called missionaries, preachers, or evangelists; he preferred the term evangelist as most descriptive of their work. The bishops and deacons officiated only within the church, and came into being only after a congregation had been established. The task of proclaiming the glad tidings abroad and setting up new congregations necessitated the order of evangelists. Their office, said Campbell, "answers to that of the prophets of old," and assumed the responsibility of carrying on the missionary work of the apostles. But, he cautioned, they were not permanent officers of the church; like the prophets they were "extemporaneous and occasional teachers," and "when Christian congregations cover the country, ... such persons will not be necessary any more than a standing army in time of peace."

The strict curtailment and limitation of power to one congregation of the officers of the church was in accordance with Campbell's contention that the Christian ministry was in no sense a substitution for the Jewish priesthood. In the Christian dispensation, he had argued, that function was performed by Christ as high priest and by all believers as priests. But the doctrine of the priesthood, of all believers, was open to grave abuses. If Campbell had not already been aware of the danger involved in his theory, his experience with the Pittsburgh church under the care of his friends, Walter Scott and Sidney Rigdon would have made him so.

Most of the members of the Pittsburgh church had come from Ireland and Scotland, and they brought with them many of the ideas on church order practiced by the Haldaneans. Among these was the custom of "mutual exhortation." The least competent often roved the most forward, and insisted on occupying the

time at meeting, much to the disgust of many, and to the edification of none. Agreeing with Campbell in warmly disapproving this
tendency, Walter Scott one day when Campbell was present at a
meeting, delivered himself of a stern exhortation to the church. At
the close, lapsing into broad Scotch as he sometimes did, he thun-
dered at his surprised audience, "What, my brethren! Is the
church to be all mouth?" His exhortation was little heeded.
Enjoying their new found liberty and "repudiating the clergy and
the pope, each member became not only his own pope, but disposed to assume this office in regard to others." Each member
conceived it as his duty to exercise a watchful surveillance, an
inquisitorial scrutiny over the conduct of others. As a result,
debates and dissensions arose frequently, and cases of discipline
were so numerous that "the public religious meetings were disturbed and the cause discredited."

With the case of the Pittsburgh church perhaps sharply in his
mind, Campbell paid very little attention in his essays on "the
Ancient Order" to the liberties due the members of a congregations. Doubtless he had decided they were likely enough to take
those—but he did emphasize the necessity of order and obedience. In an essay, which he started with the admonition, "let all
things be done decently and in order," he warned that they should
not swing from the extreme of submission to clerical dominion to
the extreme of individual independency:

> The two extremes in all associations, as respects gov-
> ernment or rule are despotism and anarchy. In some reli-
> gious establishments there is, on the part of the rulers, an
> unrelenting and absolute tyranny, and on the part of the
> ruled, a passive servility ... In other religious institutions
> there is, on the part of the ruled attribute of ecclesiastical
> authority, and on the part of the ruled there is the most
> licentious equality; which recognizes not either the letter
> or spirit of subordination. These doubtless are the

extremes between which lies the temperature zone, or the media tutissima via, the safe middle way.

The "safe middle way," Campbell believes, lay in the election of persons intellectually and morally qualified to the office of bishop and then in respectful obedience to their rule. It was the responsibility of the bishops to see that the law was understood and obeyed. Hence, the congregations, said Campbell, should "submit to their rulers, as those who watch for their souls, and as those who must give an account of their administration."

By emphasizing the doctrine of the priesthood of all believers, it was true, Campbell gave to each member the right to contribute to the corporate thought of the Church. This did not mean that he would set up each individual as a sort of infallible pope in his own right. Indeed, from the very beginning of the movement, Alexander had agreed with his father Thomas that "the consensus of intelligent opinion, the voice of the people as a whole, not of any one of them—in other words the common mind or the common reason—must check the results of individual thinking." As no one individual could be infallible in the understanding of anything, and especially of the holy word, the individual must submit his or her opinion to the qualified judgment of the Church. Nor did this mean that the Campbell's advocated the right of majority rule. On the contrary, wrote Alexander, however "natural" the principle might be "under popular government"—and the Baptists having "very generally been republicans in politics, they are republicans in ecclesiastics"—"Yet it does not well consort with the genius of Christianity to carry a point by a majority. Where the law and testimony are either silent or not very explicit upon any question, reason says we ought not to be either position or dictatorial." Majority rule did not necessarily indicate intelligent or consecrated rule; it might degenerate into mere mob rule and anarchy. Hence, it was not the Church, in the sense of a majority vote of its members, but the unanimous judgment of the intelligent and consecrated Christians, of the appointed and ordained overseers of the flock, that must have the last word in the interpretation of the Scriptures and in the administering of discipline.

Intending that the Pittsburgh congregation should especially mark his words, he added: "The subject, it has appeared to me, is very little or very imperfectly understood in many congregations, and their meetings for church discipline are generally conducted in such a way as to divest every one in the assembly of every attribute of authority, and to place every one in the character of an interpreter of the law; and if not legislators, at least, they are all executors of it."

There was another flaw in Campbell's plan of the church government as outlined in his series on the "Ancient Order," one which the passing years would make increasingly plain to him. It would be easy, merely from reading these essays, to mistake Campbell's views on extreme congregational independency to mean that, no form of organization whatever was necessary to join together in local congregations, the local units of the Church Universal. Yet, some communion between these congregations was surely desirable for the sake of the larger fellowship of Christians, and, reason itself would dictate, some cooperation between them was requisite for the most efficient work of the Kingdom. Campbell was a member of Mahoning Association, and he had insisted from the beginning of his editorial career that it was the abuse and not the things themselves he was attacking in his articles on councils and missionary societies. Furthermore, even in his essays on the "Ancient Order" he specifically stated that: "Laws governing men's moral and religious actions are the only laws which Jesus deigns to enact. He legislates not upon matters of mere policy, or upon bricks, stones, and logs of timber. He says nothing about moderators, clerks, and parliamentary deco-

rum; but upon moral and religious behavior he is incomparably
sublime. He enacts nothing upon the confederation of churches,
of delegate meetings, or any matter of temporal and worldly policy." It was true, as statements implied, that Jesus, by not legislat-
ing on matters of policy, had left the Church free to develop whatever form of cooperation the needs of the changing centuries
might dictate. Yet other statements in Campbell's essays seemed
to imply that the New Testament set up a rigidly simple and
unchanging form of government.

Campbell was chiefly concerned with, one, the abolition of
ecclesiastical courts which had power to establish infallible
canons of belief to bind the thought of succeeding centuries, and
which had authority to excommunicate those dissenting in the
slightest degree from these canons. The abolition of the hierarchy
of clergy composing these courts who extracted the last tithe from
the poor to support their good establishments and who kept the
people in ignorance to maintain their own ascendancy; (He now
wished to emphasize the fact that over-organization could have a
stultifying effect on religion and that the elaborate development of
machinery tended to become unwieldy and check the free activi-
ty of the spirit.) Hence, in these essays, Campbell was following
his characteristic method of called attention to abuses by presenting an extreme picture of the other side of the question. Also in
seeking a basis for Christian unity, he was trying to reduce church
government, as all other issues, to its lowest common denomina-
tor. Furthermore, though his thought on the questions of faith and
the sacraments was mature, his views on church government were
still in transition. As editor of *The Christian Baptist*, and as a member of an established communion, Campbell spoke as a man without practical experience in administration and could not see the
defects and limitations of the ideas he advanced. Nor was his study
of the question of church government yet deep enough to show
him that these ideas were in a sense superficial, and that the writings of the New Testament presented a far more complex picture

of this subject than he now seemed to suppose.

If in these early years Campbell's passion for unity and liberty led him to over-simplify the problem of the ministry, if practical experience and a further study of New Testament documents should in the future lead him to a broader interpretation of the problem, Campbell would be the first to admit his own mistakes and to change his position. One thing, however, he was sure from the start—he would institute a form of church government, which would guarantee the liberty of the people, but it would be liberty under law.

The same ideal governed Campbell's notion of the right and proper order of public worship. He would insist on no set and rigid form: "By the phrase, order of Christian worship," he wrote, "we do not mean the position of the bodies of the worshippers, nor the hour of the day in which certain things are to be done, nor whether one action shall always be performed first, another always second, and another always third, etc., etc." Just as a bishop suited to the oversight of one congregation might not be pleasing to another, the same order of worship would not be agreeable to all congregations. Education and taste of the worshippers would go far toward dictating the technicalities, and a spirit of liberality and tolerance should prevail on these questions. Nevertheless, Campbell did suggest that: "There are certain social acts of Christian worship, all of which are to be attended to in the Christian assembly, and each of which is essential to the perfection of the whole." The Lord's Supper was the center of the service; but the unity, the fellowship of the disciples, were also expressed and constantly realized anew in other acts of worship. Making his appeal to the primitive churches, Campbell summarized the essentials of their worship as: "They continued steadfastly in the apostles' doctrine—in breaking of bread—in fellowship in prayers—praising God." In these things, declared Campbell, Christian worship ought to and must be "uniformly the same."

These were statements that would admit a very broad interpretation. They set up no definite, legalistic formalities of worship. Nor, did the editor on the Buffaloe intend to do so. "The New Testament contains no liturgy," Campbell wrote,

> no congregational service, as did the Old Testament … An attempt to find a liturgy in the New Testament, under the terms of "express precept or precedent for every thing," is what subjected those called Sandemanians and Haldaneans to so much censure from many good men … the principle itself, if at all admitted, must lead to a stiff, unnatural, and formal profession of the Christian religion, and to a spirit and temper not exactly in accordance with the spirit of adoption, and of high-born sons of God. Most of those congregations which commenced their course with a good share of this spirit … have since found their mistake, and have accordingly changed their course …

To Campbell, the Presbyterians and Baptists were just as guilty of a cold formality in their services as were the Haldaneans. The Haldaneans missed the real significance of the Lord's Supper by their legalistic attitude toward the "ancient order." The Presbyterians and Baptists, equally legalistic, he believed, in their attitude toward a set form of worship—and any too rigid form, he was convinced, was likely to deaden the quick spirit of religion. Legalists of every school, Campbell felt, had lost the spontaneity of fellowship that characterized the early Christians. Those embracing a "low" view of the Lord's Supper had lost the vital center of worship that held the first disciples together in a glorious unity. Campbell expressed his views of social Christianity and legalistic Calvinism in emphatic language, which was not likely to

improve his standing among those Baptists who were already sus-
pecting him of gross heresies. He wrote:

> Nothing is more unlike the Christian kingdom than
> the dry, cold formalities which appear in the inside of a
> Baptist or Presbyterian meeting house. The order within
> the walls is as near to the order of a country school, abat-
> ing the ardor of youth, as it is to the order of that house
> over which the Son of God presides ...
>
> The doctrine is as cold as moonshine, and the initiat-
> ed in their arrangements and order are like so many ici-
> cles hanging to the eves of a house in a winter's morning,
> clear, cold, formal, in rank and file; but they will break
> rather than bend towards each other. A tree frog is gener-
> ally the color of the timber, rail, or fence on which it is
> found. So are the Baptists. They are, in these regions, gen-
> erally the offspring, or converts from the Presbyterian
> ranks, and they wear the same visage in their order, except
> with this small difference, that the Baptists build their
> meeting houses near ponds or rivers, while the
> Presbyterians build theirs on the tops of the hills. So long
> as they meet in memory of the reason assigned in the
> fourth commandment, or by an act of congress, they will
> have nothing to fire their zeal, kindle their love, animate
> their strains, or enlarge their hopes. And as demur and
> silent as the Quakers, except when the parson, who has a
> plenary inspiration is present, they will sit or stand ...
> until they hear the sermon, and all the appurtenances
> thereto belonging. Now if such a person were to be trans-
> lated into an old fashioned Christian assembly, they
> would be as much astonished with the natural simplicity,
> affection, and piety of the worshippers, as a blind man
> would be on the recovery of his sight.... But that stiffness
> and formality which are now the mode, and the want of a

due regard to the nature, design, and authority of every part of the Christian institution, lead us into a practice alike repugnant to reason and revelation.

Campbell had no illusion more spiritual and vital practice in regard to worship would be easy to attain. He knew full well the legalistic side of his, or any, program was the aspect most readily perceived. Here, again, he had before him an explicit example in the conduct of the Pittsburgh Church under the supervision of Walter Scott and Sidney Rigdon. As in matters of church government this congregation had tended to let liberty run to license, so in the question of the order of worship, it approached the opposite extreme of a rigid authoritarianism. Taking every apostolic precedent as a command, its members greeted each other with "a holy kiss," and in private gatherings showed forth their humility by "the washing of feet." Campbell, greatly distressed, pointed out to the Pittsburgh Church both these practices were customs, and were in no way binding on modern Christians. In insisting on the authority of apostolic precedent in regard to faith and the sacraments, he had by no means intended to imply that the example of the early Christian was to be followed in all the minutiae of their religious practices. In his essays on the "Ancient Order," he warned that the distinction must be carefully made,

> between what was their order of worship and manner of edification from what was circumstantial. To bring the Christian religion to inculcate matters of this sort, would be to convert the New Testament into a ritual like the book of Leviticus, and to make Christian obedience as low and servile as that of the weak and beggarly elements.

He had entitled his essays "A Restoration of the Ancient Order of Things," but he was anxious that emphasis on order should not take pre-eminence over the spirit of charity, without which an adherence to a correct order of worship would avail nothing. The whole history of the church proved too much insistence on a uniformity of order was ever narrowing, and not broadening, a divisive, and not unifying principle. The greater part of Campbell's essays was taken up with a discussion not of the formalities but of the spirit governing Christianity. Forsaking all theology, all attention to "order," Campbell concluded:

> ... God is, and was, and ever shall be love ... as the wisdom and knowledge of God are unsearchable, so [God's] love can never be misplaced, misdirected, never can be measured nor circumscribed. It is perfect in nature. In degree, it cannot be conceived by a finite mind, nor expressed in our imperfect vehicles of thought. It passes all created understanding.

The spirit of the Christian, wrote Campbell, was the spirit of devotion to the will of this God of love, and the perfect model lay in Christ. "The Savior was perfectly so [devout], and he is and ever shall be, the standard of perfect devotion."

Alexander Campbell gave an outline of his theology in a series of essays on the ancient order, but any expression of his religious feeling concluded in Christ. And those readers of The Christian Baptist would little understand his full meaning who did not perceive that the editor's religion was more Christocentric than his theology, and so interpret his writings.

"A Restoration of the Ancient Order of Things" had also served to illustrate another point in Campbell's philosophy; whatever his subject, there was one common theme that ran through all his writings—the insistence that Christianity is a religion of happiness.

> From the plan of the Bible, as well as from its philosophy, its claims upon the faith and admiration of

mankind may be strongly argued: Its philosophy is, that without piety no man can be happy to the full extent of his capacity for human enjoyment. All human enjoyments are reduced to two classes: one is spiritual and the other is carnal; the one is moral, social and refined, and the other is selfish, exclusive and gross; the one rises, the other sinks through all eternity. *The philosophy of the Bible is, therefore, the philosophy of human happiness*, the only philosophy which recommends itself to the cultivated understanding of man.

Though the motive to Christian action was an unselfish and noble social happiness, the motive after all was pleasure. Its authority could only be a conditional authority—an individual need obey its command only if he desired to gain a certain end. Interpreted coldly, according to his own theory, the commandments of the New Testament, Christ's law-book, were to be obeyed because happiness would follow. Regardless of the implications of his theology, Campbell's introduction of Christ lifted his religion far above the sphere of egoistic hedonism. It warmed and vitalized his whole system. Campbell's theology might admit utilitarianism, but his religion would not.

Alexander Campbell had laid before the readers of The Christian Baptist his program for Christian unity. Only the experience of the coming years would bring his thought to full maturity. But even now, as his first essay on "the Ancient Order" disclosed, he realized in some respects his system was unique; it had certain gifts of distinctive value for the Christian world. He might be the latest in the long and honorable line of reformers, but he knew that he differed from all the others. His thought was neither Protestant nor Catholic in the accepted meaning of the terms, and there was a sense in which it formed the only *via media* yet set forth between these two extremes and suggested the common ground on which they might some day come together.

The religious system, then, being propagated from the press on the Buffaloe was Protestant in the place that it gave to loyalty, love, and freedom, as opposed to regimentation and legal discipline; in its emphasis on the priesthood of all believers, as opposed to sacerdotal claims; in its stress on personal faith as trust in and loyalty to a Person, rather than as assent to intellectualized forms of Christian belief; and in place which it ... "[gave] to the Scriptures of the New Testament as sufficient witness to the essential faith, life, and order of the Christian Church."

Alexander Campbell considered his greatest contribution to Christian thought lay in his understanding of faith "as trust in loyalty to the Person of Jesus Christ as Lord, rather than as intellectual assent to dogmas, or as so-called mystical apprehension of reality." The concept would forever release the Christian world "from legalism, quasi-magic, and untenable doctrines of grace and providence." Significant, too, was his sense of fellowship and brotherhood.

Withal it was a program, which sought to unite in its highest sense the mystic communion with God and the fellowship of social service to humankind. For here was the ideal of the Church which, he had declared so beautifully in an essay in The Christian Baptist when he described the religion of the early Christians as: "the pure, clear, and swelling current of love to God, of love to man, expressed in all the variety of doing good."

While these essays were being written, the editor was busy, as usual, traveling extensively to disseminate his doctrine in person. On February 4, 1825, he wrote Philip Fall that he was receiving invitations to lecture in Western New York, but that the calls from Eastern Virginia were "peculiar urgent." So, in the summer of 1825, Campbell made his first trip to the eastern part of his own state.

His visit was brief, but he made the acquaintance of the two clergymen who wielded the power of the Baptist Church in Virginia. One was Bishop Robert E. Semple. Mild, amiable, prudent, with a shrewd knowledge of human nature, and a firm decision of character, he was one of the most popular preachers in the state. The other, Andrew Broaddus, was so excessively timid that he could not attend associations and conventions, and it was said that he would even lose his voice in the presence of strangers; but those who knew him found him a man with graceful manners, a benignant countenance, a musical voice, and so great a love of letters that many considered him one of the most thorough Bible scholars of his time.

Semple and Broaddus were almost twenty years Campbell's senior. When Alexander made his trip to the east he was thirty-seven, Semple was fifty-six, and Broaddus fifty-five. If they had been prepared, from Campbell's articles in The Christian Baptist, to meet a caustic controversialist, they were pleasantly surprised to find him instead a genial man with charming manners and an old-world courtesy; and they gave him a kindly reception and a tolerant hearing. They had no intention of surrendering an item of their orthodox Baptist faith in favor of his restoration theology, but they were determined, if possible, to save a man of so much talent and personality for the work of the Baptist Church. In hope of resolving some of their difficulties, Semple agreed to start a correspondence with Campbell through the pages of *The Christian Baptist.*

In December 1825, Semple wrote his first letter. It was generous in its praise of the editor on the Buffaloe:

> Your preaching among us reminded me of Appollos who displayed, as we moderns say, great talents, or, as the scripture says, 'was an eloquent man, and mighty in the Scriptures.' ... we all feel much interest in your welfare personally,... your mild and sociable manners, &c. pro-

cured among us not respect only, but brotherly love and Christian affection, and ... much of your preaching was admired for its eloquence and excellency, and ... if you would dwell upon these great points chiefly, such as faith, hope, charity, &c. you would be viewed by us as having a special command from Him whom we hope you love, to feed his lambs and his sheep.

The amiable bishop also felt it his duty to indulge in some fault finding. He was convinced that Campbell's opinions on some points were dangerous. "In short, your views are generally so contrary to those of the Baptists in general, that if a party was to go fully into practice of your principles, I should say a new sect had sprung up, radically different from the Baptists as they now are." Semple thought he recognized the origin of those principles: "So far as I can judge by your writings and preaching, you are substantially a Sandemanian or a Haldanian." This influence, in the opinion of Semple

> ... among the Haldanians (judging from writings) a gentle spirit is rarely to be found, Harsh and bitter sarcasms are the weapons with which they fight their opponents ... [though] I have known some of their party who have appeared, in private conversation, to be mild and gentle .... If you will bear with me, I will suggest that this seems to be the case with the editor of *The Christian Baptist*. As a man, in private circles, mild, pleasant, and affectionate; as a writer, rigid and satirical, beyond all the bounds of scripture allowance. I have taken *The Christian Baptist* now from its beginning, i.e. I have taken them from their first publication, and my opinion has been uniformly the same–That, although sensible and edited with ability, it has been deficient in a very important point, a *New Testament spirit!*

But, even on this point, Semple had an apology to offer for Campbell:

> By way of apology for you, and a small compliment to our folks, I was really struck while you were among us, that the acrimonious treatment that you had received from others had pushed you to certain severities and singularities, which, if you dwelt among us, you would relinquish.

In reply, Campbell thanked the Baptist bishop for "the benevolent Christian spirit which appears in every sentence," and assured him that he gladly accepted "the rebukes of a friend." Furthermore, said Campbell, "I have no design to plead guilty to the whole of your corrections, nor to say that I do not need some of your reproofs and admonitions." He did have "some explanations to offer, and misunderstandings to correct." In reference to his lack of "forbearance," though he assured Semple that "I hope to profit from your remarks on this subject." He offered the explanation he had given once before: If the New Testament spirit was the spirit "of meekness, of mildness, of benevolence," it was also the spirit "of hostility to all and every corruption of the gospel. The physician is not less benevolent when, as a surgeon, he amputates a limb, than when he administers an anodyne." Campbell further explained to the bishop:

> There are many topics which would lead to the exhibition of what would appear ... in your own sense of the words, 'a New Testament Spirit,' which I would have gladly introduced into this work; but owing to its circumscribed dimensions and the force of opposition, I have had to withhold ... them.

The remark of Robert Semple's that stung the independent-minded Campbell to the quickest reply was the charge that he was a follower of Sandeman and the Haldanes. Actually, it was fortunate the bishop made the charge. For in his reply, as nowhere else in his writings, did Campbell give so full a statement of some of the sources of his thought, his oath of allegiance, and his declaration of independence.

He described those, especially among the eighteenth-century theologians, who had influenced him on a rare note of whimsical humor:

> ... I was some fourteen years ago a great admirer of the works of John Newton. I read them with great delight, and I still love the author and admire many of his sentiments. He was not a staunch Episcopalian, though he died in that connection. In an apology to a friend for his departure from the tenets of that sect in some instances, he said, 'Whenever he found a pretty feather in any bird, he endeavored to attach it to his own plumage, and although he had become a very speckled bird, so much so that no one of any species would altogether own him as belonging to them, he flattered himself that he was the prettiest bird among them.' From that day to the present I have been looking for pretty feathers, and I have become more speckled than Newton or Olney; but whether I have as good a taste in the selection, must be decided by connoisseurs in ornithology.
>
> Concerning Sandeman and Haldane, how they can be associated under one species, is to me a matter of surprise. The former a Paido-Baptist, the later a Baptist; the former as keen, as sharp, as censorious, as acrimonious as Juvenal; the latter as mild, as charitable, as condescending as any man this age has produced. As authors I know them well ... I have read more of them than I approve, and more of them than they who impute to me their opinions, as hearsay ... That their views were the same on some points, is as true as that Luther, Calvin, and Wesley agreed

in many points. I was once much puzzled on the subject of Harvey's Dialogues, I mean his Theron and Aspasio. I appropriated one winter season [the winter of 1811–1812] for examining this subject. I assembled all leading writers of that day on these subjects. I laid before me Robert Sandeman, Harvey, Marshall, Bellamy, Glass, Cudworth, and others of minor fame in the controversy [on faith]. I not only read, but studied and wrote off in miniature their respective views. I had Paul and Peter, James and John, on the same table: I took nothing upon trust. I did not care for the authority, reputation, or standing of one of the systems a grain of sand. I never weighed the consequences of embracing any one of the systems as affecting my standing or reputation in the world. Truth (not who says so) was my sole object. I found much entertainment in the investigation. And I will not blush, nor do I fear to say, that, in this controversy, Sandeman was like a giant among dwarfs … I was the most prejudiced against him, and the most in favor of Harvey, when I commenced this course of reading … I have also read Fuller's Strictures on Sandemanianism, which I suppose to be the medium of most of the information possessed on that subject in this country. This is the poorest performance Andres Fuller ever gave to the world. I have not read it for a long time; it is on the shelves of my library, but I will not at this time brush the dust off it… As to James Haldane, I am less indebted to him than to most of the others. I was much prejudiced against his views and proceedings when in Scotland, owing to my connexion with those [especially Greville Ewing] who were engaged in the controversy with his brother Robert, and against the system in general … I have heard a great deal of him and his brother Robert, from members of their connexion, who have emigrated to this country; and while I do not believe that there lives upon the earth a more godly, pious, primitive, Christian, than James Haldane of Edinburgh; and few, if any, more generally intelligent in the Christian scripture, you express my views of that system generally ... Many of those [young men educated for the ministry by Robert Haldane], without the spirit of their master, became just such spirited men as you describe. Some of them, too, excellent men, caught the spirit of Robert Sandeman, and became fierce as lions in the garb of lambs, Hyper-Calvinists, Separatists, with whom 'tenth or ten thousandth broke the chain alike.' No matter if an agreement existed in nine hundred and ninety-nine opinions, if in the thousandth there was a difference, the chain was severed, and they were to one another as heathen men and publicans!

Though admitting his debt to other reformers, Campbell wished to make the nature of their influence on him clear to the bishop:

... while I acknowledge myself a debtor to Glass, Sandeman, Harvey, Cudworth, Fuller, and M'Lean; as much as to Luther, Calvin, and John Wesley; I candidly and unequivocally avow, that I do not believe that any one of them had clear and consistent views of the Christian religion as a whole ... I now believe that not one of them was exactly on the track of the apostles ... they were impeded in their inquiries by a false philosophy and metaphysics ...

While I thus acknowledge myself a debtor to those persons, I must say, that the debt, in most instances is a very small one. I am indebted, upon the whole, as much to their errors as to their virtues, for these have been to me as beacons to the mariner, who might otherwise have run upon the rocks and shoals ... though, in some instances, I have been edified and instructed by their labors.

Lest anyone should infer that even this much was too great an admission of the influence of mere men on his religious views, Campbell hastened to conclude his explanation with an extreme statement of his independence:

For the last ten years I have not looked into the works of any of these men; and have lost the taste which I once had for controversial reading of this sort. And during this period my inquiries into the Christian religion have been almost exclusively confined to the holy scriptures. And I can assure you that the scriptures, when made their own interpreter, and accompanied with earnest desired to the author of these writings, have become, to me, a book entirely new, and unlike what they were when read and consulted a book of reference—*I call no man master upon the earth*; and although my own father has been a diligent student, and teacher of the Christian religion since his youth; and, in my opinion, understands this book as well as any person with whom I am acquainted, yet there is no man with whom I have debated more, and reasoned more, on all subjects of this kind, than he—*I have been so long disciplined in the school of free inquiry,* that, if I know my own mind, there is not a man upon the earth whose authority can influence me, any farther than he comes with the authority of evidence, reason, and truth. To arrive at this state of mind is the result of many experiments and efforts; and to me has been arduous beyond expression. I have endeavored to read the scriptures as though no one had read them before me; and I am as much on my guard against reading them today, through the medium of my own views yesterday, or a week ago, as I am against being influenced by any foreign name, authority, or system, whatever.

If Campbell underestimated the degree to which he was influenced by sources, the fact still remained that he actually was a man "singularly free from prejudice and from slavish dependence upon masters." From the days when as a boy in County Armagh, he first thrilled to stories of his Huguenot ancestors' heroic flight from the tyranny of Louis XIV, first learned the history of the American and French revolutions, and first read John Locke's "Essay on Toleration," to the day when as a man in the New World he assumed his mission for the democratization of the church, Alexander's whole life was motivated by the passion for liberty— political, religious, and intellectual. As his thinking matured, he found that the natural bend of his mind was fortified by the philosophical system he had espoused. Eager to inaugurate a new era of liberty and enlightenment, and anxious to throw off the shackles of the past, the eighteenth-century philosophy gloried in its non-historical approach. John Locke once boasted that he had never read the works even of his distinguished contemporary, Thomas Hobbes. So Campbell boasted of his freedom from all human authority in religion—not because he had not read the authorities, but because he had read them and found them wanting.

His denial of any dependence on human masters was also an assumption that left Campbell completely free "to take up any current idea which seemed to him true and useful," without committing himself to any fixed system. He could thus accept the conclusions of earlier thinkers "not as authorities, but as suggestions." His writings revealed that these suggestions had come to him from many sources. His classical education had acquainted him with the thought of Greece and Rome. His study of the church carried him from the Protestant reformers back through the centuries to the apostolic and Catholic fathers—to Justin Martyr, Clement, the "great Athanasius," Origen, the lawyer Tertullian, Cyprian, Jerome, Augustine, Gregory, Scotus, Aquinas, Abelard. If, in taking a "pretty feather" from these various birds of theory, Campbell had, as he confessed to Semple, become "more speckled than Newton of Olney." It did not follow that he had issued in eclecticism. His natural independence of mind, and his insistence that beyond all these speculations lay a few simple basic truths which alone should be made the terms for religious communion, saved him from advancing an eclectic theology.

Since he had accepted Locke's theory of sensational psychology as a working basis for ascertaining these truths, he had a philosophical tool, which made it easier for him to chisel away from his edifice of religious faith the excrescences of centuries of tradition and speculation. Influenced by the sensational psychology, Campbell was no more the creature of Locke than he was the creature of Calvin or Augustine. He used the Lockian theory only when it was useful to his purpose, and unhesitatingly discarded it wherever he felt it impeded his thought as the point where it started on the path to materialism and agnosticism, he had abandoned it in favor of the common-sense Scottish philosophy of Reid and Beattie and Stewart.

If Campbell, in 1825, still remained in the bosom of the Baptist church—and he plainly stated that he considered himself "in full communion ... with the whole Baptist society in the United States"—it was becoming evident he was resting there rather uneasily. In his letter to Bishop Semple, he wrote his declaration of independence; a little later, he wrote a letter to another correspondent, which he might well consider his declaration of toleration.

A reader, signing himself, "An Independent Baptist," wrote

Campbell severely criticizing him for claiming "full communion" with the Baptists when he differed with them on so many points, and urged him to "Come out from among them" lest he be accused of "acting a part from pride, love of popularity, or singularity." Campbell's answer was equally sharp and direct.

Alexander, with his usual disarming frankness concerning his own vicissitudes of mind, admitted he himself, in his earlier years, had once been inflated with an exclusive sense of his own rightness and self-righteousness, but that as the passing years unfolded the complexities of the problem he had realized a new sense of humility:

> I have tried the pharisaic plan, and the monastic. I was once so straight, that, like the Indian's tree, I leaned a little the other way. And however much I may be slandered now as seeking "popularity" or a popular course, I have to rejoice that to my own satisfaction, as well as to others, I proved that truth, and not popularity, was my object; for I was once so strict a Separatist that I would neither pray nor sing praises with any one who was not as perfect as I supposed myself. In this most unpopular course I persisted until I discovered the mistake, and saw that on the principle embraced in my conduct, there never could be a congregation or church upon the earth.

Applying this attitude to the question of communion, Campbell said: "My full conviction is, that there are many Paido-Baptist congregations ... with whom I could wish to be on the very same terms of Christian communion on which I stand with the whole Baptist society." He was aware it was a vexing problem. The Baptists argued their position on Baptism to the position of "close communion." Campbell, doubtless, felt that there was some logic in their conclusions. But his father Thomas had been excommunicated from the Presbyterian Church partly because of the broad conception of communion, which governed his practice; his own thought had received its first great impulse from reading Locke's "Letters on Toleration." So in trying to embrace the Baptist position on "close communion," Alexander was attempting to force his mind into a rigidly logical position against which his sentiments rebelled. He could not bring himself to more than a rather vague statement of his attitude:

> ... I have thought, and thought, and vacillated very much, on question, Whether Baptists and Paido-Baptists ought, could, would, or should, irrespective of their peculiarities, sit down at the same Lord's table. And one thing I do know, that either they should cease to have communion in prayer, praise, and other religious observances, or they should go the whole length. Of this point I am certain ...

But lest any one think this was tending toward a narrow view, Alexander in the very next paragraph jumped to a passionate denunciation of sectarian intolerance:

> Dear sir, this plan of making our nest, and fluttering over our own brood; of building our own tent, and of confining all goodness and grace to our noble selves and the "elect few" who are like us, is the quintessence of sublimated pharisaism. The old Pharisees were but babes in comparison to the modern: and the longer I live, and the more I reflect upon God and man—heaven and earth— the Bible and the world—the Redeemer and his church—the more I am assured that all sectarianism is the offspring of hell; and that all differences about words, and names, and opinions, hatches in Egypt, or Rome, or Edinburgh, are like the frolics of drunken men; and that

where there is a new creature, or a society of men, with all their imperfections, and frailties, and errors in sentiment, in views, and opinions, they ought to receive one another, and the strong to support the infirmities of the weak, and not to please themselves. To lock ourselves up in the handbox of our little circle; to associate with a few units, tens, or hundreds, as the pure church, as the elect, is real Protestant monkery, it is evangelical pharisaism."

As was to be expected, the "Independent Baptist" was far from pleased with Campbell's reply. Campbell was emphatic in correcting one impression of his correspondent. The "Independent Baptist" assumed only those immersed in accordance with Baptist views were really baptized. Campbell denied any such assumption was warrantable. Ever since the day when his study of this essential ordinance of Christianity lifted him to "a new peak of the mountain of God," Alexander had been assured that he rightly understood its design and import. He often expressed his assurance in language that infuriated his Paido-Baptist opponents; but he never, even in the most heated moment of debate, suggested that those who disagreed with him about the mode and nature of Baptism were guilty of disobedience to the command of Christ. He illustrated his position to the "Independent Baptist:"

> ... there is no 'rejection' of the ordinance of Baptism by sprinkled new creatures; but a mistake of what it is. I think we can find an exact comparison which expresses the full amount of the pravity of the error and practice of the honest baby-sprinklers. It is this: Paternus says to Filius bring me a *book*; Filius, eager to *obey* his father, goes and brings him a *leaf* of paper. Paternus, Why did you not obey me? Father, says Filius, I did; I went at your command, and lo, here it is, pointing to the *leaf* . That is not a *book*, says Paternus. I thought it was, replied Filius.

Paternus says, well my son, I accept your *obedience*, and pardon your *mistake*, because it was not a *willful* one."

And he concluded his argument with this admonition to his correspondent:

> If there is any position laid down with unusual plain-nesss ... in the epistolary part of the New Testament, it is this: *That Christians should receive one another as Christ has received them*, WITH ALL THEIR INTELLECTU-AL WEAKNESSES. This you may call Latitudinarian-ism; and such a Latitudinarian, I pray you may become.

The letter closed Campbell's correspondence with the "Independence Baptist;" it had given Campbell a chance to express his protest against sectarian exclusiveness. He urged again "the duty of all Christians to maintain the unity of the spirit in the bond of peace." He admonished the "Independent Baptist to pay heed to the maxim which had been the burden of Paul's epistle to the Romans: "wherefore receive you one another without regard to difference of opinion." It was a maxim, running like a refrain through article after article in *The Christian Baptist*:

> ... a love regulated by similarity of opinion, is only a love to one's own opinion ... Christianity consists infi-nitely more in good works than in sound opinions ... It would be of infinite importance ... if ... less was said about ... sound doctrine, and the time occupied therein devoted to ... practicing that 'holiness without which no man shall see the Lord.' ... not unity of opinion, but unity of faith, is the only true bond of Christian union. I ... should never force what may be conclusion of my mind upon the religious practice of others.

Alexander, on first reading his father's *Declaration and Address*, accepted its simplicity of statement and nobility of sentiment as a new revelation, and assumed the truths it set forth were indeed "plain and obvious," and easy to follow by any who truly found the way. But the years were teaching a more realistic—and more tolerant—attitude to the young idealist. At thirty-seven Alexander knew, as he had not known at twenty-one, that perfection was not so easily attained. The ideals the road to union set forth in *The Declaration and Address* no longer seemed so simple and clear-cut. He was finding Meldenius' persuasive formula— "In essentials, unity; in non-essentials, liberty"—was by no means the panacea it might seem. With his sacramental approach to religion, Campbell naturally considered a correct obedience to the ordinances of Baptism and Communion was among the first "essentials." Yet, even here, there seemed little chance of agreement, not because of stubbornness or prejudice but because of honest difference of conviction. So it was now appearing that the third part of Meldenius' formula was its most vital element: "in all things, charity." From the first day of his career as an editor, Alexander, in protest against sectarian exclusiveness, insisted that regardless of their interpretation of essentials or non-essentials, regardless of the party name they might take, all persons who professed Christ were Christians. It was a point on which he was rarely understood.

Campbell, in spite of his protestations of love for the sincere Christians in all sects, was nevertheless convinced all sectarianism was sin, the church both visible and invisible was meant to be one. He did not believe that this unity was to be achieved merely on some vague basis of love and forbearance; there must be corporate as well as spiritual unity. The few essentials on which this corporate unity must be based had become obscured by the accumulated abuses of the ages, and *The Christian Baptist* was his medium for detecting and exposing these abuses. It was little wonder if the vigor of his attack sometimes overlaid Campbell's insistence on the broad attitude of toleration, of spiritual unity, which should govern the relations of all Christians with one another.

Even when their implication was understood, Campbell's declarations of toleration did not receive a very friendly hearing. Many other Baptists, like his correspondent "An Independent Baptist," felt such latitudinarianism was simply another evidence of his heretical tendencies. The Paido-Baptists were infuriated by the language in which these declarations were sometimes couched. To suggest he was tolerant of the "intellectual weaknesses" in his opponents was scarcely a peace offering. Though Alexander freely admitted he arrived at his conclusions by a long progression of thought, though he wrote Bishop Semple he was constantly on guard lest he read the Scriptures one day through the medium of his own view the day or week before, he was nevertheless convinced, he rightly understood a few basic principles which a divided and discordant Christendom might unite. Even his views of the ordinances of Baptism and Communion were founded in the belief that his was the most inclusive interpretation of these sacraments. It was this very assurance that he had a unique mission to perform, which, of course, was drawing supporters into Campbell's orbit. His driving conviction of his own rightness was giving vitality to his movement. It was very annoying to his opponents.

If many of these opponents were within the Baptist fold, Campbell was still confident they might be able to resolve, or at least tolerate, each other's differences. In common with all the reformers from Luther to Wesley, his desire was to work his reformation from within an established church, not to be the founder of some new movement. He was willing to admit that he was a "speckled bird," but Alexander hoped that the Baptists might treat him with the same liberality as the Episcopalians had accorded

... I do intend to continue in connection with this people so long as they will permit me to say what I believe, ... and to censure what is amiss in their views ... I have no idea of adding to the catalogue of new sects. This game has been played too long ... In one thing, perhaps, they [the Baptists] may appear in time to come, proudly singular, a pre-eminently distinguished. Mark it well. Their historian, in the year 1900 may say, "We are the only people who would tolerate, or who ever did tolerate, any person to continue as a Reformer or a Restorer amongst us. While other sects excluded all who would have enlarged their views and exalted virtues; while every Jerusalem in Christendom stoned its own prophets, and exiled its own best friends, and compelled them to set up themselves, we constitute the only exception of this kind in the annals of Christianity—nay, in the annals of the world." I think it is not very precarious perhaps, that this may yet be said of this ancient and singular people.

·10·

The Spirit of Inquiry
is Marching Forth

T THE CLOSE of his debate with MacCalla, Campbell promised to make an extended tour of Kentucky the following year. He had made his first trip almost as a stranger; now, one year later, the editor of *The Christian Baptist* was known for good or ill throughout the state. His steadily increasing correspondence had given him some indication of the strong feeling his magazine had aroused, but on his journey through Kentucky the effect came home to him in far more personal and dramatic fashion. Almost every town he visited furnished some incident to show how deep the affirmation or the disdain being excited by his writings.

After an eight day tour through Mason and Bracken counties, accompanied by William Vaughan, a popular Kentucky Baptist preacher and former moderator of the Elkhorn Association, Campbell came to the town of Flemingsburg. There for the first time he met John Smith—a frontier Baptist preacher whose manners and attire would have cut a strange figure at the University of Glasgow but whose natural abilities, vivid humor, and skill at repartee made him popular in the West. His sallies of keen wit were retold with merriment throughout Kentucky, where he was familiarly known as "Raccoon" John Smith. He was four years Campbell's senior. Two men more different in education, in temperament, and background could not be imagined. But they soon discovered they had much in common.

Smith was entirely a product of the frontier; and his only education was a little spasmodic learning dispensed in a log cabin by an itinerant schoolmaster. The family emigrated from the territory of Tennessee to Kentucky when he was eleven. His father was George Smith (really Schmidt), a Virginian of German parentage, quiet, diffident, hard-working, and an earnestly pious Baptist, who taught his thirteen children from the only three books he owned—the Bible, the Philadelphia Confession of Faith, and a collection of hymns. John's mother was an Irish woman, passionate, energetic, high-tempered, witty, with a retentive memory and a gift for satiric ridicule, who, in lieu of books, entertained her children with wild and beautiful Celtic legends and ballads. His older brothers had engaged in the Indian wars, but John knew the Cherokees only as friends who taught him their skill in hunting for deer and mountain lion, as well as their language and their traditions. He excelled in another favorite sport of the young frontiersmen—the debating society, where "his shrewd sense and keen wit always made him a champion." In time, John Smith entered the Baptist ministry, and, inheriting a full share of his mother's energy and satiric humor, he became a popular preacher. Not the least of his assets was a rich, heavy voice, with distinct enunciation, and melodious tone, which made so effective the delivery of his sermons in the "solemn, chant-like tones" admired by his listeners:

When he stood up broad-chested, in the forest, or on some rude platform, or the trunk of some fallen tree, and spoke to the multitudes around him, his deep-toned ponderous words rolled along the hollows, until the dwellers among the hills of the Cumberland have declared that they could sit at their cabin doors and hear him two miles off. Such a voice, then, had all the effect of eloquence itself; in the popular regard, it was a greater gift than learning, and awed like inspiration.

When Smith, with a naturally analytical, rationalistic mind, was able one day while working in the cornfield to come upon a satisfying solution to a problem that had been grievously vexing some of the pious old Calvinist ministers—the problem of reconciling the doctrine of the eternal justification of the elect with the fact of their actual condemnation at the time of conversion—his reputation spread abroad through the backwoods churches until some believed him "no less inspired for the work which he had done, than was Peter on Pentecost, or Paul before Agrippa."

But the cast of mind that won him this fame also involved him in difficulties. In time he found himself increasingly unable to reconcile other abstruse points of Calvinistic theology. Finally one day in 1822, while preaching at Spencer's Creek, he was suddenly so struck with the incongruity of a point he was explaining that he abruptly stopped his sermon with the remark: "Brethren, something is wrong—I am in the dark—we are all in the dark; but how to lead you to the light, or to find they way myself, before God, I know not." Leaving his astounded audience, he went home to pray and to burn the candle to the socket in many a long night's study. John Smith was an independent self-reliant frontiersman. Yet the basis of his theology was the assumption that all persons are sinners morally dead and capable of being quickened into life only by the supernatural power of the Holy Spirit and that the Spirit, having brought the elect to salvation, leaves the others to perish "not on account of their greater unworthiness, but simply because God in his own good pleasure did not elect them to eternal life." What then, pondered John Smith, was this Calvinistic "moral death" that destroyed man's free agency? And so anxiously did his friends await his opinion, that there were some who said, "the peace of a hundred churches hung on his answer to the question." Eventually he reached a conclusion—"the system which he had so long preached, was but a wind of doctrine without substantial basis." It was precisely at this moment that a friend put into his hands Campbell's Prospectus for *The Christian Baptist.*

Immediately he subscribed to the new magazine. Knowing of the Walker debate, he planned to hear Campbell's discussion with MacCalla. Sickness in his family prevented his attendance, but the report came to him that Campbell was a man of learning and piety, and he hoped that his writings would solve some of his difficulties. Ever since he pledged himself to submit all religious problems to the test of his own reason and the Scriptures and decided that Calvinism was not in full harmony with his understanding of the Bible, Smith had been trying to form a system of his own by combining tenets from various theories such as Socinianism, Arianism, Universalism, and Arminianism. Eagerly he read Campbell to discover which system he espoused. But instead of finding in *The Christian Baptist* elaborate disquisitions on the perplexing current dogmas, he read, "with variable feelings of pleasure, surprise, and painful suspicion," a sharp denunciation of all the popular systems. There were many things in the magazine of which he could approve. Like many other citizens of the frontier, he liked the editor's insistence on individual freedom and individual responsibility. His own father had fought in the Revolutionary War, and whatever he himself possessed he had wrested from the wilderness with his own hands. He liked Campbell's common-sense approach to problems, for on the frontier a person had to be practical in order to survive.

John Smith liked Campbell's manner of attack on things he opposed. Smith himself delivered some mighty blows against the Arminian Methodists and Paido-Baptist Presbyterians, and he was ready to pay tribute, as were most of the frontiersmen, to a man with a ready wit for debate. He approved of Campbell's war on sectarian persecution and ecclesiastical power, for he had learned from his father that in Virginia before the Revolution the Baptists had been bitterly persecuted, outraged, and imprisoned by the established church. Even after the war had removed religious inequality before the law, the old prejudice and proscription for opinion's sake had been so strong that John's father had emigrated from Virginia to the Valley of the Holston in the territory of Tennessee, in order that he might enjoy a more democratic religion.

Smith was not surprised at Campbell's attack on the "hireling clergy." He had been reared among preachers of the "class of hardy pioneer farmers, who had not forgotten the church tax which they and their fathers used to pay in Virginia, to support the ministry of an established religion." They "seemed to have made it a point of Christian honor, after the war was over, to preach the gospel without charge, and to support themselves independently, by hard labor, through the week." These preachers educated many of the people "into the notion that it was sinful to pay men for preaching the Gospel."

But when Campbell published his essay on "experimental religion," John Smith had been gravely disturbed. Some, whom he had induced to subscribe to the magazine, ordered him to discontinue their subscriptions. He was almost persuaded to agree with them that however great was Mr. Campbell's erudition, he was nevertheless wholly destitute of heart-felt religion. But John Smith had no intention of dropping his subscription to The Christian Baptist for this reason. He was far too curious to see what the editor would say next, and his own shrewd common-sense made him acknowledge that, though his prejudice made him resent Campbell's aspersions on "experimental religion," the article had by no means presented an exaggerated caricature. His own experience testified to the truth of Campbell's strictures. Smith's father belonged to the strictest sect of Calvinistic Baptists and had reared his children in obedience to two commandments: "to labor for their daily bread, and to wait, with humbleness of heart, for the Holy Ghost." He read the Bible to his children, but would have taken it away in terror had he thought they might be led to a presumptuous attempt to secure their own salvation by study of the Scriptures and thus usurp the sovereign power of the Spirit. No person could know their fate, and must live in dread uncertainty, unable to understand the Bible or to repent or believe or to love or obey God until some supernatural sign, some miraculous vision gave assurance of pardon and acceptance. All persons were born sinners, utterly dead, and utterly depraved. No one could please God without faith, yet no one could have faith until it pleased God to bestow it in some miraculous fashion. All these things young John Smith was taught, and many an evening around the fireside he listened to stories of conversions, to tales of spiritual adventures scarcely less filled with marvelous incident than were his mother's legends of the Banshee.

Reverent and sincere as was his belief in this doctrine of conversion, Smith was forced to agree with the editor of The Christian Baptist that the dogma was often manifested in ludicrous fashion. He himself had once turned away in pity and disgust from a testimonial meeting after an ignorant and simple-minded old man related his experience. Smith had attended some of the camp meetings during the Great Awakening in 1801 and was both offended and amused by the nervous paroxysms and excesses that characterized the scenes. He had been reared to an earnest yet calm and practical piety, and by nature he was conscientious and rationalistic rather than emotional. So, however sound he considered the doctrine "of man's moral imbecility by nature, and of his arbitrary election by grace," he thought it "unreasonable to suppose that God would send his Holy Spirit from the skies to afflict his people with convulsions—to buffet and mock them, and make them ridiculous."

Equally interesting to Smith was Campbell's attack on the role of the Holy Spirit in sending a "call" to the ministry. Smith waited long for a burning bush or some mysterious vision to assure him of God's approval of his calling. At length he decided some simple sign would have to suffice for his practical mind. One day he sat down on a log in the forest. Suddenly he noticed a rattlesnake coiled between his feet; but the snake seemed restrained by some kind of spell and left him unharmed. Thinking of Gideon and his fleece, he wondered if God had sent the charmed snake as a sign that he, too, should become a deliverer of Israel. A few days later, while trying to put a clog on a refractory ox, the beast caught him between its horns and began charging around the pen. In that moment Smith decided that if he were saved from death, God must surely mean him to preach; he escaped and soon thereafter was ordained.

Serious as he considered the nature of his "call," he had to acknowledge that there was justice in Campbell's charge that a species of magic was often substituted for knowledge, that too heavy reliance on the efficacy of a "call" often resulted in too great a neglect of study of the Scriptures. Smith himself, though he held a keen desire for an education, sternly suppressed all such tendencies while he waited for his call, thinking "a knowledge of books would make him depend less on the power of the Spirit." Smith had many times seen a preacher take his place in the pulpit and after standing a few minutes announce that the Spirit failed to put any words in his mouth and take his seat without delivering a sermon.

But there was a further reason why John Smith did not discontinue his subscription to *The Christian Baptist*. He had developed an admiration bordering on the extravagant for Campbell's style of writing. Many of the pioneer preachers had cultivated a gift for pungent expression, but their argument was crude and their attack on a rival dogma was likely to degenerate into personal insults hurled at some opposing theorist. Campbell, on the other hand, as was befitting a prize logic student of the University of Glasgow, conducted his impersonal attacks with finesse and literary allusions; he presented his arguments with simple clarity. So, when Smith's brother Jonathan informed him that he was dropping his subscription to Campbell's magazine because of the essay on "experimental religion," John counseled him: "You are wrong, Jonathan, you ought still to read that work. I do not myself endorse all that Mr. Campbell has written. But I am willing to pay him one dollar a year—were he Satan himself, and his writings destitute of truth—just for his manner of saying things. John Smith would always remain true to his own nature as an independent frontiersman, in spite of his admiration for the pen of Alexander Campbell. He was quite anxious however to meet this man who interested him so much. When he heard that Campbell intended to make a tour of Kentucky including his hometown, Mt. Sterling, and that he would speak at Flemingsburg, twenty miles distant, Smith suggested to some of his friends that as an act of courtesy they should meet the distinguished stranger at Flemingsburg. Campbell's recent essays had left them in no mood for light courtesies. Smith journeyed to Flemingsburg alone.

He arrived the day Campbell was scheduled to preach and was met by William Vaughan. Eager to hear a friend's personal opinion of this man whose writings had puzzled him so much, Smith had immediately asked Vaughan, "Is Campbell a Calvinist or an Arminian, an Arian or a Trinitarian?"

Vaughan replied; "he has nothing to do with any of these things."

"But do you think he knows anything about a Christian experience?"

"Lord Bless you! He knows everything." They went into the house, and there Smith saw a man, whose nose, he said, "seemed to stand a little to the north," taking off the "sherryvallies" in which he had ridden that morning over the muddy roads. As it was impossible to travel much among the Baptists of Kentucky without hearing stories of John Smith, Campbell was curious to meet this strange backwoodsman, and remarked when they were introduced, "And is that brother John Smith? Well, I know brother Smith pretty well, although I have never seen him before." But Smith was not ready for conversation. "I then felt," he said, "as if I wanted to sit down and look at him for one hour, without hearing a word from anyone. I wanted to scan him who had been so much talked of, and who had, in *The Christian Baptist*, and in his debates, introduced so many new thoughts into my mind."

Time soon came to go to the meetinghouse. So large a crowd had gathered to hear the editor-preacher from Virginia that the small church would not hold them. Logs and plank benches had been placed under the trees at the rear, but still many had to stand. A plank platform had been raised for the speaker and John Smith took his seat on the end of the log on which Campbell stood, "determined now," he said, "to find out to what ism he belonged in point of doctrine, for I was full of doubt and suspicion." Campbell read as his theme the allegory of Hagar and Sarah from the fourth chapter of Galatians. In obedience to his own precepts forbidding text-preaching and insisting that all passages be studied in their general context, he first gave a sweeping outline of the whole epistle and explained how he thought it should be read to best arrive at the apostle's meaning; and then he interpreted the allegory itself. It was one of his favorite themes: the coming of the Messiah to free humanity from bondage under the old law and to lead them to a new era of liberty under the gospel. John Smith listened entranced. "I watched all the time with my whole mind," he said, "to find out to what ism he belonged, but he seemed to move in a higher sphere than that in which these *isms* abounded." In a simple, plain and artless manner, leaning with one hand on the head of his cane, he went through his discourse. No gesture or any kind of mannerism characterized him, or served to call off the mind from what was being said. As soon as the sermon was over, Smith had a complaint to make to William Vaughan: "Is it not hard, brother Billy," he asked, "to ride twenty miles, as I have done, just to hear a man preach thirty minutes?" Vaughan told him to look at his watch; the sermon had lasted two hours and a half. Amused, Vaughan then asked him, "Did you find out, brother John, whether he was a Calvinist or an Arminian?" "No," replied Smith, "I know nothing about the man; but be he saint or devil, he has thrown more light on that Epistle, and on the whole Scriptures, than I have received in all the sermons that I have ever heard before."

Immediately after the dinner following his sermon at Flemingsburg, Campbell started on his way to Mt. Sterling accompanied by John Smith and several other preachers. He was glad at last for the opportunity to talk to the frontier minister of whom he had heard so many amusing stories. Lacking in formal education in comparison to Campbell and different as were their backgrounds Campbell still conceived a great liking for this straight-forward, hard-hitting, hard-thinking, independent-minded frontiersman. Knowing something of blunt frankness, Campbell was not surprised at Smith's comments. "Brother Campbell, I will now say to you what I have never said to any man before—I am, religiously speaking, suspicious of you; and as I have an unfavorable opinion of you, I am willing to give you my reason for it, I think it strange you should have written that piece on 'experimental religion' that I read in the eighth number of The Christian Baptist. You cannot be so ignorant as the piece would seem to prove. There must be something kept back or hidden behind it all; for you understand as well as anyone what the 'populars' [sic] mean by experimental religion." Campbell explained, "Well John, if all my Baptist brethren would treat me as candidly as you have done, I would think more of them; My father gave me a scolding for publishing that piece too soon; for, as he thought, the people were not ready for it. But I have a series of essays on hand, on the work of the Holy Spirit, that will explain the whole matter; this was thrown out only to call attention of the clergy."

Soon they arrived at the farmhouse where they and their traveling companions were to spend the night. Several preachers were there and they asked Campbell to present a devotional, but he deferred to John Smith. The next morning Campbell and John Smith continued on their way to Mt. Sterling alone. Smith returned to the subject of experimental religion, and asked, "I suppose you had something that the 'populars' call an experience?" "Yes, I had an experience," replied Campbell. Smith drew his horse along side of Campbell so he would not miss a word. " My father intended to make a clergyman of me," Campbell related, "and always kept me near him. From the time that I could read the Scriptures, I was convinced that Jesus was the Son of God, and was fully persuaded that I was a sinner, and must obtain pardon through Christ, or be lost forever. This caused me great distress of mind. Finally I was able to put my reliance on him; and from that time I have had peace of mind." Shortly, they arrived at Mt. Sterling.

There Campbell preached three sermons. Then Smith accompanied him as far as North Middle town, in Bourbon County, where they parted. As many things as Smith admired in the preacher from the Buffaloe, his skeptical, critical mind was not yet ready to submit to Campbell's opinions; though quite sure that his own theology had been based on error, he still doubted that Mr. Campbell's was right. But he was willing to admit that:

This interesting sojourn with Brother Campbell, led to the removal of many obstacles and to the solution of many difficulties of a religious kind, and left me persuaded of better things of him than when we first met.

All of Campbell's experience in Kentucky was not to be so pleasant as his meeting with "Raccoon" John Smith. Shortly before he started on his tour, a political newspaper in Lexington, *The Monitor*, printed a hitherto unpublished satire on the clergy that Campbell likely wrote at the request of the editor of *The Monitor*. At any rate, it did not appear in Campbell's own magazine until the following year, July 1825. The most bitingly satirical of all his attacks on the clergy, the article was entitled, "The Third Epistle of Peter, to the Preachers and Rulers of Congregations—A Looking Glass for the Clergy." It purported to be a translation from a French copy of an old manuscript found "among the ruins of an ancient city by a miserable wandering Monk." The epistle was quite long and divided into four chapters—each verse more stinging in its sarcasm than the one before:

> Now you who are called and chosen to go forth to all nations and among all people, in time present and time to come, to preach the word, see you take to yourselves marks, nay many outward marks, whereby you shall be known by men.
>
> Be you not called as men are called; but be you called Pope, archbishop, Archdeacon, or Divine, or Reverend; ... so may you show forth your honor and your calling...
>
> Let your garments in which you minister be garments not as the garments of men; ... but let them be robes of richest silk and robes of fine linen, of curious device and

of costly workmanship; ... so shall you show forth your wisdom and humility.

Let your fare be sumptuous, not plain and frugal as the fare of the husbandman who tills the ground...

And drink you of the vines of the vintage brought from afar, and wines of great price; then shall the light of your spirits be the light of your countenances, and your faces shall be bright, even as the morning sun; ... thus shall you show forth your moderation and your temperance in all things.

Let the houses in which you preach ... be built in manner of great ornament without, and adorned with much cost within; with rich pillars ... and with fine altars, ... and urns of precious stones, ... and velvet of scarlet, and vessels of silver.

And let the houses be divided into seats for the congregation, and let every man know his own seat; and let the first seats in front of the altar be for the rich that pay by thousands; and the next for the poorer that pay by hundreds; and the last for those that pay by tens. And let the poor man sit behind the door...

When you go to the church to preach ... go not ... prepared only with a soul to God and with a heart to men; ... but go you with your pockets full of papers and full of divine words; even in your pockets shall your divinity be.

And let your sermons be ... beautiful with just divisions, ... and with hyperbole, and apostrophe, ... and with sophisms, and throughout let declamation be.

And take good heed to your attitudes and gestures, knowing when to bend and when to erect, when to lift your right hand and when your left...

And be you mindful not to offend the people; rebuke you not their sins; but when you rebuke sin, rebuke it at a distance ...

If a brother shall raise up the banner of war against brother ... rebuke them not; ... but ... make them bold to kill ...

If any man go into a foreign land and seize upon his fellow man ... and bring him across the great deep into bondage; ... tell him not that his doings are of Antichrist; for lo! he is rich and gives to the church ...

Teach them to believe that you have the care of their souls, and that the saving mysteries are for your explaining; and when you explain your mysteries, encompass them round about with words as with a bright veil, so bright that through it no man can see.

And lo! you shall bind the judgments of men, (and more especially of women,) as with a band of iron; and you shall make them blind in the midst of light, even as the owl is blind in the noon day sun; and behold you shall lead them captive to your reverend wills.

In all your gettings get money! Now, therefore, when you go forth on your ministerial journey, go where there are gold and silver ...

And when you shall hear of a church that is vacant and has no one to preach therein, then be that a call to you ... and take you charge of the flock thereof and of the fleece thereof, even of the golden fleece.

And when you shall have fleeced your flock, and shall know of another call, and if the flock be greater, or rather if the fleece be greater, then greater be also to you the call...

And the more that the people give you the more will they honor you; for they shall believe that in giving to you they are giving to the Lord; for behold their sight shall be taken from them, and they shall be blind as bats, and 'shall know not what they do.'

And you shall wax richer and richer, and grow greater and greater and you shall be lifted up in your own sight, and exalted in the eyes of the multitude; and lucre shall be no longer filthy in your sight. And verily you have your reward.

… And may abundance of gold and silver and bank notes, and corn, and wool, and flax, and spirits and wine, and lands be multiplied to you, both now and hereafter. Amen.

As expected, the clergymen of Lexington were infuriated by the "Third Epistle." To help counteract the influence of so blasphemous a teacher, they published extracts from Lawrence Greatrake's pamphlet. One Presbyterian minister was so exasperated that he "had his name razed to the foundation from the subscription list of *The Monitor,* a first-rate political paper, because the 'Third Epistle of Peter' made its appearance in it." On hearing of this act, Campbell sarcastically remarked, "What a catastrophe to the Editor of *The Monitor* had all his subscribers been Doctors of Divinity!"

The Editors of *The Luminary,* according to Campbell, "also published some threats of what they were going to do with me;" When Campbell began his lectures in Lexington, he found that a Presbyterian preacher, Dr. Blythe, was endeavoring

to counteract the influence of my public exhortations, by telling his hearers that I was a bad man, and he could prove it. I called upon his reverence and requested an explanation. He then said he meant an erroneous man—not a bad man—that is, not immoral. He moreover had the goodness to tell me that he pitied me—I returned the compliment by pitying him, and after a few ceremonies and compliments we bade adieu.

The result of these attacks, of course, instead of keeping people away from Campbell's sermons, only excited their curiosity all the more; and he spoke to immense audiences both at the morning services and at those starting "at the usual hour of candle lighting."

Whatever the disapproval of the Presbyterian clergy, Campbell was finding that the Baptist elders were receiving him courteously. He made an especially good impression on Jacob Creath, Sr., whom many called "the first orator in the Kentucky pulpit." It was said that Henry Clay had pronounced him "the finest natural orator he had ever heard." Another of Kentucky's most eminent Baptists whom Campbell met was Silas Mercer Noel. Educated in both the classics and in law, Noel had emigrated from Virginia to Kentucky, where he was considered "a man of fine culture, of active enterprise, and enlarged public spirit." Campbell also seems to have met at this time two pairs of brother preachers considered most distinguished among the Kentucky Baptists—Walter and William Warder, and Edmund and George Waller. These men were by no means ready to espouse Campbell's views, but they were willing to give polite attention to his discourses in order that they might determine the worth or the danger of his new doctrine.

After several days in Lexington, Campbell made his way to Versailles. Jeremiah Vardeman was with him in the pulpit when he preached a sermon on the text from I Timothy, "Now the end of the commandment is charity." In presenting his views of "the simplicity and glorious purposes of the Christian institution," Campbell evidently drew a picture highly colored by his own peculiar bias. Vardeman, when dismissing the congregation at the close of the sermon, remarked: "We have heard strange things today. My advice to you is, Search the Scriptures and see if these things be so."

Although perplexed over some of Campbell's doctrine, Vardeman had no doubt of Campbell's power as a speaker. As he and several others were riding toward the home of a gentleman with whom they were to have dinner after the service, Campbell overtook and passed them. Vardeman remarked to his companions, "I once thought I could preach, but since I have heard this man I do not seem, in my own estimation, to be any larger than my little finger." The ludicrous comparison between the little finger and the gigantic bulk of the popular Baptist elder was eulogy enough of Campbell's ability in the pulpit. Even on the day when, at the age of twenty-two, he made his first attempt preaching beneath the shade of a tree in Washington County, Pennsylvania, his hearers had been sure that he had chosen his calling rightly. Now as he was reaching his maturity at thirty-six, it was obvious, even to those who most distrusted his theology, that Campbell was a man gifted with that indefinable magnetic quality that made him the easy master of an assembly.

When Campbell came to fill his appointment at Georgetown on November 6, 1824, he made another very important acquaintance. There, for the first time, he met Barton Warren Stone, leader of the Kentucky "Christians" whose reform movement had so much in common with his own. It was a meeting from which much could be expected. Stone, who was sixteen years Campbell's senior, could count the churches in his movement at several hundred; the most conservative estimate placed his followers at about fifteen thousand in the South and West. The churches that had openly declared themselves for Campbell's views still numbered only four, with a membership of about four hundred; but his magazine was rapidly impressing its ideas on thousands of citizens in the trans-Appalachia. And the followers of each of these men claimed as their ideals the restoring of *liberty*, *unity*, and *simplicity* to the church.

Campbell and Stone, as they likely discovered soon after meeting, had more in common than their religious ideals. Stone was also a cultured man, well born and classically educated. He, too, had been born to revolution and the struggle for liberty. His great-great-great-grandfather, Captain William Stone, emigrating from London to Virginia in 1633, became the first Protestant governor of the Catholic Province of Maryland; he was granted an estate of five thousand acres on the banks of the Potomac, which he called the "Manor of Avon." On his maternal side, Barton Stone descended from Richard Warren, said to have been a Puritan adventurer on the Mayflower, and of the lineage of the Earl of Warren and Surrey. A descendent, Col. Humphrey Warren, moved to Maryland and there on the ancestral plantation called "Frailty" was born Stone's maternal grandfather, Barton Warren, for whom he was named. He himself was born in 1772 near Port Tobacco, in Charles County in Southern Maryland. His father, John Stone, was a gentleman planter with a handsome estate in land and slaves. Nearby was the plantation, "Haberdeventure," belonging to his second cousin, Thomas Stone, who was one of the signers of the Declaration of Independence. Nearby also were "Rose Hill" and "La Grange," estates of physicians to George Washington who lived just across the river. Barton Stone's father died when he was only three, and in 1779, in the midst of the Revolution, his mother moved her family to Pittsylvania County in western Virginia, a spot that William Byrd had called "the Land of Eden." His older brothers fought in the Revolution, and in this frontier country covered with forests of great oaks Barton Stone grew up, hating the Tories and loving liberty and democracy.

Since some of his own sires had been eminent statesmen, young Barton wished to study for the bar. Coming into his inheritance at seventeen, he entered Guilford Academy in North Carolina. The school buildings were built of logs, and the entire faculty consisted of one professor, David Caldwell. A Princeton graduate, Caldwell was an excellent teacher. After completing a three years' course, Barton Stone was a proficient scholar in Latin and Greek. Years later, after he deserted his intention to study law to become a preacher, he studied Hebrew under "a Prussian doctor, a Jew of great learning."

As an infant Stone was christened into the Church of England. After the Revolution so many of the Episcopal ministers returned to the motherland that the church in western Virginia was almost deserted. Methodists and Baptists were more numerous and Stone attended the meetings of both, finding much good in each faith. But the two groups thought very poorly of each other. To the Calvinistic Baptists, the Arminian Methodists were nothing short of the "Apocalyptic locusts," and the Methodists could in sincerity and with fervor return the compliment. Nonplused by their bickering, Stone continued in his way as a young man of the world. Then he entered Guilford Academy, which was Presbyterian, and heard James McGready with his hellfire evangel turn the world "upside down." Having his feet set on another path, Stone sought to escape the influence of the revival and attend Hampden-Sydney College in Virginia. But a thunderstorm decided his future. Detained at Guilford because of the storm, he went to hear McGready preach and was thrown into the maelstrom of a conversion "experience." For more than a year he struggled and agonized. Then he attended another revival. But the evangel he heard this time was very different from McGready's. William Hodge preached a sermon on "God is Love." Stone was converted and decided that he must preach.

Meanwhile, to pay a debt owed the academy, he went to Georgia, where his brother owned several plantations, and became professor of languages at Succoth Methodist Academy, near Washington, a town noted for wealth, hospitality, refinement, skepticism, and wickedness. Beginning his study of theology, Stone, just as Alexander Campbell, became troubled by the metaphysical speculations of an abstruse divinity, which he could not reconcile with his study of the Bible. But he was to receive his license to preach from the Orange Presbytery in North Carolina, and this Presbytery was under the care of Henry Pattillo, a venerable old minister so tolerant in his doctrine that "trials for heresy were all but unknown in the Orange Presbytery." It was well that Stone, with his independent leanings, was under the guidance of leaders of liberal thought among the North Carolina Presbyterians. He had studied in school under a liberal teacher; he had been converted by a liberal evangelist; and he was examined for his license to preach by "the most explicit of this North Carolina group of independent and tolerant leaders in the Church of Scotland." Had the Campbells discovered a similar group in Pennsylvania, they would not so soon have found themselves outside the fold of Presbyterianism.

However similar up to this time some of their religious education may have been, from the day in 1796 when Stone received his license to preach he entered a life foreign to anything in the experience of Alexander Campbell. Immediately Stone had set his face to the West, a West beset by a thousand dangers and hardships that had diminished before Campbell two decades later first traveled through the states bordered by the Mississippi.

Stone, in 1796, traveled over the Wilderness Road, a long and perilous trail through the lands of the Cherokee to the remote settlements on the Cumberland in the Territory of Tennessee, which did not attain statehood until the following year. Arriving in Nashville, he found it a "poor little village hardly worth notice." He was received by the brother-in-law of professor Caldwell, the Reverend Thomas B. Craighead, a Princeton graduate who had come to the Cumberland soon after the first settlers some ten years before to establish Davidson Academy. Craighead, also a liberal, did nothing to encourage Stone in the ways of strict orthodoxy. After a short stay in the Cumberland settlements, Stone made his way across "the Barrens," following "the primitive trading path, with lingering menace of savages," to Lexington,

Kentucky, which with its fifteen hundred inhabitants was the largest town west of the Alleghenies. After two years of itineracy in Kentucky, Stone was called to the pastorate of the churches at Cane Ridge and Concord and was formally ordained by the Transylvania Presbytery. He was not sure he would be accepted, for he had not been able to resolve his difficulties. When the Presbytery asked him the usual question, "Do you receive and adopt the Confession of Faith, as containing the system of doctrine taught in the Bible?" Stone replied, "I do, as far as I see it consistent with the word of God." His reservation was accepted and as one of his irate opponents in later years remarked, Stone was "smuggled into the ministerial office."

The rest of Stone's religious experiences in Kentucky were already familiar to Campbell when he and Stone first met at Georgetown in 1824. He knew the part Stone had played in the Great Revival in the 1800s. He knew of the resulting schism in the Presbyterian Church, and of Stone's withdrawal to form the Springfield Presbytery and of the subsequent dissolving of that body in favor of an independent movement. He also knew the history of the "Christian Connection" and recognized that they had many ideals in common. He and Stone would agree on the necessity of a democratic, independent church free from the dominance of any ecclesiastical courts. They would agree on the evil of any creedal formulation of doctrine. Stone had declared creeds the "nuisances of religious society, and the very bane of Christian unity." They would not quarrel about baptism. Stone had been immersed, and the practice was popular though not universal among his followers. Stone did not object to Campbell's strictures on the "hireling clergy." When the Springfield Presbytery was dissolved, Stone had dramatically torn up "their salary obligation" before his congregations and turned to farming as Campbell had done for support.

Stone and Campbell might discuss with rueful laughter another point in common. As a leader of a new religious movement, Stone for two decades had been subject to all the *"odium theologium"* which the orthodox could heap upon his head. Campbell, especially since publishing The Christian Baptist, felt the same lash of disapproval. Similar epithets had been hurled at both of them: atheist, deist, Arian, Socinian, disorganizer, agent of hell. Peter Cartwright, the fiery Methodist circuit rider, called the Stone movement the "trash trap." In a more dignified vein, the Presbyterians officially designated it as the "New Light schism," a name that had long been current and that still carried opprobrium. The original "New Light Presbyterians" were an Irish sect that in the previous century had fallen into "many Arminian and Arian errors opposed by the orthodox Presbyterians." Often since that time the term had been indiscriminately applied to those falling under the spell of revival emotionalism. The "Last Will and Testament" was declared "both nonsensical and profane; a "sorry attempt at wit." Stone's first major Presbyterian opponent, John Poage Campbell, had called his writings "a labyrinth of quibble and subterfuge" and had said of their author:

> I have thought that many of his opinions are really infidel, and ... deistical ... and view him as an apostate from real practical Christianity ... He had sacrificed everything to popularity and has his reward. The world speaks well of him but God writes Tekel upon his character.

Not only did the orthodox oppose him; in time, all four of the men who withdrew with him to form the Springfield Presbytery and later the independent "Christian" movement deserted the new cause. Two of them joined an eccentric sect called the "Shakers;" the other two returned to the fold of orthodox Presbyterianism and charged that the Christians had become "a corrupt and shattered church." These defections only intensified Stone's ardor and zeal. Since the Kentuckians "had a temperamental edge for a game fight," they applauded his efforts, and the movement steadily grew in numbers and in respectability.

However much Campbell and Stone may have discovered they had in common, the two men were very different in person and in temperament. Stone was rather small in stature, thickset and well proportioned with blue eyes and curly, light red hair. Temperamentally he was far more like the irenic elder Campbell than like Alexander. He was excessively modest, hated controversy, was emotional and credulous, and given to melancholia. He was lacking in a sense of humor, and the mild irony of the "Last Will and Testament of the Springfield Presbytery" was as near sarcasm as he ever came. Far from being a man of action, he was the contemplative theorist, a lover of harmony, and a mediating apologist. In temperament then, Alexander Campbell probably felt that he had more in common with his new friend, the uneducated backwoodsman, "Raccoon John" Smith, than with the scholarly, retiring Barton Stone.

This difference between the two was symbolic of the difference between their two movements that Campbell, at least, could not overlook. Campbell's approach to the problem of Christian unity was fundamentally rational and intellectual. Stone's movement originated in the emotionalism of the Great Revival. It sought union more in the realm of feelings. A religion rooted in emotion was likely to tend toward fanaticism, and fanaticism had no place either in Campbell's intellectual concept of religion or in his temperament. When religious emotion evidenced itself in excessive physical manifestations, he would deplore those manifestations whether they appeared in a camp meeting on the American Frontier or in the flagellant societies and rhapsodies of saints in the Middle Ages. For this reason, though Campbell welcomed the friendship with Stone it was with reservations.

Stone had doubtless read Campbell's essay on "experimental religion" and realized how poor an opinion the editor held of all things resembling enthusiasm in religion. But Stone was a prod-

uct of the American Frontier. Campbell was not. Stone understood, as Campbell could never understand, the conditions and
the psychology that formed the revival emotionalism. He also
knew, far better than Campbell, the excesses to which these
revivals could lead. There was a Methodist camp meeting ground
about three miles from Campbell's farm; but any scene he may
have witnessed there fell far short of the abnormal excitement prevailing during the days of the Great Revival.

By the time Campbell came to America the most intense period of revival spirit had died down, and talk of impending war with
England had turned the public mind. Hence, what Campbell
knew only by hearsay, Stone knew as part of his intimate experience. Campbell had never stood among the throng of a camp-
ground during the Great Revival. But Stone had watched the
crowd gather at Cane Ridge. He knew the loneliness and isolation
of their lives that brought them together, the godly and the ungod-
ly alike. Stone had seen the revival preachers mount their ros-
trums, six or seven speaking at a time in various parts of the
ground in order to reach the vast assemblage, and had watched
them speak until, overcome by weariness or emotion, they had to
give way to others ready to take their place that the mighty relay
for righteousness might not be interrupted. He had seen the coming of night bring no thought of rest or sleep but only a heightened
zeal; while hundreds of lamps and candles suspended among the
trees to ward off the encroaching blackness of the forest, hundreds
of excited people hurrying to and fro with torches in their hands,
and the light of the campfires reflecting on the bowed heads of
other worshippers and on the rows of white tents transformed the
camp-ground into a scene of weird grandeur.

Campbell had never heard a great revival orator sway a mot-
ley throng of frontiersmen gathered in the wilderness. But Stone
had sat under the spell of James McGready who "could almost
make you feel that the dreadful abyss of perdition lay yawning
beneath you, and you could almost hear the wails of the lost and

see them writhing as they floated on the lurid billows of that hot sea of flame in the world of woe." He had watched McGready's small eyes that seemed to transfix his fascinated audience like a dart from the Holy Ghost. He had listened to his coarse, tremulous voice, with something of an unearthly quality about it, which could rise like a trumpet of doom to jangle the nerves of his hearers as he described the anathemas of God against the wicked, and which would gradually die away "on the air like the symphonies of an Aeolian harp" as he described the beauties of the Celestial City. Perhaps Stone heard him deliver his sermon on "The Character, History, and End of the Fool," the climax of which outdid itself in picturesque imagery.

Barton Stone never preached hell-fire sermons, any more than did Alexander Campbell. Most of the preachers of the Great Revival played on the emotions of their hearers by preaching the love of God rather than the terror of hell. But Stone, as Campbell never understood the appeal of McGready's type of sermon to the frontier audience.

McGready had started his ministry in the East, but so great had been the excitement attendant on his preaching in South Carolina that he was accused of diverting people from their necessary vocations and running them distracted. Finally the burning of his pulpit and the receipt of a threatening letter written in blood led him to depart with his gospel westward. There, on the "dark and bloody ground" of Kentucky, the violence of his doctrine seemed more fitting. People whose lives were a constant combat against almost overwhelming forces of nature and whose eyes had beheld the horrors of Indian massacres would be moved by no anemic prattle of peace and brotherly love. Furthermore, the crowds assembled at the camp meetings were a mixed group, representing every stratum of society. The devout and the respectable were there, assuredly; the governor of Kentucky attended Stone's revival at Cane Ridge. Also, the merely curious and those seeking a social frolic. To these were added the scoffing atheists and the drunken rowdies, and the whole was leavened with a sprinkling of prostitutes, robbers, blacklegs, and cutthroats. Realizing the vineyard in which they labored, the revival preachers came prepared to dispense "muscular Christianity as well as the Holy Ghost," and to wage a spiritual combat "as violent toward righteousness as the rest of the border was toward license."

Stone agreed with the other revival preachers that dramatic measures were necessary to gain the attention of frontier citizens "more familiar with the whoop of the savage than with the songs of Zion." Hence he could look with equanimity on even the most curious of the "exercises" befalling the people. At Cane Ridge where "the supernatural agency was present beyond all precedent," he had opportunity to observe these phenomena in all their eccentric variety. The "falling exercise" appeared first. Those affected fell to the ground and lay helpless for from fifteen minutes to twenty-four hours; some writhing and screaming; some completely insensible, as if dead; others, though motionless, experiencing visions of heavenly scenes during which "their whole soul and body were perfumed with a peculiar fragrance that rendered everything mortal disagreeable and unsavory." On recovering, they made the woods ring with their exhortations, sometimes speaking "almost without cessation for the space of five hours" and at times so loudly "that they might be heard at a distance of a mile." Many of the multitude became affected with an even more insidious exercise called the "jerks," in which the body was

> ... so transformed and disfigured as to lose every trace of its natural appearance. Sometimes the head would be twitched right and left to a half round with such velocity that not a feature could be discovered, but the face appear as much behind as before, and in the quick progressive jerk, it would seen as if the person was transmuted into some other species of creature.

Had Campbell been a witness to these scenes at Cane Ridge, he doubtless would have felt just as "Raccoon John" Smith did when he attended the revival. He would have been disgusted and repelled. He did not, and could not, believe that the power of the supernatural inspired such emotional frenzy; he was convinced that such extravagances could be explained by purely natural causes: the loneliness of life on the frontier, the consciousness of danger, and the sense of human weakness in the powerful wilderness made the people especially susceptible to impressions; the long and vivid sermons and the abnormal atmosphere of the great meetings aroused the emotional until they became afflicted with a nervous disease which sympathy or suggestion would suffice to call into action after it had become habitual from long continued mental excitement.

Stone's attitude, on the other hand, was pragmatic. He readily admitted that there were "many eccentricities, and much fanaticism in this excitement," and he deplored the excesses to which it sometimes led. Nevertheless, he viewed the "bodily exercises" with sympathy, for he was convinced that the results of the revival were good. The exercises, he reasoned, were so much like miracles, that if they were not they had the same effects as miracles on infidels and unbelievers; for many of them by these were convinced that Jesus was the Christ. Anyway, there was no doubt in Stone's mind that the phenomena, even in their excess, were true manifestations of the supernatural. One thing was sure; the newly made saints of the backwoods themselves were as convinced of the efficacy and authenticity of their experience as was any Hildegard of Bingen or Bernard of Clairvaux.

Evidently Stone and Campbell lightly passed by their differences and discussed their similarities when they met at Georgetown. Stone later wrote of their talk, "Our views were one." Campbell did not commit himself in print, but a mutual friend said of the meeting: "They conversed freely together, and were mutually led to love and highly esteem each other as brothers in the same heavenly family ... advocates of the same great and glorious principles."

✛

Campbell had an appointment to preach on Sunday, November 13th, at Frankfort, "a smart little town on the Kentucky River," hidden in "a wilderness of big trees and grape vines," and proud of its position as seat of the government for the state. The legislature was in session when Campbell arrived in Frankfort, and he accepted an invitation to address the assembly.

Then he journeyed to Louisville and immediately upon arrival called at the home of a man with whom he had pleasantly anticipated meeting for some months. He had been corresponding with Philip Slater Fall, the young minister of the Baptist Church at Louisville, and already they had discovered much in common. Fall, ten years younger than Campbell, was born at Brighton, Sussex, England, September 8, 1798. His family were people of means, his father being an officer in the British army. "I had enjoyed in England," said Fall, "all the advantages in the matter of education that wealth and social position could give." At the close of the Napoleonic wars, Philip's father resigned his commission and in 1817 moved with his wife and eleven children to Logan County, Kentucky. Both of his parents died soon afterwards, and Philip, the oldest child, became head of the family and accepted a position as teacher of an academy at Frankfort. Philip had been "carefully instructed by a most devout and excellent mother, in the way of life, according to the principles and practices of the Church of England," but after coming to Kentucky an acquaintance with a Huguenot family led him to join the Baptist Church. Young though he was, he had an excellent education, clear correct diction, and charming manners, so the Baptist elders urged him toward ministry. It was not an unusual calling in his family, for his maternal grandfather had been an Episcopal minis-

Phillip Slater Fall [1798–1890). He was minister of the Baptist Church in Louisville, KY, when he and Campbell first met in 1824. They became close friends. Fall would later become president of the Nashville Female Institute.

ter, and his paternal great-grandfather was a distinguished Baptist preacher of Hertfordshire and was buried under the pulpit from which he had preached for forty years. Young Fall was ordained in 1820 by the Forks of Elkhorn Church and became a member of the household of the Baptist preacher, Dr. Silas M. Noel. The following year he married Ann A. Bacon, accomplished daughter of John Bacon, a prominent citizen of Franklin County, who claimed a proud descent from Sir Nicholas Bacon, Lord Chancellor in the reign of Queen Elizabeth and father of Francis Bacon.

Fall first heard of Alexander Campbell from William Vaughan shortly after the Walker debate in 1820. Vaughan in "highly eulogistic language" praised "the commanding talents of the defender of the Baptist practice" to the young minister. In the following year Fall made a preaching tour to Nashville with Jeremiah Vardeman, and again he heard of Alexander Campbell, for throughout their tour Vardeman took occasion to speak "in the highest possible terms" of the preacher from the Buffaloe, "not only as a disputant, but as a man of earnest piety and wonderful scriptural attainments." Fall was curious to know more about the man who could draw such praise from two of Kentucky's most popular Baptist ministers. A few months later, while preaching in Louisville, Fall acquired a copy of Campbell's "Sermon on the Law" and a reply to the sermon. In January of 1823, Fall was called to the pastorate of the Louisville Church, and during the following winter "in the presence of a large assembly" he preached a discourse based on the "Sermon on the Law." One of the aged elders of his congregation, agitated at such heretical teaching from their young pastor, arose hurriedly at the close of the sermon and without waiting for the customary hymn and prayer exclaimed in great haste, "Let us be dismissed!" Soon after the beginning of the publication of The Christian Baptist, a friend sent Fall several issues. "Altho prepossessed in favor of its editor," later wrote Fall,

> I read many of its articles, nevertheless, with great repugnance, and, when requesting that it might be sent me, so wrote to Bro. Campbell. Still, ... truth after truth impressed itself upon me, and as it was matured was imparted for the investigation and improvement of the growing church.

The young pastor of twenty-six was slowly infusing his congregation with Campbell's doctrines while eagerly awaiting the visit of the editor-preacher from Virginia.

Campbell arrived in Louisville on a Friday, and, after "a

slight repast" at the home of Fall, he attended the regular Friday night meeting held in Fall's schoolroom. The room was well filled, and five Presbyterian ministers—Dr. Gideon Blackburn and his two sons and two sons-in-law—were present. Fall opened the meeting, and Campbell preached for nearly two hours from the Epistle to the Hebrews, "every person present," said Fall, "giving him the utmost attention. His method of reading the Scriptures, of investigating their truths, and of exhibiting their statements was so entirely new, and so perfectly clear, as to command the respect, if not the approval of all that listened." Dr. Blackburn was asked to dismiss the congregation with prayer, and while returning to the house Campbell remarked to Fall, "Dr. Blackburn does not understand the Christian religion." Asked how he knew, Campbell replied, "His prayer clearly declares that."

Saturday was a disagreeable and rainy day, but Campbell and Fall "walked together along the Canal to Portland, and about the city, to examine whatever was worthy of notice." On Sunday morning Campbell preached in the Old Court House upon the subject of spiritual gifts that the Christ had "given to men, that God might dwell amongst them." After about an hour and a half the discourse was rudely interrupted. A crowd rushed into the Court House on the heels of the officers of the law who had arrested a man for killing another in a gambler's brawl. The congregation dispersed "much to the general disappointment." In the evening he was invited by Dr. Blackburn to speak in the Presbyterian Church on Fourth Street—the Presbyterian ministers of Louisville evidently not being so suspicious of his doctrine as were those of Lexington—and there, said Fall, he

...addressed a large and very attentive congregation upon the evidences of the Messiahship. He had contracted a bad cold and sore throat on Saturday, and spoke with much difficulty, but he enchained the attention of the audience by his masterly exhibition of the claims of our Lord, to the homage of mankind.

If anything had been lacking to complete the conquest of Philip Fall to Campbell's teaching, the three sermons in Louisville had filled the need. In Fall's opinion, all who had any power to discriminate must listen in admiration to the discourses of Alexander Campbell.

The latter part of November, Campbell returned home after an absence of almost three months. Seven years before he had been discouraged by the lack of "coadjutors" in his work. Now it appeared that the field was likely to be rich with co-laborers. The pioneer Kentucky Baptists, as indeed most of the early settlers of Kentucky, had emigrated from the eastern part of Campbell's own state, Virginia, "carrying with them their princely hospitality, their indomitable energy, and their love of civil and religious freedom." Campbell had found their descendants "a highly intelligent people ... having amongst them many ... preachers ... eminently distinguished for their abilities."

Campbell informed the readers of *The Christian Baptist* in his account of the recent tour, that he was satisfied that he himself had come home richly laden with intelligence. "The kingdom and dominion of the clergy, the necessity of a restoration of the ancient order of things, and the proper method of accomplishing it, have opened with greater clearness to my view."

About three weeks after he returned from Kentucky, on December 14, 1824, Campbell's eighth child and seventh daughter, whom they named Margaretta, was born. Important as the event might be, Campbell's public duties were leaving him disturbingly little time to devote to his family. He had promised the readers of The Christian Baptist "a greater variety" in the pages of his magazine, and he had the important task of writing a series of articles explaining his views on the nature of the Holy Spirit. His earlier essay on "experimental religion" presented his negative position and discussed the points of the current doctrine that he opposed; and he had confessed to John Smith that the article was thrown out only to call the attention of the clergy. Certainly the piece had aroused attention enough. Now he had to redeem his promise to give the positive statement of his own position that, as he had said to Smith, "will explain the whole matter." Nowhere else in his writings did Campbell reveal both the extent and the limitations of his adherence to the Lockian philosophy so clearly as in his discussions of the Holy Spirit.

Both Campbell's own independent and rationalistic mind and his grounding in the philosophy of the Enlightenment caused him to rebel against the Augustinian and Calvinistic conception of humanity—a doctrine of the total depravity of the human race through the "original sin" of Adam. Through this doctrine humanity was seen as incapable through personal will or the tes-timony of the Scriptures to believe the Gospel. The direct and supernatural operation of the Holy Spirit on the human heart was necessary to restore the "lost power of believing, a process termed "regeneration" or "conversion." Such a theory outraged all Campbell's ideas of the dignity and freedom of the individual. He had to develop a concept of the work of the Holy Spirit that would be biblical and at the same time harmonize with his Lockian views on the constitution and nature of humanity.

Campbell began his discussion, entitled "Essays on the Work of the Holy Spirit in the Salvation of Man," with the statement: "To the Spirit of God are we immediately indebted for all that is known, or knowable of God, of the invisible world, and of the ulti-mate destinies of man." The Holy Spirit in its first aspect, as the Spirit of Wisdom, "dictated from heaven" the sacred Scriptures and thus gave humanity the "word of knowledge" by which individuals were to comprehend the nature and will of God. The first step toward salvation was to read and accept this testimony given through the Word; and it was as natural to believe testimony, argued Campbell, as it was to see light or hear sound. There was only one hindrance to belief—human beings, through experiencing lies and deceit, become incredulous. Doubt was to be removed, not by some supernatural act of "enabling grace" which created new human faculties, but by the presentation of evidence that would be manifest to these faculties. This evidence of the truth of its testimony was vouchsafed to human beings by the Holy Spirit in its second aspect, as the Spirit of Power.

The Holy Spirit presented its evidence, said Campbell, in three forms. The first form *miracles*, the second form *spiritual gifts* or miraculous powers bestowed on the apostles and the third form, the Holy Spirit gave proof of its testimony through bestowing the gift of *prophecy*.

All these manifestations were necessary in the early days of Christianity, argued Campbell, in order "to render the testimony credible;" and, he maintained that the Holy spirit's "distributions, as the *Spirit of Wisdom and of Power*, were confined to the apostolic age, and to only a portion of the saints that lived in that age." He did not hesitate to insist that: "the Spirit finished its work of revelation on the Isle of Patmos, in giving to John the Beloved the last secrets of the divine plan ever to be uttered in human language while time endures." Henceforth the Holy Spirit expressed itself only through the testimony of the written word in the Scriptures; but Campbell was certain that the written record of the miraculous work of the Spirit was just as potent in producing belief as the original miracles:

> The reading or hearing of these things now recorded, stands precisely in the same relation to faith, as the seeing of the apostles work the miracles, or the hearing them declare the truth. The words they spake are as much the

words of the Holy Ghost when in written characters as they were when existing in the form of sound … the miracles are recorded for the same reason they were wrought … the word written is as capable of producing faith as the word preached.

So far Campbell was concerned only with explaining the nature of the Holy Spirit's relation to the process of conversion by which people accept Christianity. So far his position was consistently Lockian. Humans were creatures who could be reached only by the importation of ideas to their intellect, and whose intellect could be reached only through the five senses. The testimony of the Holy Spirit was now revealed in ideas couched in words and confirmed by evidence that presented itself to the senses.

When Campbell came to discuss the nature of the operation of the Holy Spirit upon an individual after accepting the gospel, he was up against a different problem. Whether or not he himself realized the dilemma, he was faced with evidence of a deep religious truth, which he felt to be real and actual but which could not be fitted into his philosophical system. There was an influence of the Holy Spirit operating in the lives of Christians other than through the avenue of their intellect and their senses; and in this dilemma the religious interest triumphed at the expense of the logical. This influence he described as the *Spirit of Holiness or of Goodness.*

This influence operated to "direct or draw the whole man into new aims, pursuits, and endeavors," though it created no new faculties or bestowed "no new passions nor affections." Furthermore, it made effective the Grace of God in the human heart. Just how this grace was bestowed, whether the grace was free or sovereign, special or irresistible, were problems that Campbell did not intend to discuss. To do so would be "to run the old metaphysical race again." These dogmas were products of the "distilleries" of John Calvin and James Arminius: "That is, in other words, certain parts of the Bible, mingled with philosophy, and put through a

Calvinistic or Arminian process of distillation, issue in these abstract notions."

When one of his readers seemed to infer that he perhaps strayed too far from the regions of speculation and presented a view that was too matter-of-fact, Campbell replied:

> I am not to be understood as asserting that there is no divine influence exerted over the minds and bodies of men. This would be to assert in contradiction to a thousand facts and declarations in the volume of revelation—this would be to destroy the idea of any divine revelation—this would be to destroy the idea of any divine government exercised over the human race—this would be to make prayer a useless and irrational exercise—this would be to deprive Christians of all the consolations derived from a sense of the superintending care, guidance, and protection of the Most High. But to resolve everything into a 'divine influence,' is the other extreme. This divests man of every attribute that renders him accountable to his Maker, and assimilates all his actions to the bending of the trees or the tumults of the ocean occasioned by the tempests.

Here Campbell paused to assert his belief in the mysterious forces of the universe: "There are many things which are evident, yet altogether inexplicable … Until we know more of God than can be revealed or known in this mortal state, we must be content to say of a thousand things a thousand times, we cannot understand how, or why, or wherefore they are so."

Among these inexplicable agencies was the influence of the Holy Spirit. Further than this Campbell would not go.

In going even this far he was straying a long way from his sensational psychology. The Lockian system provided for no operation of the Spirit except through channels that appealed to the senses and could only admit spiritual influences that operated through the written Word or through the sacraments. Hence, the philosophy of Locke gave no room for a philosophy of prayer, something Campbell could not accept. "Consequently, he forsook his system at this point and stated religious truth simply as religious truth, ignoring the fact that it could not be logically coordinated with his system."

It was hard to convince the orthodox that a man, no matter what his philosophical predilections, could grow to maturity and call himself a Christian without having had some sort of proper "experience." Campbell had found it so with John Smith. As he had capitulated and related his "experience" to Smith, he finally decided to do so, somewhat more fully, for the readers of *The Christian Baptist*:

> I well remember what pains and conflicts I endured under a fearful apprehension that my convictions and my sorrows for sin were not deep enough. I even envied Newton of his long agony. I envied Bunyan of his despair. I could have wished, and did wish, that the Spirit of God would bring me down to the very verge of suffering the pains of the damned, that I might be raised to share the joys of the genuine converts. I feared that I had not sufficiently found the depravity of my heart, and had not yet proved that I was utterly without strength. Sometimes I thought that I felt as sensibly, as the ground under my feet, that I thought that I felt as sensibly, as the ground under my feet, that I had gone just as far as human nature could go without supernatural aid, and that one step more would place me safe among the regenerated of the Lord: and yet Heaven refused its aid. This, too, I concealed from all the living. I found no comfort in all the declarations of the gospel, because I wanted one thing to enable me to appropriate them to myself. Lacking this, I could

only envy the happy favorites of heaven who enjoyed it, and all my refuge was in a faint hope that I one day might receive that aid which would place my feet upon the rock.

But this account of an agonized "seeking" was scarcely calculated to please the orthodox when it became evident that Campbell related the "experience" only to illustrate his contention that "throughout Christendom every man's religious experience corresponds with his religious education;" that "what is called 'the work of conversion,' is, in many instances, but the revival of early impression." He had been reared a Calvinist; hence, his experience was "the experience of a misguided education," which he blamed for all his "darkness, and gloom, and uncertainty." He looked for salvation "independent of all the grace revealed in the gospel, but found it inseparably connected therewith;" and he would have enjoyed the "blessings of the gospel of Christ ... much sooner, had it not been for the obstacles thrown in my way by an abstruse and speculative theology." To those who would object that supernatural aid was lacking in his process of conversion, he retorted: "I have to observe that it is all supernatural, the truth believed, the good things hoped for, and the amiable one loved are all supernatural." If this explanation did not satisfy, his readers would have to make the most of it. For he could not change his opinion without denying one of the most fundamental tenets of his religion—*his conception of faith.*

The years had only increased Alexander's leaning toward the more rationalistic conception of faith. The more he learned of the emotional extravagances of American camp meetings the more he favored the intellectual position of Sandeman. Hervey's view of faith, he felt, had led to a debased Protestant mysticism that was doing untold harm to the cause of religion. Hence, he urged on the readers of *The Christian Baptist* a conception of faith that agreed with Sandeman's as to its nature and its place in the order of events, though he differed with Sandeman on the value of faith and the way in which it is produced. "Evidence also produces faith, or testimony is all that is necessary to faith," he declared. Hence, the only faith was historical faith, because it was the acceptance of an historical record. Christian faith was saving faith because it was belief in the saving fact that "Jesus is the Christ, the Son of God." All controversy about the nature or different kinds of faith were "either learned or unlearned nonsense," he declared, because the validity of a person's faith could be judged by a simple pragmatic test: What was its effect upon personal conduct?

> [I]t is not a man's eating that keeps him alive, but what he does eat; so it is not a man's believing that saves his soul, but what he does believe ... If a man really believes any fact, his faith soon becomes apparent by the influence of the fact upon him

Furthermore, he argued, this faith comes about in a purely natural way:

> To exhort men to believe, or to try to scare them into faith by loud vociferations, or to cry them into faith by effusions of natural or mechanical tears, *without submitting evidence*, is as absurd as to try to build a house or plant a tree in a cloud ... without evidence it is as impossible to believe, as to bring something out of nothing... Such is the constitution of the human mind ...

It was an extreme statement. But it was becoming Campbell's habit to use the dramatic value of an extreme statement to call attention to his position. And he wished now to insist that *no supernatural power was necessary to induce faith*; it was a matter of individual responsibility. Though the eye might be passive in receiving the rays of light, people had the power to open their eyes; so the human will had the power over the act of belief. In order to believe a person had only to lay aside blinding prejudices and antipathies and see the truth of the testimony. Hence unbelief was sin, for it was voluntary blindness.

Though he might isolate faith as a mental act for the purposes of definition, he realized that actually it was only the first step in the complex process of conversion, which also included repentance and reformation, and however theologians might separate and label them one, two, three, in reality they were so fused together that the whole process of conversion became a vital unity. Hence, Campbell in discussing faith, repentance, and reformation often let his terms overlap in meaning and included effects with causes in a manner not conducive to clearness of definition. But this characteristic of his mode of thought disclosed his realization of the complexity of the problem and saved him from falling into the "intellectualism "warranted by his philosophical presuppositions." Campbell might give a theological definition of faith in terms of Lockian intellectualism, but his religious use of faith centered in the mysterious and all-holy Person of the Christ.

While he was publishing his essays on the Holy Spirit, Campbell also had on hand another work that he started some time before. Since he was attacking various forms in current Christianity, he thought it would be well to give the origin of some of these things that he considered aberrations. It was the kind of writing he liked—a sweeping historical review.

In a series of articles entitled "Essays on Ecclesiastical Characters, Councils, Creeds, and Sects," he discussed the debt that "the modern clergy" owed to the theories of "oriental philosophy" to Pythagoras, Socrates, Plato, Aristotle, Epicurus, and Zeno, to the Cynics, the Academics, and the Eclectics and to the Jewish sects, the Essenes, the Pharisees, and the Sadducees. He maintained, with the historian Mosheim, that "the first 'theological seminary,' established at Alexandria in Egypt, in the second century, was the grave of primitive Christianity" and that the theologian, Origen, had been the chief instrument in introducing into Christianity a "new species of philosophy, extremely prejudicial to the cause of the gospel, and to the beautiful simplicity of its celestial doctrines..." "Origen," said Campbell, "disseminated more error and absurdity than any other writer of ancient or modern times." From these sources, argued Campbell, there was ushered "into existence that 'monstrum horrendum informe ingens cui lumen ademptum;' that 'monster horrific, shapeless, huge, whose light is extinct,' called an ecclesiastical court," which he defined as "those meetings of the clergy, either stated or occasional, for the purpose of either enacting new ecclesiastical canons or of executing old ones," and which he declared were "antiscriptural, antichristian, and dangerous to the community, civil and religious."

Turning to a particular work of the ecclesiastical courts, Campbell focused on creeds and confessions of faith, deeming them enemies to church union and the sowers of intolerance. "So far from being the bond of union, or the means of uniting the saints, they are the bones of controversy, the seeds of discord, the cause as well as the effect of division."

To prove his contention about the tendencies of creeds, Campbell wrote a six-part historical review entitled "A Narrative of the Origin and Formation of the Westminster or Presbyterian Confession of Faith." It was a story admirably suited to his purpose. The scene was laid in the days of Charles I when it was common to punish a religious dissenter with fine and imprisonment and even death and when it was generally accepted that the doctrine and worship of the church should be regulated by act of Parliament and enforced by the civil sword; and the Westminster assembly which formed the creed was called by Parliament in 1643 at the instigation of the Scots who would agree to assist the English Parliament in the war against its king, Charles I, only on condition that the English would unite with them in "establishing one creed, one discipline, one ecclesiastical government in both nations." Hence, considering the age and the occasion, Campbell found much historical evidence to support his allegations that "the Westminster confession owes its origin to a political contest ... it is a small morsel of the religious lava that belched forth from the crater of that political volcano which made Britain tremble from the Orkney Isles to the Straits of Dover;" that it was the fruit of the belief that "the voice of the majority is the voice of God;" and that "the whole ended in religious despotism, tyranny, and no toleration. That swords and constables, exiles, confiscations, and death, were the attendants and sanctions of this system." Campbell concluded with the comment that only when such human systems were ignored could Christianity be "attended with intelligence and liberality."

Since commencing *The Christian Baptist* in 1823, Campbell had been making frequent tours, not just to teach and debate, but also to learn. "We have been long convinced," he wrote in December 1825:

> ...that to live to purpose in any society, it is necessary to be well acquainted with the state of that society; it is necessary, in a certain sense, 'to catch the living manners as they rise' ... there is great difference between reading geography and traveling over the surface of a country; between hearing of, and seeing the religious world; between viewing men and things with our own eyes, and looking at them through the media of books and newspapers; between contemplating society in the closet, and mingling with it in actual operation.

His travels and his interaction with religious leaders had given him optimism. The reaction to *The Christian Baptist* was also giving Alexander cause for optimism: "Prejudices which existed against this paper, and the panic which its first numbers produced, are greatly subsided, and its circulation has increased with unusual rapidity." While criticism continued, others among his subscribers were sending encouraging letters. From Kentucky a reader wrote: "I do most conscientiously believe that it is doing more good than any publication in the western country." Another, after reading Campbell's attack on a supernatural "call" to ministry, wrote: "I ... am made now to wonder why the Christian world could have been kept in ignorance so long, an ignorance too which is fraught with so much distress to an honest-minded Christian." Still another reader, who thought that "A religious Archimedes has long been wanted to raise the moral world from its chaotic darkness as to true and abstract religion," assured Campbell that: "your opposers cannot hold out a fair argument with you, either upon scriptural or philosophic ground, right reason or common sense. It is for this reason, sir, that priest craft is at its very wit's end, and in the very raving paroxysms of desperation, for fear of the loss of its empire over the understandings of the multitude."

Campbell made several visits to associations in the fall of 1825. Returning from one trip of a thousand miles, he wrote in "Notes on a Tour" for his magazine:

" ... *there is a spirit of inquiry marching forth,* before which, most assuredly, the ... systems of tradition and error must and will fall."

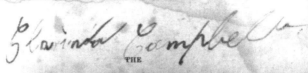

THE
SACRED WRITINGS

OF THE

APOSTLES AND EVANGELISTS

OF

JESUS CHRIST,

COMMONLY STYLED THE

NEW TESTAMENT.

TRANSLATED FROM THE

ORIGINAL GREEK,

BY GEORGE CAMPBELL, JAMES MACKNIGHT, AND PHILIP
DODDRIDGE, DOCTORS OF THE CHURCH OF SCOTLAND.

WITH PREFACES TO THE

HISTORICAL AND EPISTOLARY BOOKS;

AND

AN APPENDIX,

CONTAINING CRITICAL NOTES AND VARIOUS TRANSLA-
TIONS OF DIFFICULT PASSAGES.

PRINTED AND PUBLISHED BY ALEXR. CAMPBELL.

BUFFALOE, BROOKE COUNTY, VIRGINIA.

1826.

*Clarinda Campbell's personal copy of her father's [Alexander Campbell]
1826 translation of the New Testament. It was printed in Buffaloe, [later
Bethany] Virginia, by Alexander Campbell.*

·11·

The Printer and the Planter

WITH SO MANY great things dependent on the scriptures, Campbell was naturally much concerned about a correct translation for every word and phrase. Early in 1825 he began to publish a series of articles on the "History of the English Bible," commenting that: "It is a remarkable coincidence in the history of all the noted reformers that they all gave a translation of the Scriptures in the vernacular tongue of the people whom they labored to reform." The July issue announced that Campbell had before the public a prospectus for a new translation of the New Testament. It was to be based on the translations of three Presbyterian and Congregational divines, the work of George Campbell of Aberdeen being used for the Gospels, Macknight for the Epistles, and Doddridge for Acts and Revelations. But the prospectus announced he would make "one improvement." On the express command of King James, who wished to avoid theological controversy, his translators had retained all "the old ecclesiastical words." Campbell, bound by no such allegiance to the past, announced he would make his "a pure English New Testament, not mingled with Greek words, either adopted or anglicized." Naturally, the chief example he had in mind was the word "baptize," anglicized from the Greek "*baptizo.*" Both George Campbell and Macknight had agreed with other lexicographers that the literal meaning of "baptize" was "immerse" throughout his text. He realized the furor that would result from this innovation, but then he had never been one to seek timid support at the expense of his own convictions. He was sustained in this case by a sense of the great importance of his task. On sending his friend, Philip Fall, a copy of the prospectus, he wrote him in April 1825:

> This work I consider to be the most worthy of patronage of any ever presented to the American public—but the clergy I anticipate will oppose it. The Scriptures one way or another are very little understood ... But the time is at hand when this state of things will pass away."

Alexander needed a high conviction of importance to sustain him in this work, for it proved to be, he said, "incomparably more labor than I had any idea of." Throughout the winter of 1825–1826, he devoted every moment he could spare to preparing the translation. With his active, restless temperament, Alexander found the confinement to such a meticulous task taking a high toll on his energy. He wrote to Fall in January:

I am still nervous and often complaining but the Lord has still been gracious and merciful ... I never was more busily employed nor more laborious in study than this winter ... and do excuse this hasty scrawl which has been redeemed from the night watches ... I am so worn out writing and so nervous, that I am and I fear will be through this winter a poor correspondent. If I can only keep alive the embers of communication till I get through with this work I shall rejoice ...

Difficult though it was, Alexander still was getting pleasure from his task, for he wrote to a correspondent in *The Christian Baptist*:

It is indeed to me a delightful and profitable employment, having assembled all translations of note and even those of no great reputation, I am under the happy necessity of reading, examining, and comparing all, and in notes critical and explanatory, elucidating the text where it can be improved. But a small portion of my labor ... will meet the public eye, because, in many instances, after the most diligent examination, ... my labor simply results in the conviction that the translation of the standard works is the best. It is a work that I dare not delay, or yield to any other demands upon me, however impervious. I have more than sixty letters at this time on file unanswered, and many of my correspondents are out of patience with me; but I have ... many good apologies to make.

Spring found Alexander somewhat improved in spirits: "My health though delicate," he wrote Fall, "has been mercifully sustained through the most arduous winters study I ever spent." And the translation was off the press.

Campbell printed the edition on good paper and in large, clear type, "I am getting a new font of type of a large and elegant type in Philadelphia for the New Testament," he had written Fall in January. It was complete with prefaces, hints to readers, notes, geographical and chronological indices, and tables of every sort to assist in studying the book. Never, Campbell was sure, had so valuable a book been available for so low a price. It was to sell for one dollar and seventy-five cents.

"An Apology for a New Translation," was the title of his General Preface. Beginning with the observation, "A living language is continually changing," Campbell insisted however faithful the King James translation may have been for its day, scholarship had progressed since the days of King James until much new "sound critical knowledge" was available. Campbell added that, "after forming a better acquaintance with the idiomatic style of the apostolic writings, and of the Septuagint Greek, we have been fully convinced that what a classical scholar, or a critical etymologist, might approve as a literal version of some passages, is by no means the meaning of the writer. And the King's translators have frequently erred in attempting to be, what some would call literally correct." Campbell denied that these translators had always attempted to reproduce the exact meaning of the original. He charged, and quoted Campbell of Aberdeen as one authority, that Theodore Eza and other Genevese critics influenced the King's translators to interpolate and torture certain passages into conformity with their theology. This being so, he paused to deplore the fact that "some are so wedded to the common version, that the very defects in it have become sacred;" and in conclusion assured his readers they should have no fear that his version was distorted by bias, for:

The whole scope, design, and drift of our labor is, to see Christians intelligent, united and happy ... I do most solemnly declare, that, as far as respects my feelings, partialities, reputation, and worldly interest as a man, I would become a Presbyterian, a Methodist, a Quaker, a Universalist, a Socinian, or anything else, before the sun would set today, if the Apostolic writings would in my judgment authorize me in so doing; and that I would not give one turn to the meaning of an adverb, or position, or interjection, to aid any sectarian cause in the world.

In addition, Campbell wrote a historical and critical preface to each book of the New Testament. He laid down at the beginning the rule which he suggested every reader must follow who desired to understand these sacred books: "You are to understand the words and sentences in ... all the apostolic writings, by the application of all those rules, through which you arrive at the meaning of any other book or writing, of the same antiquity." It sounded like a simple and obvious rule, but to most of those buying Campbell's Testament the idea was revolutionary, so long had a forced and mechanical use of Scripture been the custom. The Protestant Reformation, while exalting the Bible as the sole authority, had led to a grave abuse because the quickly arising war among the various Protestant dogmatists had driven them to assert the absolute inerrancy of the Scriptures resulted in a grossly mechanical view of their nature and authority. Since from the start of his editorial career, Campbell had hurled some of his sharpest barbed thrusts against the "textuary divines" in protest against that defect in Calvinism, a lack of the idea of development, which had lead to the use of all the books of the Bible indiscriminately as "arsenals of proof-texts." He would not neglect the opportunity, in publishing a new translation, to urge his ideas for properly interpreting the Scriptures.

He established his most important exegetical principle in 1816, when in his "Sermon on the Law" he advanced the distinction between the dispensations, which would naturally lead to discrimination in the use of the documents written in the different dispensations. But along with this principle deduced from the covenant theologians, there was another and almost equally important influence brought to bear on Campbell's theories of interpretation: the common-sense empirical method which Bacon had applied to science and Locke to philosophy. Campbell believed the Bible should be interpreted according to the Baconian method of observation and deduction. Every statement in the sacred record was to be "considered as a scientific phenomenon," to be, "observed as Bacon observed the facts of nature," and "from this mass of particular instances, gathered by the empirical method," were to be, "deduced the general truths of religion and the laws of the church." According to this method, Campbell formulated his rules of interpretation: The original meaning of every word was to be carefully observed; verses or phrases were not to be lifted out of their context; the time, place, circumstances, and purpose of each utterance were to be carefully noted. Applying his own rules, Campbell, in his prefaces gave the history, circumstances and design of each of the sacred books.

Alexander made one innovation, in form, in the new edition. He had long deplored "the divisions of the Scriptures of the New Testament into chapters and verses by Romanists of small learning, and less intelligence in the meaning of the inspired writings, in imitation of the Jewish Rabbinates' division of the Old Testament." While he was preparing his translation, he had to his surprise and pleasure come across a piece by Locke, which expressed his own protest against the Bible being "chopped and minced" into verses and hence read "by parcels and in scraps" without due consideration of "what went before and what followed." Campbell's translation was divided into chapters and paragraphs according to the rules of logic and grammar, which would govern the divisions of any work of history or philosophy.

Alexander sent his translation forth with high hopes that it would be well received. "But," he admitted in a letter to Philip

Fall, "perhaps I am too sanguine—and maybe I may have to say what one of the Reformers said who thought he could convince all men of the truths of the Reformation principle—'Alas! Old Adam is too strong for Young Melancthon.'" Campbell's hopes did indeed prove too sanguine. Almost nobody was pleased with the new translation. The Presbyterians, as he had foreseen, were infuriated by his "improvement" in translating "baptize" as "immerse," though their criticism on other points was somewhat tempered by the fact that the work was substantially the translation of eminent Presbyterian doctors. But, to Campbell's surprise, the Baptists were almost equally outraged by his innovation in using "immerse." One point had evidently escaped him, if John the Baptist was rendered John the Immerser where was the authority for their name? The common people in all parties, far from liking a translation in the vernacular, felt that their Bible was taken away from them when the familiar phrases were translated into modern English. Many of them were convinced that the King James version had come directly from God, and any tampering with its language was sacrilege.

The strength of "Old Adam" soon made itself clear through numerous communications, but there were a few independent spirits whom the translation pleased. So Campbell, with his usual gusto for presenting both sides of any good argument, began to publish opinions both favorable and adverse, interspersed with some of his own acid comments.

From Kentucky, came the news that Edmund Walker, a Baptist preacher, had prayed ten days to know whether or not he should burn the Testament, and had ended by committing it "to flames with a clear conscience." After which, he sent a notice of his pious deed to the *Baptist Recorder*, a new publication being edited by his brother, George Waller, and by Spencer Clark:

> Dear Brethren: I subscribed for Mr. Campbell's
> Testament, and received it, paid $1.75 for it, kept it five or

six months and compared it carefully with one I have loved ever since I was thirteen years old. On the first reading, I condemned it but let it remain in my house some two or three months, then tried it again, condemned and burnt it.

Campbell remarked:

Can the present century equal this? I want a parallel case to put on file with it for the benefit of posterity. He compared it carefully with the common version!! Yet it is believed he could not tell the nominative case to a verb, nor the antecedent to a relative, to save himself from the Spanish Inquisition ... criticism, avaunt! This defies you!

And a reader wrote:

The man who could burn the New Testament after a prayer of the enormous length of 'ten days,' when in so good a frame of mind, certainly wanted nothing but the sanction of the law to burn the editor!! This man's orthodoxy and his amiable spirit are both from Geneva. His father John pursued the same course—witness poor Servetus!

Philip Fall, immediately on learning of the incident, wrote a protest to his friend, Spencer Clack, to which Clack replied:

... You blame us for admitting Edmund Walker's communication. You suppose it will be taken for granted that I approve it because it [appeared?] without remarks. Now the truth is I did write remarks ... and handed them to the printer, who fearing to offend Mr. W. never published them ...
... I would have been much better pleased if Brother

Campbell had made an entire new translation himself. As to myself, I am not afraid of translations, they all speak mainly the same things. In family worship, I sometimes read Campbell, sometimes the Catholic Bible, and sometimes the Common version, and sometimes I translate from the original …

To accompany the conflagration story, came another letter from Kentucky reporting that a Presbyterian minister of Frankfort, on being offered a copy of the translation, had exclaimed: "Burn it! Burn it! Take it away! He is a bad man! I would as soon see the Devil as him! He has been proved to be a liar in the public papers!" Campbell remarked:

> None who have read all the volumes of this work can accuse me of giving a one-sided view of things … If I am flattered a little now and then, I am sure to find as much censure as will ballast my cargo beyond the danger of upsetting. The following is to be put down in the hold while the wind swells the sails.

By way of adding a little more ballast, the *Western Luminary*, a Presbyterian publication, charged that Campbell, while claiming to give the translations of Campbell, Macknight, and Doddridge, had actually furnished "the public with a gospel, shaped exactly to his own views," and specified that on "the single subject of baptism" his alterations had been "upwards of eighty." Campbell, answering the "misrepresentations," retorted to the last thrust that the writer, "had told eighty lies in telling one truth, as if a man should say he had seen eighty pigeons when he had only seen one pigeon eighty times."

But the angle of attack that angered and concerned Campbell most was, as one of his correspondents expressed it: "Many of those that have got into Moses' seat would make the people believe, if they could, that the old version fell down from heaven just as it came out of the hands of the king's translators. They would feign have the people believe that it is the blackest crime that a man can be guilty of, to attempt a new translation." In the same vein, another reader informed him: "One of our teachers in this country has refused to have the new translation read in a public meeting because it is not the word of God, alleging that the common version is received as the word of God, but that the new translation is not considered such." This bit of news provoked Alexander to the sarcastic jibe:

> You will see ... that there are *two* things necessary to constitute any translation of the word of God: First, that it be *authorized* by a *king* and his court; and again, that it be finished by *forty-nine persons* ... This, sir, is not only sound, but most orthodox logic. It would, therefore, be a profanation of the pulpit, and the holy place, to read within *thirty* yards of it, the new version ... it may be read in families, just like Robinson Crusoe or any other romance; but never with the veneration of a sermon-book, and infinitely less of the word of God.

Nevertheless, Campbell realized, "so badly taught are many Christians" that they sincerely believed the King James version to be the only word of God. For their benefit, he published in full the long preface written by the King's translators, proving that they themselves made no pretensions to infallibility. He followed it with a common-sense essay on "The Word of God," which began with an obvious query:

> ... Have the French, the Spanish, the German, and all the nations of Europe, save the English, no *Word of God?* If King James' version is the only *Word of God* on earth, then all nations who speak any other language than

the English, have no Revelation… that King James' version needs a revision is just as plain to the learned and biblical student, as that the Scotch and English used in the sixteenth century, is not the language now spoken in these United States … As the boy grows from his coat, so do we from the language of our ancestors.

On the other side of the picture, were a few Baptist leaders who came forward recommending the translation. Andrew Broadus wrote Campbell that he thought it "well calculated to aid the liberal-minded reader in his study of the sacred volume." Even more gratifying to Campbell was the fact that new interest in the Scriptures was being stimulated. All of those democratic religious movements beginning even before the turn of the century that urged the common people to read and interpret the Bible for themselves had awakened the spirit of individual inquiry. The controversy that Campbell's translation provoked was pushing this inquiry still further.

There was one even more obvious concrete result. However it might be received, the new translation was rapidly selling. By September Campbell announced: "The work is almost entirely distributed." Already turning his thoughts to a second edition, he "most earnestly" solicited his readers for "all criticisms, objections, or emendations," and added the comment: "We wish to live for the benefit of our contemporaries, and of the next generation. We are indebted to those that have gone before us, and that debt we can only discharge so far as we labor for the benefit of those who are to live after us." His opponents might think the world could well do without the "benefits" that Campbell was seeking to bestow upon it. Alexander himself never doubted for a moment the necessity and importance of the work he was doing. A man of property and responsibility, he had a deep awareness of the continuity of the generations, of the obligations that each person owed to the past and to the future. Life was short; there was much to be accomplished.

✠

Meanwhile Alexander's domestic affairs were causing him grave concern. His wife had become very ill. While operating Buffaloe Seminary, they slept in a basement room to give more space to the boarding pupils; it was damp there, and Margaret had never been well since. Then too, she was not naturally robust, and bearing eight children in twelve years and burying two of them had proved too great a strain on her health.

When in May 1826, they had to carry their youngest child, Margaretta, to sleep in the cemetery on the hill beyond the orchard with her little brother and sister; Alexander had new cause for worry about his wife's failing health. Toward the last of June, he wrote Philip Fall:

> My Dear Companion Mrs. C_ has been in the hands of physicians for three months under a severe and linger-ing attack of liver complaint … We buried our youngest daughter aged seventeen months about five weeks since, as amiable and intelligent infant as I have ever seen — She died of a severe attack of croup and sore throat …

Several months before, Fall himself lost a child, and Alexander wrote him strange words of condolence:

> I cannot say that I was very sorry to hear that the Lord had taken one of your little ones to himself in the real style of condolence — 'Tis true that I sympathize with the bereavement of my friends. But I have experienced so much of the evils of this world, and seen so many of whom it might have been said that an untimely death was better than theirs that I feel quite differently from what I once felt on such losses.

✠

In the midst of these domestic worries, Alexander found that opposition to his religious movement was steadily growing. And doubtless his opponents wished that some of the "subordination to the Divine Will" which he professed to have learned from his private sorrows might be reflected in his public career by a more gentle and humble attitude. If anything, the opposite was true. His abstraction "from present things" meant, to Alexander, that his mind was seeking to free itself from some worries of the flesh in order to become more devoted to the spiritual mission, which he deemed peculiarly his own and which he felt obliged to advance by use of whatever weapons were most effective, whether those weapons be exposition, or argument, or invective, or satire. Once when Philip Fall wrote him that he had perhaps misjudged an opponent and been a little needlessly harsh toward him, Alexander bluntly answered his friend: "One thing I know I speak just as I feel and according to my judgment of propriety, and however the public may feel about it I feel satisfied with the result for my conscience approves the course." Now that the opposition was definitely organizing itself for attack on his heresy, it was not likely he would relax the vigor of his own campaign.

One of the first indications of the gathering opposition was the commencement of Baptist publication at Bloomfield, Kentucky, under the editorship of Spencer Clack and George Waller. A semi-monthly, it appeared at the beginning of 1826 with the title, *The Baptist Register*, which was almost immediately changed to *The Baptist Recorder*. The establishing of papers had not been able to keep up with the rapidly expanding frontier, and the only important Baptist publication reaching the Southwest was Luther Rice's *Columbian Star*, while a Presbyterian journal of the West, the *Pittsburgh Recorder*, boasted it was "the only religious paper in nine states and three territories." The quickly growing circulation of Campbell's *Christian Baptist* was beginning to alarm the western Baptists, who considered its editor a heretic, for they had no similar medium with which to repel his attacks. However much they might distrust the theology of Campbell, they did not make the mistake of underestimating their opponent. Those who liked him least were ready to admit that besides talents as a debater and orator, he "unquestionably possessed rare gift of expression as a writer, and a remarkable power as a journalist to turn everything that came to his hands into material that would glorify himself, his paper, and his cause." The Baptist leaders, recognizing the "immense power wielded by this man through the press," decided they must meet "his specious arguments" by a like medium. Clack and Waller took up the cudgel against the editor on the Buffaloe. Their first issue, making its bid for the attention of the same audience as *The Christian Baptist*, announced their motto: "to endeavor to strip religion of everything like the traditions of men, and to present the truth in a plain and simple manner." No one was deceived about their real object: "to expose the errors advocated by Alexander Campbell."

Least of all was Campbell himself deceived. In the May 1826 issue, he paid his respects to the new publication. Though he noticed its "belligerent aspect" toward his paper, he assured its editors he was "much pleased with their efforts:" "*The Christian Baptist* is extensively read in Kentucky, and if it is doing any injury it will be corrected and repressed in its career; and if it is doing any good it will receive a new impulse and be accelerated in its course." He further assured them that it would give him "great pleasure to be corrected by them in anything." "But," he added, "I must be convinced before I can be converted to anything. And such is the constitution of my mind, that nothing will operate upon it but truth, reason, argument, and evidence." He concluded with the suggestion that they enter into a discussion of the religious questions at issue, provided, he stipulated: "that you publish my replies in full in your paper; ... I court investigation, and only ask for what is commonly called 'fair play,' and good order in the manner of conducting it." Alexander hastened to add that he had "not stipulated these conditions" because he feared "a non-compliance, or anything like injustice on your part;" but some "insinuations" published over the name of one of the editors, George Waller, had given him "some apprehension" that the hint might not be "untimely."

The apprehension was well founded. The bishops Semple and Broadus of Virginia might consider Campbell in error, but they had a high opinion of his integrity and sincerity. Any argument he might have with them would be conducted on a high plane of truthful investigation of the issues. No man could speak more sharply and severely than Alexander Campbell himself. But he spoke against what he considered abuses in the religious systems, against sectarian bigotry and ecclesiastical tyranny. When his satire was leveled against persons, it was against religious concepts that he believed led them to wrong practices, and not against their character and personal motives. But from the day in 1822 when the "moral societies" of Pennsylvania had dubbed him the "beloved missionary" of the devil, there were always some of Campbell's opponents who would deny to him every instinct of honor and probity. It was evident that one of the editors of *The Baptist Recorder* shared this view. In one of the first issues, George Waller, whose temperament was closely akin to that of his brother, Edmund (who had consigned Campbell's Testament to the flames), published an estimate of Campbell. It began with the remark, "I take this to be the whole secret: Mr. C. has set out to cut a figure in the learned world, and no plan [is] so likely to succeed as to set himself to oppose the whole religious world;" it then proceeded to strip him of every motive save those of personal aggrandizement and greed. His attitude was reflected in a series of anonymous quips about the editor on the Buffaloe, which soon began to appear, and which Campbell sarcastically dubbed "fine specimens of sound reasoning, of good taste, of true politeness, and of a *genuine* experimental religion." Campbell believed most of these pieces of "downright billingsgate" flowed from Waller's own pen; and, with the comment, "If … their views … are to be defended and maintained by such weapons, the conquest is theirs." He reprinted one as a fair example of the rest:

> And still thou are a Baptist Bishop. Yea, verily—a Phoenix Bishop—*a'rara avis in terris*—without thy mate in all creation—without a parallel from Dan to Beer-Sheba. Oh, no! thou art not a Baptist Bishop; thou art the Chief Bishop of a rising tribe; and we advise thee to take to thyself a name quickly, lest in our notice of some other portions of thy creed, we should perchance give thee a CHRISTENING.

The editors did not prove slow in christening the "rising tribe," and Campbell's followers were soon being labeled "Restorationers" and—inescapably though disagreeably to him—the "Campbellites." With such a beginning, it was not likely that the controversy between *The Christian Baptist* and *The Baptist Recorder* would be conducted in the realm of abstract theology.

In June, Alexander wrote to Philip Fall:

> … I have got so many holdings from Georgia to Maine for my severity that I must *reform*—whether I repent or not I must reform … I have not yet read the 10th No. of *The Baptist Recorder* and cannot tell what they are to do—But I have no doubt they will repent whether they may reform or not. Great is the truth and mighty above all things and must prevail.

However sure Campbell might be of the invincibility of his cause, it was inevitable that he should occasionally weary of so much controversy. It was in this mood of weariness that he penned the first sentence of his Prefatory Remarks. In the fourth volume of *The Christian Baptist*, issued in August, he said: "On the subject of religion, I am fully persuaded that nothing but the inspired scriptures ought ever to have been published." If the application of such a principle would lay an embargo on all theological thought, the harassed editor on the Buffaloe felt that this would be an ideal condition. As he explained his idea in the preface, "the great God," in perfect and complete form in His word, had "condescended" to teach the *"one science,"* which was "the knowledge of himself, and of man in all his relations, as his creature," and the "one art," which was "the art of living well in relation to all the high ends and destinies of man." Therefore, it was presumption in man to attempt to add anything to this perfect revelation. Why then was *The Christian Baptist* being published? The answer presented no difficulties to its editor: "So many systems other than God's own system" had appeared to confound, divide, and distract the human family; it became "the duty of every philanthropist and faithful subject of the great King" to call men off "from what may prove their utter ruin." Considering himself a philanthropist, and being convinced "the religious mind is marching forward," Campbell was not to be deterred. He stated emphatically in his preface, by "the pusillanimity of our opponents, the imbecility of their attacks," the forays of religious newspapers "are as much political, commercial and facetious as they are religious."

In the fall, Campbell set out on his round of visiting several Baptist association meetings, a duty that gave him "pleasure and pain," and presented him with another example of the organized opposition to his movement. First, he went as a spectator to the Stillwater Association in Ohio, then as a messenger to his own Mahoning Association in Ohio, where he was appointed corresponding messenger to attend the Redstone Association of Pennsylvania, a fact calculated to give no pleasure to his ancient enemy, Elder Brownfield. At the first two meetings, he said "all was harmony and peace," and he returned home "edified and refreshed." After resting one day, he set out for the Redstone meeting. Elder Brownfield, determined to give no quarter to those churches in his association who, affected with the heresy of Campbellism, refused to acknowledge their allegiance to the Philadelphia Confession of Faith. Able to count on only thirty votes out of the seventy-two messengers present, Brownfield called the thirty faithful messengers together. They constituted themselves the association, appointed their officers, and proceeded solemnly to read out of the association all the dissenting messengers. Ten churches excluded thirteen. Among the churches excluded were those at Brush Run, and Washington, Pennsylvania. Campbell watched "their heads given to the guillotine and their mortal remains to Satan" until feeling "in need of some fresh air," he made his way out of the meeting. The excluded members immediately met a house nearby and asked Campbell to address them. After, they agreed to request their churches to call another meeting and constitute themselves into a new association, to be called the Washington Association. Campbell described the action of Redstone in a bitter article entitled "Ecclesiastical Tyranny," in which he declared: "No inquisitorial process was ever so *informal,* and none more shameless and remorseless. The only thing to which I could compare it was the tyranny of Robespierre during the reign of terror in the French Revolution."

This recent example of "ecclesiastical tyranny" and intolerance drew from Campbell the most sharp and biting satire he could devise, a satire to take its place beside "A Looking-Glass for the Clergy" as an illustration. To his opponents, of the complete unregeneracy of the editor on the Buffaloe, it was the:

Parable of the Iron Bedstead

In the days of Abecedarian Popes, it was decreed that a good Christian just measured three feet, and for the peace and happiness of the church it was ordained that an iron bedstead, with a wheel at one end and a knife at the other, should be placed at the threshold of the church, on which the Christians should all be laid …if less than the standard, the wheel and a rope was applied to stretch him to it; if he was too tall, the knife was applied to his extremities. In this way, they kept the good Christians, for nearly a thousand years, all of one stature. Those to whom the knife or the wheel were applied, either died in the preparation, or were brought to the saving standard.

One sturdy fellow, called Martin Luther, was born in these days, who grew to the enormous height of four feet: he, of course, feared the bedstead and the knife, and kept off at a considerable distance deliberating how he might escape. At length, he proclaimed that there was a great mistake committed by his ancestors in fixing three feet as the proper standard of the stature of a good Christian. He made proselytes to his opinions … and Luther had, in a few years, an iron bedstead four feet long, fashioned and fixed in his churches, with the usual appendages. The wheel and the knife soon found something to do in Luther's church; and it became as irksome to flesh and blood to be stretched by a wheel and rope to four feet, or to be cut down to that stature, as it was to be forced either up or down to the good and sacred three-foot stature. Moreover, men grew much larger after Luther's time than before, and a considerable proportion of them advanced above his perfect man; insomuch that John Calvin found it expedient to order his iron bedstead to be made six inches longer, with the usual regulating appendages. The next generation found even Calvin's measure as unaccommodating as Luther's; and the Independents, in their greater wisdom and humanity, fixed their perfect Christian at the enormous stature of five feet. The Baptists at this time began to think of constructing an iron bedstead to be in fashion with their neighbors, but kindly made it six inches longer than the Congregationalists, and dispensed with the knife ... and Now the bedstead is actually proved to be at least six inches too short. It is now expected that six inches will be humanly added; but this will only be following up an evil precedent; for experience has proved, that as soon as the iron bedstead is lengthened, the people will grow apace, and it will be found too sort even when extended to six feet. Why not, then, dispense with this piece of popish furniture in the church, and allow Christians of every stature to meet at the same fireside and eat at the same table?— The parable is just, and the interpretation thereof easy and sure.

Amidst all these controversies, Alexander was having new cause for worry over Margaret's health. It now appeared that she had developed consumption. As the winter winds blew cold among the hills of western Virginia, Alexander thought that a milder climate might aid her recovery. In November they set out from their farm on the Buffaloe, taking with them their oldest daughter, Jane Caroline, a young lady almost sixteen years of age and, so it was said, "intelligent beyond her years and possessed of remarkable personal beauty."

They made their trip by easy stages, stopping for visits with friends, while Alexander, of course, never lost an opportunity to fill a preaching appointment. Their journey carried them into Ohio and Indiana, and many weeks were spent in Kentucky. In January of 1827 they reached Louisville. Because Alexander had never been to Tennessee before and wished to take Margaret farther South for the coldest months, they made their way to Nashville and their friends, the Philip Falls. In 1796, Barton Stone may have found Nashville "a poor little village hardly worth notice," its some three hundred citizens forming an outpost in the wilderness, but by 1827 it was a thriving river port of more than 4,000 inhabitants, and "busier shops and stores and statelier homes were not to be seen elsewhere between Lexington and Natchez."

Philip Fall was pleased with his location and had encouraging news of the religious prospects to report to his friend. Not that everything had gone smoothly; there was an incident in the summer of 1826 that probably afforded them much laughter. Fall had delivered a sermon on the law at the Harpeth Baptist Church; it created so much excitement that, though it was communion Sunday, the ordinance was completely omitted, and a worthy elder was heard to remark, "These that have turned the world upside down have come hither also." The next Sunday Fall visited Mill Creek Church, and its pastor forbade him to speak. Most of the independent Tennesseans, who had crossed the mountains to carve a civilization out of a wilderness, were not to be frightened by a novel doctrine, not if it appealed to their common sense and their love of democracy. So Fall could report to Campbell that on his first Sunday in Nashville he had suggested the weekly observance of the Lord's Supper, and the innovation had been readily accepted. In the fall, his church, applying for admission to the Concord Association, had specified that they would not acknowledge allegiance to the Confession of Faith, nor allow that the association to have disciplinary power in their congregation. The Association, with great liberality of spirit, had accepted the church on these terms. Campbell felt it was a fortunate day for the Restoration Movement in the South when Philip Fall took charge of the church in Nashville.

Fall was also pleased with his post in Nashville for other reasons. Like his friend Campbell, he was happier when his ministry was accompanied with the role of educator, and he was delighted with his position as president of the Nashville Female Institute. The former head of Buffaloe Seminary would be interested in its curriculum, which included classes in all the "various plain and ornamental branches of Polite Literature," while the Institute was also "well furnished with apparatus necessary for necessary sciences." The academy was doing well under the supervision of Fall, for the aristocratic planters of the cotton kingdom were glad to have their daughters pursue the genteel arts under the well-born and cultured Englishman.

It is doubtful if the grand themes of religion and education were able to retain all of Alexander's interest during a visit to this rich valley of the Cumberland. Surrounding Nashville were fine, carefully tilled plantations to delight the heart of the farmer from the Buffaloe. No matter how much time and energy might be consumed by his career as editor and preacher, Campbell always remained essentially a landed gentleman. Eager to make his farm unexcelled in western Virginia, he could take valuable lessons from these planters on the Cumberland. With one of these planters, the master of the Hermitage, he might have found much to discuss besides the rotation of crops, and the proper handling of Negro slaves.

Andrew Jackson, it was true, was a military man, more given to horse-racing and dueling than to religion, and in 1827 his eyes were resolutely fixed on the President's chair in Washington, rather than on things of the Lord. But in temperament and appearance, he and the editor-preacher from Virginia had much in common. Both were born fighters; one might use the sword

Portrait of Alexander Campbell, 1826–27. It was painted by Washington Bogart Cooper. It is believed he sat for the portrait in Nashville while on tour of the south during the winter of 1826–27. The original hangs in the Campbell Mansion at Bethany, West Virginia.

and the other the pen, but neither knew the meaning of defeat, neither would give quarter to an enemy. They would fight in the same cause, one in politics, and the other in religion to make an America that would fulfill the dream of the spirited, independent, adventurous, and aggressive citizens of the western waters. Their veins flowed with the Scotch-Irish blood of North Ireland, and both would stride through life with the fierce and determined tread of a Highland Celtic chieftain. As was inevitable for men of their nature and talents, both Campbell and Jackson were destined to be fanatically loved and violently hated. Their enemies would seek to leave them no shred of honor or reputation, though both were motivated by a passionate sincerity and honesty. Loved or hated, they were born to dominate; they would always sit at the head of their own table.

Campbell took time while in Nashville to sit for his portrait. He may have done so at the insistence of his friend, Philip Fall, for the picture remained in Nashville instead of being carried back to Virginia. The artist Cooper caught a further resemblance between the soldier-politician of Tennessee and the editor-preacher of Virginia, which might have attracted the notice of more than one citizen of Nashville. The Scotch-Irish strain showed plainly in both their faces, long, fair, with strongly marked features. Their hair was abundant, inclined to be unruly, and arched up sharply from a high forehead, though Campbell's was dark brown in color and Jackson's, dark red.

Both had keen blue eyes, with a penetrating, hawk-like expression, which never seemed to be averted from the face of to whom they were speaking. But Campbell's features, though his nose, according to John Smith, did "turn a little to the north," were more regular than Jackson's, and he would grow old far more handsomely than the hero of New Orleans. As artist Cooper portrayed him, Alexander looked remarkably young at thirty-eight. The tilts with his opponents seemed to have left no scars. Though the chin was resolute, the thin nose and sensitive lips gave to his face a certain meditative, poetic look. It was the face of the young man who had made himself so charming to the ladies at the summer colony at Helensburg, who had whiled away many hours writing poems for the *Washington Reporter*. It was not the face of the crusading editor who was arousing the West with his satiric pen.

Though Alexander's visit to Nashville had given some diversion, its issue was in sadness. Margaret, growing steadily worse, realized she could not get well. Accepting the inevitable quite calmly, she tried to talk to Alexander about her death and the future of their five daughters. He refused to believe that at thirty-six she should be taken away from him and their children. She ceased trying to talk to him of death, but as spring was coming again, she wished to go home to Virginia. In March, they returned to the farm on the Buffaloe.

The editor found that work had piled high on his desk during his four months' absence. In beginning the third volume of his magazine, in August 1825, Alexander had cause to complain that there seemed to be no "excitability" in those who disagreed with them. The editors of the *Western Luminary* and the *Pittsburgh Recorder*, after promising to exchange papers and "enter in the field of investigation" with him, had retired into silence. "Not an editor in the East nor in the West of all the Luminaries and religious Heralds, has ventured to dispute one inch of the ground that we claim. And yet their snarling shows they would bite if they could." He tried to add a little fuel to the flame by the remark: "We must sympathize with them a little, for as Paul said, 'all men have not faith,' so we see all men have not courage." If these editors thought the best way to combat the new publication on the Buffaloe was to ignore it, they soon learned they were mistaken. Neither ice nor fire seemed to stop the course of its editor.

Campbell found he was receiving more communications than he could answer.

The increased correspondence, as well as, the growing circulation of *The Christian Baptist* presented a new problem. Alexander had to transport all his mail to the post office at West Liberty, four miles away, and month-by-month this was becoming more of a task. One sensible solution was to persuade the post office department that his mail was sufficiently heavy to warrant the government in designating his residence as a post office. He made his appeal to Washington, and the officials were properly impressed with the facts and figures he was able to present. The request was granted. In addition to his other occupations, Alexander was now postmaster. He could appoint a deputy to attend to the business of the office, and its advantages were several. Besides convenience, Scots thrift had also fathered Campbell's idea. The office of postmaster carried with it the franking privilege, which meant the annual saving of a good sum of money for the busy printing establishment.

Now that his farm was a post office the question of a suitable name arose. Alexander could not simply call it "Buffaloe," for there was already a post-town in Mason County by that name. Finally he decided—although the idea may have been Margaret's—to call it "Bethany." It was, after all, a very appropriate name for the home of a man who deemed it his special mission to unify and purify the church of Christ. Ancient Bethany on the eastern shoulder of the Mount of Olives, had been the scene of important events in the life of Jesus of Nazareth. Near Bethany, Jesus tarried while His disciples brought from the village the colt on which he made His triumphal entry into Jerusalem, and thence He returned in the evening to lodge after healing the sick and casting the money-changers from the temple. There, at the home of Simon the Leper, Mary the sister of Lazarus broke the alabaster box and poured the precious ointment of skipenard on His head. There he raised Lazarus from the dead; and six days before the Passover, Mary

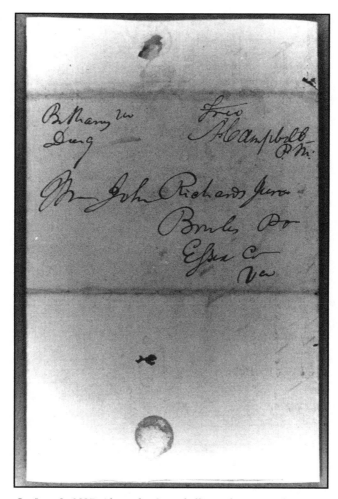

On June 2, 1827, Alexander Campbell's application to have a
post office on his farm was granted. He was appointed postmaster
of the new postal district, for which he chose the name "Bethany."
Using the franking privilege accorded postmasters, he was permitted to send his mail free of postage. This envelope contains the
name Bethany, along with A. Campbell, P.M. [postmaster].

anointed his feet with oil as He sat at supper with her brother. And
there after the Crucifixion, He blessed His disciples and was carried up into Heaven. In an appendix to his edition of the *New
Testament*, Campbell gave as the meaning of the word Bethany,

"the house of song, or of affliction." All human emotions—from joy unto sorrow—would be encompassed there.

The first number of *The Christian Baptist* to carry the legend "Bethany" was the issue of July 1827, and thereafter all Campbell's publications would carry the imprint: "Bethany, Brooke County, Virginia."

Campbell believed "there is a great advantage resulting to the community from the art of letter writing." He said, "I am peculiarly happy in having a number of correspondents of the first order in the literary and religious world." Thus began a friendly discussion between Campbell and Andrew Broadus as well as, between Campbell and Bishop Semple of Philadelphia. On the ever-present question of Campbell's satiric pen, Bishop Semple wrote to Campbell that he "by no means approved of the harsh epithets and the much sarcasm that so easily flow from your pen." Campbell responded

> The reader will see that I am still thought too severe in some of my strictures. I had thought that I had become extremely mild. In selecting terms and phrases, it is with me a matter of great self-denial to reject an appropriate one and to adopt one less appropriate merely because the most appropriate is too true—that is too severe. But as we grow older, I hope we will become wiser.

Bishop Semple warned against "Campbell's chimeras" and added he thought it best to leave Campbell's system to "conflate itself by its effect," since similar schemes had been promulgated and in time "dwindled to nothing." He further hoped that considering his "talents, conjoined with pleasant manners and apparently a pious spirit," Campbell might "be brought to a more scriptural and rational course." Campbell challenged the bishop stating he was wrong in thinking the Reformation Movement would "dwindle to nothing." On the contrary, *The Christian Baptist* was so rapidly increasing in circulation that, he said, "It is read in almost all the states in the Union, and is well received on the other side of the Atlantic."

Semple did not relax his opposition. A few months later he accused *The Christian Baptist* of "sowing the seeds of discord" to an "alarming" extent, and added, "*The Christian Baptist* has doubtless exhibited many valuable pieces and principles; but, taken as a whole, I am persuaded it has been more mischievous than any publication I have known." Campbell replied to the bishop that the clergy of all denominations would indeed agree with him that *The Christian Baptist* "has been more mischievous (to them) than even the publications of Volney, Voltaire, and Paine." But he assured Semple that for one letter like his, he received a hundred asserting that "it has done the most good, and been the most useful paper published in this country." To *The Baptist Recorder*, which was making so much capital of the good bishop's opposition, Campbell passed the suggestion that he was "always open to conviction, but never to be silenced by detraction, defamation, nor by the mere array of great and illustrious names." With the confidence in his convictions that was always so maddening to his opponents, he calmly asked: "What if Semple and Campbell are at issue—if Campbell and Paul are not at issue?"

However often his readers might think it necessary to urge he curb his satiric pen, Campbell's attitude toward Bishop Semple was indicative of the course his controversies would always take. The bishop could scarcely have spoken more severely—Campbell's ideas were "chimeras;" his movement was "sowing seeds of discord;" his magazine was "more mischievous" than any publication he had known. But the good bishop was attacking Campbell's theories not his person. He and Broadus considered Campbell, as a theologian, in error, as a man he was sincere and devout. Campbell, in turn, had the greatest respect for their integrity, a real affection for these two Virginia bishops. Like any born fighter, Campbell took real delight in combat—so long as the fight was fair. Proud of the quality of his own weapons, he preferred that his opponents come well armed; and the sharper the blows they were able to deliver, the more he respected them and the more he gloried in the contest. Such opponents always found him, as Semple and Broadus did, a "candid" and "generous" combatant. He would still not sheathe his arrows against what he considered errors or abuses in their systems, as he did not expect them to sheathe their arrows against his theories, but his attack was impersonal, his attitude was impartial and courteous.

But there was a different kind of warfare, a different type of antagonist, and a different attitude from the Bethany editor. When Campbell's opponents went beyond his theories to question his motives, when they substituted invective and slander for argument and reason, they had full cause to complain, as MacCalla had once done, of the onslaught of his "magisterial anger." Not that Campbell ever returned Billingsgate for Billingsgate; he had declined this sort of contest once and for all in his answer to the crudest of all his detractors, Lawrence Greatrake, when he said: "As I have never navigated the Mississippi on a keep boat, nor frequented the oyster market at Cheapside, I cannot enter the list here." Like one of the first saints of Christendom, Alexander was not naturally endowed with two much vaunted Christian virtues—patience and humility. With Alexander Campbell, the emotional discipline that life was forcing upon him through personal sorrow and affliction might, as he had written Phillip Fall, be teaching him "a greater degree of subordination to the Divine Will," but it did not yet include a softening of his attitude toward those whom he felt had unfairly and maliciously attacked him.

The difference in Campbell's manner toward his opponents was never better illustrated than in his correspondence, on the one hand, with bishops Broadus and Semple and, on the other hand, with Spencer Clack, co-editor of *The Baptist Recorder*. In May 1827, Clack first wrote to Campbell. He asked that Campbell consider him "not the enemy, but a friend, a brother ... who approaches you unmasked, undisguised, open and free." He reminded him that his editorials in the *Recorder* had always been distinguished by "mildness," and requested that Campbell not hold him responsible for the articles of his co-editor, George Waller. But Campbell was in no mood to be appeased by any kind words from the editorial offices of the Baptist paper that had been publishing to the world that he was a man whose highest motives were ambition and greed. So he replied to Spencer Clark:

> I cannot but express my astonishment at the greatness of your charity in saluting me 'brother.' Having been for more than one year the constant object of vituperation and detraction, of obliquity and misrepresentation in your paper; to be addressed by you as brother, sounded wild in my ear as did cousin in the ears of the fox when seized by the dog. Tis true your editorial articles were extremely mild; but while you gave free and full scope to every anonymous reveler, while your columns were surcharged with the very lowest scurrility and personal abuse, and by those too, who dare not show their face; your editorial moderation only served as a little seasoning to the dish.

One thing had been obvious to an impartial reader from the first number of *The Christian Baptist*: the editor's passionate conviction that Christians were meant to be united corporally, as well as, spiritually. Convictions, which led him to denounce sharply all the sects and the abuses in their systems, he believed were dividing the church. Nevertheless, he repeated over and over like a refrain, that, whatever their differences in interpreting the will of God, "I do love all of every name under heaven that love my Lord and Master." So now, however harshly he may have begun his letter to Spencer Clark, Campbell closed it with the remark, "believe me to be most sincerely attached to every one who loves my Lord and Master, whether Baptist or Paido-Baptist, New Light or Old Light."

In a subsequent letter, Clack claimed Campbell was opposed to creeds "because they were not in the Bible," and yet was erecting his conception of the "ancient order" into a creed. Campbell replied that Clack had completely misunderstood him; he had no objection to a creed being published every year provided it was not "made a test of Christian character nor a term of Christian communion"—an exalted position he would never wish for any of his own views no matter how right he considered them. Hence, Alexander remarked, "You must, I think, now see that you are fighting with a phantom of your own creation. It is not the editor of *The Christian Baptist* that you assail, but an apparition or a ghost that has some monocles who might have appeared to you in the vicinity of Bloomfield."

Spencer Clack, in his second letter, abandoned the theological arguments to make another appeal to Campbell to return from his erring ways. "In the western country you have friends," he assured Alexander, "As a man, they love you; but as a teacher, you do not possess their confidence." Again bringing the weight of Semple's name to bear, he said:

> … a worthy bishop of Virginia, whom some time since you had occasion to praise; he is your friend; he loves you, but does not approve of your opinions. Hear what he says: … 'What shall we do with Campbell? He is certainly wise, but not with the wisdom of God, at least not often. He seems to be misled by an ambition to be thought a reformer; but he will fail, or I shall miss my guess (as the Yankees say.) He may be as learned as Luther or Calvin or Melancthon, but they fell on other days than our friend Alexander. It is one thing to reform Popery, and

another to reform the Reformation ... yet, after all,... I can't throw him away as a good man, nor am I without hope of his veering about until he gets to the right point of the compass and his last days be his best days.'

In reply, Campbell assured him he was convinced of "the firmness and correctness of the ground" on which he stood, and apropos of bishop Semple's sentiments remarked, "The greatest calamity that has befallen the Protestants is this, that they imagined "the Reformation was finished when Luther and Calvin died..."

If, in establishing the *Baptist Recorder,* the Kentucky Baptists opposing Campbell had wished to have the contest conducted on the plane of theological discussion, they had, in selecting George Waller as one of the editors, made a strange choice. If they had wished the paper to sound the tocsin to warn the pious of the approach of a dangerous enemy and arouse them to violent action, they had, perhaps, chosen well. For George Waller was a man of positive character with almost no education and resulting strong prejudices and fixed convictions. In 1805 he wrote in his diary two resolutions, which, considering his editorial career, would sound strange in the ears of Campbell: He resolved to "speak evil of no man," and "never to enter into a strenuous argument with any man." At the same time, he was motivated by "a great aversion to innovation," which in view of the novelty of Campbell's doctrines proved stronger than his resolutions. Perhaps Campbell's Kentucky opponents responsible for the management of the *Recorder* thought to have one editor to supply the passion, another to furnish the argument. Spencer Clack was the antithesis of his co-editor; a man of "learning and culture," he had studied under a distinguished Pennsylvania theologian, and since coming to Kentucky had established in Bloomfield an excellent school. If Campbell had not been put thoroughly out of sorts by the method of attack launched against him by George Waller, he and Spencer Clack might have conducted a reasonable examination of their differences, just as he and Broadus were doing. The result would have been far better for the Kentucky churches.

Clack was sincerely convinced Campbellism was a dangerous threat to the Baptist doctrines in which he believed. He was determined to leave no stone unturned in an attempt to stop the spread of its influence. Philip Fall seemed to have fallen under the spell of the Bethany editor. Even after Campbell's visit to Nashville, he had hopes he might divest Alexander of some of his glory in Fall's eyes, and save the talented young preacher from utter heresy. Clack wrote Fall a long letter in May, 1827, critical of Campbell, and urging Fall to distance himself from the Campbell reformation.

In the midst of all the conflicts with Baptist bishops and editors, Alexander's mind was still chiefly concerned with Margaret. There now seemed little hope of her recovery, and Alexander's letter on July 28, 1827, to Philip Fall carried the sad prophecy:

> ... My dear companion is so extremely low that she has for some days past been scarcely expected to live from day to day ... she has wasted away in body; but like the setting sun, in mind, has grown greater and greater. More patience, composure, resignation and Christian confidence and hope I have never before seen exhibited ... and although our affliction is overflowing with mercy [and] goodness—yet still it is grievous and arduous to be borne.

The summer days seemed to bring new color to Margaret's face, and when the time came for the August meeting of the Mahoning Association, she was strong enough that Alexander could risk leaving her for a few days. Accompanied by his father-in-law, John Brown, he set out for New Lisbon, stopping at

Steubenville, Ohio, to invite Walter Scott to go with them. Scott had given up charge of the Pittsburgh church in 1826 and moved to Steubenville. There he opened a school and lectured to the small Baptist church. At first he declined to accompany Campbell to the meeting, because in the spring he had issued a prospectus for a magazine to be called *The Millennial Herald,* a notice of which had been published in *The Christian Baptist.* He was busy preparing the first issue for the press when Campbell arrived. Alexander finally persuaded him.

New Lisbon proved to be a memorable meeting. Two preachers associated with Barton W. Stone in the Christian Connection movement, John Secrest and Joseph Gaston, were present. In accordance with the liberal principles of the Mahoning Association, these two visitors from another denomination were cordially received and invited to seats. One of the churches in the Association sent in a request that an evangelist be selected and employed to travel among the churches, and the unusual suggestion was readily approved at the meeting. Campbell and the other messengers thought there was only one choice for the task of itinerant preacher, the young man who had been so loathe to attend the meeting, Walter Scott. Scott accepted the appointment, and it was voted that Campbell was to write a circular letter on the subject of itinerant preaching for the next Association.

Though Margaret's health seemed a little improved during the summer months, with the coming of fall she grew steadily worse. Alexander had to admit, as Margaret herself had done long ago, her recovery was hopeless. In October when Margaret again tried to talk to him of death, Alexander did not demur. She talked to him of the five daughters she would leave—Jane Caroline, age fifteen; Eliza Ann, age fourteen; Maria Louisa, age twelve; Lavinia age nine; and Clarinda, age six. She also talked to him, of her friend Selina Bakewell of Wellsburg. Selina had been a frequent visitor to the mansion on the Buffaloe for several years, and since Margaret had been ill she came more often. She was eager to show a tender concern for her friend, her friend's children, and her friend's husband. Having a sweet voice often raised in song in the Wellsburg church, Selina sometimes would spend almost an entire day at Bethany singing hymns for Margaret. Touched by Selina's sweet attentions, Margaret seems to have conceived the idea that she could leave her children safely in the care of her friend. And so expressed her wish to Alexander: If he could find it in his heart, once she was gone, would he make Selina his wife and the mistress of Bethany? Alexander gave his promise.

Margaret also had some words of counsel and farewell to her daughters. She had long ago expressed the prayer that she might live to hear her youngest child able to read to her from the Scriptures. Six-year-old Clarinda had sat by her bedside and read from the sacred book. Margaret was ready, so she called her daughters about her and bid them an eloquent farewell:

> My Dearly Beloved Children—It appears to be the will of our Heavenly Father to separate me from you by death … You are all able to read the oracles of God, and these are your wisest and safest instructors in everything. But I am reconciled to leave you from another consideration. I was left without a mother when I was younger than any of you; and when I reflect how kindly and how mercifully our Heavenly Father has dealt by me; how he watched over my childhood, and guarded my youth, and guided me until now, I am taught to commit you without a fear or anxiety into his hands … I have said you can all read the Holy Scriptures. This is what I much desired to be able to say to the youngest of you, and it is with great pleasure I repeat it … The happiest circumstance in all my life I consider to be that which gave me a taste for reading and a desire for understanding the New Testament. This I … consider to be one of the greatest

blessings which has resulted to me from my acquaintance with your father.

Although I have had a religious education from my father ... it was not until I became acquainted with the contents of this book ... that I came to understand the character [of] God ... And now I tell you, my dear children, that all your comfort and happiness in this life, and in that to come, must be deduced from an intimate acquaintance with the Lord Jesus Christ. I have found his character as delineated by Matthew, Mark, Luke and John exceedingly precious; and the more familiarly I am acquainted with it ... the more I desire to be with him ...

With regard to your father, I need only, I trust, tell you that in obeying him, you obey God. For God has commanded you to honor him ... It is my greatest joy in leaving you, that I leave you under the parental care of one who I know will teach you to choose the good part ...

Consider him as your best earthly friend, and next to your Heavenly Father, your wisest and most competent instructor, guardian and guide ... Never commence, nor undertake, nor prosecute any important object without advising with him. Make him your counselor ... As to your conversation with one another, when it is not upon the ordinary business of life, let it be on subjects of importance, improving your minds. Everything vain and fantastic, avoid ... Persons of discernment, men and women of good understanding, and of good education, will approve you; and it is amongst these I wish you to live and die ... But there is one thing which is necessary to all goodness ... and happiness; and that is to keep in mind the words that Hagar uttered in her solitude, 'Thou God seest me.' My desires for your present and future happiness cannot be surpassed by any human being. That God that made me your mother, has, with his [one] finger, planted this in my breast, and his Holy Spirit has written it upon my heart ... and I once more say to you, remember These words ... This will be a guard against a thousand follies. I feel grateful to you for your kind attention to me during my long illness; I must thank you for it; and the Lord will bless you for it. I cannot speak to you much more upon this subject. I have upon various occasions, suggested to you other instructions ... As the Savior, when last addressing his disciples, commanded and entreated them to love one another, so I beseech you to love one another ... and to seek to make one another happy by all the means in your power. I once more commend you to God and to the word of his grace, that we all may meet together in the heavenly kingdom is my last prayer for you.

On the first of October Alexander wrote his friend in Nashville: "Mrs. C. is reduced to a mere skeleton, unable to speak above breath except by a great effort." Three weeks later, on October 22, he sent him the terse message:

Dear Brother Fall,
Though overwhelmed in affliction but not sorrowing as those who have no hope, I feel it my duty to inform you that Sister Margaret Campbell departed this life at eleven o'clock this morning in the confident expectation of a glorious immortality.
Yours as ever,
A. Campbell

Margaret was laid to rest beside her three children in the cemetery overlooking the clear waters of the Buffaloe. On her plain brown tombstone, Alexander had carved a simple obituary closing with the last lines of a hymn Margaret had loved to sing.

No terror the prospect begets
I am not mortalities slave;
The sun beam of life as it sets,
Paints a rainbow of peace on the grave.

The obituary that he wrote for his magazine was brief and simple, as Margaret would have wished.

It was good that Alexander Campbell had much work to do. It kept his mind from traveling too frequently to the cemetery on the

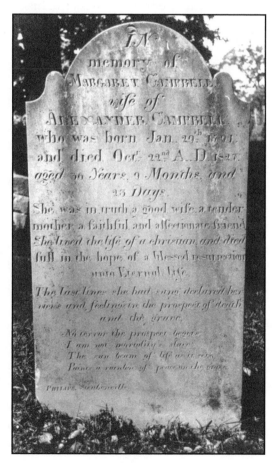

Margaret Brown Campbell, wife of Alexander, died October 22, 1827. She was buried in the family cemetery along with three of her eight children who preceded her in death—Amanda, John, and Margaretta. The photo is of her gravestone as it stands today.

hill. His work was not by any means confined to his magazine and his ministry. As Alexander's responsibilities expanded, he increased his efforts to make his farm profitable enough to support the other enterprises. Gradually he had added to the original three hundred acres that John Brown had deeded to him. On March 28, 1820, he secured an additional hundred and thirty-six acres from John Brown and Anna, his wife. On June 5, 1827, he bought one hundred and fifty acres from a Caleb Jones; and, on September 1, 1827, he bought forty-two acres from a James Robinson. He now held a total of 628 acres on Buffaloe Creek.

The problem was to make these acres as productive as possible. Soon after he became master of his own land, Alexander had found productivity was a problem of serious concern to all his neighbors. They were learning the sad lesson that even the richest of domains might be eventually destroyed by abuse. Wasteful methods of farming had nearly ruined the virgin freshness of their soil, until not more than ten or twelve bushels of wheat could be produced per acre. Then came a price slump. In 1821 the farmers of western Virginia were selling wheat for twelve and a half cents a bushel and flour for a dollar and a quarter a barrel, other products were selling proportionately low. Even the whiskey trade that had proved a boon to the first settlers began to be unremunerative. Kentucky soil could produce corn much cheaper than the hills of western Virginia, and Cincinnati and Bourbon whiskies were supplanting the "old Monongahela" manufactured on the banks of the Buffaloe. Something had to be done. Production must be diversified, and an export product found which would be concentrated in bulk and easy of handling. They were still faced with a serious transportation problem, but one solution readily suggested itself—the raising of fine wool. From the days of the earliest settlers herds of native sheep had roamed the western hills, "a hardy, long-legged, course-wool breed, with speed and endurance equal to a fox hound and hardiness not much inferior to the deer of the wild woods." The busy fullers and hand looms of the pioneer women converted their fleece into hardy garments for the frontiersmen. The wool was not of a quality to compete in the markets with the older settlements, those east of the mountains and in Europe. But the more enterprising farmers of western Virginia saw no reason why they should not raise wool of a fine quality. Several of them imported Merino and Saxony sheep direct from Europe for distribution throughout the section, and thus an experiment was launched.

Alexander was an enthusiastic pioneer in the new venture. Certainly a man who was accused of introducing all kinds of strange, novel ideas into religion would not be slow to embrace a plan for improving the farming in Brooke County. He, too, imported a flock of Merino and Saxony sheep "from a distance;" he may have been one of those bringing his flock direct from Europe. The daring adventurous quality of the idea would have appealed to him, but it is more likely he bought them from some dealer east of the mountains. The wool was selling between seventy-five cents, and a dollar and a quarter a pound, with two or three pounds to the sheep. The whole produce of a large farm could be loaded onto one wagon and carried to market. Alexander rapidly increased his flock, until the hillsides of Bethany were covered with white sheep. The fine wool could be converted into ink and paper for *The Christian Baptist* and into necessities for the family of a young reformer who had pledged himself to preach the gospel without pay.

The expanding activities of Bethany farm also brought the necessity of additional farm laborers since most of Alexander's own time was necessarily consumed in his study and printing office. He had first secured the service of a female slave, a woman of about forty named Nell, who along with her one-year old son, Ben, he had bought for two hundred dollars. Then, the summer before Margaret's death—June 11, 1827, according to the bill of sale—he had acquired two male slaves, Charles and James Pool, brothers of eighteen and twenty years old respectively, and men

ESSAY
ON
SHEEP:
THEIR VARIETIES—ACCOUNT OF THE ME
RINOES OF SPAIN, FRANCE, &c.
REFLECTIONS
ON THE
BEST METHOD OF TREATING THEM,
AND RAISING A FLOCK IN THE
UNITED STATES;
TOGETHER
WITH MISCELLANEOUS REMARKS
ON
SHEEP AND WOOLLEN MANUFACTURES.

BY ROBERT R. LIVINGSTON, LL. D.
President of the Society for the Promotion of Useful Arts, Mem-
ber of the American Philosophical Society, President of the
American Society of Fine Arts, Corresponding Mem-
ber of the Agricultural Society of the Seine,
Honorary Member of the Agricultural
Society of Dutchess County.

CONCORD, N. H.
PUBLISHED BY DANIEL COOLEDGE.
Sold also by Thomas and Andrews, West and Richardson, Bradford
and Read, and Caleb Bingham, Boston.
1813.

without family whom he bought from a Methodist preacher for the sum of four hundred and fifty dollars. Intending eventual emancipation for all his slaves, in the case of the two brothers, he wrote the provision for their freedom directly into the sale contract which specified that James after a period of eight years and Charles after a period of ten would be released from servitude.

New hands were also needed in the Bethany printing office. *The Christian Baptist* had increased in circulation and many of Campbell's later subscribers were requesting copies of the early numbers to complete their files. He was busy preparing a second edition of the first three volumes—August 1823 to August 1826. As early as August 1826, Campbell had remarked to his subscribers that he might publish a new edition, since the first was "almost sold." At the beginning, he explained, it had been too expensive to print a great many extra copies and, "besides, hundreds of volumes have been lost through the negligence of postmasters and the remissness of subscribers in notifying our agents." In February 1827, while Alexander was on the tour of the south-west with Margaret, his printer announced this proposed second edition was "now in the press." The November 1827 issue announced that this second edition was "now out of press." It also announced plans for a second edition of the new translation:

> From the demands for the New Translation, its superiority now being so generally acknowledged by those who

Opposite: Campbell produced a finer quality of wool than was possible with native sheep. Seeking a better market for his wool, Campbell wrote to Mssrs. King and Harding, "I have sent you several lags wool, a specimen of my fleece of Saxon wool, my flock being made out of the best New England Saxon sheep now amounting to 1,500 head." The volume entitled Sheep by Robert Livingston is from Alexander Campbell's personal library.

have read it, it is intended in a few days to issue proposals for a second edition of it. The intention of this notice is to solicit from the colleges in the United States; from the learned teachers of Christianity of all denominations; from the students of the sacred writings ... their objections to the work.

The December issue carried the news that the new edition of *The Christian Baptist* had been mailed to all those subscribing and informed them that it was "prepared for being bound three volumes in two with indexes. We have added to the new edition the famous Epistle of Clement to the Corinthians ... It is very scarce in this country."

Meanwhile, Alexander was not allowing his personal sorrow to interrupt methodical attention to his usual duties. Regularly he fulfilled his pastoral obligations at Wellsburg and cared for the new Bethany Church, which had been erected on his farm. Many members of the original Brush Run Church had never given up their early plan of emigrating in a body farther westward. In the spring of 1826 James Foster had announced his intention of carrying out the idea. Several joined with him, and they moved west, Foster buying a thousand acres of land on which they established a settlement and a small church. Though weakened by these removals, the Brush Run Church sent four messengers, Thomas Campbell among them, to the first meeting of the new Washington Association in September 1827. Soon afterwards it was decided that, out of convenience a church should be constituted in the neighborhood of Bethany. At the time of Margaret's death, Alexander was also in the midst of editorial work that could not be delegated to other hands. He was just concluding his series of essays on the "Ancient Order," and the controversy with Semple and Clack was still under way.

The October issue of *The Christian Baptist* that carried Margaret's death notice, also carried the first communication to its editor from the editor of another new Kentucky magazine. But this time the communication was friendly. In November 1826, Barton W. Stone started publication of the *Christian Messenger* at Georgetown. Campbell made some remarks on the magazine under the heading "New Periodicals" in his issue of June 1827. Stone's first letter to *The Christian Baptist* appeared in October. It began with a friendly appreciation of Campbell's work, that he deemed much like his own:

> Brother Campbell—Your talents and learning we have highly respected; your course we have generally approved; your religious views, in many points, accord with our own; and to one point we have hoped we both were directing our efforts, which point is to unite the flock of Christ, *scattered in the dark and cloudy day.* We have seen you, with the arm of a Samson, and the courage of a David, tearing away the long established foundations of partyism, human authoritative creeds and confessions; we have seen you successfully attacking many false notions and speculations in religion—and against every substitute for the Bible and its simplicity, we have seen you exerting all your mighty powers. Human edifices begin to totter, and their builders to tremble. Every means is tried to pre-vent their ruin, and to crush the name who dares attempt it. We confess our fears that in some of your well-intend-ed aims at error you have unintentionally wounded the truth. Not as unconcerned spectators have we looked on the mighty war between you and your opposers; a war in which many of us had been engaged for many years before you entered the field. You have made a diversion in our favor, and to you is turned the attention of creed mak-ers and party spirits, and on you is hurled their ghostly thunder. We enjoy a temporary peace and respite from war where you are known.

Stone, though he had been first in the field, was willing to admit he had learned something from Campbell's campaign: "From you we have learned more fully the evil of speculating on religion, and have made considerable proficiency in correcting ourselves." But now he had a complaint to make about the remarks Campbell made on the subject of John's "In the beginning was the word, and the Word was with God, and the Word was God." Stone charged that in these remarks Campbell had theorized on the most important point in theology, and in a manner "more mysterious and metaphysical than your predecessors;" and he advised him "not to soar too high on fancy's wings, above the humble grounds of the gospel, lest others adventuring may be precipitated to ruin." Stone then launched into a series of metaphysical objections to Campbell's remarks and asked that his fellow editor reply. He closed "with sentiments of high respect and brotherly love."

Campbell's reply was polite but firm. He refused to enter the realm of metaphysics, and he was sorry Stone had "said and written so much on *two* topics, neither of which you, nor myself, nor any man living can fully understand … You do not like my comment on John, Ch.1. Ver.1 — Well, then, just say so, and let it alone. I said in presenting it I was not about to contend for it, nor to maintain any theory upon the subject." He also warned Stone lest his movement in adopting the "sacred name Christian," and yet contending for some peculiar theory of the Atonement or the Trinity should make the title "Christian" as much a sectarian name as Lutheran, Methodist or Presbyterian." But, he assured Stone, he was his brother, however they might differ on some opinions and however the Baptist might object to their friendly relations: "Some weak heads among my Baptist brethren have been scandalized at me because I called you *brother* Stone." Immediately after this friendly exchange, Campbell's Baptist brethren again saw fit to protest his attitude toward the Kentucky heretic. Spencer Clack deemed a policy of "fire brands, arrows and death" the proper attitude toward such a heretic. Campbell retorted, "I cannot thank you for your advice, … inasmuch as it was not solicited."

If Campbell's reply to Stone's letter was perfectly courteous, it was also a little wary. He did not intend that anyone should question his right to call the Kentucky reformer his brother, but he was not going to commit himself too far. However he might respect the deep piety and noble purpose of Stone, he did not forget that Stone's movement had its inception in the revival hysteria of the Second Awakening. And it was difficult for Campbell to see any good in this type of fervor, even when it seemed to react to his own advantage. At present, Kentucky was being agitated anew by a great revival among the Baptists; it was beginning to be evident that the greatest interest was centering where Campbell's teachings had the most weight. Nevertheless, Alexander wrote to Philip Fall on December 4, 1827:

> I concur with you in your views or rather fears about the tendency of these big meetings. I am reconciled to them only as an expedient to bring down the opposition and to gain ears into which to pour the voice of God.

In January 1828, the mansion on the Buffaloe became even more lonely. The trip to Nashville with her parents the winter before had proved eventful indeed to lovely Jane Caroline; she had won the heart of a young gentleman of Tennessee, Albert Gallatin Ewing. They were married on January 24th in the parlor at Bethany. Alexander could not perform the ceremony in this room where he and Margaret had been married just seventeen years ago, and his friend, a Methodist preacher, the Reverend Waterman, officiated at the simple service. The young couple left for Nashville and the already harassed master of Bethany was left with another problem, since fifteen-year-old Eliza Ann could scarcely be expected to take full charge of so large a household. But the problem was soon resolved with the advent of a white housekeeper from Wellsburg, the choice of Eliza Ann herself. A happy choice it proved, as Elizabeth Patterson remained "upwards of forty years" at Bethany, to become the beloved friend and nurse, "Aunt Betsey," to two generations of Campbell children.

To the frequent visitors at Bethany, Alexander tried to show little evidence of his sorrow, and only an occasional extract in *The Christian Baptist* showed the trend of its editor's thought—once he printed Washington Irving's "Sorrow for the Dead" and again "The Dying Mother" from Pollock's *Course of Time*. But to his friend Philip Fall Alexander wrote on March 24th after urging him to come to Bethany:

> I still feel very lonely in the midst of the best company which I certainly have had for months past and am like a stranger in my own house. No person could feel a greater loss in losing a wife as respected society than I have felt in the loss of mine. And I find that no other society can compensate for hers.

The same letter to Fall also carried information on more impersonal matters:

> Brother Duval [evidently an employee in the printing office] is just on the verge of the Eternal world. I think he has been sinking in consumption for three years ... This is the reason why your order has not been attended to. He would not trust any person to fill it unless he could stand by and see it done; and therefore it is not likely to be filled soon.
>
> Bishop Semple after proposing to discuss the points at issue in secret correspondence has finally abandoned the

field. I would not agree to a private discussion unless it should be afterwards published if I pleased. *Sic transit Gloria mundi.*

I will send you one hundred hymn books after I get them bound.

… I am beginning the 2nd ed. of N.T.

The publication of the hymn book had been concerning Campbell for some time. A corrected translation of the New Testament needed as its handmaiden, a corrected hymnal of praise and worship. In the concluding two essays of his long series on "A Restoration of the Ancient Order," Campbell published extracts from his "Preface to a new selection of Psalms, Hymns, and Spiritual Songs about to be issued from the press." The preface was a treatise on Psalmody. Among other things, it made clear his reason for publishing a new hymnal: "Hymn singing like every other act of Christian worship has been corrupted by sectarianism." Hymns had been made to conform to the peculiar theology of each sect until in singing, he said, "instead of *praising* God, we are often *scolding* men who differ from us." His hymnal, of course, would correct these abuses. But in announcing that the books were "just out of press" in the April issue, he had an apology to make for the smallness of the hymnal; he had "explored all the good selections, European and American," he said, and "could find but very few songs adapted to the genius of the Christian religion and of pure speech." The whole selection contained only one hundred and twenty-five pieces, thirty of which were psalms of David. Five of the hymns were written by Campbell himself, those beginning "On Tabor's top the Savior stood;" "Tis darkness here, but Jesus smiles," "Upon the Banks of Jordan stood," "Come, let us sing the coming fate," "Jesus is gone above the skies." Whatever they lacked in poetic content, they made up in correct theology.

Meanwhile, throughout the winter of 1827–28, strange reports had been coming from the Western Reserve where Walter Scott, as instructed by the Mahoning Association, was working as an evangelist. Reports came of great meetings and many hundreds of conversions. Reports came of cooperation between Scott and evangelists of the Christian Connection movement. Campbell was disturbed. Had Walter Scott embraced some popular hysteria? Campbell had been preaching since 1810. He had been publishing a magazine since 1823, and there had been few conversions under his ministry. Not that Alexander was distressed by this fact. He conceived his mission as a work of education. He was a lecturer rather than an evangelist, a teacher rather than a preacher. He sought not so much to arouse the emotions of the unconverted as to attract the minds of Christians to the ideals of the Restoration Movement. Not wishing to start a new sect, he was attempting to work within an established communion to spread the gospel of unity and simplicity. Now Walter Scott, presumably preaching the same gospel was converting people by the hundreds. Alexander himself could not leave Bethany to investigate the reports from the Western Reserve; Margaret's death was so recent and his attention was needed every minute at the printing office. But his father was ever ready to another migration. And the territory was not strange to Thomas, for the previous fall he and his youngest son, Archibald, who was just making his debut as a preacher, had made a tour of the churches on the Western Reserve. So now in the spring of 1828 Thomas saddled his favorite sorrel and again rode to the west, this time to see what strange things young Scott was teaching.

A letter soon came back to Bethany and Alexander was reassured. On April 9th his father wrote him: "We have spoken and published many things correctly concerning the ancient gospel … but I must confess that … I am at present, for the first time, upon the ground where the thing has appeared to be practically exhibited …" Scott was preaching no new doctrine but was merely putting into practice what Thomas and Alexander themselves had been talking and writing about for many years.

The story of recent events on the Western Reserve was simply told. When he was appointed evangelist for the Mahoning Association, Scott was immediately faced with a problem that had not much concerned the Campbells. They had been working to restore what they conceived to be the simplicity of early Christianity in order to regain unity and harmony within the church. Scott had to convert these ideas into a program for the conversion of those without the church. He had read and pondered long upon the question and some of his musings, over the pen name of "Philip," he had contributed to *The Christian Baptist*. He had absorbed Campbell's writings on the subject of conversion, especially on the nature of the Holy Spirit and on the connection between baptism and the remission of sins; but where would a practical application of these ideas lead? Just what was the exact position that baptism should occupy in relation to the other requirements for salvation? He knew that Calvin and Wesley, as well as Alexander Campbell, and every creed in Christendom did lip service to Peter's words on the day of Pentecost and proclaimed a connection between the sacrament of baptism and the remission of sins. But Scott did not feel that any of them made a practical application of their theory. Campbell admitted as much: "We can sympathize with those who have this doctrine in their own creeds unregarded and unheeded in its import and utility; for we exhibited it fully in our debate with Mr. MacCalla in 1823, without feeling its great importance and without beginning to practice upon its tendencies for some time afterward." Scott had an orderly mind. It was not sufficient to have the right elements in the process of conversion; they must also come in logical order.

Finally he emerged from his study. He had reduced the steps necessary to salvation to a simple five-point plan: faith, repentance, baptism, remission of sins, gift of the Holy Spirit. The steps were not only in strict accord with apostles' practice but also with

Campbell's teaching. For some time, as "Philip" in *The Christian Baptist,* he had been "consciously playing Melanchthon to Campbell's Luther." Now his work as evangelist to the sinners of the world would be a complement to the work of his friend, as a teacher, and he was no less sure than Alexander had been when he stood upon "a new peak of the mountain of God" that his discovery had come almost like a new revelation. Some years later he wrote: "In 1823 a plea for a particular ecclesiastical order was put forth publicly by Bro. Alex. Campbell. This, for distinction's sake, was called 'the ancient order' ... In 1827 the True Gospel was restored. For distinction's sake it was styled 'the ancient Gospel.'"

Once he had decided on the proper steps for restoring the "True Gospel," Scott made plans for putting his theory into practice. Fearing to offend the churches that had appointed him, he decided to present it first at a meeting outside the grounds of the Mahoning Association. When Peter spoke to the multitudes of Jerusalem on the day of Pentecost and they had asked "what shall we do," he had simply replied, "Repent, and be baptized every one of you in the name of Jesus Christ for the remission of sins, and ye shall receive the gift of the Holy Ghost." So Walter Scott spoke to his audience in the western territory. But the results he obtained were very different from those who heard the Apostle Peter. The apostles baptized three thousand that Pentecostal day, but Walter Scott had not a single response to his plea. The "true Gospel" might have been "restored," but his audience did not seem to be aware of the momentous occasion.

In fact, they were thunderstruck. However familiar might be the words of Peter, the orthodox Calvinist and Arminian alike knew that people were not converted by any such simple process nor in the order of events preached by Walter Scott. First, not last, and after a long siege of agonized waiting and praying came the gift of the Holy Spirit, which enabled the hardened human heart to embrace faith and repent of its sins; then came baptism, which was regarded as little more than a means of admission into the church, a command to be obeyed by those already converted, and with which no special promises were recognized as being connected. Now a preacher was telling them that penitents should no longer be subjected to this long and arduous process, that the "mourners' bench" should be abandoned, that "divine assurance" should replace "delusive feelings," and that "intelligent obedience" and not "visionary theories" of a supernatural visitation would bring victory over sin. They did not know what to think. Those familiar with the writings of Alexander Campbell had heard these ideas often repeated, but now these ideas were being applied to a simple and practical plan for evangelizing the world, a plan radically different from the revival messages they were accustomed to hear. They were not at all sure they approved the strange innovation.

Scott might easily have been discouraged by the failure of his first attempt to preach his "Ancient Gospel" message, for he was naturally timid and vacillating. But whatever the effect on his audience, the experiment had filled Scott with a divine assurance. Hereafter he would preach his evangel with a full sense of its power. Boldly he gave notice that he would deliver a series of discourses on "the Ancient Gospel" at New Lisbon, Ohio, within the bounds of the Mahoning Association. On the day appointed a large crowd collected, for news had spread that Walter Scott would preach a novel doctrine. Near the end of his long sermon, it was noticed that a stranger entered the assembly. Scott closed by repeating Peter's words and inviting any of those present to be baptized for the remission of their sins. The stranger shouldered his way through the crowd and presented himself. Every one was astounded, and none more so than Walter Scott himself. The stranger had not even heard the sermon, yet he did not hesitate to accept the gospel invitation. But on being questioned this man, who gave his name as William Amend, seemed to understand the matter as perfectly as did Scott; so his confession was taken and he was baptized the same hour of the day. The date was November

18, 1827. Scott himself, and those who accepted his message, had no doubt about the importance of the occasion. The purpose of baptism "now, on the 18th of November, 1827, for the first time since the primitive ages was fully and practically realized;" William Amend "was, beyond all question, the first person in modern times who received the ordinance of baptism in perfect accordance with apostolic teaching and usage."

But Scott was curious to know how William Amend had arrived at his decision so quickly. He wrote him a letter, and Amend replied; he was a Presbyterian, but could not accept such Calvinistic dogmas as election and foreordination; becoming "wearied" in "this wilderness," he took up the Bible "as if it had been dropped from heaven," and read it for himself in "just one year;" he often studied Peter's Pentecostal sermon, and a few days before he attended Scott's meeting at New Lisbon he had said to his wife, "this is the gospel ... Oh that I could hear the gospel in these same words as Peter preached it. I hope I shall some day hear it. The first man I meet who will preach the gospel thus, with him I will go."

The strange news spread abroad. Daily, Scott's audiences increased. Baptizing seventeen at New Lisbon, he went on to other fields. "Aflame with zeal," he "passed rapidly, like a meteor, throughout the Western Reserve, startling the people by the abruptness and directness of his appeals." He made his five-point program into a "five finger exercise" that men could easily remember. Riding into a town, he would hold up his hand and bade the school children memorize his five point show of fingers, and go home and tell their parents a man would preach on that at the school-house in the evening. The parents would come and carry away the sermon outline on the five fingers of their hand. The preaching tour became a crusade. Meetings were often held out-of-doors, for village churches and schoolhouses would not hold the crowds. Everywhere those whose thought had been leavened—or perverted, according to the viewpoint—by Campbell's teaching were welcoming Scott's message. Leading preachers in the Association and some from the Christian Connection were joining him in the crusade. Thus, Thomas Campbell found affairs when he arrived on the Western Reserve.

Nor was he long in recognizing why Scott's crusade was achieving such surprising results. It was succeeding for the same reason *The Christian Baptist* was daily adding new subscribers to its lists. While he and Alexander had been laboring for eighteen years to reform and unite the body of Christ by getting the church to restore the New Testament order, Scott was now "restoring the church by building it anew out of the common people—sick of sin, tired of creeds, and anxious to know what God required of them to be saved." The ideas which the Campbells had been teaching, translated into Scott's evangel, furnished the best possible preaching program for converting these common people of the western territories. It was a common-sense program; it was sane, practical, definite, non-theological. It was authoritative, and yet it gave full reign to individualism and independence. It eschewed all vagueness and complex theological dogmas. Assuming both human rationality and the moral ability to take the first step toward salvation, it placed the responsibility squarely on the individual. There was something positive to be done and each person could do it. The church could not presume to determine the right of the candidate to be baptized; each decided for her or himself. Above all, it was a profoundly spiritual process. God had given promise that any one who believed, repented, and obeyed should be saved, and the convert who took the Word of God at its face value would be ennobled by a divine assurance of salvation.

But there was another element that was entering into the success of the evangelism on the Western Reserve. It was the personality of Walter Scott. However legalistic and intellectual might be certain aspects of his message, his musical voice, his lean, tense face, his dark lustrous eyes, his lively wit, his vivid imagination, which clothed his thought in poetic eloquence, and his fiery and impassioned zeal all enlivened his "Ancient Gospel" far from the realm of cold rationality. Intellectualism might be implicit in the content of his message, but Scott's own enthusiasm gave to his preaching a deeply emotional appeal. His enthusiasm also added another element to his appeal. Scott was convinced that he had made a new discovery of epochal importance, and he was able to impress his hearers with the same conviction, especially in the regions where *The Christian Baptist* had copiously sown its seeds. His message had an urgency, a freshness sure to create excitement in the small towns of the frontier country. When he descended upon a settlement, "it was not just another preacher holding another meeting but a man announcing the discovery of that true gospel which had not been preached in its purity for nearly eighteen centuries." Other communions might boast of apostolic succession; the Baptists might claim that through all the dark ages of the church faithful Baptists had held aloft the faith pure and undefiled from the days of primitive Christianity; but "here was a man who actually made a merit of the fact that the true Gospel had been entirely lost from the apostolic age until 1827 and that he himself had been the agent of its discovery."

Thomas Campbell decided the method of approach had great merit. So after sending word to Alexander that all was well, he stayed on the Western Reserve to help Scott spread the word.

Reassured about affairs on the Western Reserve, Alexander went quietly on with his work. He would leave others to their calling. He knew that his work lay in his study and his editorial office. As he wrote to a Kentucky friend, Colonel James Mason of Mount Sterling, on April 4, 1828:

> Accounts from all parts of the country rejoice my heart exceedingly. I should like to be in the field—but the Lord seems to require me to wield the press at home. I

have considerable difficulty to keep to my post for I feel strong inward propelling powers, but as before said, a sense of duty reconciles me to be casting the shots and cleaning and refitting the arms for the warriors.

As spring ripened into summer, Alexander's thought turned toward more personal matters. It may be that, as a friend later recorded, he had given his promise to Margaret to make her friend, Selina Bakewell, the mother of their children. But Alexander needed no pledge to decide him in taking a wife. It was not well for a man to feel, as he had written Philip Fall, "like a stranger in my own house." He might "find that no other society can compensate" for Margaret's. But he thought that Selina Bakewell might make an excellent substitute.

Selina was tall and slender, with raven black hair, and she was young—only twenty-five. She had been born on November 12, 1802, at Lichfield, England, in a house where, so it was said, Samuel Johnson had once lived. Selina's father, Samuel R. Bakewell, who had married a woman of Shrewsbury, Anne Marie Bean, came to America in 1805 and a short time later settled his family at Wellsburg, in Western Virginia. Selina was becomingly educated at the Old Brick Academy. She was also becomingly pious. But, unlike Margaret, her piety seemed to bring her no joy. Completely lacking in a sense of humor, she was naturally inclined to look on the worst side of things. Perhaps Alexander thought he possessed optimism enough for both. If Selina lacked Margaret's cheerfulness, she was a person of tireless energy and, so she herself said, "unvaried health, combined with a good English constitution." Selina was also by her own admission, endowed with courage and determination, along with a suitable respect for the abiding value of life, which more than once had been evident to the husband of her friend during her numerous visits to Bethany through the years.

Selina Huntington Bakewell, age twenty-five, and Alexander Campbell, age thirty-nine, were married at the home of Selina's brother in Wellsburg, Virginia, July 31, 1828, by Dr. Edward Smith, a Methodist minister. This photo of Selina was taken late in life.

As summer came to the Bethany hills, Alexander asked Selina to be his wife. Without undue hesitation, she accepted. Once before, said Selina, she had been approached by a man with intentions of matrimony, "one, too, possessed of riches and high social standing;" but he was "a man of the world," and so, "sympathetic and kind" but "firm and immovable," she had refused him. Now, by "a remarkable interposition of Divine Providence," "faith and trust" had their reward. "After I had resolved not to marry any man who was not a Christian, in the abounding goodness of God, He gave me a distinguished Christian husband, and one, too, possessed of ample means." The practical Selina knew she was not mistaken about the "ample means;" the comfortable "mansion" on the Buffaloe, the great herds of sheep covering the hill-sides, the busily turning wheels of Bethany Press, and the hard common sense of their master, all spoke to her of security. Being mistress of Bethany would be no easy task, but to lighten her burdens there would be Nurse Betsy and there would be the Negro slaves. With a discerning eye on Alexander's abilities and on the scores of visitors who were beginning to make their way to Bethany to talk with him, she knew, too, that he was well on his way to being "distinguished." She might have added that she felt for his person an admiration amounting to worship, which was by no means strange. Alexander was not a man whom women would pass without a second glance. Like all intense masculine men, he felt a constant need for his complement, the feminine, and once a woman knew him, she was charmed and flattered by his manner. Secure in his own dominance, he was never attempted to assert a petty authority over women, as most weaker men did. Confident of his own superior strength, he could encourage a woman to her best endeavor. He never treated a woman just as a woman but always paid her the subtle compliment of accepting her as a person, as an individual with a peculiar value all her own. He was interested in her mind and her talents, and he made her feel that interest. It was little wonder that Selina felt God had been good in sending her such a husband.

On July 31, 1828, they were married. Dr. Edward Smith, a Methodist minister, performed the ceremony at the house of Selina's brother in Wellsburg. Nine months and nine days after the death of Margaret, Bethany mansion had a new mistress.

Important as the taking of a wife might be, Alexander could not allow it to interrupt his labors. The only indication to the readers of *The Christian Baptist* that its editor's mind was concerned with matrimony was the publication of an extract, "Bishop Beveridge's Resolutions concerning the Choice of a Wife." For a wedding tour, Selina accompanied Alexander to the annual meeting of the Mahoning Association at which he was to deliver the introductory address. Jane Caroline and Albert Ewing were visiting at Bethany, and they accompanied the Campbells on the trip.

After the summer tour, Alexander spent the winter of 1828–29 quietly at home, for he had much to do. The second edition of the New Testament was coming off the press. His request for criticism had brought many replies and on the whole he had found them favorable: "the intelligent and liberal of different parties [admit] that this New Testament is the only one that can make any reasonable pretensions to being divested of a sectarian character;" "Its claims for … universal acceptance, are … said to be, superior of those of any other version hitherto offered to the public." The March 1929 issue of *The Christian Baptist* announced that the New Testaments had been forwarded to agents in various cities in New York, Pennsylvania, Maryland, Virginia, Georgia, Tennessee, Kentucky, Ohio, Indiana. and "other places too tedious to mention."

Campbell also had on hand several new series of essays. While Walter Scott was busy preaching his "Ancient Gospel" on the Western Reserve, Alexander had started in January 1828, a group of nine articles entitled the "Ancient Gospel." In the lengthy series on the "Ancient Order," that was not yet finished, he was expounding his ideas of the proper order to be observed within the church. His new essays turned attention, as Scott was doing, to the steps or process of becoming a part of the church.

Though Campbell's mind, like Scott's, was logical and tended to arrange ideas into neat symmetrical patterns, it was by no means so legalistic or mechanical as the young evangelists. A dual tendency was always present in Campbell's thought. His mind might be logical, but his temperament was broad and free. Hence, in his writings he was always pulling away from some narrow view or some bold authoritarian principle. So in his essays on the "Ancient Gospel," though he arranged and numbered the steps in conversion as did Walter Scott (substituting the term "reformation" for "repentance" and adding a sixth step, "eternal life"), he immediately remarked, "We do not teach that one of these preceded the other, as cause and effect; but that they are naturally connected."

Selina, too, was having a busy winter, and she might well be glad that his editorial work was keeping Alexander close at home during the first months of their marriage. She was not brought up on a farm, as Margaret Brown had been, and she had many things to learn about being mistress of a house in the country. The task was not made easier by the almost incessant stream of strangers who came to see what manner of man was the editor of *The Christian Baptist*, and Selina soon found that some of them were not inclined to leave very quickly. There were also servant problems … one of the Negro slaves, Ben, the son of Neel, proved an especial blessing to a wife burdened with the entertainment of numerous guests, for, said Selina, being a "good and obedient boy," "possessed of a wonderful musical talent," Ben "frequently sang for visitors and charmed them with the sweetness and pathos of his voice." As if to try Selina's patience to the utmost, an epidemic of measles broke out during the winter, and she had to care for no less than thirteen cases in the family. There were five motherless children to look after, and then in the spring, on April 23, 1829, she herself gave birth to a daughter, whom she named Margaret Brown in thoughtful tribute to the first mistress of Bethany. Perhaps she may have found some comfort and assistance from the presence of Alexander's sister, Dorothea Bryant, on an adjacent farm that was part of the Bethany lands. Just before his marriage to Selina, Alexander had bought a 236-acre tract on Buffaloe Creek from Richard McClure, and this was most likely the farm where the Bryants now lived.

There was one duty falling to the lot of Bethany's mistress that Selina found very gratifying, busy with household tasks though she might be. As had been his custom with Margaret, Alexander always wished to read his essays to her before they went to press. Well aware of his satirical vein, he wanted her criticism. He was also wont to remind her of the preacher who read all his sermons to his housekeeper to judge what would be the effect on his congregation, a remark Selina, having a proper respect for her own good taste and judgment, took as a standing pleasantry. Being quite fond of Young's "Night Thoughts" and the more melancholy prose and poetry of English literature, she had no doubt that she might be a good judge of the literary quality of her husband's work.

Alexander was finding that having a woman at his side was making life pleasant again. Doubtless he no longer felt like a stranger in his own house, and the guests who came now to Bethany found its master very different from the lonely and abstracted man of the previous winter. One of these visitors, a young doctor named Robert Richardson, who had recently moved to Wellsburg and was making his first acquaintance at the mansion on the Buffaloe, was especially delighted with his host. He had been a student at Walter Scott's academy at Pittsburgh and, though reared an Episcopalian, had been converted to the Restoration Movement under Scott's ministry. Setting up practice at Wellsburg very soon after his baptism, he lost no time in making the acquaintance of the leader of the movement. Many years later he would become Campbell's biographer and write of these first impressions as a guest at Bethany:

> It was delightful to witness with what unstudied cour-
> tesy he welcomed his visitors, and with what genial pleas-

antry he placed everyone at his ease, so that no one could long feel like a stranger. Without apparent effort he constantly kept up the charm of social converse, adapting the theme to the feelings and circumstances of the company ... He seemed to be always at leisure to entertain his guests, and that, too, with a mind so full of gayety and free from preoccupation that no one could have suspected for a moment the immense business constantly resting upon him.

But, as young Dr. Richardson also observed, Campbell's "immense business" as editor, publisher, postmaster, preacher, farmer, and sheep-raiser was only accomplished by a most careful schedule and long hours of work. Usually Campbell arose at three o'clock in the morning and went to his study. By the time the house bell rang for morning worship he had often prepared enough manuscript to keep his printers busy all day. After breakfast he would arrange his affairs for the day and bid adieu to any parting guests. Then he would call for his horse or set off on foot, sometimes accompanied by visitors, to inspect the work in progress at the printing press or on the farm and to give instructions to his workmen. After dinner he usually corrected proofsheets, reading them aloud if anyone was prepared to listen. Then the carriage was often brought round so that he and Selina and perhaps some guest might pay a promised visit to a neighbor. Conversation on these visits was likely to be occupied with discussing the problems confronting the Virginia farmer, with national politics and its effect on their internal affairs and with improvements in their methods of agriculture. If there were no visits to make, Campbell would often spend these hours in his study, or they might find him in the parlor or on the portico reading or talking. "It was the evening," said Richardson, "that was always devoted to social and religious improvement." But before the "social" always came the "religious." Family, guests, and servants alike were expected to gather in the parlor for evening worship; everyone must recite some hymn or Bible verse and show an intelligent comprehension of the Scripture read. Selina would lead in singing a psalm or hymn and, before kneeling for the closing prayer, Alexander always had "something novel and agreeable to impart zest and interest to the exercises" lest they "become monotonous by frequent repetition."

Certainly Campbell never considered that he was establishing his magazine and press for any other reason than to advance what he conceived to be the cause of God. It was true that the circulation of *The Christian Baptist* had increased daily. Campbell now had agents for the paper in at least twenty of the nation's twenty-four states, and most likely subscribers in the other four states. The January 1829 issue announced an agent in Canada and two in Ireland. But whatever profits the future might bring from his press, its early years were fraught with risks and uncertainties. In fact, so great was the expense and so precarious the returns Campbell was often hard pressed for the money to keep it going, and the magazine began to voice some of its publisher's worries.

In the issue for November 1826, he was forced to ask some of his delinquent subscribers to pay up: "We are constrained at this time to be somewhat urgent, as justice requires us to liquidate the debts of the establishment." The same month the following year found Campbell telling his readers that publishing the second edition of *The Christian Baptist* had exhausted our funds" and informing them: "Bank notes, paying specie, not further south than Virginia, nor north than New York, are receivable by us. United States is generally preferred; but Virginia, Ohio, Maryland or Pennsylvania bank bills are generally at par here. We have never been much in the habit of dunning, and we did not like to get into such a habit; we therefore hope that it may not become necessary." But it did threaten to become necessary, for in July 1828, he reported "more than 1,200" delinquent subscribers for the current volume, "some hundreds in arrears for several volumes back," while "many subscribers" had not paid anything from the commencement of the magazine in 1823; "I should be sorry," he concluded, "to have to *dun* the readers of *The Christian Baptist* as other editors have to *dun* their readers, and still more sorry should I have to threaten them with those invaders of our happiness, called the *officers of the law.* As I have never done so, I hope none will give us an occasion for so doing." Evidently the response was not too great, for November still found Campbell "in much need of funds." "While our subscription list," he remarked "has continually augmented there has been, on a large majority of the agencies, a falling off in collecting and remitting to us ... I would rather write a volume of essays than write one such notice as this. We have a great many excellent agents, and very punctual subscribers; but there is a large majority whom we would wish to commend, and yet we cannot. We hope this notice will suffice for a long time to come." Several months later he wrote an "Essay on the Duties of an Agent," considering himself, he said, now "pretty well qualified to write on this subject from experience," since he had "had all sorts of agents" from the best to those "in the superlative degree, approaching to zero" who "got as many subscribers as they could, collected punctually as any agents could; but finally decamped with the cash!"

An article in the issue for May 1830, was far more specific about the financial condition of *The Christian Baptist.* It was written in answer to a piece in the *Columbian Star* by a Baptist minister, Abner Clopton. Repeating the old charge that Campbell was motivated by a desire for wealth and fame; a note appended by Clopton gave an impressive array of figures to prove that

Campbell, on the four thousand subscribers of which he "boasted," annually cleared a profit of twenty-five hundred dollars. Campbell replied that Clopton's charge was ridiculous. Wealth and fame could scarcely be the objective of "a 'little' unpopular paper" dressed in "plain, unvarnished, and humble garb" and "issued in the county of Brooke, by one who had concealed himself in the backwoods, and kept aloof from all the hobbies and from all the great undertakings of the day, during ten of the most ambitious years of human life." In the first place, said Campbell, he had never "boasted" of four thousand subscribers. In the second place, the twenty-five hundred dollars annual "clear gain" was a myth. There were no profits whatsoever! "My clerk," said Campbell, "has just now handed me the amount, which in the aggregate gives the sum of $1,487 dollars, 62 ? cents as the whole amount received during the last year, and the most prosperous year in the way of receipts since the commencement of this work." Not a cent of this amount represented profit. On the contrary, *The Christian Baptist* was constantly in the red, though its editor was frank to admit he hoped it would not always be so:

> I can assure my friends that, averse as I am to being in debt, and determined as I have been to pay off all claims against me on the account of my printing office with all the works issued from my press ... I have never since the commencement of this paper been able to pay for a lot of paper for a new work when it was ordered; and had I not had other means to rely upon than the press for its own support, the enemies of reform would have triumphed long ago.

Whatever its financial risks, Campbell never once considered discontinuing his magazine. From the beginning he had conceived of his work as a work of education, and the press was its medium. Without *The Christian Baptist* the Restoration Movement would be denied its most effective voice. And, as he had once remarked to a correspondent, breath was free—hence, he could and did preach without pay—but ink and paper cost money. So it behooved him to pay strict attention to the business affairs of Bethany farm. Those who shared Campbell's religious ideals and wished to see them disseminated might well be glad that the acres on Buffaloe Creek were increasing, that the sheep on Bethany's hillsides were multiplying, and in Campbell's veins flowed the blood of canny Scots and thrifty Huguenots.

If Campbell had any doubts about the growing influence of his work, they would be dispelled by his daily increasing correspondence. "Numerous and interesting essays," he said, were beginning to be "sent us from all parts of the country;" and he was six or eight months behind with his communications.

Many of these letters were fulsome in their praise of *The Christian Baptist.* From Ohio a correspondent wrote: "It is by far the most valuable human production that I ever saw. It not only discovers to us … our maladies; but it points out to us the only antidote for all our diseases." Another communication said:

> … it possesses this decided advantage over every other religious publication of the day—that it does not present a cross-eyed, one-sided view of things, and that it does not shun nor hate truth and investigation, and that all questions which are comprehended with the field of reason, sound philosophy, and revelation, are fairly answered.

Still another wrote:

I believe it is calculated to do more good than any other writings now extant, (the scriptures alone being excepted). Although there be some who will not dare read it, for fear of imbibing its truths, (as I heard a gentleman say), yet I rejoice to know that its light is spreading far and wide, and will soon cover the whole country.

From Kentucky came a letter:

I … ever will feel grateful that it was placed in my hands. Though I had been licensed as a preacher, I found upon divine subjects, I was and had been as ignorant as an ox, and as stupid as an ass.

Another reader encouraged:

Persevere, brother. You are conquering, and will conquer. One of your most bigoted opposers said not long since, in a public assembly, that, in traveling twenty-five hundred miles circuitously, he only found four Regular Baptist preachers whom you had not corrupted.

One correspondent assured him that even his opposers were borrowing their ideas from him, saying of one of them: "that two thirds of his sermon is sometimes made up of extracts from *The Christian Baptist* and that the other third is employed in abusing it." Several members of "a Church of Christ" in Hartford, Connecticut, wrote that his magazine had "afforded" them "joy." While from one reader came the remark: "… that all his communications were being examined more carefully "than any other writings of this day." Another wrote, "I approved of your writings because I saw, generally, a clearness and candor in them, rarely to be met with in these dogmatical days … No man probably in

America has as much in his power as *you*. The eyes of thousands are upon you."

Other reports coming to Bethany were no less encouraging. Six years earlier, Campbell had established his magazine, confident in the power of the press to disseminate his ideas, and he now found his expectations more than justified. The news of Walter Scott's unique preaching program had spread throughout the West, and his five finger exercise was rapidly adopted by evangelists in Virginia and especially in Kentucky. In Kentucky the revival fervor was reaching great heights, and even Campbell's strongest opponents there had to admit that: "The revival greatly favored the reformation. In those portions of the state where Campbellism was most prevalent, the additions were much the largest." Under the excitement such staunch Baptist elders as Jeremiah Vardeman and Walter Warder were "shaken by the storm from Buffaloe," while Jacob Creath and "Raccoon" John Smith had unequivocally accepted Campbell's reform principles. From his friend Colonel John Mason of Mount Sterling, Campbell received news of Smith: "the people are following him in crowds, and he is teaching them the ancient gospel with astonishing success. Indeed, sir, I am persuaded you would be amazed yourself were you present, and see with what adroitness he handles those arms which have been cleaned up and refitted in *The Christian Baptist*." The Kentucky revival fervor carried over from 1827, into 1828, and into 1829. In one issue Campbell announced that Vardeman had baptized five hundred and fifty persons in six months, and that Smith in less than three months had baptized three hundred and thirty-nine. The Kentucky Baptists claimed that during the revival something over fifteen thousand were baptized throughout the state.

Campbell viewed these revival accessions with mixed feelings—aside from his inherent fear and distrust of revivalist emotionalism. They were bringing to the front a new type of leader to disseminate his restoration theories. His own attack on clerical pretensions and on distinctions between clergy and laity, which had from the first made a strong appeal on the frontier where leveling tendencies were already rampant, was reflected in the support of many an independent-minded backwoods preacher. John Smith named one of the first churches that he organized, "Liberty;" and within the bounds of his Association, a young licentiate, inspired by the ideas of *The Christian Baptist*, arose one day in church and indignantly challenged the preacher in charge who had been predicting the speedy downfall of Alexander Campbell. When the congregation, outraged by his presumption, voted that the church was not "pleased with her young gift," he retorted, "... I was born free; and, as the Church of Christ is not a prison, I withdraw myself from you!," and out from among them he walked. This impulse to liberty implicit in all Campbell's doctrine was greatly fortified by Walter Scott's reduction of the plea to a simple five point evangel, which almost anyone could preach.

So far the movement had been in the hands of educated men. Alexander, his father, his friends, Walter Scott—all were acquainted with university halls in the Old World. Now Alexander realized the message should be taken up by less educated persons. While he would rejoice in the triumph of the simplicity of the Gospel, he would anxiously watch lest it be abused and perverted into some new enthusiasm. But no such qualms disturbed the thought of those frontiersmen, long confused by the complex dogmas of a supralapsarian Calvinism, to whom the new yet "ancient gospel" seemed heaven-sent in its simplicity. Many of their experiences would agree with that of Samuel Rogers, a child of the West who had emigrated from Virginia to Kentucky, to Missouri, to Upper Louisiana then under Spanish rule, and, at the age of nineteen, back to Kentucky again where he was converted under the revivalism of Barton Stone. Later, he was ordained and began to preach, but it was not until he came upon the writings of Campbell that he really found peace and assurance; as he himself recorded his story:

> ... I was ordained by Stone at Cane Ridge ... He then gave me a Bible saying: 'Preach its facts, obey its commands and enjoy its promises.' I was greatly troubled about my call. I contended that if I were called as were the apostles, I ought to have their credentials ... I attempted to draw from dreams and visions and vague impressions, some supernatural aid ... I thought I ought to perform miracles. My mind was often in a wretched state. About this time I got the 'Christian Baptist' and found relief ... Alexander Campbell taught as no other man, but with a clearness and simplicity that carried at once conviction to the mind of every man of common sense ...

Anxious that his relatives in Ireland should know something of his work in the New World, Alexander had, in 1825, sent some copies of his debates and of *The Christian Baptist* to his uncle Archibald Campbell. These Irish relatives likely read the volumes with mixed emotions, their pride in Alexander's accomplishments mingling with amazement at his strange opinions. Archibald Campbell was still a staunch Seceder, and he was not apt to change his views very easily, for he had inherited more than his name from his father, the crusty old soldier in his Majesty's army who had seen service at the Battle of Quebec. But he thought that his nephew's writing would suit his friend, Robert Tener of Dungannon, who was a member of one of the independent churches. Archibald was right. Robert Tener did enjoy the works and after some initial suspicions were removed, the entire church at Dungannon came to share his agreement with Campbell's principles. When, in 1827, a commercial traveler from Liverpool, a zealous Independent, called on his brethren at Dungannon, he was enthusiastically informed about the American movement and given some of Campbell's works. The Bethany theology made its way into the Independent churches of Liverpool, Nottingham, and Manchester. By 1829, Archibald Campbell, Seceder or not, was acting as agent for his nephew's magazine in Ireland. William Tener of Londonderry, a son of Robert Tener, was also an agent. On November 5 of that year William Tener wrote to Campbell commending "that ably edited periodical, *The Christian Baptist.* Many of my friends in this your native land have reason to bless God that ever they saw it; and although their prejudices were against you at first, they yielded to the evidence of all pow-erful truth." And he concluded: "In America you are a century before us. All the churches with which I am acquainted request me to present their Christian salutation to you." While they still did not agree with everything he had written, they consider him "a zealous, fearless, and able champion of truth."

But there was no danger of Campbell lacking ballast to keep his cargo from upsetting. Censure would always keep pace with praise. A letter from Illinois informed him: "'*Campbellism,*' and '*Campbellites,*' have become very common terms in Illinois, and they are not infrequently pronounced with a bitterness that reminds me of the '*Christian Dog*' of the Turks." From Kentucky came the opinion: "In the estimation of many among us, you are considered the arch-heretic, and did you live in other lands and other times, "woe would be to you." One Ohio correspondent wrote, "I have occasionally to hear that Alexander Campbell has 'denied the faith, and is worse than an infidel;'" while another reported that he had heard a sermon on "Campbellism," in which some of the preacher's "mildest compliments to the authors and supporters of 'ancient things' were the following: 'They are vessels of wrath and agents of the Devil.' 'Hell never was more pleased than when she enlisted them.'" Another Ohio minister preached a sermon on "Alexander the Coppersmith," of whom Paul counseled Timothy "he hath greatly withstood our words," the apostle adding the anathema, "I have delivered [him] unto Satan" that he "may learn not to blaspheme." The preacher made a triumphant application of the text: "I must warn you to beware of Alexander the coppersmith; for *he has greatly resisted our words,* making the Bible a mere history." A preacher in Kentucky delivered a sermon on the theme that it was not "God's time" to reform the church, hence, "the Great Alexander Campbell, with all his master talents, will fall, and he ought to fall." A western newspaper remarked "many, very many of every sect and denomination of Christians speak of him as a most dangerous heretic and a desperately wicked man." A "young gentleman in Lexington, Kentucky" wrote to a friend at Bethany: "You are aware that the sentiments of Bishop Campbell are greatly misrepresented in this place, and that whatever comes from him is shunned by the *'orthodox'* as they would shun a pestilence; vituperation and slander are hurled from a thousand engines."

The *Baptist Recorder* was vigorously continuing its campaign to stamp out the pestilence; and before 1830, it was joined by the *Baptist Chronicle* edited at Frankfort.

But Campbell's editorial opponents were by no means confined to the Kentucky press. *The Columbian Star and Christian Index,* under the management of William Brantly, was located in Philadelphia. Editor Brantly lost no time in expressing his opinion of the Bethany press and its owner whom he contemptuously dubbed the *"Brooke County Reformer."* He referred to Campbell's publication as "insolent, pugnacious, insidious, falsely called *The Christian Baptist;*" its editor was "self-willed, self-conceited, merciless, arrogant," a man who, "as he never appears to write or think in a serious mood," was wont to indulge in odd fancies "to ascertain how far he can lead his blind admirers upon the implicit faith which his authority alone challenges." Campbell dryly remarked, "Paul ascribed to the dyspepsia, rather than to the head or the heart, the opposition of his opponents; so, for the sake of all parties, I do adopt and pursue the same course."

The Presbyterian press was keeping pace with the Baptist in its attacks. The *Pandect*, published in Cincinnati by the rigid Calvinist, The Reverend Dr. Joshua L. Wilson, was free in making sarcastic references to the "much water scheme" and in publishing extracts from Campbell's works followed only by the words, "Look at this absurdity!!!," to which Campbell remarked, "Pope Leo ... could have, by one such line ... answered all the writings of Luther, Calvin, Beza, and all the old Reformers." Another Presbyterian attack appeared in 1828, in pamphlet form. It was from Campbell's erstwhile debating opponent, the Reverend MacCalla, who had moved from Kentucky to Philadelphia, and it was entitled "Unitarian Baptist." Campbell was not surprised at the charge "Unitarian;" it was one he had frequently heard. A friend in Missouri had written him as early as 1825 saying that the Unitarians in that country claimed him as one of them; the Western Luminary of September 1826, charged him with "fast winging his way towards the cold regions of Unitarianism;" and as time went on, the reports increased. If for no other reason, Campbell's tolerant attitude toward Barton W. Stone would have labeled him a Unitarian. The letter Alexander received from William Tener of Ireland in 1829, severely took him to task "for calling that creature named Stone a brother," and was frankly aghast that Campbell in a friendly correspondence with Stone should have said that neither the Trinitarian nor Unitarian theory was "worth an hour." But even without any association with Stone, Campbell would inevitably have been termed a Unitarian. But the Unitarian accusations in MacCalla's pamphlet, objected Campbell, had consisted of invective instead of sound argument and good logic. He addressed Campbell as a "clerico-anticlerical knight errant, with his Sancho, Sidney Rigdon;" and fervently prayed, "The Lord rebuke thee; child of the Devil, enemy of all righteousness!" This led Campbell to the remark that after reading the "Unitarian Baptist" a man "is as well qualified for devotion as if he had risen from a game at cards." Campbell then offered a sad observation on the nature of religious controversy: "There is less of the gentleman, and more of the rancor of disappointed ambition, manifested in most of our religious discussions, than in our political controversies."

Anxious lest his own associates give cause for like censure, he counseled them through his magazine: "Let our brethren everywhere be courteous and forgiving, affable and familiar, rendering to no man evil for evil, and by good works and a good teaching put to shame the ignorance of foolish men." However popular and customary in the West might be a violently sectarian pulpit oratory, in which the proponents of all rival theologies were roundly denounced, twenty years residence in the West had not changed Alexander's opinion of such practices. Even now, when so much of that oratory was being directed against "Campbellism," he still felt as strongly as ever that to engage in controversy while occupying the "sacred desk" was unseemly and irreverent. And he said so in print. "Indeed I know many brethren of the first talents who do not agree with the views offered in this work ... I hear patiently all their strong reasons and proofs. As I claim forbearance, I can cheerfully exercise it." Opponents of Campbell who considered him arrogant, self-willed and opinionated would assume that all such sentiments issuing from Bethany press were merely sound and fury and signified nothing. But those who were watching the course of *The Christian Baptist* with open minds and an unprejudiced curiosity were likely to hold a different opinion. Quick spirited and gifted with a satiric pen its editor certainly was, and when invective was launched against him he could not refrain from lashing back with a cool, pointed sarcasm, which his opponents found more infuriating than a barrage of expletives. But this by no means negated Campbell's insistence on forbearance and fair play.

Quite the contrary, from the day when his young thought had first been quickened by reading John Locke's "Letters on Toleration," Alexander was animated by a hatred for the twin demons of bigotry and intolerance. If he was to ask freedom of thought for himself he knew that he must grant the right of dissent to others; and it was only when his opponents denied him the right to differ with them in opinion and damned him as a heretic because he so dared, that Campbell arose in what MacCalla had once called his "magisterial anger." In fact, it appeared to Campbell, that the opponent who refused to attack him with reason and logic and resorted instead to calling him a "child of the devil" and an "enemy of all righteousness" must be actuated by one of two motives—deliberate malice or blind prejudice. There seemed little doubt that there were some in the first category, men who envied Campbell his ability to sway an audience by his oratory and command a following by his pen, who envied the seeming ease with which he could give of his time and talents more freely than most, and yet steadily increase his own earthly possessions. There were even a few among the clergy who feared and opposed him chiefly because they saw in his attack on an established hierarchy a threat to their own power and incomes. Those in the second category, those who sincerely believed Campbell to be a "child of the Devil" intent on destroying the very bases of their religious faith, were more numerous.

But there was another kind of opponent, whom Campbell always welcomed to his pages. They were persons of broad minds and free souls who, considering the opinions of the Bethany editor erroneous and sometimes even dangerous, were ready to give their reasons and support their arguments with logic, courtesy, and good sense. Whatever the nature of the opposition, Campbell reserved to himself the right of a citizen of a Republic to present his own theories and to defend them from all attack. So he closed one of his essays in *The Christian Baptist*:

> ... as long as life endures, I shall pray, Lord teach my hands to war, and my fingers to fight with the weapons of truth and goodness; from love, good will, and a zeal according to knowledge.

DEBATE

ON THE

EVIDENCES OF CHRISTIANITY;

CONTAINING

AN EXAMINATION

OF THE

"SOCIAL SYSTEM,"

AND OF

ALL THE SYSTEMS OF SCEPTICISM OF ANCIENT AND
MODERN TIMES.

HELD IN THE CITY OF CINCINNATI, OHIO, FROM THE 13th
TO THE 21st OF APRIL, 1829; BETWEEN

ROBERT OWEN,

OF NEW LANARK, SCOTLAND, AND

ALEXANDER CAMPBELL,

OF BETHANY, VIRGINIA.

Reported by CHARLES H. SIMS, *Stenographer.*

WITH

AN APPENDIX,

WRITTEN BY THE PARTIES.

VOL. I.

What then is unbelief?—'Tis an exploit,
A strenuous enterprize. To gain it man
Must burst through every bar of common sense,
Of common shame—magnanimously wrong!

——Who most examine, most believe;
Parts, like half sentences, confound.
Read his whole volume, Sceptic, *then* reply!

YOUNG.

O Lord of Hosts! blessed is the man that trusteth in thee!

DAVID.

BETHANY, VA.
PRINTED AND PUBLISHED BY ALEXANDER CAMPBELL.
1829,

*The printed debate between Alexander Campbell and Robert Owen, April
13–21, 1829.*

· 12 ·

Mr. Robert Owen
and the Social System

ONE JULY DAY in 1826 Campbell received a letter that launched a chain of interesting events. It would carry him from the discussion of technicalities of Christianity to the discussion of the very basis of religious belief. It would precipitate for Campbell a study of the rising gospels of socialism and communism. It would lead him to a debate in 1829 with the English socialist, Robert Owen.

The ramifications were by no means evident from the beginning. At first, there was merely a letter from a puzzled boy who feared that his inability to reconcile certain religious teachings would lead him to Deism or to skepticism. This was not the only letter Campbell received. Many of those who unwillingly found themselves being propelled towards unbelief by the intolerant bickering of the churches and by religious dogmas, which they thought inconsistent with reason, recognized that the editor of *The Christian Baptist* was a man in whom they could confide their perplexities without fear of being subjected to denunciation or abuse. He would not label them "infidel" or castigate them as children of the Devil. On the contrary, he seemed to share many of their own doubts about the existing state of religion. Yet his belief remained unshaken. They were anxious to know how this could be and wrote him letters of inquiry. On his various tours Campbell would spend many evenings discussing the knotty problem of skepticism.

It was not a question he was loath to discuss. Rather, the prize logic student of Professor Jardine still found a unique pleasure in exercising his ability to distinguish between false and true arguments, and to exhibit the correct relations of proposition and proof. Plus, he considered himself something of a master of the various fields of skeptical thought.

It was inevitable, of course, that a young man who had journeyed to Scotland to enter the University of Glasgow in the year 1808, bringing with him an inquisitive and penetrating mind and a deep admiration for the philosophy of John Locke, should have acquired some knowledge of the various conflicting philosophical theories that were so much occupying the more serious students of the University.

Alexander, at the age of twenty-one, had been taken from the quiet certainties of life in his father's parsonage in County Armagh and plunged into the confusing vortex of one of Europe's great universities, where no belief was too sacred, no concept too ancient to be called into question and brought before the bar of investigation. Some of his later calm assurance arose from the fact that his faith had passed trough this ordeal and emerged whole and vital.

Through the years in America Campbell had pondered the things he brought from the University of Glasgow. The oil had frequently burned low in his Bethany study while he sought to learn the ways in which humans thought, from the days of antiquity even unto his own century, and had solved the riddles propounded by their souls. He would bring to God not a dumb devotion, but an intelligent understanding. Sir William Drummond had said: "He who will not reason is a bigot; he who cannot is a fool, and he who dare not is a slave." Alexander had no intention of being bigot, nor fool, nor slave. Once he remarked in one of his essays:

> It is well for man, that *faith* and not *reason* is the principle on which all revealed religion is founded. For although some skeptics scowl at the idea of faith, and extol the superiority of reason, as a guide, yet the truth is, that faith is incomparably a more safe guide than reason. Not one in a thousand reason infallibly or even correctly. Hence it was that the Grecian and Roman philosophers erred more extravagantly, and ran into wilder extremes in religion, than the tribes which implicitly followed tradition, or acted upon the principles of faith … The wise man rests upon experience, that his ancestors have erred … he that drinks water to extinguish the burning sensations occasioned by swallowing vitriol, though he reasons plausibly, does not reason more discordantly with fact, than the majority of reasoners who reason themselves into universal doubt.

No one who read *The Christian Baptist* would doubt that its editor, who indeed was being accused of advocating "head religion," had proper respect for human reason. He was merely making a distinction between truths that must be accepted on testimony, and truths which could be ascertained by the unaided natural reason. In a letter to Barton Stone he phrased it: "The truths of the bible are to be received as first principles, not to be tried by our reason, one by one, but to be received as new principles, from which we are to reason as from intuitive principles in any human science." This, to Campbell's mind, was simply applying to religion the Baconian principle, the "practical and truly scientific mode" of "our scientific men," who "have stopped where human intellect found a bound over which it could not pass." Certain spiritual principles were to be accepted, just as were the axioms of mathematics or the laws of physics. But, Campbell further insisted, once these principles were accepted, the evidence on which they rested made its appeal to natural reason. As he once expressed it: "The things revealed are all reasonable when all the remises are understood."

To reconcile religion and reason was a task that Campbell found necessary both on the basis of his philosophical assumptions, and by the dictates of his own temperament. Campbell might be living in the midst of the romantic revolution—he was born the same year as Lord Byron—but he remained little touched by its emotions and sentimentalities. He was, and ever remained, a robust eighteenth-century rationalist. His pen was impelled by the satiric vigor and sometimes, so his enemies were quick to say, by the skeptical spirit of the philosophy of the Enlightenment, rather than by the attitude of "sweetness and light" characterizing nineteenth-century romanticism. Not that he was out of key with his century. Far from it. Freedom and simplicity were his watchwords, as they were the watchwords of the young revolutionists who were his contemporaries. A good parallel might be made between Campbell's religious movement with its cry, "Back to Christ and the Christianity of the New Testament," and the rising literary movement with its cry, "Back to Nature." Campbell was seeking to free religion from the fetters and complexities of theological dogmas. Poets like Wordsworth were seeking to cast off the fetters of classicism and a tiresome formalism, and find "a freer and a truer view of life and art" by a return to naturalness, and by urging that their "only rule was to be free from rules."

Though Campbell might in these respects represent the impelling motives of his century, he by no means accepted its accent on emotion and sentiment. His method was the method of the Enlightenment. He would defend his ideals by the appeal to reason, not by the appeal to romantic emotionalism. Indeed, temperamentally, he would decry the comparison, but Campbell was nearer Voltaire than Rousseau. He had given no indication in his writings that he had read Rousseau; perhaps he had not done so, or perhaps he had read his works and considered them unworthy of comment. At any rate, he would feel no kinship with the sentimentalities of the French romantic. He might sympathize with Rousseau's attempt to combat the atheism and materialism of the French Enlightenment, but he would not respect his method. He could not agree that instinct and feeling were more trustworthy guides than reason; he would deny Rousseau's contention, that a thinking man is a "depraved animal." Campbell by no means rejected all of Rousseau's emphasis on feeling. The high place Campbell gave to faith in his system discounted the charge of it being a "rational theology." With John Locke, he "considered the intellectual element of human experience based on the sensations, as the universal element; emotions are purely individual and incommunicable, except when translated into terms of intellectual concepts." Campbell remarked in a series of essays entitled "Sermons to Young Preachers;"

All evidences are addressed to the higher and more noble faculties of man. The understanding, not the passions, is addressed; and therefore an appeal to the latter, before the former is enlightened, is unphilosophic as it is unscriptural. As the helm guides the ship, and the bridle the horse, so reason is the governing principle in man.

In the 1820s a new specter in very real and substantial form was arising to disturb the thoughts of the orthodox citizens of the West. Its name was Robert Owen, who quite obviously, was a far more formidable threat to established religion than Thomas Paine had ever been. Owen's skepticism appeared in noble guise; it was a mere handmaiden to his benevolent scheme being propagated from the Owenite community at New Harmony, Indiana. Desiring, perhaps to provoke a concrete antagonist, Campbell began a new series of essays. The first that appeared in the April 1827 issue, he entitled, "Mr. Robert Owen and the Social System," and it was followed by four others entitled "Deism and the Social System."

In itself there was nothing either new or alarming in the idea of a community founded for mutual benefit and co-operation. On the contrary, the practice had played an important part in the settlement of the New World, and certainly Campbell had no objection to the plan. Had not the Brush Run church contemplated a similar project when they planned to emigrate farther west in a body in 1815? Furthermore, his young friend, Robert Richardson, later recorded that Campbell "had himself, at a former period, engaged in a project of this kind, and looked with approval on the management and prosperity of such industrial communities as he had found at Zoar in Ohio and elsewhere." Richardson was likely referring to Campbell's part in planning the Brush Run removal.

But the nineteenth century was seeing the rise of a different type of social co-operative community in America. The beginning of the Industrial Era, which might mean wealth and influence to the rulers of capital, was bringing oppression and a train of sordid evils to the working classes. To save the working classes from their fate was a mission beginning to intrigue the minds of more than one socially conscious reformer. In France, captivating and ingenious theories of communism were being broached by Charles Fourier. In Scotland, a plausible philosophy of the "social system," — to be exemplified in "Villages of Co-operation," — "founded on the principles of united labor, expenditure and property, and equal privileges" was being earnestly advocated by Robert Owen. Adherents of these social theories, dreaming of a new world order in which the progress of science and industry might be used to secure, not wealth for the few, but a better life for the many, had naturally turned their attention to the young American republic. In its vast expanse lay rich and uncultivated lands. There, individuals, nearer to a natural order of society, breathed a freer air. Class hostility and vested interests were weaker, and conventions less importunate.

Enthusiastic foreigners flocked to America, secured lands, speedily organized communities, and began a barrage of propaganda through lectures, pamphlets, and magazines bringing converts into their ranks. The condition would not have been especially alarming to the majority of democratic citizens, except for one circumstance. While the earlier communal settlements either had been religious in inception, or had confined themselves to regulating temporal affairs and left entirely free the religious sentiments of individuals, most of the new co-operative systems assumed that religion was inimical to their plans for remodeling society, and hence sought to destroy its influence. The church was part of the old order and must go.

It was this aspect of the new co-operative societies that had caused the Bethany theologian to propose his series of essays on Robert Owen and Deism, and the "social system." And never did

Campbell show his open-mindedness, never did he prove that it was no mere lip service that he paid to Locke's *Letters Concerning Toleration*, more clearly than in these essays. From the very first sentence he made his attitude plain:

> Mr. Owen has attracted much attention to this country as well as in Britain from the singularity of his views … I have waited for a better acquaintance with his principles and managements before I even ventured to form an opinion for myself, either of their wisdom or practicability; and am not yet able to form a satisfactory opinion of the social system as advocated by him. I have long endeavored neither to condemn nor approve any opinion either because it is old or new, popular or unpopular. Paul's maxim I esteem of equal importance in all things — 'Bring all things to the test, and hold fast that which is good.'
>
> The benefits resulting from a co-operative system have been apprehended in theory and proved by experience, before we heard of Mr. Owen in this country … but that a social system of cooperation can at all exist without religious obligations has never yet been proved; but this appears to be the experiment now on hand at New Harmony, Indiana … I have no notion of getting angry with Mr. Owen, or of belaboring him with harsh epithets for hazarding an experiment of this sort.

Alexander had a great deal of respect both for the man and his ideals, Robert Owen's career was one to win admiration, no matter what one thought of some details of his plan for social betterment.

✠

Born in 1771 in Wales of humble parentage, and without much formal education, Owen, at eighteen, became partner and manager of a cotton factory at Manchester, England, employing forty hands. At twenty-nine he was part owner and managing director of the mills at New Lenark, Scotland. He had purchased the mills from his father-in-law, David Dale, and close to two thousand people depended on him for support. David Dale had initiated certain benevolent projects for the improvement of the workmen at his mills, but his son-in-law had more far-reaching ideas of reform. And reform was sorely needed.

The Industrial Revolution was bringing in its wake a train of cruelties and miseries to disturb the conscience even of men less philanthropic than Robert Owen. Owen rebelled against the sight everywhere around him of squalid mill towns with their "men, women and children maimed, stunted, and demoralized by the slavery of the new factories, condemned to work impossibly long hours under incredibly vile and unhealthy conditions, treated not as human beings but as mere instruments for the accumulations of riches." With industrial discoveries, rapidly opening new and easy avenues of wealth to those with capital to invest, "it had become customary to employ children regularly in the mills at six years of age or even earlier, and to work them, with only one pause, for fourteen hours a day or even longer." "Most of the overseers," wrote Owen after a tour through the manufacturing districts, taking with him his fourteen-year-old son, Robert Dale Owen, "openly carried stout leather thongs, and we frequently saw even the youngest children severely beaten … Their stories haunted my dreams. In some large factories, from one-fourth to one-fifth of the children were either cripples or otherwise deformed, or permanently injured by excessive toil, sometimes by brutal abuse. The younger children seldom held out more than three or four years without serious illness, often ending in death."

Portrait of Robert Owen made by Rembrandt Peale in London four years after the debate.

Owen had no intention that such conditions should exist at New Lanark. Other manufacturers and statesmen might defend the enormities of the Industrial Revolution in the name of progress, but Owen stood out against them, preaching "the virtue and efficiency of good factory conditions and humane treatment." He sought the passage of reform legislation in Parliament; other industrialists might sing the praises and virtues of competitive capitalism, but Owen said "the vision of another system, based on co-operation and human fellowship." Believing that the roots of character and happiness were embedded in education, he claimed education "not for a favored few, but as the common right of all children, however poor their parents might be." The reforms he preached, he put into practice at New Lanark. And since Owen's good management enabled the mills to pay good dividends, he gave a practical illustration to those who would learn, industry could be both profitable and humane. The fame of his experiment spread, and visitors came from the continent to view his model industrial community at New Lanark.

Owen's ideas had begun to spread to America only a very few years after the Campbells crossed the ocean from North Ireland. In 1814 copies of Owen's *New View of Society* were circulated to the leading governments in Europe and America. John Quincy Adams, then Ambassador to Great Britain, sent copies to the governors of all the United States. Between 1821 and 1822, a Society for Promoting Communities based on Owen's principles was started in New York. Soon thereafter, failing to get his "plan" adopted by the Tory government of England, Owen himself turned his thoughts to the New World, which he thought might "redress the balance of the Old." Owen, fired by a kindred impulse, realized his dream by establishing New Harmony on the banks of the Wabash. He began his work in America with a series of lectures, the first being delivered in the House of Representatives in Washington, in the presence of the President of the United States. "By a hard struggle," he said to his American audience, "you have attained political liberty, but you have yet to acquire real mental liberty." New Harmony, based on the full equality of all the settlers and divided into six departments—agriculture; manufactures; literature, science and education; domestic economy; general economy; and commerce—was to point the way to the acquirement of this "mental liberty." Quite fittingly it was dubbed the City of Mental Independence.

Wishing to give Owen due credit for his philanthropic ideals, Campbell remarked at the beginning of his essay on "Mr. Robert Owen and the Social System;" "his talents, education, fortune and extraordinary zeal in the prosecution of his favorite object, entitle him to a very liberal share of public respect. It is, I believe, very generally admitted that he is perfectly disinterested as far as respects pecuniary gain, in all that he has done, and is doing, for the establishment and development of the social system." When it came to some details of Owen's "Plan," Campbell had an entirely different idea. At the very basis of Owen's system lay his almost boundless belief in the effect of "environment and training on the character of the child," which was naturally accompanied by a thorough contempt for the concept of individual development. "Man's character is made for and not by him," he never wearied of saying—an idea not likely to find favor with the self-reliant master of Bethany.

Owen declared, in his famous address of 1817, that the pernicious influence of the church must be removed before his "new moral world" might be realized. "My friends, I tell you, that hitherto you have been prevented from knowing what happiness is, solely in consequence of the errors—gross errors—that have been combined with the fundamental notions of every religion that has hitherto been taught to men ... By the errors of these systems, he has been made a weak, imbecile animal, a furious bigot and fanatic; or a miserable hypocrite; and should these qualities be carried, not only into the projected villages, but into Paradise itself, a paradise would be no longer found." Some of the philosophers at New Harmony, carrying this restriction farther than Owen himself, were contending that marriage was among the outworn institutions of religion that must be abolished in the interests of society.

Surveying these tendencies, Campbell commented: "This I regret from my regard for the social system in particular, and also because of its pestiferous influence on certain classes of society, who need the benefits of something more than the social system to improve their morals and their circumstances." Remarking

Lithograph of the Campbell-Owen debate by the French artist Auguste Jean Jacques Hervieu. Campbell is seated on the right.

whimsically, "There is a deistical, atheistical, political, economical as well as a Christian enthusiast." He continued in a tone of ironic amusement:

> Mr. Owen seems to have paid so much attention to the influence of circumstances upon human character, an influence very great indeed, as to have ascribed omnipotence to it, or rather to have deified it … To make every thing in human character depend upon the power of circumstances, is to me as great an error as to make nothing depend on it. These are the two extremes. *Media tutissima est.* The True and the safe way lies between. Education may do as much for the animal man as cultivation may do for plants, I think it can do little, if anything more. The moralist who conceives that he could, by an

entire change of circumstances, effect an entire change of character, is not less deceived than the botanist who thinks he could make grapes grow on thorns, or figs on thistles, by a change of climate and of culture ... No change of circumstances could make a Nero out of Mr. Owen, nor a Bonaparte out of General Hull. There is more born into the world than flesh and blood, and yet a great deal depends on corporeal organization. No change of circumstances could make a painter or a musician where the eye and the ear are not bestowed by nature, so no change of circumstances can make the naturally indolent, selfish, envious, ambitious, the contrary characters. I cannot, then, ascribe the attributes of Deity to the circumstances of birth or education, and therefore I cannot be *so mentally independent* as Mr. Owen.

So spoke the philosopher of Bethany, always the rationalist, never the extremist.

The organ of propaganda for Owen's Indiana "Village of Co-operation" was the *New Harmony Gazette*, where Campbell, in his essays, next turned his attention. There was scarcely an issue of the magazine, he said, "in which there is not either a popgun or a blunderbuss discharged at Revelation." It "is the *focus of the lights of skepticism*, to which, as Tacitus said of Rome, flows all the cream, shall I call it, of *enlightened* infidelity ... The conductors of that journal are among the most assiduous, devoted and persevering Skeptics of the 19th century." Nevertheless, speaking as a free and tolerant man, Campbell would ironically add: "For my part I rejoice to know that so much of the reflex light of Christianity shines in our political institutions that no *Bastille*, no *auto da fe* awaits the man who vends his skeptical reveries in books or papers, or publicly declaims against the Bible and in favor of Deism." Likewise claiming his right freely to reply to their charges, he made it clear that he did not come forward "to be attacked through the media of other men's sophistical technicalities ... Although not so rich in mental independence as the conductors of the social system, I have some little property of this sort of which I would be parsimonious."

A current writer, signing himself "Inquirer" in the *Gazette*, was attacking the Scriptures because Moses's account of the creation showed "no correct knowledge either of astronomy or of natural history." Campbell had no intention of conducting his discussion on any such trivial plane. Having a mind neither narrow nor literalistic, he did not consider his Bible a handbook on science, or geography, or history. He had already brought down on his head the fury of the orthodox by declaiming against the "textuary divines" who used all parts of the Bible that were "properly denominated a Divine Revelation," and those parts which were "no more than true and faithful history." Taking this high view of the spiritual intent of the Scriptures, he could answer the objections of the Gazette with the passing remark that the record of Genesis "is neither contrary to, nor incompatible with any established truth in the principles of Sir Isaac or of Galileo ... I would not give a pin for an arithmetical defense of the size or of the contents of Noah's ark, nor for an astronomical explanation of the Mosiac account of the creation, to confute or refute the puerile cavils of any conceited skeptic." Campbell informed the New Harmony skeptics, "It is the *rationale* of the system I first attack:"

> You have erected a temple, in which you have constructed a throne, and on it you have crowned REASON, arbiter of every question. I approach the altar you have dedicated—I have read the inscription thereon. I will date to enter barefoot into your sacred edifice, and will make my appeal to your own goddess.

Thus approaching the question in philosophical temper, he asked "the enlightened Deists at New Harmony" to answer three questions which he proposed concerning immortality and the existence of God.

☩

The editors of the *New Harmony Gazette* were surprised by the essays issuing from the press on the Buffaloe—surprised by their manner no less than by their method. They were generally used to being attacked with harsh anathemas, or on the basis of what Campbell had called "sophistical technicalities." But the Bethany editor's approach was as rational as their own, and his attitude was as tolerant as could be desired. They commended his "liberality" and opened their pages to the discussion. An answer to Campbell's queries soon appeared; it read: "We can reply to these propositions neither in the affirmative nor in the negative, for we possess no positive knowledge on any of these subjects. A God, the Soul, Heaven and Hell, … can never, from their nature become cognizable by the senses of man." Campbell commented on this reply in jubilant vein. The "people of the city of Mental Independence" were "said to have the best *library* on this continent." They boasted of living "in the best approved condition of human nature;" yet they had admitted that to them evidence of things spiritual was unknown and unknowable:

> This is the identical conclusion to which I knew most certainly, by all the knowledge of philosophy which I possess, they would be constrained to come. For, as I have frequently said, there is no stopping place between Deism and Atheism; and they are lame philosophers who, taking philosophy for their guide, profess to hold with Herbert, Hume, Gibbon, and Payne, that there is a God, an immortal soul, a heaven, or a hell. I give great praise to the New Harmony philosophers for their candor and their honesty in frankly avowing the conclusion which all the

lights they have authorize them to maintain. I say they are *good philosophers*. They have reasoned well.

Throughout the winter of 1827–1828 Campbell had no further word to say to the skeptics of New Harmony. His other work was pressing, and his heart was heavy because of the death of Margaret. In the spring another and perhaps better way of answering the New Harmony philosophers presented itself.

A letter came from Canton, Ohio, dated February 22, 1828, informing Campbell that a certain Doctor Underhill, "an emissary of infidelity, of considerable talents," had been sent to the nearby town of Kendal, Ohio, a co-operative community established on Owen's principles. Underhill was winning so many converts in that section of Ohio, and the "freethinkers" were becoming so bold, that "even the apprentices in the workshops, and boys in the streets, begin to reason away, and rail at religion." Declaring that none but a Roman priest, and he not very effectively, had undertaken to contradict the skeptic, the letter urged Campbell to come to Ohio and meet Dr. Underhill in debate. Campbell answered the Ohio correspondent that he considered Dr. Underhill "too obscure to merit any attention from me on the Atheism or Deism of his philosophy" and hence, "to go out of my way to meet such a gentleman would be rather incompatible with my views of propriety." But, proposed Campbell, "if his great master, Mr. Robert Owen, will engage to debate the whole system of his moral and religious philosophy with me ... if he will engage to do this coolly and dispassionately ... I will engage to take the negative and disprove all his affirmative positions ... But in the meantime I will not draw a vow, save against the king of the skeptics of the city of Mental Independence." His enemies might call his answer proud if they chose, but Alexander felt that he had dedicated his time and his talents to the Lord, and they were not to be wasted.

Soon after publishing his reply to the Ohio correspondent in the April issue of *The Christian Baptist*, Campbell came upon a challenge that Owen had issued to the clergy of New Orleans. Suggesting that each group should choose a half dozen gentlemen to debate, Owen proposed to prove:

> ...that all the religions of the world have been founded on the ignorance of mankind; that they are directly opposed to the never changing laws of our nature; that they have been and are the real source of vice, disunion, and misery of every description; that they are now the only real bar to the formation of a society of virtue, of intelligence, of charity in its most extended sense, and of sincerity and kindness among the whole human family; and that they can be no longer maintained except through the ignorance of the mass of the people, and the tyranny of the few over that mass.

The words of the challenge convinced Campbell. He had been puzzling his mind to decide whether Owen was a Deist or an Atheist, whether the "sage philosopher of New Harmony" was an outright enemy of religion in every form, and that a bold attack must be made to halt "the apparently triumphant manner in which Mr. Owen, a gentleman of very respectable standing as a scholar and capitalist, of much apparent benevolence, traveling with the zeal of an apostle, through Europe and America," was disseminating his "most poisonous sentiments," and advocating "this libertine and lawless scheme." Since none of the clergy seemed anxious to do so, Campbell published Owen's challenge and his formal acceptance. He agreed to meet Owen "at any time within one year from this date, at any place equi-distant from New Harmony and Bethany, such as Cincinnati, Ohio, or Lexington,

Kentucky." Campbell further proposed that a disinterested stenographer should take down their speeches for the privilege of publishing the debate. He closed his challenge by quoting Owen's own words: "With feelings of perfect good will to you, which extend also in perfect sincerity to all mankind, I subscribe myself your friend in a just cause."

As it happened, before Owen received this acceptance of his New Orleans challenge, he saw Campbell's reply to the correspondent from Canton, Ohio, and immediately through the *New Harmony Gazette* of May 14th wrote Campbell a letter agreeing to meet him in debate. Campbell replied, specifying that he would meet the champion of agnosticism in single combat, though, he added, "I have no objection to your assembling all your brethren skeptics, from harmony to Lanark, if any place could be found large enough to hold them." In conclusion he assured his contemplated opponent: "I have, from a little experience in public discussion, no doubt, but that I shall be able to maintain perfect good humor throughout the whole; and I have reason to believe that your philosophy has improved your good nature so far as to make you an acceptable disputant."

The arrangements for the debate had to be made, and as Owen on his way east to take ship for England, paid a visit to Bethany in the summer of 1828. Immediately they liked one another, these two men, each in his way the apostle of a new order, the prophet of a millennium. Brought up in the same era, they had revolted against many of the same things in the old order. The failure of the church in the eighteenth century to meet the challenge of the new conditions, the hatred and conflict between the rival sects, the greed and intrigue of the ecclesiastics had driven the idealistic young Robert Owen to the conviction that something was fundamentally wrong with religion. Now, at fifty-seven, having repudiated the worship of God, he was seeking to find the outlet for his humanism in a new religion of service to humanity. Alexander Campbell, recognizing and deploring the failure and corruption of the church as much as did Owen, had made the distinction that Owen did not perceive—something was fundamentally wrong with the church but not with religion. He was seeking "a new moral world" for humanity through a reform of the church.

However different their points of view, the two philosophers had a pleasant visit. Each gave credit to the other for the sincerity and intellectual honesty that he himself possessed. Owen's friends found him a man who combined an almost childlike simplicity with the manners of a courtier. If he often bored and wearied them with ceaseless reiteration of the same arguments and doctrine, they forgave him for the sake of his candor and cheerfulness, his charm and benevolence. But the sage of New Harmony could not outdo either in charm, or in courtesy, the master of Bethany. They lingered over tea in the wainscoted parlor of the mansion. They visited the little cemetery beyond the orchard and talked of immortality. They went for long walks through the lovely summer hills and viewed the numerous operation of Campbell's press and farm. Owen might have in his mind a conception of a model community; Campbell could show him a model farm. Owen "assured Mr. Campbell" that "persons of taste in England would go many miles to see "his beautiful Virginia countryside." Eventually, "after an agreeable and desultory conversation," said Campbell, they decided to hold their debate the following year, 1829, in Cincinnati, Ohio. It would begin in April "as it is to be expected that facilities of steam boat navigation and the mildness of the weather at that season will be favorable."

On Tuesday, April 7, 1829, Alexander Campbell set out for Cincinnati to meet the champion of New Harmony. The debate had been postponed several days for the convenience of Robert

Owen, who was in Mexico trying to persuade Santa Anna, military leader in that country's current revolution, to cede him a large tract of land for an experimental community.

Campbell departed in good spirits to meet "the Champion of Infidelity in two continents," as he described him. Writing a few "Desultory Remarks" for his magazine the night before he left Bethany, he said to his readers:

> Although I have not for months written any thing upon the skeptical system, it has not for a single hour of the day been absent from my thoughts. I have put myself upon the skeptical premises, and made myself, as far as I could, doubt with them. . . . I start in the most confident expectation …

Not that everything was harmonious. As Alexander was well aware, some of his opponents felt that Christianity had better go undefended than be defended by such a champion. Among the irreconcilables was Dr. Wilson, editor of the Cincinnati *Pandect*, who had sarcastically commented that "if two blind men met to argue about colors" the debate "would excite curiosity, but on one would feel bound to lay aside his work and go."

Saturday, April 11th, found both disputants in the city of Cincinnati. Alexander was accompanied by his father, Thomas. Selina, being with child, could not come. For a time it was feared that with a long sea voyage ahead of him Owen himself would not arrive; but Admiral Fleming, a personal friend of Owen, conveyed him on a British warship from Mexico to New Orleans. One account claimed that a "gun brig of the British navy sailed up the Ohio with the missing champion of humanity on board."

Conveniently situated on the banks of the Ohio, Cincinnati attracted many visitors for the debate. The debate had been well advertised. Notices had appeared in the Edinburgh *Scotsman* and in the *London Times*. Campbell noted the presence of people from New York, Pennsylvania, Virginia, Kentucky, Indiana, Tennessee, and Mississippi.

Considering the large crowd, the city arrangements committee sought a place for the debate large enough to accommodate the numbers. The largest facility was the Presbyterian Church. The minister, Dr. Wilson, editor of the *Pandect*, refused, remarked Campbell sarcastically, with his "usual politeness and liberality." The committee next approached the Methodists for the use of their large meeting-house, which, said Campbell, "was readily and cheerfully granted."

On April 11th Owen and Campbell "set their hands and affixed their seals" to "The Laws of Discussion," Thomas Campbell and John Smith acting as witnesses. Seven moderators were to preside with Judge Burnet as chairman. Owen was to open the discussion, and the debaters were to speak alternately, thirty minutes each.

On Monday morning, April 13th, the debate opened. Every seat in the church was occupied, and many who came to hear were turned away, disappointed. Most of the audience, perhaps, had never seen either of the disputants. Campbell now at forty, his foretop a little mixed with gray, had never made a better appearance. Dignified and self-possessed, he had the air of a statesman far more than that of a clergyman. His clear and exceedingly rapid enunciation still retained a trace of Scotland's brogue, which so well became the name of Campbell. Owen was seventeen years Campbell's senior. Not nearly so handsome as his younger opponent—some even considered him ugly—he was almost as tall, and his courtly manners and "exceedingly neat and fine suit of black broadcloth" made him appear a proper gentleman to his Cincinnati audience, even while his chaste English accent fell strangely on their ears.

One fact became evident very soon after the discussion started— namely, that contrary to all expectation, a debate was not to be held. And for the reason that Robert Owen simply refused to debate! Campbell had prepared in advance only his opening address, thinking that the rest of his time would be occupied in answering Owen's arguments. But Owen appeared with reams of paper in hand setting forth his whole social and moral philosophy, and these he continued to read calmly, hour after hour, scarcely noticing the remarks of his supposed opponent. Campbell protested "It seems a very hard matter, indeed, to reason logically when we have nothing to reason against." "Mr. Owen's course in this debate has been irrelevant, impertinent, and out of the purview of the discussion contemplated, and to which the public have been invited ... This morning we have had a disquisition upon marriage, commerce, and a code of natural laws—none of which has any bearing upon or logical connection with the question at issue; ... I am at a loss to reconcile this equivocal course with what I must think is the honesty, frankness, and candor of my friend's character and disposition." The moderators likewise protested: "Mr. Owen wandered from the point of discussion immediately before the disputants ... The Board of Moderators suppose that you ought to prove the falsehood of the existing religions before you proceed to the discussion and explanation of your substitute." Owen, with a sweet and disarming unreasonableness, continued on his course—heedless of protest or reproof.

Campbell had an indication of this before the debate opened, when a copy of the *London Times* came into his hands. Both the *Scotsman* and the *Times,* judging from the words of Owen's New Orleans challenge, had stated that he and Campbell were to "discuss the truth or falsehood of the Christian religion;" Owen had protested in a letter to the *Times* that they had misstated his and Campbell's purpose, which was "to ascertain the errors in all religions and thus to form from them collectively a religion wholly true and consistent, that it may become universal." Even when Campbell directly challenged this letter on the first day of the debate, Owen, according to one of his own biographers, "was unable to recognize" that it "was not a fair statement of his original purpose," for the simple reason was he "was at all times incapable of seeing a point of view differing from his own, or even of conceiving of the possibility of such a view, except as the result of ignorance or prejudice."

Of the two men debating in Cincinnati, the religious reformer and the social reformer, there was no question which was the fanatical dogmatist. Even Owen's friends admitted that he always thought "he had proved a thing when he asserted it in the force of his own conviction." While commending his benevolence, they had to deplore this habit "of dogmatic assertion treated as equivalent to proof, and of obvious pity for all who doubted his conclusions." Campbell had a talent for positive assertion, but the master of Bethany was a man of many and varied interests, and the inquiring and philosophic temper of his mind kept him constantly on the search for new facets of truth and made him eager to explore the reasoning of other men. Owen, on the contrary, was a man of only one idea and interest. His mind seemed completely closed to any influence from without; "he believed that his own experience had unlocked for him the gates of truth, and that he had no need for other guides." Hence, his attitude toward debate. He might have said of the meeting at Cincinnati, as he said later of another debate: "It would have been the loss of most precious moments for me to have attended to anything Mr. Brindley might say, instead of using them to tell the world what I wished it to learn from myself."

Campbell perceived that this was the drift of Owen's attitude, and after a final protest on the third day of their discussion, he ceased trying to persuade his opponent to adhere to the rules of debate. He instead settled down to affirming his own stand on the truth of religion and to attacking what he conceived to be the errors in Owen's plan for regenerating society.

Among the visitors in the audience was a woman from England, Mrs. Trollope, mother of Anthony Trollope, the novelist. She watched the proceedings with especial care, for she was gathering material for a book that she published soon after her return to England. The book, entitled *Domestic Manners of the Americans* devoted four pages to a description of the Campbell-Owen debate. When it is considered that Mrs. Trollope, following the best tradition of British tourist to America, saw in the new republic almost nothing to approve, and much to ridicule, her account of the debate was rather flattering:

> ... a small stage was arranged around the pulpit, large enough to accommodate the disputants and their stenographers; the pulpit itself was throughout the whole time occupied by the aged father of Mr. Campbell, whose flowing white hair and venerable countenance, constantly expressive of the deepest attention, and the most profound interest, made him a very striking figure in the group. The chapel was equally divided, one-half being appropriated to ladies, the other to gentlemen; and the door of entrance reserved for the ladies was carefully guarded to prevent crowding ... I suspect the ladies were indebted to Mr. Owen for this attention; the arrangements respecting them on this occasion were by no means American.
>
> When Mr. Owen arose, the building was thronged in every part: the audience, or congregation (I hardly know which to call them), were of the highest rank of citizens ... It was in the profoundest silence, and apparently with the deepest attention that Mr. Owen's opening address was received ... when I recollect its object, and the uncompromising manner in which the orator sated his conviction that the whole history of the Christian mission was a fraud, and its sacred origin a fable, I cannot but wonder that it was so listened to ...
>
> Half an hour was the time allotted for each haranguer; when this was expired, the moderators were

seen to look at their watches. Mr. Owen looked at his (without pausing), smiled, shook his head and said in a parenthesis "a moment's patience," and continued for another half-hour.

Mr. Campbell then arose; his person, voice and manner all greatly in his favor. He quizzed Mr. Owen most unmercifully; pinched him here for his parallelograms; hit him there for his human perfectibility, and kept the whole audience in a roar of laughter... Mr. Campbell's watch was the only one which reminded us that we had listened to him for half an hour; and having continued speaking for a few minutes after he had looked at it, he sat down with . . . the universal admiration of his audience. Neither appeared to me to answer the other; but to confine themselves to the utterance of what they had uppermost in their own minds when the discussion began. I lamented this on the side of Mr. Campbell, as I am persuaded he would have been much more powerful had he trusted more to himself and less to his books. Mr. Owen is an extraordinary man and certainly possessed of talent, but he appears to me so utterly benighted in the mists of his own theories, that he has quite lost the power of looking through them, so as to get a peep at the world as it really exists around him.

The debate lasted eight days, exclusive of Sunday, ending on April 21ˢᵗ. The sessions began each morning at nine and lasted until twelve, and recommenced at three in the afternoon to continue, as specified in "The Laws of the Discussion," " until the parties agree to adjourn." The adjournment was likely to come rather late, since "it was once said that when Owen called a meeting no man on earth could say at what hour it would close," and "he had met a kindred spirit in Mr. Campbell." Nevertheless, according to the *Cincinnati Chronicle*, every session was attended by an audience of "more than twelve hundred persons." People had come to Cincinnati expecting intellectual stimulation and entertainment. And they were not disappointed.

Campbell brought the best product of his mature thought to the debate. Whatever philosophical discipline had been evident in the pages of his magazine was given its fullest expression. Some details of his theological system might become outworn with the passing years, but in defending the basis of religious faith against the onslaughts of materialistic skepticism, he was defining his attitude on a timeless question. Owen, in expounding his social system, was lighting a beacon for future generations of social materialists. Campbell, in opposing that system, was seeking to find a rational *via media* for harmonizing the demands of personal righteousness and social responsibility for all persons who would be concerned about dividing the things that are Caesar's from the things that are God's. Campbell informed his audience at the outset: "I have rummaged antiquity, and the systems of philosophy, ancient and modern." They were ready to believe him, when in the course of debate he quoted from Bacon, Locke, Hume, Hobbes, Mirabaud, and Godwin, from Herbert's *De Veritate*, Paine's *Age of Reason*, and Cudworth's *Systema Intellectuale*. He illustrated his remarks by references to the ideas of Berkeley, Reid, Isaac Newton, Spinoza, Rousseau, Voltaire, Swedenborg, Franklin, and Gibbon, to Godwin's *Political Justice*, Darwin's *Loves of the Plants*, and Montesquieu's *Spirit of the Laws*, to Aristotle, Pyrrho, Democritus, Epicurus, Orpheus, and Solon. He embellished his thoughts with literary allusions. He quoted Addison, Scott, and Lord Chesterfield, Herodotus and Tacitus, and in the Latin Horace and the *Ecologue* of Virgil. He brought in reference to Milton's *Paradise Lost* and Homer's *Illiad* and the writings of Cicero, Plutarch, Demosthenes, Xenophon, and Sallust. He explored the systems of the various "sects" of Deists, Theists, Atheists, Pantheists and Polytheists—"There are more versions of the volume of nature, than of the volume of revelation"—

as well as their "dogmas and mysteries." He investigated the concepts of various pagan religions. He entered on a thorough analysis of human "mental powers" and of the nature of the five senses. He told his audience, "to adduce the alphabet of mental philosophy in order to lead you to relish and apprehend the truth of our reasonings upon our external senses, and mental faculties." Withal, it was an array of learning more than sufficient to impress the audience gathered in Cincinnati.

On the part of Owen, the debate furnished a detailed picture of the Utopia that he was sure would result from the application of his social and moral philosophy. In later years a biographer of Owen (who termed Campbell "a fiery and fluent Universalist preacher") declared that the discussion gave one of "the most reasoned and elaborate statements of Owen's creed." This creed was embraced in his "Twelve Fundamental laws of Human Nature," which he read on the first morning of debate, and then re-read and elaborated day after day, until Campbell protested "that these laws should not be commented on more than ELEVEN times." These "Twelve Laws," with the exception of one that declared that "man's belief in no case depends on his will," were simple commonplace truisms affirming the power of organization and circumstances to mold and modify human character; but from them Owen argued to his amazing conception of human nature and ideal environment. Since a baby does not control the circumstances under which it is born (a fact solemnly set forth in one of the "Twelve Laws"), Owen concluded that human beings are entirely helpless creatures of circumstance, unable in any way to direct their own destiny. Hence, since man had no personal will and was "a being irresponsible for his thoughts and feelings" and for his actions, it was obviously foolish and unjust to attribute to him either blame or praise for his conduct or character. Moreover, argued Owen, people "cannot be bad by nature."

Once people had become aware of these "fundamental laws" of their nature, Owen was convinced, the millennium would be at hand. Some may have accused Alexander Campbell of pride of mind, but compared with Owen, Campbell appeared the most modest of men. "There never was," averred Owen, "in the imagination of any human being, a collection of facts so truly valuable to the whole of mankind as those which are contained in these twelve laws." They were truly "divine revelations;" they were "a perfect system of moral laws;" they were the twelve "most valuable jewels." The application of these laws, he had not the slightest doubt, would prevent one bad or irrational creature being formed. Every person would be beautiful, healthy, happy, and rich. Aided and abetted by the new march of education and science they would, in Owen's imagination, usher in a new era of peace and joy which put to shame St. John's vision of the Isle of Patmos.

Owen reasoned that humankind was a passive mass that could be molded by the application of a purely mechanical formula into any desired form. Control of environment was control of destiny; science and sociology were sufficient to cure all the ills of humankind; the salvation of the world could be realized by the enforcement of a communistic, egalitarian scheme of living. To work this salvation, said Owen, "We shall discover a mathematical mode of training the rising generation, by which they shall be prevented from receiving one error, one bad habit, or acquiring one injurious passion." These perfect creatures would want for nothing, for they would "be made wealthy" by "the enormous scientific power obtained within the last half century," "by the enormous mechanical and chemical power for the creation of wealth, now at the disposal of society, and which admits of unlimited increase." This wealth would be obtained by laboring no more than two hours a day and, though people might differ in "natural qualities," was to be distributed equally so that all might have the same "conditions of life." No longer would work be conducted for gain or profit. Large cities being injurious, the citizens of the new order—the family was no longer to be considered a unit—were gathered in communities not exceeding two thousand in population, while society furnished free and easy travel from place to place. These happy, irresponsible citizens were also to be relieved even of the necessity of caring for their children, for all children were to be reared by the community.

There were, to Owen's mind, three institutions of the present society which would have to be removed before this perfect social system could be put in order. First was religion, "because all religions are diametrically opposed to the immutable laws of nature as exhibited in man." Religion taught the baleful doctrine that "man has a free will, forms his own character, and determines his own conduct," and hence is liable to praise or punishment for his actions. To Owen the revelation that "ignorance, vice, and misery and free will notions were inseparably connected" and that "man can be no more responsible for his nature ... than ... any other animal" had been vouchsafed. The second institution to be discarded was marriage. One of the twelve fundamental and universal laws being that "human nature required for its happiness, health, and well-being a change of sensations," it naturally followed that neither man nor woman, except in strange cases, could remain faithful to one mate; "the artificial bonds of indissoluble marriage, and the single family arrangements are more calculated to *destroy* than to *promote* affection." Third to go was private property. In the new order every person should have "a full supply of everything that is best for human nature," while selfishness, poverty, and jealousy—"the innumerable evils arising from private property"—would be terminated. Thus would come the millennium: "In these new arrangements, the countless evils which have been engendered by conflicting religions, by various forms of marriage, and by unnecessary private property, will not exist; but, instead thereof, real charity, pure chastity, sincere affections, and upright dealing between man and man, producing abundance for all, will everywhere prevail."

Alexander Campbell—though he had come to understand the nature of Owen's closed mind which made it impervious to all argument—was ready to show the audience numerous errors and inconsistencies in Owen's social system. For it was a system in opposition to Campbell's every instinct as a self-reliant and democratic citizen of a new republic. That republic was trying a great experiment in free government, and that experiment, Campbell was convinced, could never succeed on a theory of mechanistic materialism.

Entirely aside from the religious issue, Owen's scheme, Campbell insisted, could be attacked on the basis of common sense. It was, and ever would be, unworkable because it was founded on a false conception of human nature. Human nature could not be completely explained in terms of, or controlled by, the physical sciences, for there was a mystery of personality and character that would defy all scientific formulas. No mechanical regulation of environment, no system of education could ever create a genius or even produce a group of uniformly good and happy persons.

On the one hand individuals were creatures of values and potentialities ignored in Owen's system. The materialistic conception of human nature, argued Campbell, in a biting indictment, denuded humanity of all its rightful "dignity and honor" and reduced individuals "wholly to the earth:"

> ... a colony of bees co-operating in the building of store-houses and cells ... is the grand model of what man would be and what he would do... my benevolent oppo-

nent labors to show us that matter—solid, liquid gaseous matter—is the height and depth, the length and breadth of all that deserves the name of knowledge. As for *souls*, and their appurtenances, they are mere nonentities ...

... when he [man] is taught to annihilate the Creator, he is next to be taught that he is himself neither *Creator nor creature*, but a sort of self-existent particle of a self-existent whole ... Lest he should be too uplifted in his own imagination, he is to be taught that he is no more than a two-legged *animal*, as circumscribed by *sense* as a mole or a lobster.

To complete the process of degradation, man is to be taught that he has no faculty, or power of learning or knowing any thing but by his senses.

Campbell repudiated Owen's "Twelve Fundamental Laws of Human Nature," not because they assumed too much, but because they recognized too little. He was even perfectly willing to admit that, with the exception of the one denying free will, they were true. However, he added, they "might, with the same logical propriety be affirmed of a goat." Much to Owen's disgust, and the audience's delight, he reread the "Twelve Laws," substituting the words "kid" and "goat" for "child" and "man." The whole scheme of Owen, he continued, was "defective and at variance with all experience," for "every rational theory on the nature of man must be predicated, *de rebus spiritualibus as well as de rebus naturalibus.*"

Owen had "lost sight of the creature man," charged Campbell, and he pointed to the New Harmony experiment to prove his contention. The Indiana community project had collapsed the year before the debate took place, and with it had gone most of Owen's private fortune. The magic of his "Twelve Laws" simply had not been sufficient to mold into harmony the wide social and racial differences of the citizens of New Harmony.

Young ladies with a fondness for music took it ill when called from their pianos to milk cows; and they did not always approve the gentlemen with whom they had to dance when lots were drawn for the cotillion. Only the most aristocratic members, it was noticed, would wear the distinctive community dress. Mothers retained a strong predilection for wishing to care for their own children. Owen, of course, not at all ruffled by these results, blamed failure on the fact that members of the community had not been reared from birth in accordance with his principles. Campbell had a different explanation: Owen's was "a lame and blind philosophy." And "in every point of view in which we regard it, this system is at war with human nature ... sooner can he reverse the decrees of gravitation than abolish religion, marriage, or even private property." Under Owen's scheme, said Campbell, "Man at his zenith is a stall fed ox. Mr. Owen has mistaken the capacity of man as much as the vintner did the capacity of a vessel, and who strove to fill it with two gallons when it held four ..." Campbell believed Owen had failed to recognize that individuals were possessed of a thirst for knowledge, of a desire for immortality, of a longing to inquire into their origins and destinies.

In Owen's animalistic conception of humanity ruled only by the laws of "blind Fate and inexorable Necessity," morality, Campbell pointed out, became nothing more than "a due regard to *utility*. Bees are *moral* as well as people; and he is the most moral bee which creates the most honey and consumes the least of it." Campbell pointed out the fallacy in Owen's argument, from the doctrine of necessity to the conclusion, that religion was predicated upon the ignorance of humanity. It was an *argumentum non sequitur*, since, contrary to Owen, all religions were not based on a belief in the free will and responsibility of persons. The Calvinistic predestinarians, as Owen seemed unaware, were also "philosophic or systematic necessarians." Owen, in some respects, would have made a good Calvinist! And, therefore, "these reasonings and speculations of Mr. Owen upon the social system are not more objections to the truth of Christianity than are the Alleghany protuberances to the theory of the earth's sphericity." In fact, Campbell remarked, Owen's own career disproved his own theory: "Mr. Owen was himself educated in a family of Episcopalians; is he now an Episcopalian? We see that the circumstances of his education could not shackle his active mind. We see that he had broken the chains, and that his emancipated mind now walks abroad, as if it had never know a fetter. This shows that there are some geniuses formed to overcome all disadvantage, to grasp a whole system, as it were, by intuition; that in some minds there is a renovating and regenerating power, paramount even to the influence of circumstances, omnipotent as my friend represents them to be." Campbell contended that "Mr. Owen's system, as far as it has any peculiar benevolence proposed in it … is a plagiarism from Christian society."

In Owen's mechanistic society the individual counted for little; the individual had a merely functional role, like an ant in an ant-hill. Since people must worship something, Owen deified the state, which he termed "the social system," and he made human beings the creatures of that system. Campbell approached the question from the opposite side: Society existed for the individual, not the individual for society. His conception of men and women as spiritual beings, as children of God, capable of reason and the free will to make their own choices and mold their own destiny, capable of the aspiration to develop and perfect themselves in the image of their spiritual ideal was the basis of democracy; and insofar as democracy allowed the encroachment of the secular, materialistic philosophy of society, insofar would it endanger its heritage. William Penn had said that humanity would either be governed by God, or be ruled by tyrants. For so long as humanity's first loyalty was to God, to the highest good within itself, then there were definite limits to the power which an organized society might wield. Also, only the religious person, with a high concept of humanity, with a respect for his or her own dignity and that of others, with a due regard to the sacredness of the individual as a being made in the image of God, was capable of establishing and safeguarding a free and moral society. Alexander Campbell could not see the future; he could not realize to what death grips these two concepts of human beings—the spiritual and the mechanistic—would some day come. He knew the theories of Robert Owen represented a threat to the very foundation of the American way of life; he knew that the American people must not forget that the essence of liberty lies within the framework of religion.

Radical as were these differences in opinion between Campbell and Owen, the debate proceeded smoothly, and the opponents repeatedly expressed their mutual admiration for each other. But Owen also remarked to the audience that "Campbell is in the depth of mental darkness:

> blind as a mole ... his mind is completely overwhelmed with the theological learning he has been induced to acquire. Mr. Campbell has little or no practical knowledge of the present state of the human mind, or of society, out of the western districts of this country ... The most intelligent of the population of Europe never think of introducing religious subjects for argument. They are well aware that all religious mysteries and miracles are opposed to reason, and are useless for any good purpose ...

As Owen at another point succinctly expressed it: "The difference between Mr. Campbell and myself is this: I have for many years attended to nothing but facts; and Mr. Campbell to nothing

but imagination." All of his own ideas, Owen was unalterably convinced, were not theories but established facts while all of
Campbell's arguments rested on mere fancy. "Mr. Campbell's
learning and ingenuity seemed to me mere wordy wanderings ...
I could not ... prevent myself feeling the baseless fabric of the
whole of his fanciful vision."

On the morning of the fifth day of debate, Friday, the 17th,
Owen finished reading the manuscript elucidating his "cause,"
and he suggested that Campbell, without the usual half-hour
interruptions, should take the floor as long as he wished. The
moderators concurred, and Campbell was pleased with the opportunity to resent his case in connected form. He began his connected address about a half-hour before the noon adjournment on
Friday. The debate reconvened at three, and Campbell spoke the
entire afternoon. On Saturday morning he launched into his subject, and he continued until evening when the debate was
adjourned until Monday. On the intervening Sunday he delivered
the morning sermon in the Methodist Church (of which Owen
later remarked, "Never did I see so much fine talent so miserably
misdirected."). On Monday morning Campbell resumed speaking. He yielded the floor to Owen on Monday evening at four
o'clock. In all, his speech had occupied a little more than twelve
hours.

Campbell began with the "historic evidence of the Christian
religion." With scientific care he arrayed the testimony of an
imposing number of the church fathers of the first three centuries along with a brief outline of the prophetic evidences. But
it was the third grand topic of his speech—"The genius and tendency of the Christian religion"—which carried Campbell to
his highest eloquence. "A free, a just and equitable government," he declared, "has always developed the powers of the
human mind ... Political and civil liberties are essential to the
expansion and development of the human intellect. All history
is appealed to in proof of this. To this liberty we ascribe the great

improvements in all the arts of civilized and social life." Campbell contended it was not the skeptics, but to the liberalizing tendencies of true Christianity, that man was "most indebted for the improvements in government." Christianity alone, he said, was predicated upon a "philosophic view" of the whole man, of all the facets of human nature. Campbell concluded his twelve hour oration with his most biting analysis of the weaknesses of Owen's "social system."

> I feel too much interest in the eternal welfare of my fellow-creatures to remain a mere passive spectator. I feel myself called upon to put on the armor of reason, true philosophy, and religion, and to stand to my post, lest in the midst of such morbid excitements, in this age of extravagant theory and licentious philosophy, many over-ardent minds might be allured by the speciousness and false glare of this tinseled philosophy, which, I trust, we have shown to be any thing else but consentaneous with the constitution, experience and history of the world.

Even Owen found himself impressed by this lengthy and eloquent exhibition of his opponent's creed, and his first words that Monday afternoon were generous:

> That which I admire in him above all, is his downright honesty and fairness in what he believes to be the cause of truth. Now, this is a straightforward proceeding in the investigation of truth, which I have long sought, but which until now, I have sought in vain. The friends of truth, therefore, on whichever side of the question it may be found are now more indebted to Mr. Campbell than any other Christian minister of the present day.

The debate continued all through the next day, Tuesday, the 21st, as each of the opponents, in conclusion, summarized his most pertinent arguments. The polite and decorous behavior of the audience, might, Campbell felt, have one bad effect. Owen and others might take their calmness for apathy, might assume that they embraced Owen's position and were exhibiting "the social indifference of fatalism." He wished to have the matter settled before the debate ended. So he made a proposition: All those who believed in Christianity and wished to see it "pervade the world" should stand up; there was, said the reporter, "an almost universal rising up." Then he asked who were "doubtful of the truth of the Christian religion" to stand, three arose. Chagrined by this show of support for religion, Owen commented tartly, "Truth requires no such support."

Mrs. Trollope concluded her account of the debate with the remarks:

> ... it was said, that at the end of fifteen meetings, the numerical amount of the Christians and infidels remained exactly what it was when they began. This was a result that might have been perhaps anticipated; but what was much less to have been expected, neither of the disputants ever appeared to lose their temper. I was told they were much in each other's company, constantly dining together, and on all occasions expressed most cordially their mutual esteem.
>
> All this I think could have only happened in America. I am not quite sure that it was very desirable it should have happened anywhere.

But most of the citizens of the West, contrary to Mrs. Trollope, had thought the discussion desirable and were mightily pleased at its results. Timothy Flint, one of the moderators of the debate chosen by Owen, wrote a report for his *Western Monthly Review* in which he found Campbell "self-possessed, quick of apprehension and at retort" but did not like his severely logical way of building up his religious system." According to Flint's biographer, "The liberality of Campbell's theological views was the one thing that especially attracted Flint to this west theologian." He concluded his review by expressing the hope "that the empire of bigotry in this quarter will be shaken to its center; that the two extremes of Calvinism and Atheism will be alike rejected by the sober good sense of the people ..." These concluding remarks from Flint brought him into disrepute with the orthodox Presbyterians, and a few months later found him active in forming the "First Congregational Church" in Cincinnati.

Campbell liked the report of the debate in the newspaper *The Cincinnati Chronicle and Literary Gazette*—"the fullest and upon the whole, the most satisfactory I have seen." Said the *Chronicle*:

> All admit that the talent, the skill in debate, and the weight of proof were on the side of Mr. Campbell. Those who believed this philosopher [Owen] of circumstances and parallelograms to be a great man, appeared to be sadly disappointed; any of those inclined to his theory of social compacts have relapsed into a state of sanity; while the disciples of infidelity have either been shaken in their faith, or mismanagement and feebleness.

In contrast, the *Chronicle's* estimate of Campbell was flattering indeed:

> ... He is undoubtedly a man of fine talents, and equally fine attainments. With an acute, vigorous mind, quick perceptions, and rapid powers of combination, he has sorely puzzled his antagonist, and at the same time both delighted and instructed his audience by his master-

ly defense of the truth, divine origin, and inestimable importance of Christianity.

As soon as the debate was over, Alexander Campbell hurried back to Bethany and to Selina. But as the discussion did not close until the 21^{st,} and Margaret Brown was born on the 23rd, Selina had to bear her first child without the reassuring presence of her husband.

Thomas Campbell, anxious to turn to account the interest aroused by his son's discussion, remained in Cincinnati several weeks preaching and baptizing all whom he could convert. Robert Owen also stayed in Cincinnati about two weeks to correct and rewrite the stenographer's report of his speeches. Part of this time was spent very pleasantly with Thomas Campbell to whom Owen referred as the "reverend gentleman." "There is something so kind and evidently sincere in his manners, that I had great pleasure in all my communications with him."

After this fortnight in Cincinnati it seems that Owen made a second visit to Bethany, concerning which Selina wrote:

> Mr. Owen ... manifested his natural kindness of heart in coming to our house and spending several days writing up and comparing notes. He was courteous and affable, but consistent in his course, for although he conversed freely, yet he retired before worship, not taking any part, shunning to be present either morning or evening at the family devotions.

Following this visit Owen went on to Washington to seek an audience with Andrew Jackson and Secretary of State Martin Van Buren, while Campbell settled down to the labor of preparing the debate for the press.

It was a task he had not sought, being as he said "already oppressed with much more than an adequate share of business." According to original plans, a Mr. Gould of Philadelphia was to have published some twenty or thirty thousand copies of the debate for his services as reporter. But Owen tarried so long in Jamaica that Gould despaired of his arriving in Cincinnati in time for the debate and broke the contract. Campbell then offered the same proposition to Charles Simms, a Cincinnati reporter, who declined. Owen and Campbell were compelled to publish the work themselves. But Owen, wishing to return to Europe, requested that Campbell buy out his interest in the work, and thus Campbell became sole proprietor.

Owen made a strange maneuver. When he arrived in Bethany after his fortnight in Cincinnati, he had presented the astonished Campbell with a booklet whose title page bore the grandiose legend:

Robert Owen's Opening Speech and his Reply to the Rev. Alex. Campbell, in the Recent Public Discussion in Cincinnati, to prove that the Principles of all Religions are erroneous, and that their practice is injurious to the Human Race. Also Mr. Owen's memorial to the Republic of Mexico, and a Narrative of the proceedings thereon, which led to the promise of the Mexican Government, to place a District, one hundred and fifty miles broad, along the whole line of frontier bordering on the U. States, under Mr. Owen's jurisdiction, for the purpose of establishing A New Political and Moral System of Government founded of the Laws of Nature as explained in the above debate with Mr. Campbell.

Cincinnati: Published for Robert Owen and sold by all Booksellers in America and Europe, 1829.

The title would be dramatically changed.

Debate
On the
Evidences of Christianity
Contains
An Examination
of the
Social System
and of
All the Systems of Skepticism of Ancient and Modern Times
Robert Owen
Alexander Campbell
Printed and published by Alexander Campbell, 1829

Campbell issued contracts for materials, type, and press. He was very well pleased with stenographer Simm's report of the discussion. Campbell did not doubt the importance of the discussion, announcing in *The Christian Baptist* "To say the least, it was perhaps the most interesting discussion which has occurred since the Reformation ... No work of the same kind can be found in any language or country." The October issue announced that the debate was out of press and on its way to six different bookbinders. As he had to send part of the debate out of his office to be printed, Campbell divided it into two volumes, the two were bound in one book. Owen having spoken fifteen hours during the debate and Campbell twenty-five, the two volumes totaled 551 pages.

The published debate immediately found a large audience. One of the many letters of commendation: "I believe you have a duty to perform in this age of immense magnitude; Nothing less than that of placing Religion on her native seat of common sense. While reading your evidences of Christianity, I was of opinion that you ought to visit every town and village in the United States, and preach to the people." So rapidly did the copies of the debate sell, that before 1829 had expired, a second edition was published.

CONCLUDING REMARKS.

TO the co-operation of a few friends, under the divine government, is to be ascribed the success which has accompanied this first effort to restore a pure speech to the people of God—to restore the ancient order of things in the christian kingdom—to emancipate the conscience from the dominion of human authority in matters of religion, and to lay a foundation, an imperishable foundation, for the union of all christians, and for their co-operation in spreading the glorious gospel throughout the world. I had but very humble hopes, I can assure the public, the day I wrote the first essay or the preface for this work, that I could at all succeed in gaining a patient hearing. But I have been entirely disappointed. The success attendant on this effort has produced a hope which once I dared not entertain, that a blissful revolution can be effected. It has actually begun, and such a one as cannot fail to produce a state of society far surpassing in the fruits of righteousness, and peace, and joy, any result of any former religious revolution, since the great apostacy from christian institutions.

Having been educated as Presbyterian clergymen generally are, and looking forward to the ministry as both an honorable and useful calling, all my expectations and prospects in future life were, at the age of twenty-one, identified with the office of the ministry. But scarcely had I begun to make sermons, when I discovered that the religion of the New Testament was one thing, and that of any sect which I knew, was another. I could not proceed. An unsuccessful effort by my father to reform the presbytery and synod to which he belonged, made me despair of reformation. I gave it up as a hopeless effort: but did not give up speaking in public assemblies upon the great articles of christian faith and practice. In the hope, the humble hope, of erecting a single congregation with which I could enjoy the social institutions, I labored. I had not the remotest idea of being able to do more than this; and, therefore, I betook myself to the occupation of a farmer, and for a number of years attended to this profession as a means of subsistence, and labored every Lord's day to separate the truth from the traditions of men, and to persuade men to give up their fables for the truth—with but little success I labored.

When pressed by some of the most influential Baptists in the cities of New York and Philadelphia, in the year 1816, to settle in one of those cities, I declined the friendly offers and kind persuasions of both Deacon Withington of New York and Deacon Shields of Philadelphia, alleging that I could not take the charge of any church in those cities, because I did not think they would submit to the government of Jesus Christ, or to the primitive order of things. They asked me what that order was. I gave them my views. To which neither of them objected. Deacon Withington alluded to Mr. M'Clay's church in that city as practising in part that order; and said that for himself he preferred it. I replied that however well disposed he might be towards it, I could not

The first and final paragraphs of Campbell's concluding remarks in The Christian Baptist.

The October issue of *The Christian Baptist* contained Campbell's "Proposals" for a new magazine. It was to be named *The Millennial Harbinger*. Its object, according to the "Prospectus," was

think that many of the members of that church would (Mr. Williams' it was then,) and rather than produce divisions among them, or adopt the order of things then fashionable in that city, I would live and die in the backwoods. The same or similar remarks were made to Deacon Shields in Philadelphia.

Such were my views and feelings at that time, and so slight were the hopes which I entertained of seeing the least impression made upon the kingdom of the clergy. But my own mind labored under the pernicious influence of scholastic divinity, and the Calvinian metaphysics; and although I greatly desired to stand perfect and complete in the knowledge of the will of God, and my conscience could bow to nothing but the authority of the King Eternal, yet a full emancipation from the traditions of the elders I had not experienced. This was as gradual as the approaches of Spring.

In the year 1820 when solicited to meet Mr. Walker on the subject of baptism, I hesitated for about six months whether it were lawful thus to defend the truth. I was written to *three* times before I gained my own consent. I did not like controversy so well as many have since thought I did; and I was doubtful of the effects it might have upon society. These difficulties were, however, overcome, and we met. It was not until after I discovered the effects of that discussion, that I began to hope that something might be done to rouse this generation from its supineness and spiritual lethargy. About two years afterwards I conceived the plan of this work, and thought I should make the experiment. I did so, and the effects are now before the public.

Little is done, it is true, compared with what is yet to be done; but that little is a great deal compared with the opposition made, and the shortness of the time in which it has been done. He that sails against both wind and tide sails slowly, and if he advance at all it must be by great exertion of the mariners. The storm now rages more than at any former period; but the current is more favorable. The winds of doctrine are raging up on the great sea; but they are continually shifting, and though we may be tossed and driven sometimes out of our course, the vessel is good, the Pilot the most skilful, so we cannot fear to reach the desired haven.

Many apologies ought to be made for the execution of the prospectus of this work. Things changed so much from our expectations that we were compelled to change with them. Our series of essays upon some topics were much shorter and longer between, than was contemplated. The publication of two debates, and of two editions of the New Testament, unexpected when we issued our proposals, distracted our attentions, and so increased my labors, that more was done than could be done well. The compositions for this work were almost universally written in the despatch of ordinary letter writing, the half of an essay being often in type, or in the press, before the other half of it was conceived or written. During the last two months we have issued three numbers of the Millennial Harbinger, and this is the sixth number of this work in nearly the same period. Besides we have written scores of long letters. These things ought not to have been so, but a wil-

to combat skeptics and sectarianism, and to develop and introduce "that political and religious order of society called THE MILLENNIUM, which will be the consummation of that amelioration of society proposed in the Christian scriptures." Besides this grand object, the work proposed to help disentangle the Scriptures "from the perplexities of the commentators and system-makers of the dark ages;" to give general religious news and reviews of religious publi-

lingness to do all that the most unremitting attentions could do, and the demands upon our services in various departments having been so urgent, we were compelled to undertake too much. We hope to avoid these excesses of labor in future, and to rally and concentrate our energies upon one work.

Many subjects introduced into this work have not been fully and systematically discussed. General views have been submitted, rather than full developements and defences. Not a single topic has received that finish, or that elucidation which it is in the compass of our means to bestow upon it. Many queries are not formally and fully answered which have been proposed; though most of them, if not formally replied to, are still substantially discussed in some of the essays in this work, such as that proposed by 'A Friend' in the present number, page 273. I have thought if life should be prolonged, and an opportunity offer, that I would one day revise this work, and have a second a edition of it published, with such emendations as experience and observation might suggest.

I have commenced a new work, and taken a new name for it on various accounts. Hating sects and sectarian names, I resolved to prevent the name of *Christian Baptists* from being fixed upon us, to do which, efforts were making. It is true, men's tongues are their own, and they may use them as they please; but I am resolved to give them no just occasion for nicknaming advocates for the ancient order of things. My sheet admonishes me that I must close, and as usual on such occasions I ought to return than's to all those who have aided in the circulation of this work and patronized it, were it not that I cannot consider it as a favor done to me. Those who write for a subsistence should feel grateful to those who sustain them; but the patrons of this work, its real friends, were actuated by other considerations, than personal respect for me; and as it was not to sustain an individual, but to promote the truth they bestowed their patronage, I can only say that the God of truth has blessed them, and will bless them, having acted sincerely in this matter. To him I commend them, and to him to whom I owe my being, and all that I call mine, to whom I have vowed allegiance never to be recalled, to him I will now and forever ascribe praise for the good which he has made me to enjoy, and for the good, if any, he has enabled me to do to others. I have found myself blessed in this undertaking—my heart has been enlarged, and no reader of the Christian Baptist, I think, will ever derive more advantage from it, than I have from the writing and conducting of it. To Jesus Christ my Lord be everlasting praise!

EDITOR.

cations; and to present a miscellanea of "religious, moral and literary varieties." Campbell had no intention of restricting his new magazine to questions that were exclusively religious in nature. A man of many interests himself, he expected to discuss whatever educational, social, and even political issues he thought concerned the spiritual welfare of humanity. He listed among subjects to be addressed: "The injustice which yet remains in many of the politi-

THE

MILLENNIAL HARBINGER,

EDITED BY

ALEXANDER CAMPBELL,

I saw another messenger flying through the midst of heaven, having everlasting good news to proclaim to the inhabitants of the earth, even to every nation
and tribe, and tongue, and people—saying with a loud voice, Fear God and
give glory to him, for the hour of his judgments is come: and worship him who
made heaven, and earth, and sea, and the fountains of water.—John.
Great is the truth and mighty above all things, and will prevail.

VOL. I.

BETHANY, VA.

PRINTED AND PUBLISHED BY THE EDITOR.

1830,

Proposal for the Millennial Harbinger *as it appeared on pages sixty-two and sixty-three of the final issue of* The Christian Baptist *in 1829. The first page of the* Millennial Harbinger *as it appeared in 1830, Volume I.*

cal regulations under the best political governments," as well as, "The inadequacy of all the present systems of education, literary and moral, to develop the powers of the human mind, and to prepare man for rational and social happiness." Finally, to bring these rather high-sounding generalities down into the realm of the concrete, and to prove that in his new publication he had no intention

PROPOSALS,

By Alexander Campbell for publishing by subscription, a monthly paper, to be denominated "THE MILLENNIAL HARBINGER."

PROSPECTUS.

THIS work shall be devoted to the destruction of sectarianism, infidelity, and antichristian doctrine and practice. It shall have for its object the developement and introduction of that political and religious order of society called THE MILLENNIUM, which will be the consummation of that amelioration of society proposed in the christian scriptures.

Subservient to this most comprehensive object, the following subjects shall be attended to:—

1. The incompatibility of any sectarian establishment, now known on earth, with the genius of the glorious age to come.

2. The inadequacy of all the present systems of education, literary and moral, to develope the powers of the human mind, and to prepare man for rational and social happiness.

3. The disentanglement of the Holy Scriptures from the perplexites of the commentators and system-makers of the dark ages. This will call for the analysis of several books in the New Testament, and many disquisitions upon the appropriated sense of the leading terms and phrases in the Holy Scriptures and in religious systems.

4. The *injustice* which yet remains in many of the political regulations under the best political governments, when contrasted with the *justice* which christianity proposes, and which the millennial order of society promises.

5. Disquisitions upon the treatment of African slaves, as preparatory to their emancipation, and exaltation from their present degraded condition.

6. General religious news, or regular details of the movements of the religious combinations, acting under the influence of the proselyting spirit of the age.

7. Occasional notices of religious publications, including reviews of new works, bearing upon any of the topics within our precincts.

8. Answers to interesting queries of general utility, and notices of all things of universal interest to all engaged in the proclamation of the *Ancient Gospel*, and the *Restoration of the Ancient Order of Things*.

9. Miscellanea, or religious, moral, and literary varieties.

Much of the useful learning which has been sanctified to the elucidation of those interesting and sublime topics of christian expectation, will, we intend, be gleaned from the christian labors of those distinguished men of liberal minds, who are ranked among the most renowned fathers of christian literature; and much aid is expected from a few of the more enlightened brethren of our own time, who are fellow-laborers and pioneers in hastening this wished-for period. It is intended to give every family into which this work shall come, so much of the religious news of the day, and such a variety of information on all the topics submitted, as to make it a work of much interest to the young and inquisitive.

of side-stepping a discussion of even the most controversial of all the social and political problems facing the country, he also promised his readers; "Disquisitions upon the treatment of African slaves, as preparatory to their emancipation and exaltation from their present degraded condition." Those who had followed closely the full career of the little press on the Buffaloe might have remembered, this was not editor Campbell's first declaration on the subject of slavery. Indeed, writing the introductory essay to the very first num-

Vol. VII   THE CHRISTIAN BAPTIST.   63

The indulgence and patronage which have been extended to me as editor of the *Christian Baptist*, embolden me to attempt a work of still greater magnitude, expecting that if that work, written, as the greater part of it was, under very disadvantageous circumstances, and while my attention was divided between other works and a multiplicity of other business, obtained so general a circulation, and was so well received—a work to which a much larger portion of my energies shall be devoted, will not fail of obtaining, at least, an equal patronage, and of proving proportionably more useful, as the range will be so much greater, and the object one in which all christians, of every name, must feel interested; and, especially, as there is not perhaps, in the christian world, any work published with the same design, and embracing the same outlines.

CONDITIONS.

Having purchased a large fount of beautiful new type, of a good medium size, and a first-rate new printing press, we may promise a beautiful impression, on good paper.

1. Each number shall contain 48 pages large duodecimo, equal to a medium octavo, or equal in superficies to more than 63 pages of the Christian Baptist. Being printed on super-royal paper, it will cost to the subscribers only twice as much postage as the Christian Baptist, though containing more than twice and a half times as much matter. With a good index it will make a volume of 600 pages per annum.

2. It shall be published on the first Monday of every month—the first number to be issued on the first Monday of January, 1830.—Each number shall be stitched in a good cover; and all numbers failing to reach their destination shall be made good at the expense of the editor.

3. It shall cost, exclusive of postage, Two Dollars and Fifty Cents per annum, to all who do not pay until the close of the year, but to those who pay in advance, or within six months after subscribing, Two Dollars will be accepted.

4. Postmasters, who act as agents, shall have ten per cent. for obtaining subscribers, and for collecting, and remitting the amount of their subscriptions.

5. All other persons, who obtain and pay for five subscribers, within six months from subscribing, shall have one copy gratis. But to those who do not guarantee and pay within that period, ten per cent. on all the subscribers, for whom they make payment, shall be allowed.

6. Persons who subscribe at any time within the year, will be furnished with the volume from the commencement. And no person, unless at the discretion of the editor, shall be permitted to withdraw until arrearages are paid.

7. All who do not notify their discontinuance to our agents in such time that we may be informed a month before the close of each volume, will be considered as subscribers for the next volume.

N. B. Let all subscribers be careful to name the post-office to which they wish their papers sent.

ber of *The Christian Baptist*, he had in a paragraph painted a dark and bitter picture of "glaring inconsistencies" of Christendom in which central place went to

those Christians who are daily extolling the blessings of civil and religious liberty, and at the same time, by a system of the most cruel oppression, separating the wife from the embraces of her husband, and the mother from her

It is contemplated to issue the first number of this work bearing date the first Monday of January. It may not, however, appear till late in the month, as circumstances which we cannot control have thrown us back in our calculations. The 7th volume will not be finished before the first number of the *Millennial Harbinger* appears. As this enlarged periodical is undertaken at the request of many of our friends, we will follow the following rule in addressing the first number of it, unless otherwise directed:—

1. To all persons who have taken and paid for the back volumes of the Christian Baptist, or who have been subscribers from its commencement, and have paid up to the close of the sixth or seventh volume.

2. To all who have subscribed for the Millennial Harbinger, and forwarded to us their subscription before the end of December

If we should send the first number to any other persons than those above specified, or to any who do not think it worthy of their patronage and support, they will please send it back to us, and we will then desist; otherwise we shall consider them as authorizing us to send it, and as bound, on the principle of justice, to pay for it. It rust it will prove itself worthy of the patronage of all the intelligent and benevolent friends of humanity and religion into whose hands it may fall.

Those holding subscriptions will please to return them on or before the first day of December next; and those wishing to be supplied with proposals, shall be furnished on their application by letters to us. Whatever numbers of the seventh volume are wanting to complete it after the first of January will be as speedily forwarded as possible after that date. We wish to begin the new work with the new year, as more consistent with easy arrangement and keeping of accounts.   EDITOR.

BETHANY, Brooke county, Va. 1829.

FOR THE CHRISTIAN BAPTIST.
ELECTION.—No. III.

THE following sentence is found in our last essay: "Having ascertained in a summary way, the elector, the person first elected, the ends of the election, the time when it began, and when it shall terminate, I shall speak of the principle on which it proceeds," &c. Let us then speak of the principle on which a person might, at any time, be admitted into the elect institution, or church of God and Christ.

1. This election divides itself into two great departments, the Jewish and Christian churches, the *first* receiving its members on the gross, limited, and partial principle of *flesh*, i. e. relationship to Abraham by the line of Isaac and Jacob. The *second*, admitting its members on the exalting, universal, and impartial principle of *faith* in Jesus Christ.

2. The election of individuals to church privileges in the first of these principles, viz: Fleshly relationship can be justified only by the fact that the infancy of the world, the rudeness of the age, &c. rendered the introduction of the higher and more refining principle of faith, if not impossible, at least altogether impolitic, in regard to the ends to be accomplished by the institution

tender offspring; violating every principle, and rending every tie that endears life and reconciles man to his lot; and that, forsooth, because *might gives right*, and a man is held guilty because his skin is a shade darker that the standard color of the times.

After this original declaration he had returned to the subject no more, perhaps thinking he had his hands full enough in this first

The building constructed by Alexander Campbell to house the printing operation for his new magazine, the Millennial Harbinger. *It is located one block east of the old church in Bethany.*

venture with trying to persuade the public to a more rational view of "Original Christianity." But with the advent of the *Harbinger* he was determined, as the "Proposals" pledged, to lift his voice until the nightmare of slavery should be banished and all alike be free to pursue the American dream of liberty and happiness.

The "Proposals" also gave more interesting details concerning the new monthly periodical. *The Christian Baptist* had not been very much to look at, but Campbell meant *The Millennial Harbinger* to be inspiring to the eye as well as to the mind. "Having purchased," he said, "a large font of beautiful new type, of a good medium size, and a first-rate new printing press, we may promise a beautiful impression, on good paper." His old press and plant had served him well. By the time the seventh volume of *The Christian Baptist* was completed, no less than forty-six thousand volumes, according to the estimate of Dr. Richardson, would have issued from this little country printing office. But Alexander was determined to make an entirely new beginning, so he laid plans to erect another and more imposing structure to house his new printing press. It was to be a two-story frame building, located several yards from Buffaloe Creek and on the opposite side from the mansion.

The "Proposals" further stated that the new magazine, though still small, was to be larger than the old—"48 pages large duodecimo, equal to a medium octavo" (about six by nine and a half inches)—and was to be printed on "super-royal paper," so that "it would cost to the subscribers only twice as much postage as *The Christian Baptist*, though containing more than two and a half times as much matter. With a good index, it will make a volume of 600 pages per annum." Of course, this superior publication could not sell for as low a price as the smaller magazine; rates were two dollars a year in advance or two-fifty in arrears. The editor promised that the first number would be issued on the first Monday in January 1830.

It was an optimistic promise. For Campbell well knew that the next few months would demand his attention and presence in a field far removed, both spiritually and physically, from theology and the Bethany press.

·13·

The Charms of Political Life

THE YEAR 1829 was, indeed, proving a time of dramatic events for Alexander Campbell. In April at Cincinnati, he had sought to lay low the specters of atheism and materialism in single combat with Robert Owen. In October he was to enter the political arena at Richmond to cross swords with the entrenched oligarchy of Eastern Virginia. There, in a three months' debate on the revision of Virginia's antiquated state constitution, he would match wits with John Randolph of Roanoke and sit in council with James Madison, James Monroe, and John Marshall.

With the attempt to reform Christendom on his hands, he had been careful not to divert attention to political controversy in the pages of *The Christian Baptist*. Even the two tempestuous presidential campaigns, which had been waged since the establishment of his printing press on the Buffaloe, had elicited only a single comment, in the January issue of 1825, when the editor had made a passing but scathing protest.

The aloofness of the *Baptist* from political comment was in no way to be interpreted as a lack of interest on the part of Campbell in the public affairs of the nation. Far from it. The country's leading political, as well as religious, journals found their way to his study. On those evenings when he and Selina called for their carriage and went visiting neighbors, the conversation of the menfolk was certain to turn on politics, particularly on the economic problems of the farmer and the questions of tariffs and internal improvements. Moreover, it was a rare evening that the talk did not reveal something of their growing anger and resentment over conditions in Virginia. Though as a young man, in his first flush of delight at finding himself in the New World, Campbell had written to his uncle in Ireland that "the farmer here is lord of the soil, and the most independent man on earth" Twenty years residence in the Trans-Alleghany country had taught him that his neighbors, the small farmers of western Virginia, along with artisans and other non-landholders throughout the state, by no means possessed the independence they considered their due; and the root of the trouble lay in the state constitution.

Written during the conflict and confusion of 1776 by a body not selected for that purpose, it had remained unchanged for over a half century despite repeated protests from Thomas Jefferson, and a constantly rising flood of petitions to the legislature demanding reform. The constitution, it was true, contained a Bill of Rights guaranteeing those freedoms and equalities which the founding fathers hoped to see materialize in the new republic, and for which the common soldiers of the Revolution had believed they were fighting. The Bill of Rights was appended to an undemocratic document framed to keep the power in the hands of a minority owning the bulk of the state's property in land and slaves. Representation to the General Assembly was based not on numbers but on the English idea of representation for local units—each county, regardless of size or population, sending an equal number of members to the House of Delegates. In accordance with old colonial free-hold privilege, the right of suffrage was restricted to persons owning twenty-five acres of improved or one hundred acres of unimproved land. The executive branch of government was a mere tool of the legislative: The assembly elected a governor, who shared his duties with an Executive Council of eight men. And the state judiciary was dominated by county courts with such far-reaching powers that they had become "closed corporations of leading families."

Disgruntled Virginians grew more discontented when they surveyed the states about them. Campbell himself had become aware of the sharply varying complexions of government when he first traveled westward into Ohio, Kentucky, and Tennessee. The empire had marched away from the established and conservative seaboard to bring into the federal union new states motivated by the individualistic, democratic spirit of the frontier. They came with constitutions that granted white manhood suffrage, and claimed no representation for property even when those states were in the slave-holding south-west. A reaction had swept back eastward until practically all the states recognized the rights of universal suffrage. With his liking for the broad view, Campbell could see that his course of empire in the nation had operated in miniature within the confines of Virginia. First, it was the plantation, slave-owning gentry of the two main divisions east of the Blue Ridge Mountains, the Tidewater and the Piedmont, who had largely written the constitution of 1776. They had made sure that it retained for them most of the privileges granted by royal charter to the over-lords of the Virginia colony. Then, gradually, both populations and wealth had begun to shift westward. The shift bled into the rich valley lying between the Blue Ridge and Alleghanies; and, finally, into the lands of the Trans-Alleghany. The citizens, independent yeomen owning small farms with few or no slaves and imbued with all the egalitarian spirit of their frontier neighbors farther to the West, were demanding that the abstract guarantees of the Bill of Rights be put into practical operation in their state government. Furthermore, the political leadership of western Virginia came from the Scotch-Irish. Alexander Campbell was only one of many settlers who had learned their fierce attachment to liberty through years of persecution and bloodshed in their North Ireland homeland. They had no desire to exchange oppression by the nobility of Great Britain, for control by the aristocracy of the Tidewater and Piedmont. Yet neither the letters of Thomas Jefferson, nor the reform conventions held at Staunton in 1816 and 1825 had seemed to get results until 1828. The General Assembly, at last, authorized a vote of the people, which resulted in the call for a constitutional convention.

The year 1828 was good for democracy. And democracy, as Campbell was well aware, had run a turbulent course in his adopted country. At the time of the Revolution, of course, democratic hopes had run high. Once peace was restored, Toryism had soon revived itself in Federalism with its aristocratic psychology and stake-in-society theory of government. Then the French Revolution had come to stir party passions afresh and provide a new and rich body of democratic philosophy. In 1800 the common citizens of the new American Republic had reasserted themselves and swept the Federalists from office in order to make the author of the Declaration of Independence their chief executive. Gradually, plain people had seen the stream of national benefits diverted from the public domain and channeled through government pipelines to water the private gardens of Hamiltonian gentlemen of property. Now, in 1828, the spirit of 1800 had risen to sweep the purveyors of special privilege again from office. The first man from the West was placed as president. Alexander Campbell had been a schoolboy in Ireland when the first American Revolution, by ballot, had sent Thomas Jefferson to the White House. But in 1828 he was a citizen of the United States, and his fertile acres in Brooke County entitled him to a vote, even in aristocratic Virginia. He would have a voice in this second uprising of the people as he cast his ballot for the Democrat from Tennessee.

The common faith of the West might seem on the way to becoming the common faith of America, realistic men still remembering the past, would not become prey to an easy optimism. Virginians intent on constitutional reform had no illusion about the entrenched power of their Eastern oligarchy. Their jubilation over the calling of the convention was sobered by thoughts of the grave responsibility in selecting their delegates. The convention, the legislature had decided, would be composed of ninety-six delegates, four from each of the state's twenty-four senatorial districts. It soon became evident that nothing was to be "required of the successful candidate but a character for integrity and the acknowledged possession of undoubted talent." In some cases, the people of one district were looking into others "for such men, as they thought best fitted to represent them." Everywhere the alignments of federal politics were being ignored; and Campbell soon became aware that citizens of his district were disposed to ignore religious predilections and prejudices as well.

To his surprise and somewhat to his dismay, his neighbors, foes and friends alike of his religious views, began to importune him to run for a seat in the convention. At first he rebuffed the overtures, but they continued. The men of the Virginia panhandle knew they were making no mistake in urging Alexander Campbell to represent their cause at Richmond. His approaching debate with Robert Owen was attracting national and even international attention. Of more importance was his obvious kinship, in both political principles and personal qualities, with the aggressive general in the White House. All could be sure that the combative reformer who had waged such war for a decade against clerical dominion over the people could be trusted to deal in a proper manner with the aristocratic assumptions of the East. The very ones who had smarted under his lash in *The Christian Baptist* had best reason to know that this attack would be conducted with satisfying proportions of logic and sarcasm.

On that fundamental issue was the basis of all other discussions at Richmond—the right of majority rule versus the stake-in-society theory of government—left no question to what rank of political philosophers the master of Bethany belonged. The editor who had sent independent, hard-working citizens of the West chuckling about their chores from the Western Reserve to the valley of the Tennessee by his merciless lampoon of the money-seeking clergy in "The Third Epistle of Peter" would naturally share all of Jefferson's quiet contempt for Federalist arguments for rule by "gentlemen of principle and property." Jefferson's dry rejoinder "I have never observed men's honesty to increase with their riches," was well matched in Campbell's acid observations on an avaricious priesthood, which had long since discovered that "the most artful and … effectual way to get hold of the purse, is to get a hold of the conscience." Indeed, it was obvious that the underlying stimulus of the Bethany reformation itself was the conviction that the common people, if properly informed, are capable of judging wisely for themselves. Its leader, who as a young preacher had once signed after his name the letters V.D.S, *Verbi Divini Servus* to shame the lordly D.D.'s of a reverend synod, was clearly of a mind and temper with that redoubtable Yankee poet and journalist, Philip Freneau. Freneau put to shame the pretensions the tie-wig Federalists had attached to his pen-name, Peter Slender, the letters, O.S.M., One of the Swinish Multitude. Now, in issue after issue of the *Baptist*, Campbell was warning those who would keep the people in ecclesiastical bondage in words almost identical with fiery Sam Adam's warning to the Colonial Tories, "in these times of Light and Liberty, every man chuses to see and judge for himself." The men of his district, intent on sending to Richmond only those delegates certain to fight for the essentials of Jeffersonian-Jacksonian democracy, urged Alexander Campbell to enter the race for a convention seat. They were completely confident that he fully shared with Jackson, a belief in the right of linsey-woolen to be equal with broadcloth and that he, actuated by the same Puritan conviction of the sacredness of stewardship, would, like their president, return to the people who put their trust in him an honest reckoning of that trust.

At length Campbell had allowed himself to be persuaded. If he had been slow to consent, there had been nothing coy in his hesitancy. With the Owen debate and its subsequent publication at hand, he knew that he would have little time for proper study of the constitutional questions at issue. In any event—as he wrote concerning the decision to his old friend William Tener in Ireland—he truly had "no taste or longings for political matters or honors." Yet he had to admit the weight of the argument pressed by friends of his candidacy: That the issues to be decided at Richmond were "not like the ordinary affairs of legislation," rather they, concerned "the most grave and solemn of all political matters," involving the fundamental law and liberty of the state. Advocates of his religious views added another, eminently practical argument: that the most distinguished men of Virginia were sure to sit in the convention. Therefore, his presence there, far from compromising his dignity as a religious teacher, would give him a unique opportunity to advance the cause of reform. Attuned to this point, Campbell frankly and cannily admitted to Tener that he was well aware that a seat in the convention offered an excellent means, as he phrased it, "of gaining an influence in public estimation to give currency to my writings, and to put down some calumnies afar off that I was not in good standing in my own State." But these were not to be the decisive factors impelling him into politics. For a long time he had been concerned over what he considered Virginia's two major failures in the realm of human rights—the failures to educate her children and to free her slaves. It was, therefore, in the hope of helping write a new constitution for his state which would contain provisions for "a system of common school education" and, which more importantly, would lay "a foundation for the abolition of slavery" that he finally consented to announce his candidacy.

At first the campaign went smoothly enough. The senatorial district in which Campbell lived was comprised of five counties— Ohio, Preston Tyler, Monongalia, and Brooke—would be represented by four delegates. The choice of one of the four delegates was a foregone conclusion. Philip Doddridge, a Wellsburg attorney who already represented his district in the United States Congress and had previously served three terms in the Virginia House of Delegates, was generally expected to take a seat in Richmond as the great champion of the West. The congressman was a brother of Campbell's good friend, Dr. Joseph Doddridge, the Episcopal minister at Wellsburg. Campbell entered the race with the understanding that he had the support of Philip Doddridge and, therefore, he would have to do little active campaigning to assure his seat.

The elections in the five counties were to be held not simultaneously but successively. They began soon after Campbell's return home at the close of the Owen debate in Cincinnati on April 20. Ohio County held the first balloting. Campbell was present at the polls on election day and was one of the four successful candidates, receiving more votes than either of Ohio's own candidates, one of whom was Samuel Sprigg, a lawyer of Wheeling and a personal friend of Philip Doddridge. Nevertheless, Doddridge seemed pleased with the results, according to a letter that Campbell wrote to his personal friend, Colonel Charles S.

Morgan of Morgantown, who was also a candidate for the convention. "After the Ohio election," wrote Campbell, "Doddridge promised to aid my election all in his power ... and said that he would personate me in Brooke and Tyler—and that if I and he were elected there was nothing to be feared from the Eastern oligarchy." Preston County next held its election; again Campbell was present at the polls and received "a large majority" over both the candidates from Ohio County. On election day in Tyler County, Campbell was not present—perhaps because of Doddridge's promise to "personate" him there. As a result, many citizens in the county did not know he was a candidate, and he "therefore got but few votes in it."

The defeat in Tyler presaged a radical change in the whole complexion of the campaign. Doddridge withdrew his support of Campbell, and Campbell—after firing a volley of protests in letters to Doddridge—took actively to the hustings. Loyalty to friendship on the part of both men was at the root of the trouble. Doddridge, for some reason not publicly explained, was violently opposed to the candidacy of Campbell's friend, Colonel Morgan. Campbell, also for reasons not publicly explained, was equally opposed to the candidacy both of Samuel Sprigg and Eugenius M. Wilson, another lawyer and close personal friend of Doddridge's. The rift apparently began when Campbell, accompanied by his brother-in-law, Horatio N. Bakewell, had an interview with Doddridge just after returning from the Preston elections. Campbell reported in a letter to Morgan, "Bakewell ... heard Doddridge say to me that he hoped I would not recommend you to the citizens of Brooke; and ... he would not be obliged to come out at the election and expose you—but if compelled he would tell such a story as would put you down in Brooke and ought to put you down in the District. This was evidently said to deter me from recommending you." Naturally, considering Campbell's temperament, the threat had the opposite effect and no doubt precipitated his open opposition to Sprigg and Wilson. In any event,

Campbell's report to Morgan continued, "As soon as the Result of the Preston and Tyler election was known, he [Doddridge] and Campbell [Dr. John Campbell, of Wellsburg] changed their tone all at once—and began to oppose me as coming in contact [conflict?] with Sprigg ... As soon as I recommended you and opposed Wilson and Sprigg all the lawyer interest in Brooke was put in requisition against me." If by this marshalling of forces the opposition hoped to drive the Bethany theologian from the field, they very little understood his character. Marshalling his own forces, he determined, at all hazard, to win the elections in the remaining counties of Monongalia and Brooke despite the opposition of the most popular men in the district; and the campaign became a battle.

As he could scarcely hope to personally canvass all the voters, his printing press was put to excellent use in the preparation of handbills for distribution throughout the two counties. Though he might be a political novice, the printed *Address To the Citizen of Monongalia County, Virginia*, which he issued on May 20, six days prior to the election there, proved that he could frame a vigorous republican document as effectively in the political field as in the religious. The opening paragraph shrewdly played upon the fact that he had no personal political aspirations to distract him at Richmond from the exclusive service of the "Fellow Citizens":

> YOU are now called upon to commit the most important trust have ever confided to any political representative ... The importance of this crisis ... [has] compelled me to consent to have my name laid before you; although, as may be known to all, I have never sought political offices, honors, or profits; nor do I now ... I have been long known to some of you as the advocate of religious liberty, and as an opposer of all clerical and sectarian intolerance; and in the private circle I have always been an advocate of republican principles, of internal improvements and domestic manufactures ... I have long wished

A *Campaign Address by Alexander Campbell published in the Brooke County papers during his campaign to become a delegate to the Virginia Constitutional Convention in 1829.*

for the arrival of time when this state might be politically renovated. I believe that time has come, and ... that I can contribute to this political regeneration, and, therefore ... I have, for this once, but for this once, consented to become a candidate for your suffrages.

The body of the handbill described the "system of reform" comprising his platform. He called upon the testimony of "the immortal Jefferson" to enforce his advocacy of "the abolition of the present county court system ... [to divest] this little county aristocracy of its wide dominion over our purses and our liberties," and of "the removal of the executive council, those *political drones* which eat so much of the people's honey ... without carrying a drop ... to the hive," and to the discerning there was a hint of his feeling about slavery in the phrasing of his advocacy of "the extension of the right of suffrage to every free *white* (I am sorry that I have to use the words *free white*,) male of twenty-one." The last paragraph returned to the theme of the first and, with only a passing reference to the opposition (to note that he had "outpolled Mr. Sprigg in his own county"), he closed in proper confident vein:

> ... Being known never to have sought for political honors; to have plead the cause of reform before it was popular; to have always been in the ranks of the republicans before and during the last way; I can hazard nothing in submitting my pretensions to republicans ... I only wish to ... assure you that, if elected, my best efforts shall be devoted to your interests, which, in this case, are perfectly identified with my own.

Monday, May 25, election day in Monongalia County, found Campbell at one of the most doubtful and important precincts. There, too, was Samuel Sprigg, eager to harangue the voters. He took the platform first, and after some pointed remarks on the gen-

eral unfitness of a preacher to fill such a political trust, he des-
canted learnedly and at great length the technical aspects of the
subjects of suffrage and the basis of representation. When he finally sat down, little time remained for Campbell to speak. But it was
time enough. Before him was an audience of farmers, weary and
bored by the lawyer's long doctrinal disquisition. With astuteness
worthy a more veteran politician, Campbell chose the words
surest to please and make sense to them.

First he won their laughter, with a few sharp sallies that disposed of his opponent's remarks on the clergy, and suggested several reasons why the legal profession might not be worthy to merit
the exclusive confidence of the public. Then he began to talk
plainly of the economic basis of politics and of the simple fact that
each state's "own peculiar interests" must govern the course of its
legislation:

> If the people of Virginia, he said, were a manufactur-
> ing community, then its legislation should be directed to
> the fostering and protecting of manufactures. If we were a
> commercial people, then the interests of commerce
> should demand our special attention. But, gentlemen,
> our State ... contains almost exclusively an agricultural
> population, and I hence argue that the interests of the
> farmer should be chiefly considered in whatever changes
> may be proposed in the organic law ... while my oppo-
> nent has been descanting upon the white basis and the
> black basis, you will permit me to observe that agriculture
> is with us the true basis of prosperity and power, and that
> the honest farmer, who by his daily toil increases the
> wealth and well-being of the commonwealth, becomes its
> truest benefactor.

If he continued a while to enlarge on the dignity and virtue
inherent in a farmer's life, and remarked on the furrows down

which his own hand had guided the plow, there were perhaps none present to accuse him of demagoguery. It was well known that the editor and theologian on the Buffaloe was also a working a farmer, who often happily forsook his books and studies for his fields and flocks. It was common knowledge that he had more than once refused flattering offers from the city to remain close on the quiet land among his Virginia hills. But while he spoke eloquently, in whole agreement with Jefferson's dictum, that, "Those who labor in the earth are the chosen people of God," and the surest guardians of the state's welfare and independence, he also, out of regard to the lateness of the hour, spoke briefly and to the point. He closed with an anecdote from his youth to drive home his final point that the farmer's interest should be chiefly consulted. Campbell noted, it's the farmer "who has to bear at last the burdens of government:"

When a lad on a visit to the city of Belfast, I recollect that my attention was particularly engaged by a large sign over one of its extensive stores. This sign contained four large painted figures. The first was a picture of the king and his royal robes, with the crown upon his head, and the legend issuing from his mouth, 'I reign for all.' Next to him was the figure of a bishop, in gown and surplice, with the inscription, 'I pray for all.' The third was a soldier in his regimentals standing by a canon and uttering the words, 'I fight for all.' But the fourth figure, gentlemen, was the most noteworthy and important of all in this pictorial representation of the relations of the different parts of human society. It represented a farmer, amidst the utensils of his calling, standing by his plough and exclaiming, 'I pay for all!'

To the sound of cheers and laughter, Campbell took his seat. The voting began—the votes being cast by acclamation, not by written ballot—and nothing save the name of "Campbell" was heard for so long that it seemed the election would be unanimous. When at last a lone voter came forward and announced the name, "Sprigg," the lawyer proved he could take defeat in gentlemanly fashion. He arose, bowed pleasantly toward his supporter, and remarked, "I thank the gentleman for his vote, for I was really beginning to think you had all forgotten that I am a candidate."

The campaign in Brooke County also went well as Campbell expected, though not without heated skirmishing. His printed address to the citizens of Brooke, unlike the Monongalia handbill, dealt sharply with his opponents. In any event, the broadside so incensed Doddridge that by election day in Wellsburg, he had lost his accustomed joviality in a fit of anger, which betrayed him into summoning all his gifts of eloquence for a tirade against Campbell. The speech, in fact, was so vituperative that apparently he was made "conscious of his error" as soon as he "came off the Bench" and "was attacked by sundry citizens for his remarks." As a result, he went into the courthouse and voted for both Campbell and Sprigg in order "to appease the resentment"—a maneuver, it proved, which did little to satisfy Campbell or his friends. Throughout the contest, one stratagem of the opposition that had particularly annoyed Campbell, was the persistent spreading of a report that Sprigg would outpoll him in his own county. To scotch the rumors, he had taken the occasion, while speaking at Morgantown in Monongalia County, to make a few bold predictions of his own: that out of three hundred votes cast in Brooke he would get two hundred and Sprigg one; that Morgan himself would outpoll Doddridge there; that a candidate named McClean would outpoll Sprigg; and that Wilson would not receive more than forty votes. When the final results of the Brooke County elections were in, he was proved a political prophet of uncanny accuracy. The final tallies read: Morgan, 247 votes; Doddridge, 242, Campbell, 215; McClean, 141; Sprigg, 131; Wilson, thirty-eight.

In writing of the Brooke County returns to Colonel Morgan, Campbell showed himself "well enough" pleased by the results but not a little irritated still by the course of the campaign.

"Dr. Campbell and P. Doddridge," he wrote:

> ... opposed me with all their might, and actually persuaded some of my friends that there was a probability of electing Sprigg and me and hence he got some 80 votes on the same ticket with me—They have both sunk 50 percent since the election, and are now the dullest commodities on the Wellsburg market ...
>
> On the whole I am glad to get to my writing chair again; for I was fairly tired of the canvass—I am however constrained to call Doddridge to account for some things he said concerning me in his address at Wellsburg—But he has been so drunk that when in Wellsburg last I could not see him ...

A week later, however, inured to battle he may have been by his service for more than a decade in the bitter war of the frontier churches—he was still smarting under the castigation he had received from Doddridge. The interval had brought him some satisfaction, for, in a letter to Morgan he wrote, he was "now in correspondence [with Doddridge] relative to "the affair," and had got a letter from him yesterday in which he ...promised to *apologize* for a part of his speech, and to *explain* at length the rest of it ... and it is universally agreed." He added, with frankly malicious relish, "that I have humbled Doddridge more than any person he had come in contact with—in this one instance at least—He took a hard spell of drinking on the head of it—and is now tapering off." Yet, like an old campaigner, the aggrieved Campbell had no intention of retiring from the field until he had won a clear victory. If Doddridge did not "make a full retraction," he informed Morgan, he would feel "compelled in self vindication to come out in the newspapers" and publish their correspondence, telling "a story in no way flattering" to his late opponents. But, he concluded, "I hope I may not be pushed to this necessity." And, seemingly, he was not.

Perhaps he and Doddridge agreed—or perhaps mutual friends persuaded them—that their personal differences were of little moment. The voters had decided they were going together to Richmond to fight the common cause of the West. The final election returns from the five counties showed that the four delegates chosen to represent the district in the Constitutional convention were to be: Alexander Campbell and Philip Doddridge of Brooke County, and Charles S. Morgan and Eugenius M. Wilson of Monongalia. The personal contest between Campbell and Doddridge had thus ended in a draw: a friend of each was elected.

News of Campbell's election, not to his surprise, of course, brought tart comment from more than one quarter. He himself reprinted, for the amusement of his own readers, a sarcastic jibe from the *Columbian Star*:

> Mr. Campbell ... is maturing the whole doctrine of Constitutions, and means to bring in Moses as the first Exemplar. The fable of the river fish which played off into the sea, and was soon overmatched, one might suppose, would offer a seasonable hint to him.

Evidently a few wild rumors concerning the political intentions of a delegate already known as a religious incendiary also became current. Philip Fall, in Nashville, received a letter from a certain William Anderson who was considerably agitated because he had heard that a certain Mr. Butler had said that, "Brother Campbell was aiming to overthrow the government of the United States."

But as the summer months rapidly passed, Campbell had little time to concern himself with such rumor or accusation. His

Alexander Campbell was elected a delegate from Brooke County, to participate in the Virginia Constitutional Convention that opened October 5, 1829. The famed artist, George Catlin painted a watercolor of the gathering. Campbell is seventh from the right on the back row. James Madison is standing. Seated immediately in back of him is John Marshall. James Monroe is in the speaker's chair on the left of the picture. Opposite: A close-up of Alexander Campbell as he appeared at the Virginia Constitutional Convention.

father had promised to take charge of Bethany press during his absence; still, he had to lay out the issues of the magazine and write his own advance copy. Above all, there was the exacting job of preparing the Owen debate for publication and seeing it in press—a job that was to detain him at home until late September.

As he had anticipated, these duties did not leave him much time to study and prepare for the forthcoming convention. On August 12 he wrote Morgan:

> I am so enormously oppressed with writing this summer that ... on the subject of the Constitution—I must rely upon my past stock of information as far as reading is concerned—and then the reason and nature of things.

But tell me can we not ride down together and talk the matter all over on our way to Richmond ... I intend to ride on horseback, how will you travel?

In particular, he wanted to talk over these two special projects that he had in mind to introduce at Richmond. The first he and Morgan had already been discussing, for, he wrote, "I am much pleased to find you and I so simultaneously have been thinking and concurring, too, on the subject of a system of *common school education*. The Remarks you have made upon the Resources of the State furnish some new ideas to me." The second he was broaching for the first time to his friend.

There is ... one other original idea ... which induced me to have my name laid before the people more than any other consideration—I call it *original* idea because it has been on my mind for years relative to the new constitution. I will tell you the secret though I have not said a word about it except to two or three friends—Perhaps you anticipate me already—I have always been of opinion that *some day* ought to be fixed in the New Constitution as the *Last day* on which any person should be born a *slave*—In other words that from the 4th of July 1840, 35 or 50 or some such period all persons then within the territory shall become free. I hope we will pull together on this oar.

There was a terse but illuminating postscript, indicating that he and the Colonel were interested in getting a political appointment for some friend: "I have written a warm recommendation of Mr. Dougherty (?) to President Jackson." Also, the remark obviously indicated that Campbell was well known as an active Jackson supporter, otherwise such a recommendation to the president would have been a futile gesture.

In any event, on Tuesday, September 22, the radical reformer of Brooke County—his debate with Robert Owen safely in press at last—set out on horseback toward the East, full-panoplied to defend the essential of Jacksonian democracy against the well-armored knights of conservative aristocracy.

At two o'clock on Sunday afternoon, October 4, Campbell rode into Richmond, wearily astride his spirited mare, "Miss Fanny." In thirteen days she had brought him the long, hazardous, beautiful journey over the lofty ridges and through the great valley of the Appalachians, across the Piedmont Plateau, and into the lush lowlands of the Tidewater. Brought him safely, though not without skittish incident, he noted, in a letter, "My mare was no more apparently fatigued when I arrived in Richmond than when I left home. She is however dangerous to ride. Very scary and she well-nigh pitched me off. I felt much fatigued." Not too fatigued for the pleasant observation that, "I was hailed on the streets two or three times before I got to the tavern. I have been welcomed by preachers and people civil and religious." Moreover, by evening he was sufficiently rested to preach "at seven to an immense congregation."

The convention was scheduled to open promptly at noon on Monday, October 5. The morning proved "lovely and auspicious as could have been chosen." In walking the short distance from his tavern to the Capitol, Campbell had to make his way through a great crowd of people of all ages: Some were young men, spoiling for the promised display of verbal fisticuffs, who had ridden horseback from Kentucky, Tennessee, and other states to the South; some were leading statesmen of the Republic and eminent citizens of "every profession and class," many of them with their families; and there, too, were colorful ministries of foreign powers "who wished to see men whose names had become historical." A few days later a newspaper correspondent would report the scene: "People are daily flocking here in vast multitudes ... All feel a deep interest in the matters of debate; and the discussions are not only in the convention, but in the boarding-houses, taverns, shops, public streets and market places." Indeed, Richmond had not seen such crowds since 1824 when the Marquis de Lafayette had returned to the streets. He had marched with Washington, and all Virginia had turned out to do him honor in a three-day celebration. A celebration replete with triumphal arches and an obelisk to Revolutionary heroes, a parade, fireworks, races, a dinner at the Jockey Club, and a grand ball under the canopy of the Eagle Hotel. Campbell had not journeyed to Richmond to see the French hero of the Revolution; and by only three years, death had cheated him of seeing the Virginians with whom he would have most liked to sit in convention — "the immortal Jefferson."

But everywhere about him were the spirit and the handiwork of the author of the Declaration of Independence. Soon after the close of the Revolution, Jefferson had headed the committee that laid out the eight-acre Capitol Square on the top of Shockoe Hill. He made it a place of pride and beauty for all Virginia, with its

straight well-graveled paths and numerous plantings of the
European linden, the City Hall, decorated at each end by a Doric
portico of four columns, standing in one angle of the square and,
in another, Governor's Mansion, a house of "democratic hospitality" where, during sessions of the Legislature, "a bowl of toddy
stood on the sideboard every day for members who chose to drop
in to partake of as they pleased." Commanding the center of the
square and lending an "imposing and imperial air" to the city,
whose population of seventeen thousand was spread over its two
hills on the left bank of the James, was the State Capitol itself.
Jefferson had designed the state capitol at the request of his fellow-
citizens while minister to France in 1785, "thinking it a favorable
opportunity," he had written, "to introduce into the State an
example of architecture in the classic style of antiquity." He selected the Maison Carée at Nîmes, an ancient Roman temple, as a
model, and his was carried out, though, in his opinion, "with
some variations, not for the better." Mounting the steps of this
Capitol, in whose Hall of Delegates the convention sessions were
to be held, Campbell took his first look at the men assembling on
the floor. He was impressed anew with the quality of leadership
that for half a century Virginia had been furnishing the nation.
Seated about him were two ex-Presidents of the United States,
James Madison and James Monroe; the Chief Justice of the
Supreme Court, John Marshall; the Governor of the State,
William Branch Giles; the former Governor of the State, James
Pleasants; the two United States Senators, John Tyler and
Littleton W. Tazewell; and eleven members of the House of
Representatives, among whom were Charles F. Mercer and Philip
P. Barbour and former member, John Randolph of Roanoke. Also
there were Judge Abel P. Upshur, John W. Green, and William A.
G. Dade; and lawyers favorably known at the state and federal bar,
like Benjamin Watkins Leigh, Chapman Johnson, Robert
Stanard, and Robert Barraud Taylor. Many, too, were here to
whom honors would come in the future. John Tyler would

become President of the United States; two others would serve in his cabinet as Secretary of State, and John Y. Mason as Secretary of Navy; still others would distinguish themselves as judges and governors, as members of Congress and representatives of their government to foreign courts.

Amid this array of talent, Campbell realized that he sat alone and unique, an editor-preacher from the westernmost mountains of the State, whose peculiar religious mission was so little comprehended by the majority present that even those who wished to be most complimentary could designate him only as "the celebrated Baptist divine." Having spent the past seven years fighting for his ideals of religious liberty—the right of private judgment and the quality of clergy and layman—he would welcome now the opportunity to assert his ideals of political liberty—the right of every citizen to a vote and equal representation. For a man of pride and self-assurance, it would be good to pit his talents against the best that Virginia—and the nation—had to offer.

Nor, Campbell perceived, were these talents likely to go unheralded. At the reporters' table sat two Richmond editors whose reputations carried far beyond the boarders of their own state—John Hampden Pleasants of *The Constitutional Whig* and Thomas Ritchie of *The Democratic Richmond Enquirer.* Both were "prominent socially and powerful politically," and both were so "stubbornly partisan" that their enmity would not cease until one lay dead at the hand of the other's son. At the table also sat Mr. Stansbury of Washington, whose "skill," it was said, "in reporting the proceedings of Congress, is well known to the citizens of the United States." He had been engaged to keep, as nearly as possible, a word-for-word record of the convention. This record would be published the next year under the title *Proceedings and Debates of the Virginia State Convention of 1829–30*—a volume which, "all local self-conceit aside," Virginia might consider "one of the most remarkable gifts that the political genius of the Anglo-Saxon race has ever made to Parliamentary History." Over the

next few months, "constitutional questions of high import" were
to be "agitated with a range of knowledge, a philosophic breadth
and insight, a strength and clearness of reasoning, an animated
eloquence, an academic gloss, and a punctilious courtesy such as
has rarely distinguished any convention, parliament, or congress
in the annals of free institutions." Reporters from other states were
present, too; and South Carolina's *Charleston's Mercury* summed
up the general expectation with the comment: "It constitutes, perhaps, one of the most enlightened assemblies that has ever been
convened in the United States ... Public curiosity is, therefore,
naturally and highly excited to witness the display of intellect,
which will no doubt mark its session as an epoch in our history."

When, just at the stroke of twelve noon, the gavel sounded the
opening of the convention, every foot of space in the gallery occupied by citizens eager not to miss an act of the anticipated drama.
"The eyes of the world are upon us," wrote Thomas Ritchie.
Campbell, possessing a fine sense of the dramatic, would fully
appreciate the quality of this opening scene as the assembly's triumvirate of elder statesmen held center stage. James Madison
speaking in his small, barely audible voice, nominated James
Monroe for president of the convention, and, elected by acclamation, Monroe was escorted to the speaker's chair by Madison and
John Marshall.

Madison was the sole survivor of the revolutionary convention
that had met at St. John's in 1775; but the three had sat together
in the small, white church for the convention of 1788 and determined the course of the new nation by ratifying the Federal
Constitution. In Madison, delegates and visitors now beheld an
old man of seventy-eight, small in stature, with wizened face and
ample forehead; and though he had attended the convention of
'88 "exquisite in dress with his blue and buff clothes and immac-
ulate ruffled shirt and wrist-hands, and his hair powdered on top
and queued and tied with ribbon at the back," today his "dress was
plain; his overcoat a faded brown surtout." John Marshall in '89

had been "gaunt, dark, tousled-haired, but perfectly at ease in an ill-fitting summer coat bought for the occasion for a dollar." Now, only four years Madison's junior, wearing a long surtout of blue and silk stockings and shorts and a queue in the manner of the last century," he made an appearance "revolutionary and patriarchal," though he was still somewhat careless in dress and looked more the simple farmer than the nation's most distinguished jurist. Between these two, the youngest of the trio, James Monroe, appeared frail, feeble, and "very wrinkled and weather-beaten." Even in 1788, as a young man of thirty, he had been "awkward in speech and manner;" and after having filled every high office his state and country could bestow, he was still "ungraceful in attitude and gesture." Chief among his talents was the ability to conciliate; and in the fact that his term in the White House was known as "the era of good feeling," the assembled delegates might seek a hopeful augury for the weeks of debate ahead.

Accepting the presidency of the convention, Monroe made a short opening address: "our Constitution was the first that was formed in the Union," he reminded the delegates, and they were assembled to amend it "and thereby give a new support to our system of free republican government." The roll call of delegates was read. And the Constitutional Convention of 1829 was underway.

The preliminaries over, Campbell hastened back to his tavern to write Selina. It was a brief note—a swift report on his journey, "Miss Fanny's" bad conduct, and his first reception in Richmond, a couple of lines on the opening of the convention: "It was a most imposing spectacle. No body ever met on this continent more venerable." Then, a hasty conclusion: "I can only find time to inform you of my safe arrival and to send you all my warm affection. It is not with me out of sight out of mind. But I need not write about it."

A week later, he was feeling much need to "write about it." If Selina had been somewhat disappointed in Alexander's first letter from Richmond, she had nothing to complain of in his second. Evidently, for all her outward air of prim piety, the second mistress of Bethany had a proper regard for connubial pleasures. Certainly, it was apparent, fourteen months of marriage and the birth of their first child had but increased her husband's ardor. The greater part of the long letter was filled with expression of a lover's longing: "Your loneliness and my want of your smiles and company," he wrote:

> bear heavily upon me, my dear Selina. I find privation alone teaches us the value of possession ... I feel as I had lost the half of myself. I have ear into which to whisper a secret which I cannot communicate to any other, and there are not lips I can embrace in this strange land ... Here I am among many friends and strangers but ... none can narrow the place which you occupy—none can supplant my own little Rib at Bethany ... I am extremely anxious to get a line from you that I may have the memorial of your love before my eyes.
>
> How does our little Margaret, that dear pledge of our love, grow... I cannot tell you anything about my business at home. I have forgotten that when I think of home—I only think of my dear Selina and my dear children.

So far as the convention matters went, he had only a brief prophetic word: "I cannot tell you very much about our business here—we are preparing for war—Sharpening our swords and lances—You will hear from us soon."

In truth, except for the novelty of his surroundings, Campbell found little of interest in the first week of the convention, occupied as it had been with routine proceedings. Rules had been adopted, one of which tacitly recognized the "war" at hand:

"When any member is about to speak ... he shall rise from his seat, and without advancing from thence, shall, with due respect, address himself to the President ... avoiding all indecent and disrespectful language." Four committees were appointed, composed of one delegate from each of the twenty-four senatorial districts; on the Bill of Rights and on the Legislative, Executive, and Judicial departments of government. Campbell was placed on the Judicial Committee, of which John Marshall, naturally, was chosen chairman.

With the beginning of the committee's sessions, Campbell no doubt found his interest considerably enlivened. His pledge to the voters of his district to fight for the abolition of Virginia's dictatorial county court system was bound to bring him in quick conflict with the arch-conservative jurist who was the committee's chairman. The second week of convention was also enlivened by an ironic duty that fell to the lot of the conservative Marshall. As the delegate from Richmond, he was forced—to the sardonic amusement of Campbell and other reform delegates—to present "The Memorial of the Non-Freeholders of the City of Richmond." It was a long and impressive document, stating clearly and boldly the democratic demands of the disenfranchised who, as it said, "have been passed by, like aliens or slaves, as if destitute of interest or unworthy a voice, in measures involving their political destiny; whilst the freeholders ... have seized upon sovereign authority ... [and] have made [themselves] ... not the representatives of the people, but the organ of a privileged order."

For the better part of two weeks the convention met in committee; and when the committee reports were at length brought to the Hall of Delegates, Campbell took the floor for the first time, on Saturday, October 24. He did not rise to make a speech, he explained, but as "he was in a considerable minority in the Judicial Committee," he "would beg leave" to dissent from majority opinion and "submit his own ... resolutions" on judiciary reform. While he was about it, he also presented three other resolutions advocating an extension of suffrage far more radical than that provided in the report of the Legislative Committee just read by its chairman, James Madison. His resolutions were laid on the table, to be taken up in due time.

On the afternoon of the twenty-seventh, Campbell again took the floor. Still, he said, "he did not rise for the purpose of making a speech ... but to offer a remark or two ... [on] the order of the ... proceedings. Order he considered the first law of heaven; but if he were to judge ... by what he saw here, he should conclude that ... confusion and darkness were likely to accompany their proceedings." Obviously, events for the past two days had not gone to suit Mr. Campbell.

In the first place, there was the tabling of the Bill of Rights. The reformers naturally favored adoption of a statement on "right" as a preliminary to subsequent discussion. But the conservatives had no desire for debate on the ticklish matter of these abstract rights before more "practical details of Government" were agreed upon. They won the day, and the convention had thus, Campbell declared, put aside "as mere abstractions ... the grand principle which lay at the bottom of the science of government, ... the sub-basis ... of the fundamental law of the community." In the second place, there was Judge Green and his bland assumption of the right of property rule. Having tabled the report on the Bill of Rights, the convention had turned to consideration of the report of the Legislative Committee. The strength of the reformers became apparent when the first resolution was read, recommending that representation to the House of Delegates should be based on "the white population exclusively." Judge Green of Culpepper County immediately countered with a move to amend the report by striking out the word "exclusively" and adding instead the words "and taxation combined." The battle line was drawn, majority rule, or rule by the propertied minority. Moreover, in presenting his amendment, the judge had blandly suggested that the right of property rule was already established and, therefore, the burden of proof lay on those favoring the white basis resolution. Campbell, of course, took the opposite view, and so he now sharply concluded: Judge Green's assumption "was as great an aberration from the correct principles of order as that which had taken place yesterday ... In a word, I consider the order yesterday to have been 'no principles;' that today seems to be 'proof.'" The convention was getting its first taste of the salt that was making Campbell's name both applauded and denounced throughout the West.

As the debate continued through the week, Campbell paid particular attention to the speech of Judge Abel P. Upshur of Northampton County—a fair, blue-eyed, young man, rather stout in stature but graceful and easy in manner; and one of Virginia's most able young jurists, with a "clear, calm, and convincing" style of oratory. To one observer at least, his speech on the basis question was the "most elegant ... delivered during the session, a philosophic essay on the science of government." And all its logic was marshaled to prove that: "There are two kinds of majority. There is a majority in *interest*," said Upshur, "as well as a majority in number ... It is precisely the principle for which we contend ... that those who have the greatest stake in the government shall have the greatest share of power in the administration of it." A remark from another representative of the East also lodged in Campbell's mind to irk him considerably. Philip P. Barbour of Orange County, member of Congress and lawyer distinguished for his "logical acuteness," summoned his logic to declare in his address that: "While *faith* is the surest of all foundations in matters of religion, the very reverse of faith, is the true foundation of all free Governments. They are founded in *jealousy*, and are guarded by caution."

While the Tidewater was pressing her claims, Campbell's colleagues were by no means silent. John R. Cook of Frederick County and Philip Doddridge presented the case for the West with statistics and with passion. Doddridge, already the "hero of many triumphs," both at the bar and in the political arena, took the floor, of course, "with the eyes of the whole West fixed upon him ... a champion so well armed ... so confident in himself and his cause, and so well sustained by his constituents, and supported by his colleagues, that few men" in the assembly were ready to "meet him without some misgivings." As he spoke on the basis of representation, upbraiding the East for its enslavement of the West, it seemed to many in the hall that the stream of his eloquence "bore down upon his adversaries with impetuosity" of one of "his native mountain torrents." Nevertheless, by the end of the week, the other delegate from Brooke County felt it was time that he had his own say on the subject.

So on Saturday morning, October 31, Alexander Campbell arose to make his first address.

Just as though, only four days earlier, he had not called the body to task for a lamentable disregard of both "order" and "principles" in its proceedings, he began with a graceful, and humorous, gesture of deference:

> Mr. Chairman—I have never been in the habit of making apologies; I have never liked them. When I hear apologies from gentlemen, who, either have acquitted ... or expect to acquit themselves well, I am reminded of the lady in the play, Who in hopes of contradiction, oft would say, Methinks, I look so wretchedly today.
>
> But really, Sir, ... When I rise to address an assemblage ... of such illustrious patriarchs ... and politicians ... and [consider] that I am not only little experienced, but without experience in such addresses as I am now to make I cannot but feel embarrassed and intimidated.

But immediately he made it plain that this "embarrassment" arose "most of all" from fear that he might "not be able to do justice to the cause, which reason and conscience," he continued, "have compelled me to espouse ... It was *principles*, Mr. Chairman, which brought me here ... I know, Sir, that local interests and district feelings can only yield to principles." And with this reference to "principles," his mood again changed swiftly as he renewed, even more vigorously, the first warning to his colleagues:

> We are entirely at sea in this debate. We set sail without compass, rudder, or pilot ... [and] are now a thousand miles from land ... It will be well if the *rari nantes in gurgite vasto* apply not to us ... For my part, I never could reason without some principles to reason from, and some point to reason to ... Call me orthodox, or call me heterodox, I confess I believe, that in the science of politics, there are as in all other sciences, certain fundamental principles, as true and unchangeable as any of the fundamental principles of physics or morals.

Obviously, the tabling of the Bill of Rights was still rankling in his mind. To temper with scorn his rebuke of those who were proposing, he charged, that the assembly should "build the house and then lay the foundation; ... heal the constitution, and then feel the pulse." Moreover, Campbell and his colleagues were certain, their own insistence on the Bill of Rights as first order of debate was no mere quibbling over procedure. Rather, they realized all too well, that recognition of its guarantees was fundamental to the cause of the West. These guarantees were based on the philosophical assumptions that the "rights" it set forth are self-evident, inalienable, and eternal, derived from God and the laws of the universe itself, the origin of individual liberties being in the very nature of persons, in their worth and dignity as rational beings made in the image of the Creator. Therefore, they are expressive of universal principles that no government and no majority may justly or safely violate. Having marshaled his greatest eloquence at Cincinnati in April to defend this conception of the "nature of man" and society against the materialistic, mechanistic assumptions of Robert Owen, Campbell now welcomed the opportunity to expose, point by point, what he considered the equally erroneous and cynical political assumptions evident to him in the speeches of Judges Green and Upshur, and of Philip Barbour.

To begin with, he declared, their argument was "based upon views of society" which were "anti-republican." If Green's amendment—calling for representation based on population "and taxation combined"—was adopted, "the radical principles of our Government" expressed in the Bill of Rights would be abandoned. He contended,

> A new principle will be sanctioned; the very principle on which the Aristocracies and the Monarchies of the old world have been founded. Give men political power according to their wealth, and soon we have a legalized oligarchy; then come the thirty tyrants; then follow the *Quin decemviri*; then triumvirate; and last of all, comes Julius Caesar ... Men love power and in proportion as they possess it, does that love increase.

To confirm this charge he pointed out that the Eastern delegates in the assembly were rather opposing the Bill of Rights or, at best, seeking to nullify it with sophical arguments. Barbour admitted its first article ("All men are born free and independent") "to be true doctrine in theory, but dangerous in application; "or Green affirmed that "all men have equal Natural Rights, but not equal political rights."

Secondly, said Campbell, such line of reasoning was not only "anti-republican," it was "unphilosophic" as well. Particularly unintelligible to his mind was the assumption that wealth is the prime factor in determining man's value to society. And so he came to pay his "devoirs to the honorable gentleman from Northampton," Judge Upshur:

> This gentleman starts with the postulate, that there are two sorts of majorities: of numbers and interest; in plain English, of men and money. I do not well understand, why he ought not to have added, also, majorities of talent, physical strength, scientific skill, and general literature. These are all more valuable than money and as useful to the State. A Robert Fulton, a General Jackson, a Joseph Lancaster, a Benjamin Franklin are as useful to the State as a whole district of mere slave-holders. Now, all the logic, metaphysics and rhetoric of this Assembly must be put to requisition to show why a citizen, having a hundred negroes, should have ten times more political power than a Joseph Lancaster, or a Robert Fulton with only a house and a garden.

To compound the absurdity, he ironically suggested that "the property basis of representation, never can become tolerably rational, until each vote is valued at a given sum and every man have as many votes, as he the stipulated price." Before turning to define his own philosophy of majorities, he hurled a few parting shafts of sarcasm at all three of his chosen antagonists:

> This gentleman [Judge Upshur] could find no law, or right, as he termed it, in nature, but the right of the strong to devour the weak. Brutal force governs everything. He presented the lion devouring the ox; the ox driving the

lamb; the lamb something weaker, but last of all, the worm eating the elephant.

This, Sir, is but a small part of the incongruity of this honorable gentleman's doctrine with Republican principles. But he concludes there are no principles in government, and his honorable associate [Judge Green] from Culpepper, declares, that men are governed by *interest* only. And as for the poor, they have no affection, no love of country, no social feelings, no conscience, no religion; they are all governed by mere cupidity. No wonder the eloquent gentleman from Orange [Barbour], affirmed that there is no *faith* in politics.

Certainly, to the "natural rights" men of the West, these contentions of the gentleman on Tidewater bordered dangerously close to Alexander Hamilton's contemptuous demands for a government of the propertied minority safely removed from interference by that "great beast," the common people. They also alarmingly affirmed those political and economic concepts of Hume, Hobbes, and Adam Smith and Machiavelli, which viewed the social state as a ruthless class struggle and judged men as impelled not by ideals but by needs, not by principles but by self-interest, not by reason but by desire for goods. In contrast and in reply, Campbell, of course, drew his inspiration from quite a different line of thinkers. His political philosophy, like Jefferson's, was an amalgam of seventeenth-century English and eighteenth-century French liberalisms, supplemented by the influence of the American frontier. Campbell asserted the rights of individuals apart from, and superior to, the rights of property and disdaining units of Adam Smith; and deemed the great end of statesmanship to be not the material power and glory of the state, as did Hamilton, but the well-being of the individual citizen, as did Jefferson. Having passed with Rousseau beyond the liberalism of Locke to translate politics and economics into terms of social justice, having accepted the revolutionary doctrine that reason and not special interests should determine social and political institutions, and having long advocated that the sanction of the government rests not on coercion, but on good will, on the consent of the governed, he held this belief in the sovereignty of the majority, a concept of government that assumed the compact theory of the origin of the state. He considered its function to be that of a public-service corporation. Here, moreover, he found his theology reinforcing his political thinking. For these concepts of government were all ideas implicit in the theory of church and state, which had been clarified by the great Independents, Thomas Hooker and Roger Williams, as well as Milton. In the New World the compact idea had established itself from early colonial days through the Mayflower Compact and the church covenant of the Pilgrims, and Campbell's own championship of the social contract theory of government was a natural outgrowth of his early avowal of the Dutch Covenant Theology with its conception of the relation between God and humanity as a covenant.

At the very beginning of his address, therefore, he had cogently stated his concept of the function of government: "It is just as true that Government ought to be instituted for the benefit of the governed, as that a whole is greater than a part; or that a straight line is the shortest distance between two given points." Now he was ready to support this thesis by elaboration of his concept of the origin of government. "The gentlemen on the other side," he remarked, "have triumphantly called upon us, to find the origin of majorities in the State of Nature." In meeting their challenge, he would follow the classic theory, as expounded in Rousseau's *Social Contract*, that individuals in the primitive state existed as unsocial units and human government began when these individuals agreed to surrender some of their natural rights in exchange for the benefits they could enjoy by joining with neighbors in forming a social compact. "We all know," he admitted at the outset, "that men roaming at large, over the forest, could have no ideas of majorities." But, he continued, human beings "are social animals ... who seek society," and as soon as they begin to seek recognition of the sovereignty of the majority will, as expressed in a social compact, "is one of the first things, which, from nature itself, would present itself to them." In short, he summed up, "The true origin of this idea, is found in the nature and circumstances of men."

To give dramatic point to his argument and to answer those who denied "the existence of a state of nature altogether," he proposed an historical analogy drawn from the unhappy record that throughout history "political communities have been broken up, and from their ruins, new ones have been formed." Suppose, he suggested, that "some foreign enemy should invade our country, and spread devastation, ruin and death... [and that] a few might escape and flee to the most distant wilds ... beyond the Rocky Mountains," where, after several years of separate wanderings, they happen to come together. They agree to form a social compact. In making his escape, A—an old Virginian," Campbell quipped—had "snatched a bag of dollars; B had taken his wife; C, his rifle; D, his children; and E had only himself but possessed a useful knowledge of Indian languages. For a while each man claims himself entitled to the major share of influence in the new government." At length A rises to purposes:

> Gentlemen, I see we all have claims for various portions of political power. I think we must abandon the idea of forming a social compact upon these principles ... I will agree that we all surrender ourselves, our property, our talents, and our skill, *pro bono publico* ...

And, thus, Campbell concluded with a sardonic twist of humor:

> Mr. Chairman: Here we have in miniature something analogous to this state of nature, of which we have so

often heard. And here we have the only true philosophy of the social compact ... [where] every man surrenders himself to the whole community, and the whole community to him. We have no occasion to travel so far *South*, as the gentleman from Northampton [Upshur], who penetrated these regions until he saw a *white devil*. Nor need we go so far *North* with the gentleman from Orange [Barbour], who found a nation composed entirely of *women*. He seemed greatly concerned for the political rights of such a nation. But, Sir, he need not have troubled himself much on this account, for such a nation could not continue for more than five hundred years.

But Campbell had something more than political theory to offer the convention. Though he had remarked at the outset he would leave to others the "dry details" of a technical discussion of wealth and population while he dealt with these "rights" which the gentlemen of the Tidewater seemed so loath to have introduced into the discussion. He, nevertheless, had a plan for reapportionment of representation, one that, to his mind, would guarantee both the safety of property and the rights of individuals. Both the Tidewater and his own Trans-Alleghany frontier, he proposed, should surrender certain delegates to the General Assembly to be redistributed in the central part of the state along the base of the Blue Ridge and in the Valley. Then, he reasoned, "the power lost in the counties on tide-water and west of the Alleghany would be deposited in that part of the State which, from its central position and from its dense slave-population, would be the safest deposit which the fears of the slave-holders could devise." "We are not, then, Mr. Chairman," he concluded, "contending for power for ourselves, but for the principles which ... cannot fail to benefit the whole State by distributing power where it ought to be and by divesting our government of those odious aristocratic features, which ... are daily causing the sceptre to depart from Virginia."

With this plan and the conciliatory tone obviously worded to reassure the Eastern planters they need not fear radical eruption of anti-slavery sentiment from the West, Campbell was resigning, albeit reluctantly, his cherished intention of laying before the convention a scheme for gradual emancipation. Immediately on coming to Richmond he had broached his scheme, and an informal caucus was held to discuss the question. With the general tone and sentiment of the caucus he had been well pleased. In fact, he was "agreeably surprised" to hear "the largest slaveholder in the State" express his readiness to free the whole of his six hundred slaves at any moment Virginia might pass a statute of abolition. In general, he found the Tidewater planters no less willing than himself to declare slavery "the greatest curse, the most unendurable incubus on the prosperity of Virginia that could be imposed upon it,—a burden ... which they ... would not much longer endure." Yet, it was the consensus of the caucus that it would be "impolitic and inexpedient" to introduce this vexed and complex subject into a convention already oppressed with many issues certain to be almost impossibly difficult to resolve. In the end, Campbell yielded to the "matured judgment" of the caucus, and even did so with tolerably good grace. There were several reasons.

For one thing, he was bound to recognize that the introduction of an abolition amendment might, indeed, so greatly prolong and embroil the debate as to endanger the whole basic program of republican reform. The West was contending, and Campbell's discovery of the fact that the Eastern gentry "were as alive to this subject [of slavery] as we could be" buoyed his belief that Virginia would, in any event, rid herself of this "incubus" at no very distant date. Meanwhile, as a slave-holder himself, well acquainted with the general working of Virginia's slave economy, he need not be plagued with exaggerated notions of the plight of the Negro laborer. Robert Owen had come to America for the debate by way of Jamaica, where he had taken particular interest in the condition of the Negro slaves. In all honesty, he felt compelled to admit that most masters treated their slaves well, if for no other reason than that it was to their interest to do so, and to report that "The West Indian slave, as he is called, is greatly more comfortable and happy than the British or Irish operative manufacturer or day-labourer." Here was a phase of the issue which the two men, the socialist and the religious reformer, were certain to have searched out as they had walked together the previous year over the Bethany hills and observed the operations of Bethany farm. Moreover, Campbell could cheer himself with the fact that the caucus did achieve on concrete result: All its members were agreed "to guard against the insertion of a single word in the con-stitution recognizing the existence of this evil" so that the problem of emancipation would rest "constitutionally within the power of the ordinary legislature to take any measures, at any time, which in its wisdom it may think expedient."

Having yielded on the issue of slavery, he was, more than ever, adamant in pursuing the fight for a democratic plan of represen-tation. As he concluded his argument, he warned the Eastern oli-garchy that its "money basis" policy not only was both "anti-repub-lican" and "unphilosophic," it was also "short-sighted." "Do we not daily," he asked, "see that riches are forever taking to them-selves wings?" Therefore, he reasoned the fathers on the Tidewater, blinded today by "the fascination of wealth and power" and fear of "an imaginary evil," were seeking constitutional provi-sions that might well tomorrow disenfranchise their sons and "pro-scribe their own posterity." To point up the moral, he closed with a story taken from Dr. Johnson's *Rambler*:

> A young man much afraid of thieves and robbers breaking into his room at night … put his ingenuity to work, to invent a new lock and key, which could not be violated. He succeeded … [and] one day called in a

friend to exhibit ... his ingenuity. It required some two or three minutes to lock and unlock the door. The gentleman, after admiring ... his ingenuity, remarked, 'Why, Sir, ... this is certainly a great defense against thieves and robbers, but it is so difficult to unlock, I should fear that if the house were to take fire you might be consumed before you could ... escape.' 'I declare, Sir," said the young gentleman, I never thought of that. Hereafter I will sleep with my door, not only unlocked, but half open.'

A few days later, on November 4, in replying to a letter just received from Selina, he made no reference to his maiden speech before the convention. There were, however, a few revealing sentences concerning himself and convention affairs in general:

> I expect we will have a long session. We have splendid oratory ... on both sides of the one great question whether man with wealth or man alone shall be the basis of government.
>
> I do not know that I have ever seen so many great men assembled together before—But I find myself much more at home amongst them now than I did at first—They all know me from the East and West and they all watch my movements ... this meeting ... will give me a new kind of Education ... which will be profitable to me and I hope to some of them.

Chiefly, the letter was concerned with affairs at home; particularly it spoke again of this lover's longing for his wife, declared with an explicit ardor certain to have brought a bright flush of remembrance to Selina's checks:

... your most affectionate letter yesterday ... gave me much joy ... and carried me over all the hills and valleys which separated me from your embrace. O that I could as easily transport my body as I can my soul to my dear half that I left behind me ... I am ... in point of company indulged in the evenings ... more than I could wish—But then I am reminded that there is no one into whose ear I can whisper one word of love or upon whose bosom I can lay my head—or my hand ... I need not tell you my dear, that I send my love to you for I keep it here.

By return post, a reply from Selina sent another letter hastening from Richmond to Bethany. This time some admonitions to the virtues of "self-denial and patience" were coupled with the expressions of longing; " ... you must know that I always open your epistles with a palpitating heart—when I am breaking open the seal I think of the fingers that made it secure—and of the heart that is sealed to mine ... I long to be restored to your bosom and company—I must however exercise a due degree of patience for some time yet." Only thus obliquely, in this letter of November 9, did he refer to his business at Richmond.

And, in truth, he had nothing to report from the convention that might have been of cheerful import. As the weeks passed it was becoming increasingly apparent the drama in Richmond was likely to play itself out in misunderstandings and strange confusions. Though the beginning of the Western delegation had been animated by high optimism, and Philip Doddridge had made "his great speech on the basis question" with "the hope of triumph ... bright before him," by November 5 the *Richmond Enquirer* felt forced to remark, "The lemon has been a little more squeezed and a few drops of acid infused into the debate." By the 17th the paper was wondering if the "ominous discussion" shouldn't be closed. Two days later, the *Daily Richmond Whip*, convinced that "too diplomatic a temper" was reigning in the convention, suggested that "it would be better for members to fulfill the character of representatives of the same people, than to act as the negotiators of separate and hostile nations."

Certainly, Campbell's speech on the basis question had struck no answering spark of approval from Tidewater flint. The elegant and accomplished Benjamin Watkins Leigh of Chesterfield County spoke the general attitude of the East in the sarcastic rejoinder: "It seems to be imagined that no Government is a *civilized one*, unless it be founded *on the natural rights of man, in a savage state.*" Robert Stanard of Spotsylvania "possessed powers of denunciation ... hardly ever ... equalled" and that these powers seemed merely enhanced by a defect in his delivery, almost amounting to stammering. He often turned these to his advantage when, after hesitating for a word to riddle an opponent, he would "finally select one, the hardest and bitterest that had risen to his tongue."

"Let me tell the Reverent gentleman from Brook," said Stanard,

> (for among the fallacies of the day is his attempted application of analogies drawn from the exact sciences to that of Government) ... that geometry ... furnishes but a poor guide, when we would ... fix the relations of moral and political quantities.
>
> Under the guidance of a fallacious analogy, the gentleman thinks it would be wise to set out with certain *a priori* principles, certain postulata and axiomata, and then to keep ourselves within the exact parallel lines which these guides shall prescribe to us ... All these guides will fail him, and he will find himself betrayed into the most desperate and fatal errors ... he will go on, linking consequence, and induction to induction ... like Jacob's ladder, which led from earth to Heaven—only, that this, I fear

takes the opposite direction ... (... it leads to the hell of anarchy, not to the heaven of peace) ... I fear that the downward tendency of his scheme is so strong, as to put in requisition all the wisdom, prudence, and firmness here assembled to arrest its career, and even that may be unavailing.

Another sharp, if minor, irritant was the injection of John Locke into the discussion. In his scriptures on Philip Barbour, Campbell had reminded the assembly that the proposition, "*All men are born free and independent* ... is a position much older than these United States, and flowed from a gentleman, to whom, more than any other, these American States, are indebted for all their civil and religious liberties ... the statesman, the philosopher, and the Christian who is the legitimate father of the first article on the Bill of Rights. I need not tell you ... I allude to the Author of the 'Essay on Toleration,' ... of the Essay upon the 'Human Understanding.'" The name of Locke was far too potent a factor in American thought for the gentlemen on the Tidewater to allow this invocation of his authority to pass without protest. They hastened to brand the philosophy of the West with the epithet "Jacobin," and contended that it was their own position that fulfilled the true intent of the philosophy both of Locke and of the founding fathers. "I am unwilling," retorted James S. Barbour, "to surrender the principles of Locke, and of Milton, for the fancies of Rousseau, aye, as unwilling as I am to disregard the lights of our own revolution for the *ignus fatuus* of French ... anarchy and atheism." Leigh vehemently seconded him: "Locke has had a singular fate .... He exploded the *right divine of Kings*—he showed that all government is of human institution; yet he is supposed to have established the *divine right of democracy* .... It does not follow that because all men are born equal and have equal rights to life, liberty, and the property they can acquire by honest industry,

therefore, all men may rightly claim ... equal political powers—
especially equal power to dispose of the property of others."

Here the gentlemen of the Tidewater were posing a neat
point, as Campbell, Locke's thorough disciple, knew full well. He
knew Locke was the apostle of Whiggery, not of democracy; he
was a constitutional monarchist arguing the sacredness of property rights and conceiving the social compact as a contract between
ruler and subject, and not between the several members of a free
community. But these considerations would trouble Campbell little. Remembering Locke's dictum, "The end of government is the
good of mankind," he was secure in his conviction. While Locke
sought the protection of property against ruthless taxation by a
king, for a king's own ends, he never intended his argument for
property rights to be used as an instrument of class exploitation.
Perceiving that Locke's noble words, "Chains are but an ill-wear-
ing how much so ever we gild or polish them," sounded man's
perennial defiance to arbitrary power. He was certain that they
now should serve Western Virginians, as well in the fight against
the assumptions of the Eastern oligarchy, as they once had served
Locke himself against the "divine right" claims of James II and the
American colonials against the tyranny of George III.

As for the charge of "Jacobinism," it would disturb Campbell
and his colleagues even less. The epithet had sounded the conservatives' tocsin of alarm for so many years, it was worn a little
thin by 1829. Three decades earlier, the Tie-Wig Federalists, in
terror of infection by the *bacillus gallicus*—and adept at employing the dogma of total depravity to dispose of the validity of all
democratic aspirations—made it common practice to denounce
"infidel French Mobocracy" and its American offspring, the democratic clubs of the "Illuminati," which they dubbed "demoniacal
clubs" and "nurseries of sedition." So now, in the Richmond convention, while Stanard was denouncing the whole "scheme" of
the Scotch-Irishman from Brooke County on the assumption that

its "downward tendency" led straight to the "hell of anarchy," Western delegates were likely to hear his words as but outworn echoes from the past. They would hear echoes of that "Hartford Wit," Theodore Dwight, who had once exclaimed of the democracy of Connecticut, "Can imagination paint anything more dreadful this side of hell!" or of another New England gentleman who, traveling among the Scotch-Irish of Pennsylvania in the 1790s, had written home, "I have seen many ... Irishmen, and with few exceptions, they are ... the most God-provoking Democrats on this side of Hell;" or of still another who, in 1798, had gloomily predicted that the "indiscriminate admission of wild Irishmen" to the right of suffrage would soon put "an end to liberty and property."

One fact was significant and more than a little amusing. For all their fulminations against the radicalism of the West, the conservatives of 1829 no longer equated the term "Jacobin" with the term "democrat." After all, wanting a more orthodox candidate and detesting the nationalism of John Quincy Adams, a majority of Virginia's voters in the East had cast their ballots with the West in 1828 to send a democrat to the White House. So, however they might actually fear "democracy" and pride themselves on being "republicans" in best seventeenth-century tradition, they politely refrained from aspersions on the newly-adopted name of the political party they had, albeit reluctantly, espoused. Nevertheless, gentlemen like Barbour and Leigh managed to make their meaning clear. On the other hand, Campbell, realizing the strength of their aversions, made one concession: In support of his arguments he was careful to invoke only the reasonably respectable names of Jefferson and Franklin, and to employ only the older Jeffersonian term, "republic." He did not offend gentlemen of the opposition by calling on the testimony of Sam Adams or Tom Paine, nor harass their feelings by use of the Jacksonian term, "democrat." Obviously, and unhappily, this caution was availing him nothing at the hands of Stanard and other gentlemen well versed enough to recognize a suspect political theory by whatever name it might be called.

Yet, in truth, Campbell's political philosophy was not so radical, nor so completely at variance with that of the Tidewater gentry as they seemed to imagine. Though ready to battle for "equal rights," he would make no fetish of the doctrine of egalitarianism, nor erect it into a grand abstraction after the French manner. With as healthy a contempt of sentimentalism as his esteemed Dr. Johnson, he had, only a few months before at Cincinnati, warned his countrymen not to be duped by fine hopes of social regeneration through the romantic schemes of Robert Owen. Much as Dr. Johnson, more than a half century earlier, he had urged a hard lesson in realism on his countrymen being carried away by the romantic panaceas of Rousseau. Here, he stood firm again with Locke and Jefferson, cautious Anglo-Saxons both. Locke had written, "I cannot be supposed to understand all kinds of 'equality' ... Excellency of parts and merit may place others above the common level." In speaking of men being "by nature all free, equal, and independent," he was implying such an equality as is "the foundation of that obligation to mutual love [fraternity] amongst men ... which ... they owe one another." In short, a God-fearing equality that is an assertion of the common clay, of a sense of community even with the poor and most humble, and a realization of how precarious is the salvation even of the mighty and most proud. In the words of Jefferson, "the mass of making has not been born with saddles on their backs, nor a favored few booted and spurred, ready to ride them legitimately, by the grace of God."

On the question of "majority rights," the tough-minded master of Bethany was no blind worshipper of majorities, no "slavish adorer" of those "sovereign lords the people." Though he might agree with Paine that in the long count of history the majority is more likely to be just, he would not succumb to Rousseau's romantic dictum that the majority is always right. Realizing human weakness as well as Hamilton or Adams, he simply reasoned, with Jefferson, to a different conclusion: The will to power being strong, no group of persons is good enough to be entrusted with unrestrained power for a class will serve class interests and, therefore, mastery is safest in common hand. Joel Barlow had said, with Yankee wit and realism, "If government be founded on the vices of mankind, its business is to restrain those vices in all, rather than to foster them in a few." In fact, if any gentleman of the convention were readers of *The Christian Baptist*, they would realize that no delegate on Tidewater could have stated the issue more sharply than had Campbell. He enlivened some "Notes on a Tour," written in 1825 with a few pointed comments on the dangers of both "democracy" in the state and "independence" in the church:

> We learn ... from experience, as well as from books, that the human mind is prone to extremes in all circumstances .... When a tyrant is dethroned ... his [former] vassals ... convert his palaces into ... strong holds each other in rotation. So in the church. They who call the Pope Anti-Christ ... set themselves up as Popes, and thus a whole congregation of protestors become a college of cardinals .... Democrats in politics, and independents in religion, are not infrequently the greatest tyrants in the world. I am a democrat because I love kingly power, and don't want to part with it to other hands. And you are an independent because you like papal supremacy and wish to have your share in full. I only mean to say (for I am called a democrat and an independent) that such is the issue of both, if not closely watched and constantly guarded.

By the same token, those who had either heard Owen debate, or carefully read the *Baptist*, would know the master of Bethany would embrace no theory of "property rights" that might endan-

ger his own rich and, in part, slave-tilled acres on Buffaloe Creek.
True, he scorned Hobbesian psychology of "my interest." The
affirmation of his philosophy of religion as a "philosophy of happiness," seeking a present good for all humanity, naturally
inclined him to the revolutionary shift which Jefferson had given
the doctrine of natural rights when he changed Locke's classical
enumeration, "life, liberty, and property," to read, "life, liberty and
the pursuit of happiness." But, in the Owen debate, Campbell had
nowhere spoken more forcefully than where he contended that
his opponent's socialistic system was "at war with human nature,"
that one could sooner "reverse the decrees of gravitation" than
abolish the right of private property. In the Preface to his magazine, which he had written shortly before leaving for Richmond,
he had proposed a new enumeration of "natural rights" to include
the categories of both Locke and Jefferson. The "equal, inherent,
and unalienable … rights of all," he wrote, are the rights to liberty, to "preserve life," to "pursue happiness, or to seek food and
entertainment for both mind and body," and to "acquire … [and]
defend … property."

Conservatives like Stanard and Leigh were not comforted by
consideration of such philosophic abstractions. However moder-
ate their bent, the concrete differences and the tug of special interests were alienating East and West. Foremost among these was the
question of slavery. As the discussion lengthened and tempers
grew shorter, Campbell appreciated more and more the wisdom
of those who had advised him not to introduce his emancipation
amendment. It might be true that the small, thinly settled counties east of the Blue Ridge had the same representation in the
General Assembly as the large, populous counties of the West; but
so long as there were four hundred thousand slaves in the East and
only fifty thousand West of the mountains, the conservatives
would demand some representation based on this slave population. On the convention floor, as Campbell found in the caucus
room, there was no debate on the merits of the slave system. Both

sections were agreed that it seemed to be a necessary evil, which the Southern planters must endure for the present. Therefore, Campbell had insisted in his basis address, the conservatives were founding their argument "upon assumption only" when they contended that if the "white basis of representation were adopted," then the non-slave-holders would have the exclusive control in all governmental arrangements, and would, at once, "interfere with the rights of masters to their slaves."

On the other hand, delegates from the Trans-Allegheny, whatever Campbell's personal protestations, had not come to Richmond exclusively to wage a pure fight for abstract principles. The West, too, had its special interests, centering chiefly in the questions of internal improvements and of protection for domestic manufactures. A major complaint of the conservatives was the fact that, while the counties east of the Blue Ridge paid nearly three-fourths of the state taxes, the slave population alone supplied 30 percent of the entire revenue. The Westerners, with "many mountains and hills to pass, and rapid rivers to descend" to get their produce to market, asked for large state expenditure for the building of roads and canals. Yet, the West very logically argued, only through these internal improvements could its property be increased in value sufficiently to assume a proper share of the state's taxes. Campbell pointed out: "Sir, the disproportion between the east and west in the tax-paying department will every day diminish. As the west increases in population and improvement, its ability to pay will increase ..."

In Campbell's home county of Brooke, the issue of internal improvements was to project itself into the presidential campaign of 1832 with some amusing and very human results. In 1806 the U.S. Congress approved a national road from Fort Cumberland to the Ohio River. Charlestown [Wellsburg], in Brooke County, and Wheeling, in Ohio County, became formidable rivals as the western terminus of the route, and in 1808 Brooke County secured a charter for a Wellsburg and Washington Turnpike. In 1817 the western terminus was fixed in Wheeling. But by 1825 the road between Brownsville and Wheeling was in such bad repair that there was serious talk of changing the route via Wellsburg. The old controversy was renewed and work began on the turnpike chartered by Brooke County in 1808. Henry Clay explored the merits of the two routes and in his report to Congress, made, it was said, some "sarcastic allusions" to "Panther Mountain," a high hill some two miles east of Wellsburg. The Wheeling route again triumphed; and when Clay ran for the presidency against Jackson in 1832, Brooke County did not forget "Panther Mountain." Clay was burned in effigy at Wellsburg, and in the entire county "Harry of the West" received only one vote, that of "Prov. Mounts, an eccentric, hair [sic] brained individual, whose solitary vote was for a long time a subject of amusement among his neighbors"—and to Clay himself.

Thereafter, Ohio County was to be persistently pro-Clay and Whig, Brooke County uncompromisingly anti-Clay and Democratic, a political complexion it maintained for a generation. Brooke County was for internal improvements—provided the internal improvements were for Brooke County. [Brooke County Record, 32–37] Judge Upshur admitted this fact and then reversed himself in curious fashion when he argued that "the character of the western country" was not conducive to the use of slave labor, and would not be "until a general system of roads and canals, shall facilitate their access to market. And when that time shall arrive, the worst evils which we apprehend will have been experienced; for it is to *make* these very roads and canals, that our taxes are required." Surely such a circular course of reasoning had little logic, unless it was realized that the East was being motivated by considerations not at all local in character: The real issue was between states rights and nationalism.

However the West might decry the "special privilege" of the East, the Southern planters feared far more the "special privilege," which the encouragement of manufactures under the development of Clay's "American System" were fostering in the North. Sharing Leigh's conviction that "every commercial operation of the federal government has been detrimental to the Southern ... planting states," they felt justified in opposing any act calculated to extend the power of the federal government into the states. It was this attitude that dictated the intense concern for their slave interests so evident in the convention. Robert Morris of Hanover County, in a speech just preceding Campbell's, expressed the common fear that any concession to a free white basis in the state would endanger the principle of federal numbers (basing representation in Congress on the white population plus three-fifths of the slave population). And they would not be reassured when Campbell, in reply to Morris, ironically attacked the "fallacy of the hypothesis ... that we were ... in danger of losing our power in the Federal Government, if the doctrine of putting five souls into three bodies, should cease to be the popular practice in Virginia. He did not tell us, indeed, why Virginia gave up two-fifths of her slave population to the Union; in this she erred, unless she intended to give up the other three-fifths to her own white population."

Likewise on the subject of internal improvements. It was not so much that the East begrudged roads and canals to the East as that this scheme of improvements had become a federal project, and, as Leigh expressed it, "the Federal Government points a road along 'the Valley,' ... and States Rights fall or tremble at the very sight of this tremendous ordinance." The question of tariffs was not an issue, except indirectly, in the debate at Richmond. But the recent passage of the "tariff of abominations" had given the planters a new and just cause for alarm. Governor Giles spoke for them all when he took occasion to denounce it on the convention floor as an act "addressed to the worst passions of the human heart." The gentlemen of the seaboard would not forget that this "ubiquitous" tariff of 1828 had been passed with the support not only of the salt and iron manufacturers of the West, but also of the

Western wool-growers, one of the most prosperous of whom was not sitting in the convention as one of the most troublesome spokesmen for Western democracy.

✠

If the Richmond drama should ultimately play itself out in tragedy, the tragedy would spring from the emphasizing of these differences, which were obscuring a fundamental identity of interest. For, of course, as Campbell himself had so effectively argued a few months earlier in his speech before the farmers of Monongalia County, the ideal society of all Virginians, east and west, was a prosperous and secure agrarian state. When Campbell assured the voters of Monongalia that he shared their advocacy of "internal improvements and domestic manufactures," and when the individualistic freemen of the West voted for the tariff of 1828, they were thinking in simple immediate terms: of the need to get the produce of their farms to market, and the desire to protect their small, private enterprises and the great flocks of sheep grazing their Western hills from the importation of foreign wool and foreign salt and iron manufactures. They had no idea of promoting a system that would develop monopolies of corporate wealth or government paternalism conducive to corrupt sovereignty. They would agree with Campbell, saying at an election precinct in Monongalia that, "agriculture is with us the true basis of prosperity and power." Yet they would embrace an "American System" holding the germs of a philosophy likely to produce that society anathematized by Campbell as one that makes the rich man richer, and the poor man poorer. And the complexity of the issues, the confusions of the multiple economic and political factors involved, prevented their seeing anything illogical in this position—a deficiency, in truth, shared with a majority of their countrymen including most of the politicians, among them Henry Clay himself. Nor was Campbell, on this score, wiser than his neighbors. In reality, Clay's American System was the mainstay of his political party which, in turn, was but a revival of old Hamiltonian Federalism with its principle of a centralizing government as the dispenser of special favors, of the state in *loco parentis* to the economic interests of its citizens. All the lights of Campbell's philosophy, both political and religious, aligned him with Rousseau and Godwin and Paine and Jefferson in their conceptions of political justice and the minimized political state. In fact, in preparation for the Owen debate, he had read over Godwin's *Political Justice*, dubbing its author, "a highly gifted writer." Godwin's jealousy of delegated power was clearly inherent in the Bethany reformation, with its jealousy of ecclesiastical prerogative and its insistence on the principle of "least government" in the church. Undoubtedly, when he advocated protection for domestic manufactures, Campbell was thinking—not of the great industrial metropolis of Glasgow spawning its extremes of wealth and poverty that he had observed during his university days in 1808—but of the domestic economy observed during his boyhood in County Armagh where the people prospered by maintaining a just balance between agriculture and industry. From this he might draw a happy analogy to the small manufacturing enterprises of his neighbors in Brooke County. Though his realism should have counseled him to caution, he shared Clay's own complacency in believing that devotion to republican principles might safely be coupled with trust in a paternalistic federal government to distribute favors with an impartial hand. Likewise, to his fellow-citizens of the vast undeveloped West where such improvements as roads and canals were an everyday necessity, the view of the federal government as in *loco parentis to* the rising commonwealths was a persuasive argument, which appealed alike to farmer and to speculator, to town and to country. Thinking to embrace both the American System and the American Dream, they were, in effect, seeking to graft a Hamiltonian limb of special privilege on the Jeffersonian trees of liberal republicanism. So, at Richmond, blinded by their desire to obtain some immediate benefits from the federal government, Campbell and his colleagues would fail to see that the Eastern conservatives were opposing a system fundamentally antagonistic to their common agricultural interest, and their common philosophy.

On the other side, the conservatives denounced the hell-bent "downward tendency" of Campbell's theory of majority rights. The East, having embraced the tenets of individualism and the minimized state, had long since, in effect, grafted a limb of eighteenth-century liberalism on the tree of Tory privilege, Tory will-to-power of the wealthy; so now at Richmond, blinded by concern to protect their own wealth invested in slaves, they would fail to see that this concern might make it appear to the West that old aristocrats of Tidewater plantations were no better than new aristocrats of "banking institutions and moneyed corporations;" for whether the wealth be owned in bank stocks or in slaves meant little to those from whom it withheld the power of self-government.

After listening for some time to the troubled debate, the aged president of the convention took the floor. And in a single sentence he crystallized the root of the differences and difficulties. "I am satisfied," said Monroe, "if no such thing as slavery existed, that the people of our Atlantic border, would meet their brethren of the West, upon the basis of a majority of the free white population." So he proposed a compromise plan. He asked that the East yield, to grant the white population basis for the House of Delegates; that the West yield, to concede the compound basis, consisting of population and taxation combined, for the Senate.

It was the conservatives who quickly put an end to any hope of agreement on these terms. "If George Washington were to rise from the dead ... to propose such a compromise," said Leigh "... so ruinous ... so damnatory to the dearest interests of the people who had sent him here, he should find the moral courage in his heart to reject and to oppose it." Then, carried away by zeal for these "dearest interests," he launched into an address extending over part of two days and calculated to outrage every instinct of the self-respecting yeomen of the West. They were "peasants," he declared fit to be compared only with the slave labor of the East and equally unqualified for any voice in "political affairs." There was more. In his basis address a few days earlier, Campbell had sharply reminded the East that in the war year of 1814, when the Eastern militia "were all needed to prevent insurrections among your own discontented population," it was "the Valley and the west," men with "no suffrage, no representation in your Government," who "fled to your succour and protection from an invading enemy." Far from acknowledging this debt, Leigh passed what the *Niles Weekly Register* termed "certain unkind, if not con-temptuous remarks on the western militia, many of whom per-ished at Norfolk, when called from their mountains to defend the homes of the low-landers during the last war." On Leigh's speech being published, the result was swift and dramatic in at least one town of the West. The "peasants" of Harrisonburg assembled on the public square and burned in effigy a figure of Leigh bearing a copy of the offensive address; and according to a newspaper report of the incident, "although nearly all the male citizens of the place were engaged in this affair, there was no noise except the voice of the officer, who commanded, nothing was heard." All appeared to be feeling the effect of a deep, silent, indignant feeling of resent-ment.

It was little wonder that by mid-November the *Richmond Enquirer* was speculating whether the "ominous discussion" at the Capitol shouldn't be closed. The discerning would see in the Harrisonburg affair no incident of passing anger, but the symbol of a tragic irony of Virginia history and one of the unhappiest auguries of the convention. Had the East matched the generosity of the West in acknowledging their opponents as gentlemen worth of respect and granting their bond of affinity as Virginians, the drama at Richmond might well have moved to a very different conclusion. It had long been a form of amusement with the seaboard, of course—this affectation of superiority over everything to the West. And though by 1829 the frontier had moved its outposts across the Mississippi and started its trek toward the Rocky Mountains, nothing could convince the Tidewater Virginian still that all lands west of the Blue Ridge were not wild and uncultivated, and their tenants crude and uncouth. The common mind of the East was speaking when Leigh sarcastically derived western influence as "the weight of a Back-woods vote," and which another conservative described the great quantity of western land as "unfit for human use and not desirable as haunts for wild beasts."

These aspersions fell strangely on Western ears at Richmond. The "frontiersman" who occupied the White House had ridden away to Washington from a white-columned mansion in the rich and beautiful Cumberland Basin of Middle Tennessee, where his study overlooked a garden with handsome flower beds and curving brick-edged walks laid out by a "regular bred English Gardner," and where hospitality was daily dispensed with a graciousness and dignity that would do credit to any mansion of the Tidewater. In Western Virginia, the rambling white farm-house which Campbell's neighbors were pleased to call "Bethany Mansion" might not be so impressive as Andrew Jackson's Heritage, but the courtesy and conversation enjoyed by visitors to this house on the banks of the Buffaloe would equal in quality any that might be found in the great plantation houses on the banks of the James.

In his basis address, therefore, Campbell had summoned up his own talent for fine raillery to mock the air of condescension and suspicion with which the East seemed to view the Western citizenry. Noting that Judge Green, speaking for his "taxation combined" amendment, had appeared so oppressed with fear of the rapidly growing West that "his mental lights were, for the time being, eclipsed" and he had strained all the laws of logic "to show, while the wise men all came from the East, the march of empire was to the West," Campbell commented with amused irony:

> But, Sir, it is not the increase of population in the West which this gentleman ought to fear. It is the energy which the mountain breeze and western habits impart to these emigrants. They are regenerated; politically, I mean, Sir. They soon become *working politicians*; and the difference, Sir, between a *talking and a working politician* is immense. The Old Dominion has long been celebrated for producing great orators; the ablest metaphysicians in in policy; men that split hairs in all abstruse questions of political economy. But at home, or when they return from Congress, they have Negroes to fan them asleep. But a Pennsylvania, a New York, an Ohio, or a Western Virginia Statesman, though far inferior in logic, metaphysics, and rhetoric, to an old Virginia Statesman, has this advantage, that when he returns home he takes off his coat, and takes hold of the plough. This gives him bone and muscle, Sir, and preserves his Republican principles pure and uncontaminated.

Since it was all too clear that the East did in fact distrust the quality of Western citizens as much as their numbers, Campbell dropped his air of ironic raillery to protest in high seriousness: "I have been sorry, very sorry, Sir, to observe in sundry gentlemen on this floor, a disposition to treat us as aliens, or as persons, who have no *common interest* with the people of the east."

Though all such protests appeared unheeded, the representatives of the Western "peasants" gathered their strength on November 14 to vote on Judge Green's amendment. It was defeated, forty-nine to forty-seven. But the margin of victory was far too small for the reformers to dare risk a final vote on the report of the

Legislative Committee at this time; so the convention turned its attention to an aspect of the issue scarcely less inflammatory in character, the right of suffrage.

As these lines were taking form, Campbell gradually began to identify the leaders of the opposing parties; and the drama itself was proving no less interesting than the character of its actors.

Of the triumvirate of sages, Monroe and Madison were to play but minor roles in debate; and it soon became ironically clear to Campbell and his colleagues that they could expect no assistance from the two Republican ex-presidents in achieving republican reforms at Richmond. On the rare occasions when Monroe spoke "his ideas appeared to be confused ... his manner perplexed," and even his limited use as moderator was to be cut short by illness. Madison did not take the floor at all until the convention had been in session many weeks, and then he spoke only thirty minutes and in so low a tone that "the members rushed from their seats and crowded around" to hear him. A visitor in the gallery reported that "although a pin might have been heard to drop ... I could distinguish only one word, and that was 'constitution.'" His argument, however, was "simple and lucid"—and a scholarly exposition in defense of minority rights. Indeed, though at first it had seemed that he would maintain a neutral position, as the convention progressed, this man who in the early days of the Republic had fought so ardently by the side of Thomas Jefferson, gave his vote more and more often to the side of the conservatives. But in 1776 Madison had been a young man, eager—as Campbell and the other young reformers of 1829 were eager—to battle for his ideals of justice against any caution or expediency. Now he was an old man, and he feared radical sentiments he once had welcomed as liberal.

The third member of the triumvirate, still robust, his faculties undimmed at seventy-four, would take an active part in the convention. To know where his influence lay, one had only to know that he had gone to the polls to vote but twice in the past twenty-four years. He first cast his ballot, in 1804 against the re-election of Thomas Jefferson, and then in 1828 to vote against the Democrat from Tennessee. Appointed chief justice at the beginning of the century, John Marshall had used his high office for three decades "to do even more perhaps than Hamilton in molding the yet malleable Constitution into an instrument for a powerful and high centralized government, emphasizing the rights of property over those of man." Now, at Richmond, "displaying no vision, no aspiration, no devotion to human rights" he would consistently maintain the role of practical statesman who believes that the best and safest government is government removed as far as possible from control by the common people.

Another of the elder statesman was Virginia's governor, William Branch Giles. A man of sixty-seven, leaning on crutches and pale and shaken from a recent illness, he was generally regarded "as the leader of the reserve corps, ready to bring up his powerful reinforcement" at any time it was needed to aid the conservatives. But whenever the governor did speak, Campbell, having won his own first reputation of the debating platform and with his own penchant for the quiet, reasoned manner of speaking, would pay particular attention. For in Giles, he was listening to the man whom Jefferson had pronounced America's greatest debater. Some even declared the equal of England's greatest, Charles James Fox, and whose style of delivery another observer at Richmond described as "perfectly conversational—no gestures, no effort; but in ease, fluency, and tact, surely he had not there his equal; his words were like honey pouring from an eastern rock."

But very early in the convention it had become evident to the reformers that the active leader of the seaboard cohorts was to be not an elder statesman but the young conservative whose manner so well became the name of his county of Chesterfield, Benjamin

Watkins Leigh. A lawyer of forty-eight, he was small and so grace-ful in person—a slight limp, instead of impairing the ease of his carriage, seeming rather to heighten its effect—that even the sea-soned newspaperman, Hugh Rose Pleasants, called him "uncom-monly well made ... with a hand that would have formed a study for Kneller, eyes of uncommon brilliancy, a forehead of striking beauty, hair as black as the wings of a raven, and glossy and fine as a lady's, and features ... [almost] classically handsome." Though his basis address had driven the men of Harrisonburg to coldly furious protest, a visitor in the convention gallery remarked: "He never lightens, never thunders; he can charm, he can convince, but he can scarcely overwhelm." Opposite as were their views, Campbell would recognize one trait they had in common: Leigh, even as he, seemed to seek out difficulties "for the mere love of the excitement produced by overcoming them."

The competent second to Leigh was a young conservative whom Campbell had already met in debate, Abel P. Upshur, who at the age of thirty-nine, was Judge of the General Court of Virginia. Two lawyers at the Richmond bar whom Campbell had likewise met in debate and with whom he was also serving on the judiciary committee, Robert Stanard and Richard Morris, were adding support to the conservatives. Able support it was, for, what-ever its evils, the establishment by the Virginia constitution of the Court of Appeals and the Chancery Court in the city of Richmond had one good effect, that like the Inns of Court in London, it concentrated in one place the state's highest legal tal-ent. Though Stanard had served at the Richmond bar for twelve years, his talents—both for logic and, as Campbell had good rea-son to know, for effective invective—were so well remembered in his home district that Spotsylvania had sent him as her delegate. As Morris was a delegate from Hanover—the county which had given America Patrick Henry and Henry Clay—it was fitting that even in this assembly of orators, he should have inspired Hugh Pleasants to describe him as pouring "forth without effort, and

apparently without consciousness, a torrent of magnificent eloquence, combining all the elements of a great oration, powerful
argument, classical imagery, and finished wit." Morris' speech on
the basis question preceded Campbell's, and it moved John
Randolph to comment, "I see that the wise men still come from
the East." But Campbell himself was far from overwhelmed by
Morris' "display of ... rhetorical powers." Rather, Campbell
remarked with quiet irony, "I wish I could comment his logic, as
sincere as I do his rhetoric. His whole speech was founded upon
two or three assumptions ... And, Sir, allow me two or three
assumptions, and I don't know what I could not prove."

While he was assessing the quality of the opposition,
Campbell was also taking stock, these first few weeks, of his
Western colleagues. In the forefront, of course, was his colleague
from Brooke County. Whatever their personal differences,
Campbell would be the first to admit that the West had placed its
confidence well in the powerful logic and eloquence of Philip
Doddridge. One of the seaboard delegates might have found him
somewhat slovenly in dress and his voice lacking "freedom of
play;" but Hugh Pleasants grew almost lyrical in describing how
his origin among the lofty mountains, the precipitous torrents,
and the "primeval magnificence" of the unbroken forests of the
West had imparted to Doddridge a fresh and different quality and
a habit of thinking for himself that "gave a breadth to his views,
and a boldness to his language that sometimes startled the tamer
denizens of the city, "even though his language," with all its
impetuosity, was remarkable for its classical purity," his words
seemed "indissolubly wedded to the meaning they were designed
to convey." Yet, another writer had another discerning critique to
offer. Doddridge, he pointed out, shared "similar faults and excel-
lencies" with his opponent Leigh; "sociable, lively, and agreeable,
their company was too much sought for their own good" so that
neither quite "accomplished as much as was expected of him, or
filled that place to which his powers seemed to call him."

In any event, early in the convention, it became evident—to the dismay of the conservatives and the delight of the reformers— that the West was to find its "Ajax Telamon" in a native of the East. Chapman Johnson, a member of the Richmond bar and a native of Louisa County in the Piedmont, was a friend of Benjamin Watkins Leigh, and had sided with the seaboard in its attempt to stave off the convention. But he had once been a resident of Augusta County in the West; and his old neighbors, remembering his quality of "wisdom and fairness," had called him to represent them at Richmond, and he would fully honor their trust. He was no orator like Doddridge, and his style was diffuse. His speech, on the basis of representation, occupied the better part of three days, a fact that drew sarcastic raillery from John Randolph; but so "gigantic" was his strength of understanding it revealed that an eminent New York jurist called him "*par eminence*, the great man of the convention." In contrast to his friend and chief antagonist, the "slight graceful, and handsome" Leigh, he was "a man of noble and commanding presence ... [with] a head whose intel- lectual developments would have delighted a phrenologist, and a countenance more strongly indicative of extreme benevolence," wrote Pleasants, "than that of any other human being we recollect to have seen ... [He was] the very incarnation of truth, honor, jus- tice, and generosity. Even those who most bitterly disputed his peculiar opinions, could not but bow in reverence to the majesty of his virtues." Withal, Chapman Johnson was a man with whom "the Reverend gentleman from Brooke" would especially delight to be associated.

Indeed, theirs were some of the same qualities; and though Campell's style of oratory, in contrast to Johnson's, was clear, calm, and concise, they would make something of the same impression on observers of Richmond. For, even as Campbell was observing others, so he himself was being observed. Of the ninety- six delegates in the convention, the majority were signifying their position only when the roll was called on a ballot. But the master of Bethany had not come to Richmond to express his will merely by his vote. Almost immediately he was marked as "one of the most controversial figures in the convention." His name found its way often onto the pages of the *Richmond Enquirer,* and few later accounts of the convention would be written that did not assess his contribution. One historian, who considered it doubtful whether any body in the "world's history" had ever "included so much talent, eloquence, experience, and intellectual power," listed him among its "most notable and distinguished members." Another, John P. Little by name, described him in detail for the *Southern Literary Messenger:*

> Alexander Campbell, the Baptist reformer ... contended stoutly for the Western plan of representation and for the spirit of reform generally. A stout, rugged looking man, a Scot by birth, yet brought up in the mountain region of Virginia, he possessed much vigor and originality of mind; he was learned too in many languages, and had his natural shrewdness and keenness increased by the excitements of American culture, and improved by the workings of an intellect deeply exercised on religious subjects, and fully inspired with the great idea of reforming the church and the world. He presented that singular spectacle—a cool and cautious Scotsman, thoroughly imbued with, and active in carrying out, the most enthusiastic ideas. And this enthusiasm was accompanied by the firm decision of character, instinctive wisdom, honorable fairness of conduct, abiding sense of religious truth, and persevering resolution which honorably distinguished the Scottish people. It would be better for the world if a people so honest, firm and wise had more enthusiasm; for we may be sure that it would be exerted in advancing the cause of religion and morals, and thus benefiting the race of man.

But having said all this, Little, who himself had no sympathy with the cause of the West, apparently felt nothing illogical in adding the sharp reservation: "Mr. Campbell was too much carried away by his love of reform; and his views, embracing every subject, made him, like most reformers, too much a citizen of the world to be a perfectly safe counselor for Virginia."

For his own part, Campbell, it seems, in the midst of all the assembled talent at Richmond, found one of his happiest associates with a young conservative from the Norfolk district, Hugh Blair Grigsby. The wide divergence in their political sentiment, of course, offered no bar to friendship for him, who had so recently scandalized the good citizens of Cincinnati by his friendly relations with the "infidel" Robert Owen. One day Grigsby was to become distinguished as an historian of Virginia and leave a lively record of the men and issues of 1829. At the opening of the convention, the delegate from Norfolk had been General Robert Barraud Taylor, a portly, graceful, and extremely able Tidewater gentleman who, naturally, had come to Richmond to defend the *status quo*. But after a month's exposure to Western republicanism, he startled the convention with a strong speech declaring: Locality cannot alter right; "whatever fifty votes can do in the county of Norfolk, then fifty votes should do the same in the county of Brooke." His outraged, slave-owning constituents in Norfolk immediately and firmly requested that he reverse his stand. Instead, Taylor resigned his seat, explaining in a letter to the convention on November 7, "They ask what is impossible. They require me to violate my conscience and the sentiment of filial devotion, which I owe to my country." In his stead, the Norfolk district then sent to Richmond young Grigsby, age twenty-two, an exchange by which the West lost a champion on the Tidewater, and Alexander Campbell gained an agreeable companion. As was to be expected from his youth, Grigsby took no active part in the debates. But he used his powers of observation well; and when in 1853 he wrote his historical sketch, *The Virginia Convention of*

1829–30, he made room for an affectionate and humorous tribute to his reverend friend from Brooke County. Since he otherwise was limiting description to members of the assembly by then deceased, he explained: "The member ... whose election to a seat in that body was a topic of remark at the time, from his unique position requires, though still living, a short notice." "There was a strong distrust of theologians in Virginia," he continued,

> and it was feared that by the presence of a popular divine in the convention the element of religion might be mixed up with topics sufficiently exciting in themselves. But the course of ALEXANDER CAMPBELL soon dispelled all such fears. He indeed belonged to a sect the most numerous in the Union—a sect, however, most devoted to religious freedom in its largest sense; but, if it had been otherwise, of this powerful sect Campbell was a schismatic. There was no danger to religious freedom from him. He needed it more than anybody else. With the doctrines of his church and with the constitution of the State he was equally at war. In his personal appearance, in his dress and manners, in his style of speaking, he was a man of the world ... He was a fine scholar, and, with the younger members of the body who relished his amusing thrusts, his pleasing address and social feelings rendered him very acceptable. As a controversialist he had some great qualities; he was bold, subtle, indefatigable, and as insensible to attack as if he were sheathed in the hide of a rhinoceros ... With the exception of Col. Bierne, he was, I think, the only foreign-born citizen in the body.

Years later, after Campbell had died and he himself was become an old man, Grigsby again wrote of his happy association with the elder man as he had known him in the convention in 1829:

The ground of our communion was that he was a Scotsman, and ... a good classical scholar. On my mother's side I am of Scotch descent, and have made the merits of Scotsmen a theme of study through life. And as I was when I knew Mr. Campbell but two and twenty, and was fresh from my Latin and Greek studies, I was at no loss in starting topics of conversation; and in our genial intercourse the exciting subject of the fierce contests of that day were held in abeyance. His mind was of a masculine order, and his temper was aggressive. He would rather gain the day by a hard fight, than by the retreat of his enemy. He was a good logician; but his mode of reasoning was better adapted to the pulpit and the professor's chair than to the forum and the bar. In private life he was a delightful companion, free of guile, full of talk, hearty in his feelings, and scorning that dread of misrepresentation, which in this country so often seals the lips and represses the earnest impulses of the heart ... I have said that he was of Scotch descent; for, though born in Ireland, he was an offshoot of the great clan of Argyle.

But whatever interest the "unique" Reverend gentleman from Brooke or the great national figures in the assemblage might excite, there was one delegate above all, others whom the crowd was most anxious and impatient to hear; and he seemed determined not to be heard. Campbell himself, with his own talent for trenchant satire fast becoming a by-word in the West, would wait with especial eagerness for the first address of the Virginian whose sarcastic, bitter wit and invective had rebounded from the halls of Congress to keep the country amused and scandalized for three decades. Others might surpass John Randolph of Roanoke in logic and statesmanship, but for sheer brilliance of oratory he was considered unrivaled, and his uncommon and compelling person had long since caught the imagination of the nation. The anxiety to hear him, it was said, "amounted almost to frenzy. Many persons, greatly to their own inconvenience, remained in town days longer than they would otherwise have been induced to do." It was thought he would answer the first speech of Chapman Johnson, and such a throng packed the galleries and the spare seats in the hall that there was "no room even to breathe, much less to turn around." But whether from caprice or from art—he was "a consummate actor, ... adept as ever trod the boards of Covent Garden or Drury Lane"—he did not condescend to speak. Nor did he for days to come—though he arrived at the Capitol every morning wearing a full suit of black with crepe upon his hat and arm; and when questioned, he would answer that he was in mourning for the old Constitution of Virginia since in this convention he expected "to witness its death and burial."

Then, finally, on November 14, at a time when nobody was expecting it and the lobby and galleries were almost empty, the delegate from Charlotte rose slowly from his seat and pronounced the words, "Mr. President." "Never," said Hugh Pleasants, who happened to be in the hall at the moment, "have we seen two words produce the same effect ... Where the crowd came from, or how they got intelligence that Randolph had the floor, we could never learn, but it poured in like the waters of the ocean when the dyke gives way." And all attention was centered on the tall, quaint "unearthly-looking figure" of the speaker, whose "pair of dark hazel eyes reputed to have a 'petrifying effect upon those [on] whom he chose to fix them in anger or disdain.'" Now, at last, Campbell was hearing the melody of that "inimitable voice," "shrill and pipe-like ... musical in its lower tones and like a clarion in its upper ones," now, at last, observing the style of an orator who, even as himself, employed "very little gesticulation," usually speaking "with the greatest deliberation, his left hand resting on his cane, and his right ... giving emphasis to his words." Now, at last, he was watching the effect on an audience of that "admirable acting," which changed Randolph's "most airy nothings into golden precepts," watching as the "immense crowd" sat enthralled, "still as death, save when it indulged itself in shouts of laughter." But above all, he was listening to the content of Randolph's argument, listening closely and carefully, for the full two hours of the address, so that he might remember and reply. If Alexander Campbell was already marked as the most radical spokesman for the Western democrats, John Randolph spoke as the most uncompromising voice of the ultra-conservatives.

A few days later, on November 19, Campbell took the floor for his second address—on the right of suffrage. This time he spoke extemporaneously. A scheme for extension of suffrage presented by his colleague, Eugenius Wilson, having failed, he rose to present his own resolutions. No one was surprised that they demanded full, free, white manhood suffrage.

In his basis address he had digressed long enough to declare the right of suffrage, man's God-given right "of thinking, willing, and expressing his will," a right possessed "anterior to his coming into the social compact," a right *natural and underived,* to the exercise of which, every man by nature has a good a reason as another." Now that this question was before the convention, he began by defining a citizen, as "a freeman, who has a voice in the Government under which he lives;" then proceeded immediately to the acid comment: "[In Virginia], though we admire the term, and in a sort of complimentary way, address all men as citizens ... we have comparatively few citizens ... No disenfranchised man is a citizen." In contrast, he felt that his own resolutions both fulfilled the true intent of the Bill of Rights, which required evidence only of "permanent common interest with, and attachment to the community" as the qualification for voting, and also satisfied the dictates of common sense, since, to his mind, no artificial restrictions upon the right of suffrage were either intelligent or desirable.

To levy any tax, even a poll-tax, as a restriction on suffrage was to invite corruption, for, "If we desire to see men act a dignified part, we must treat them according to the dignity of human nature. If you put the tax at one dollar, you make the price of a thousand votes only a thousand dollars." Therefore, simple nativity and residence in the state were evidence of "attachment to the community" preferable to any "pecuniary or property qualification," and "must appear so to all," he concluded ironically, "except those who think that virtue, intelligence, and patriotism, spring up out of the soil, and grow like mushrooms upon its surface, after a person has paid a stipulated price for it."

The position made clear, he then turned to a searching analysis of Randolph's address delivered five days before. And in the process, the polished wit of Roanoke was himself to be the recipient of a considerable same of polished raillery, Western style.

Foremost in Campbell's mind was Randolph's scornful denunciation of "this monstrous tyranny" of majority rule, the "all-prevailing principle that *vox populi vox dei.*"

Were he a young man, Randolph declared, "I would not live under King Numbers. I would not be his steward—nor make him my task-master. I would obey the principle of self-preservation—a principle we find even in brute creation, in flying from this mischief." Now, Campbell answered him:

> I was sorry to hear, the other day, the eloquent gentleman from Charlotte [Mr. Randolph], protest against his majesty *King Numbers*, and declare his readiness to revolt from his dominions. King Numbers, Mr. Chairman, is the legitimate sovereign of all this country. General Jackson, the President of these United States, is only representative, the *lawful representative* of King Numbers. And, whither Sir, can that gentleman fly from the government of this King? In the North, in the South, in the East and in the West, he can find no other monarch. Except he

cross the ocean he can put himself under no other King. And whenever he may please to expatriate himself, he will find beyond the dominion of King Numbers, there is no other monarch, save King Cypher, King Blood, King Sword, or King Purse. And, Sir, permit me to add, there is none of those so august as our King. I love King Numbers; I wish to live, and I hope to die, under the government of this majestic personage. He is, Sir, a wise, benevolent, patriotic, and powerful prince—the most dignified personage under the canopy of Heaven.

Randolph had suggested that the blame for producing "this great and grinding oppression" of King Numbers was to be laid to the silent operation of "time, the greatest of innovators"—a descriptive phrase borrowed from a translation of a Latin maxim of Lord Bacon's. Campbell, the classical scholar, was quick to seize the opening, and replied by quoting the entire maxim correctly in the original, which neatly turned the expression to his own advantage:

> I heard the same gentleman, Mr. Chairman, with pleasure, too, refer to a saying of the immortal Bacon. Twice he alluded to…the great *innovator*, Time. I did wish to hear him quote the whole sentence, and apply it. Lord Bacon said, (I think I give it in his own words)— *Maximus innovator tempus; Quidni igitur tempus imitemur?* Why then, says he, can we not imitate Time, the greatest of all innovators?

Young Grisby was so amused by this "successful rejoinder" to a gentleman who generally had the last word himself that after twenty years, he was to remember and repeat it in his history of the convention. But the gentleman from Charlotte, neither amused nor mollified by Campbell's thrust, sharply rejoined a few days later: "This lust for innovation—this *rerum novarum lubido* has been the death of all Republics."

At that point the conservative and the reformer were farthest apart. Fearful and suspicious of every new departure in government, Randolph was clearly ready to go further than any other conservative at Richmond to contend that George Mason and his revolutionary compatriots, with unapproachable wisdom and infallible judgment, had conceived in Virginia's present constitution a perfect instrument for expressing the will of her people. Indeed, as his first address made plain, Randolph's policy and purpose in the convention was not to open or discuss any of the numerous questions at issue, new or old, but "simply to insist doggedly and scornfully upon the strength of Sir Robert Walpole's maxim, *quieta non movere*, that the existing constitution of Virginia should undergo no substantial change." In contrast, the reverend gentleman from Brooke who had long since started the West with the novelty of his religious views, and for two decades had urged the people to sweep the "rubbish of the ages" from their minds to make room for the advent of new light, to recognize that progress in all affairs, religious or civil, results from experiment would scarcely be so shackled by reverence of the past.

"I am no friend to mere theories, but," he reminded the opposition, "all reformations and all improvement are first theories." To those gentlemen dismayed by the idea of novelty, he suggested humorously that even if General Suffrage were a novel idea "that would not prove it false. Steamboats are a novel invention, and … [the] new race of iron men which modern science has created … I mean the wooden, brazen, and iron men, which neither eat, drink, sleep nor get tired … are all revolutionists and will as surely revolutionize the world as ever did the art of printing or any conquering invader." Then continuing in the same vein, he proceeded to offer a lesson in history to these gentlemen so addicted to the virtues of antiquity. They had affirmed that General Suffrage was a "novel doctrine" sprung up in the age of Cromwell;" but, declared Campbell:

> ...not withstanding the general historic accuracy of the gentlemen on the other side, they have mistaken the date ... It is now three thousand three hundred and twenty-nine years old ... When Israel became a Commonwealth ... they received a Constitution from him who led them through the Red Sea. ... After it was written, it was submitted to every man upon the muster roll of Israel ... and they voted for its adoption as their national compact. So old, Sir, and so venerable is the origin of General Suffrage.

Here was another *touché* which Hugh Blair Grigsby thought worthy of record in his history of the convention, where, after remarking that Campbell appeared "a man of the world," he continued:

> ...and it would not have been suspected that he was other than a layman, if in his speech on the basis [*sic*] he had not drawn his illustrations at length from the Jewish system. ... He had a great fund of humor, and, observing the zeal with which the East pressed the antiquity of the constitution, he proved easily enough the superior age of his own system, and urged that the East on its own principles might without self-abasement lay George Mason at the feet of Moses.

At another point, Campbell also sought to correct an historical assumption of Randolph and his fellow conservatives who, in their eagerness to maintain the *status quo*, were quite prepared to fall back on Edmund Burke. They might even claim the assent of the founding fathers in support of Burke's theory of a changeless constitution, based on the conception of a static, non-revocable civil compact—the legal doctrine of inviolability, which had provoked the tart rejoinder from Thomas Paine. Paine wrote in *Rights of Man* this answer to Burke: "The vanity and presumption of governing from the grave is the most ridiculous and insolent of all tyrannies." Thomas Jefferson, too, had written sharply of those men who "look at constitutions with sanctimonious reverence, and deem them like the ark of the covenant, too sacred to be touched." And John Locke, in his two *Treatises on Civil Government*, "had forever laid down the right of resistance to encroaching sovereignty, the principle that any violation of the civil compact, of the rights of the subjects, on the part of the government may rightfully lead to revolution."

Therefore, at Richmond, arguing with Paine, Jefferson, and Locke against the principle of "government from the grave," of the rigid constitution, the perpetual contract, Campbell reminded the conservatives that, "the great error of mankind, and the common error of all ages, has been, to suppose that all reformations are perfect." "It is equally true in religion and in politics … After many ages of darkness and superstition … Luther and Calvin," he continued, in the only allusion to religious reformation he was to make during the whole convention, "effected … a real reformation … and … during an interval of three hundred years, their adherents have not advanced an inch. So in politics." The "illustrious fathers of the American Revolution" had framed a constitution that was "the best production of nearly six thousand years." But, since "it was not to be expected that these sages, great and wise … as they were, could have perfectly emerged" out of the long-consecrated "political darkness and errors … of the old world … experience and the progress of political light have discovered some defects" in their handiwork. Moreover, in spite of what all the conservatives might say, Campbell insisted—and here he was on solid historical ground— the sages of '76 had themselves foreseen "that changes would take place and that the human mind ... would progress," and so had "devised, and most prudently advised, a frequent recurrence to fundamental principles." Principles, of course, contained in the Bill of Rights, which instrument, as he was more convinced with the passage of each day's debate, "has been our palladium, and the only bulwark against the demolition of our republican citadel."

On coming to Richmond, he continued on a plaintive note, he had hoped that the gentlemen assembled there in 1829 would carry on the political torch handed them by the gentlemen of 1776: " ... present to the world the best model of Government the world ever saw." But, he added, "I am, Sir, beginning to despair." The situation was all the more distressing because the anticipated "thorough amelioration of our condition" was being frustrated by "the monosyllables *mine* and *thine*," by contests "about mere local interest which a few years will change in defiance of all our efforts." "No Government which has paid a due regard to the rights of man," he declared, again calling on the lessons of history, "has ever been subverted. Where are all the ancient empires of the world? The Egyptian, Assyrian, Persian, Grecian, Roman? All, all ... gone to ruin. And what was the cause? Either they were not founded on a just regard of social rights, or ceased justly to regard man according to his nature." Here was the heart of that passionate concern for social justice, and for economic justice, which he so fully shared with Jefferson and Paine, Godwin and Rousseau— the demand that every concept of government be judged and every act of government be held strictly to account, not by the balance sheet of corporate business or the power and glory of the state, but by its returns on the social ledger. And here he was returned once more to the delegate from Charlotte. As one further defense of the *status quo*, Randolph had referred the convention "to, the great men, which the present system in Virginia had produced." Campbell now answered him with the stinging rebuke:

We doubt it not, Sir. I have lived in a country in

which there were many great men, very learned and powerful men. But how were they created, Sir? For one noble Lord, there were ten thousand ignoble paupers, and for one great scholar, there were ten thousand ignoramuses. That is the secret, Sir. I never wish to see this mode of making great men introduced into this great Commonwealth. I trust, Sir, we will rather strive to make many middling men, than a few great or *noble* men.

In concluding, Campbell insisted that General Suffrage was in "the spirit of this age," and he rejoiced to find himself "associated with many gentlemen on this floor, who ... have not only grown up under this age, but grown up with it," gentlemen "who feel the current of time," and so "have no idea of making Chinese shoes for American feet; or of constructing a new bedstead after the manner of Procrustes, for men of American stature." There was "one most august tribunal to which ... Time will make us all do homage"—the tribunal of public opinion. And public opinion in "no less than half the States in this Union" had already decided to disregard the property qualification for electors. Furthermore, the idea was proving practical. Half of those states were slave states, and "so far from impairing the safety of property of all of them." For, indeed, said Campbell, and all his former air of raillery was dropped as in his closing words he reiterated the solemn warning with which Chapman Johnson had sought to arouse the convention a few days earlier:

When we disfranchise one class of men, or deprive them of their political and natural rights, to secure any property or privilege we possess, we endanger that very property and those very privileges, more ... than we protect them.... It is in the nature of man to hate, and to attempt to impair and destroy, that which is held at his expense, and which degrades him in his own estimation.

For the safety, then, and the preservation of those very interests, I would conceive this extension of the Right of Suffrage indispensible.

The *Richmond Enquirer* tersely summed up the result of his oratory: "Mr. Campbell['s] propositions in favor of an extended suffrage ... were rejected by a strong vote." It was strong, indeed, only eleven members "rising in the affirmative." Even the reformers, in the main, were not ready to battle for so radical an extension of the franchise. Yet, as the *Enquirer* pointed out a few days later, other propositions from both sides of the Hall, from Doddridge and Cooke, from Stanard and Leigh, shared the same fate with Wilson's and Campbell's. The debate continued for days, and Campbell interposed frequently with remarks, as did John Randolph of Roanoke.

Though he had remained silent for weeks, from the time of his first address Randolph was, in fact, to occupy so large a place on the floor that in Hugh Pleasants' opinion: "He was like the musical Director in the midst of an immense orchestra; the players and the instruments seemed to obey the slightest motion of his hand." He was "literally the hero of the convention," and even the "boldest and most impassioned speakers" would turn "their eyes to watch his approving nod, and seemed to catch inspiration from his recognition." But Randolph held his mastery by a two-edged sword. Young Grigsby, observing his amazing influence day by day from the floor, was in later years to record the other side: "He inspired terror to a degree that even at this distance of time seems inexplicable. He was feared alike by East and West, by friend and foe ... He called himself on one occasion a tomahawker and a scalper ... and as he knew the private as well as the public history of every prominent member, it was impossible for his opponents to foresee from what quarter ... the attacks would fall. He also had political accounts of long standing to settle ... and none could tell when the day of reckoning would arrive ... . Moreover, it was impossible to answer a sneer or a sarcasm with an argument." But one delegate obviously did not fear these remarkable powers of retribution or of sarcasm. Rather, having thrown down the gauntlet in his address on suffrage, the master of Bethany had seemed with almost careless bravado to signal his willingness to cross the swords of debate with the redoubtable master of Roanoke.

Certainly, no field at Richmond was more bitterly contested than that where this question of suffrage was settled. Denying that the right of suffrage was anything more than a mere "conventional" right, the conservatives in general would have none of the arguments from the Bill of Rights and Thomas Jefferson. "We are not to be struck down by the authority of Mr. Jefferson," said Randolph; "If there be any point in which the authority of Mr. Jefferson might be considered as valid, it is in the mechanism of a plow."

And apparently he didn't think much of the plow. As for the abstract rights of suffrage, he tossed off this appeal with an insolent, "Sir, the only good I ever knew these abstractions to do is to abstract money out of he pockets of one great division of the country, to put it into the pockets of another." Leigh also, with his usual success, searched his mind for offensive epithets: "If any plague originate in the North, it is sure to spread to the South: ... the influenza ... the small-pox... the Hessian fly ... Universal Suffrage—all come from the North." He, too, assailed Jefferson. Even the conciliatory Monroe warned that other governments had fallen when the populace attained too great power and urged retention of the voting privilege to "some hold in the territory itself ... something that we own, not as passengers or voyagers." Randolph enthusiastically seconded Monroe: The "only safe ground" for the right of suffrage in Virginia was "*terra firma*: literally *firma*: The Land," surely not an unreasonable contention in framing a constitution "for the people emphatically agricultural; where land is ... accessible to every exertion of honest industry."

Returning to the field comment on these latter arguments, Campbell remarked that the downfall of ancient governments was no warning against an extension of suffrage in Virginia, for their position had not been analogous to hers; and as "to the case of procuring a freehold, no man with due respect to himself and his rights would stoop to purchase what he had a right to demand." An alarmed conservative quickly "expressed his opposition to cutting down the venerable tree planted by our forefathers and planting another in its stead"—to which Campbell retorted that he "thought the gentleman's alarm about the ax imaginary; it was only a pruning knife to lop off a few aristocratical branches." As other Eastern delegates continued to attack by painting lurid pictures of conditions in states given up to these wild ideas of Jacksonian democracy, Campbell again replied, in milder vein, that:

> He had traveled extensively over the new States, and had never seen any of those formidable evils which seem to haunt gentlemen's imaginations in reference to Universal Suffrage. He believed it was owing to the restraints upon the Right of Suffrage, that Virginia was so far behind her neighbors in the culture of her soil and the progress of general improvement.

Here—on charge of retrogression—was a home thrust that the East could not deny. For while industrial development increased, the wealth of the North and the invention of the cotton gin attracted vast numbers of Virginia's citizens into states farther South more adapted to cotton-growing, her land values had drastically declined and vast areas of worn-out lands were given over to broom-sedge and pine. Other reformers in the convention, like Campbell, were quick to press this advantage, and offer the remedy. "I could weep over her desolation; for I love Virginia," said Naylor; and to what was the desolation due? To "a defect in her frame of government.... Engraft the scion of genuine Republicanism upon the old stock of Virginia patriotism, and see whether it will not bud ... and bear precious fruit." But for the East to admit the thrust was not to accept the remedy. On the contrary, the spectre of her abandoned lands and stationary population was the basis of much of her fear and suspicion of the rapidly growing West, and of her resulting aspersions on the quality of Western citizens. Early in the convention, Campbell had protested this attitude with light, mocking raillery. But tempers were now growing shorter. As the Eastern delegates—not at all deterred by remembrance of the cold, quiet anger of the people of Harrisonburg silently burning Leigh in effigy—continued their aspersions. Fenton Mercer protested in sharp exasperation that they were acting "as if they apprehended, from the West, an irruption of barbarians."

Ignoring the taunt, the East gathered its strength; and when the final ballot on the right of suffrage was taken, the gentlemen on the Tidewater could feel that they had again, for a time at least, made themselves "secure against the barbarians." The number of men of legal age who remained disfranchised in Virginia still numbered more than thirty thousand.

After the basis of representation and the right of suffrage, there was one other major question before the convention, that of judiciary reform, in which Campbell, being a member of the Judiciary Committee, had a particular interest.

Stormy sessions must have marked the meetings of the Judiciary Committee as the Brooke County reformer faced the implacable conservative who was its chairman; the fact Campbell was a leader of the opposition there had been evidenced when he took the convention floor for the first time on October 24 to present a minority report on action of the committee. These sessions had prepared him for the realization that in the struggle for judicial reform, the delegates bent on a more democratic constitution would meet their greatest odds. Staunchly they had stood their ground on the issues of representation and of suffrage. Here, one delegate's theory was as good as another's. But the Judiciary was a different matter. For, there stood John Marshall. The nation's most famous jurist might be careless of dress and unspectacular in debate, with a voice almost as inaudible as Madison's and a monotonous "song in his speaking" to which his right hand harmonized "in a most ungracious manner, but he wore the halo of this office as Chief Justice of the Supreme Court of the United States properly. He awed anyone who might dare dispute the validity of his opinions; and with him were arrayed many of the most brilliant and distinguished minds in the convention. It would take courage in any man not used to arguing legal matters to stand against them. But the Bethany editor had long since demonstrated that he was not a man to veer from battle because his adversary had a larger force and had been longer in the field than he.

So on December 1, Campbell arose to make his third, and last, address—a plea for a more democratic judiciary. On this question, he and the other reformers at Richmond were to stage, in miniature, the same struggle that had plagued the councils of the nations from the very beginnings of the new republic. Marshall—believing absolutely in the doctrine of the ethical absolute, the *vox justiciae, vox dei,* worshipping the body of the English Common Law, which a Speaker of the House of Commons had once declared "drawn from the Law of God, the Law of Nature, and the Law of Reason, not mutable"—had for three decades been rendering judicial decisions that constantly negated the Bill of Rights, and served as a causeway over which the eighteenth-century doctrine of the sovereignty of the law was passing to unite with the new philosophy of capitalistic exploitation. Through his verdicts, the American Constitution was emerging as an instrument for the propertied minority much as English constitutional theory had received a pronounced Tory bias in filtering through the mind of the great Tory commentator, Blackstone. But he had to fight every step of the way against the bitter opposition of Thomas Jefferson. Concerned lest the rights won by the Revolution be interpreted away by lawyers resting their case on the legal fiction of an "abstract justice" above constitutions and statutes and the majority will, Jefferson, on the one hand, had warned against unquestioning veneration of a Common Law grown up under English absolutism and the "wily sophistries" of the Tory Blackstone whose books had "done more towards the suppression of the liberties of man, than all the millions of men in the army of Bonaparte." On the other hand, he had warned against Marshall's demand for unquestioned supremacy of the Judiciary with the blunt assertion that it "is a misnomer to call a government republican, in a which a branch of the supreme power is independent of the nation." Thus, Marshall and Jefferson had long since posed the question: How much authority may be invested in the Judiciary without endangering the liberties of the republic?

Campbell was little prepared to answer at Richmond. Marshall was not surprised to find his assumptions about the consummate blessings of Virginia's County Court system being maligned in Jeffersonian terms. Virginia justices of the peace sat together to form her County Courts; and in judging their efficacy, the testimony of "the immortal Jefferson," "one of the most illustrious sages which Virginia has produced," was of far greater value, suggested Campbell, than the testimony of those gentlemen in the convention, some of whom, from twenty-five years experience as justices of the peace, had declared these courts "one of the wisest and most beneficial institutions in the country, if not in the world." For, he commented dryly, "without imputing anything to their motives ... I may be permitted to remark, that the relations in which we stand to persons and things ... often imperceptibly, influence our judgment ... Were we, Mr. Chairman, to ask the Autocrat of all the Russias, what he had to testify concerning the Government over which he presides, he would doubtless say it was the best on earth."

First, Campbell had a word about the majority report presented to the convention as the will of the Judiciary Committee: It "is not," he said, "to be regarded with all the authority ... commonly attached to the reports of Committees." He considered its passage secured by an adroit rouse, a neat trick of parliamentary maneuvering. The reformers were evidently strong on the Committee, and they had at first defeated one of the most important clauses of the report, that concerning the County Courts. But as a conservative member had been absent when the vote was taken, Marshall had later called for a reconsideration of the vote, carefully selecting a time when a friend of reform was absent. And thus, the report had been passed—by a mere majority of one. Therefore, Campbell thought careful consideration was due the substitute resolution that he had presented on October 24. Marshall's resolution provided that the County Courts be explicitly written into the new constitution, thus entrenching them in power forever as constitutional courts. Campbell's resolution proposed that they be included only under "such Inferior Courts" as the General Assembly "might from time to time ordain and establish," thus leaving their operation to the discretion of "future Legislative bodies."

This point clarified, he then turned to dissecting the body of intricate, extraordinary powers held by the County Courts and show, point by point, how they violated fundamental principles of republican government, the Bill of Rights, and even the state constitution itself. In later years, he was to write a surprisingly generous eulogy of John Marshall:

> There is none of the rulers of our nation, with whom
> I have a ... personal acquaintance, that I esteem more

highly than the venerable Chief Justice. For good sense, sound wisdom, uncorrupted integrity, profound knowledge of our institutions, and extensive acquaintance with all that pertains to his own office and duties, he has, in my judgment, no equal on this continent and no superior on the other.

Campbell himself, it was true, was establishing an entire religious program upon the insistence of liberty under law; anarchy, contempt for law, having no place in his well-ordered thought, he was in full accord with Locke's re-establishment of the Aristotelian formula, "Above all men is the law." Yet this would not soften, at Richmond, his opposition to Marshall's primacy of judicial over human rights or his attack on a County Court system which, he declared, made every county in the Commonwealth "necessarily subjected to the government of a few individuals by a legal investment." To the reform delegates, in general, its judiciary system was one of the most odious features of their state government. Not merely a matter of courts and judges, it involved the whole social and political organization of the state. The heart of the system being its rigid and self-perpetuating County Courts, Campbell warned that if all the functions enjoyed by the justices of these courts could be "safely lodged in the same hands, at the same time, then it must follow … that all the doctrines on which our political system is founded are erroneous and fallacious."

Did not, he asked, one of these fundamental doctrines declare that all power is derived from the people and magistrates must be amenable to them? Did another teach that no office of magistrate, legislator, or judge shall be hereditary? Yet, the justices of the peace were appointed by the governor for life, and vacancies, in practice, were filled only on recommendation of the remaining justices—for obvious reason that no man could hope to be elected to the General Assembly without approval of these justices, and the Legislature appointed the governor. So the dangerous circle was complete! Clearly, then, said Campbell, these tribunals are "not amenable to us, not *responsible* to us; because not created by us;" and the privilege of naming their successors tended to "make the magistracy *hereditary* in certain families," a practice Montesquieu had eloquently warned against since "corrupt men will appoint *corrupt successors.*" Furthermore, asked Campbell, did not the Bill of Rights provide that no persons "be taxed … without their own consent or that of their [elected] Representatives" and the state constitution itself assert that the Legislative, Executive, and Judicial departments of Government, in both powers and personnel, be completely "separate and distinct?" Yes, the County Court, at the local level, exercised all Legislative and Executive as well as Judicial authority. It fixed the county rate of taxation, thus giving rise, "in my opinion," said Campbell, to "as real a grievance … as was the complaint of this Commonwealth when a Colony, against the right [of taxation] usurped by the English Government." Also, it appointed civil officers and all military officials below the rank of brigadier general and, of course, generally saw that the posts of honor and profit went either to its own members or to their relatives. Such was the Court's widespread tentacles of power that the justices of the peace even, in effect, named the state's representatives to the lower House of Congress, and the Legislature dared not elect United States Senators whom they disapproved. Naturally, all other county officials were appointed by the governor only on their recommendation; and, since they served gratuitously as judges while the office of sheriff paid a salary, they were able— through an exception in the old constitution which allowed them to serve both as judges and as members of the Legislature—to attach the sheriffs' responsibilities to their own offices, a system obviously liable to the worst abuses. The sheriff's office was commonly passed on from one member of the Court to another. Far too often, once acquired, it was farmed out to deputies, the disgraceful practice of selling it at public auction unknown. Little wonder, Campbell reminded the convention, that Patrick Henry in 1788 had so roundly denounced "our state sheriffs, those unfeeling blood-suckers, [who] have under the watchful eyes of the Legislature, committed the most horrid and barbarous ravages upon our people." "But," added Campbell sarcastically, "we love a cheap magistracy, and the justices serve for nothing! It is true, they only divide among them, between 50 and 50,000 dollars per annum, in ... sheriffs' fees."

Despite all these abuses, he declared in closing: "I am not an enemy to the County Courts, but I wish to leave them ... subject to the wisdom of Legislation ... [and] not ... bind them irrevocably ... upon posterity by Constitutional provision. If they are so wise and useful, as gentlemen suppose," he shrewdly concluded, "they need not fear the Legislative ... control ... which can best adopt them to the ever-changing exigencies of society."

Nevertheless, his resolution could muster only twenty-two votes of approval. Still he did not quite surrender. If the clause in Marshall's resolution providing for "*the* County Courts" was changed to read "*a* County Court," he suggested, then it might be construed to "admit of [future] Legislative provision." Marshall thought if the change "tended to reconcile any gentleman to the resolution, it had better be adopted;" Randolph testified that he "wished to hear what good it would do;" and the debate passed back and forth for a time. Finally, Campbell's motion carried, 48–42, with Monroe, Madison, and Marshall all voting in the affirmative. Weeks later, the convention reversed its decision, denying even this minor concession to reform. And this was only an initial defeat. At one point, Campbell presented a resolution which actually provided that the justices of the peace be elected by the people. But the reformers, generally, were demanding nothing so drastic. They would be content if the self-perpetuating features of the County Courts be abolished. In the end, quite the reverse was provided. The old constitution left the governor technically free to accept or reject the recommendations of the justices in making his appointments; the new constitution specifically required him to accept their recommendations. Thus, shunting aside all republican protest and argument, the convention had greatly strengthened "the very foundation of Virginia's aristocratic political organization."

Drawing his regal robes of office about him, cloaked in the myth of Judicial infallibility, the Chief Justice had led his cohorts to the safe haven of an independent Judiciary, untroubled and untrammeled by fear of any intervention from the common people. Though by now they were getting a little used to defeat, it was a bitter blow to the reformers—and especially to the passionate democrat from Brooke who had dared, both in Committee and on the convention floor, to raise his protest against the majestic assumptions of John Marshall and his Judicial aristocracy.

For many days, far too many, busy with his two addresses on the right of suffrage and on judiciary reform and their attendant debates, Campbell did not find the time for his accustomed letters to Selina. The Friday after his judiciary address, on December fourth, he finally settled himself to the task of writing home, but still he had to be content with penning a brief note on the activities:

> I must ask a hundred pardons for my long silence—I am as much oppressed as in my thorniest days at home. I have always to do the work of two or three persons in every vocation—I have been preaching, debating politics, baptizing, and last night I married a fine young couple—So that I have to do a little of all sorts of business—I am tired out in Richmond—I do not know but may get leave of absence in a few days as we are not likely to do anything.

If so I will hasten over the mountains—But when or how I shall be at Liberty I can not with certainty say ... A son of Bishop Henley's is to accompany me home—and to stay with me 3 years...I do not know what I shall do with the hands I shall have but I can get plenty of them.

I can do more than inform you I am busy—and although you have my heart and thoughts every day and every night—yet the public have may hands and my tongue. Remember me most affectionately to all the children and to all enquiring friends relatives and neighbors—and be assured that I am ever and always yours in the flesh and in the Lord. You may expect a letter from me in a few days—

Your loving husband
A. Campbell

On December tenth, he redeemed his pledge. This time he again found space enough for a lover's words of warm affection—though he sought to lighten his tale of longing with a bit of teasing about the ladies of Richmond which may or may not have hit its mark in view of Selina's highly undeveloped sense of humor.

Impatient and anxious as he was for this return to his beloved Bethany, in the next few weeks, Campbell would be glad that other lesser questions which came before the convention were quickly settled.

Another of the minor questions brought before the convention held peculiar interest   for "the Reverend gentleman from Brooke." The resolution guaranteeing religious freedom, notwithstanding its stipulation that men's religious opinions should in no wise "affect their civil capacities," carried a proviso that no "minis-

ter of the Gospel, or Priest of any denomination ... be eligible to
either House of the General Assembly." John R. Cooke, perhaps
out of courtesy to his reverend colleague, moved that this proviso
be struck out of the resolution. In spite of any campaign quarrel he
and Campbell may have had, Doddridge supported Cooke's
motion. "He disapproved the election of ministers to a legislative
body as much as most men," he said, but, he added:

> ... he would not vote to prevent the people from mak-
> ing whom they would their delegate to their own Hall of
> Legislation. He considered the exclusion as at war with
> the principle of the whole resolution: which allowed men
> to promulgate their religious opinions free from all politi-
> cal consequences...

Randolph immediately arose to deliver an oration in disagree-
ment, which might have made Campbell extremely uncomfort-
able had he been less used to withstanding thrusts of sarcasm—
had he not been as young Hugh Blair Grigsby expressed it, "as
insensible to attack as if he were sheathed in the hide of a rhi-
noceros." For, after stating that there were conditions "that every
well-regulated mind belonging to the clerical profession ought of
itself to suggest" in favor of the proviso, Randolph continued:

> I have had the pleasure (I was about to say I have had
> the honor, but the term would be misplaced) to be
> acquainted with many of them; with men ... clothed with
> that humility which is the Alpha and Omega of the
> Christian character ... and I never knew one of them who
> dared trust himself in such a situation ... The task of leg-
> islation is at war with the duties of the pastor ... Sir, no
> man can busy himself in electioneering (and in these
> times who can be elected without it?) ... can mingle in

Legislative cabals; I say no man can touch pitch without being defiled.

Randolph was making use of an old familiar ruse, whereby, as one historian phrased it: "The real purpose of preventing the church from gaining even a semblance of political power is veiled in solitude that ministers may not be diverted from the great duties of their calling." Randolph also might, if he had thought it necessary have called upon historical precedent, for the Virginia convention of 1775 had refused to admit clergymen to its councils, and the Constitution of '76 had disqualified them. There was, it was true, excellent reason for fearing the power of the clergy at the time of the Revolution and a few years thereafter. Other states had felt like Virginia—that stringent measures must be taken to prevent the new republic from falling under an Old World ecclesiastical tyranny.

Even Thomas Jefferson, in another draft for the Virginia constitution that he had drawn up in 1783, had continued the disqualification clause. But by 1800, Jefferson had been convinced that the clergy had thoroughly "absorbed democratic principles" and, hence, ought no longer be denied the right to represent their districts in legislative assemblies. "The clergy here," he wrote "seems to have relinquished all pretensions to privilege, and to stand on a footing with lawyers, doctors, etc. They ought, therefore, to possess the same right." With the provision now being argued on the floor of the convention of '29, the one minister in the body saw fit to stay out of the discussion. Only once—when Governor Giles said that ministers already had two privileges, preaching and exemption from military service, and that they might have political privileges only if these other two were removed—did Campbell break silence to remark pointedly that "these objections applied with equal force to justices of the peace, and nobody contended for excluding them." But the convention of '29 seemed bound to illustrate again "the persistency of a constitutional fetish." It refused to strike out the disqualifying proviso by the overwhelming majority of eighty-one to fourteen.

One of the fourteen delegates voting for the admission of clergymen to the General Assembly was James Madison. Some time later Campbell had more concrete evidence that this venerable statesman had not been unfavorably impressed by the role, both religious and political, which "the Reverend gentleman from Brooke" played in Richmond. Campbell, of course, had by no means been neglecting his religious calling while pursuing his political duties. Every Sunday found him in the pulpit of the First Baptist Church preaching to audiences that often included members of the convention, of whom none was more regular in attendance than James Madison. After the convention was adjourned and Madison had started home to Montpelier, he stopped over the first night with his cousin, Col. Edmund Pendleton. Pendleton was the presiding justice of the County Court of Louisa and grand-nephew of the Edmund Pendleton of colonial and revolutionary fame, who, incidentally, even though a cripple unable to rise from his chair, had been unanimously chosen president of the Virginia Constitutional Convention of 1788. Col. Pendleton was an admirer of Alexander Campbell, and the next morning as he walked the porch with his guest, Madison, he asked him what kind of a figure Campbell had made at Richmond. Madison commented favorably on Campbell's ability in the convention and then added: "But it is as a theologian that Mr. Campbell must be known. It was my pleasure to hear him very often as a preacher of the gospel, and I regard him as the ablest and most original expounder of the Scriptures I have ever heard." Madison may have voted against the clause disqualifying ministers from the Assembly partly as an act of courtesy toward the clerical delegate in the present convention whose ability he had come to respect. At any rate, with so much of the conservatives' attack being obviously leveled at him, Campbell doubtless found very gratifying this action of the elder statesman whom, ever since arriving as an immigrant boy from Ireland, he had so much admired.

At least one observer of these proceedings believed that the presence of "the Reverend gentleman from Brooke" accelerated the dispatch with which the convention agreed to deny ministers a seat in future political assemblies in Virginia. In his article in *The Southern Literary Messenger,* John P. Little, who obviously disapproved of any clergyman—and of Alexander Campbell in particular—taking part in legislative councils, remarked:

> He was evidently out of place in this body, and as he stood very much alone, as well in his religious opinions as in his political views, it might be said to him more truly than to a wiser man, who meddled not in politics, 'Thou art beside thyself.' The clause in the old Constitution prohibiting clergymen from serving in the Legislature was continued in the present one after debate, and was evidently meant to exclude one who possessed such radical notions and was so anxious to enforce them.

If Mr. Little had but realized it, there was an ironic jest in his comment. Even the most rabid conservative would not have voted to debar all ministers just to make sure that one particular preacher from the Buffaloe would never again bother their legislative councils with his radical notions. The actions of this preacher in their midst could not possibly have resurrected any old fears that the onus of ecclesiastical tyranny was rearing its head in republican Virginia. For of the ninety-six gentlemen gathered in the convention hall at Richmond, "the Reverend gentleman from Brooke" hated and had fought every aspiration of the church toward worldly, political power. Having grown to manhood in a country where an authorized state religion dealt persecution and suppression to every nonconformist, he could know, better than any person born to the liberty of the new republic, how great the evils were when a religious establishment gained control of government. Alexander Campbell had learned his love of tolerance and freedom in a hard school, and he would not see these priceless heritages depart from Virginia.

In fact, the "Reverend gentleman from Brooke" presented a resolution of his own which proved that he was ready to go further than any delegate there in restraining the power of the churches. One which was, doubtless, in part, an outgrowth of his efforts through *The Christian Baptist* to persuade the state legislature of Kentucky and Ohio that the incorporation of sectarian colleges was contrary to the Bill of Rights:

> Resolved that no incorporation for any ecclesiastical or religious purpose, shall ever be granted, or have validity in this Commonwealth.

Even Marshall and other conservatives thought this resolution went too far; it would deprive churches of the right of securing property and, anyway, was needless from the natural aversion of every American legislature to any act tending to build up religious establishments. It was moved indefinitely to postpone the amendment.

Another resolution presented by Campbell was to be dismissed even more summarily. Though he had yielded to expedient advice on the subject of slavery, he did not give up without a fight on the floor that, second of the two projects of which he had written Colonel Morgan before the convention, the question of common school education for all the children of the commonwealth.

Other delegates, too, had come to Richmond with high hopes that some provision for education, which had been omitted entirely from the Constitution of 1776, might be written into the new Constitution; and the subject surfaced early in the convention. Charles Fenton Mercer, as might have been expected from his long years of service in the battle for free public schools on the floor of the General Assembly, had fired an opening gun in his speech on representation and taxation:

> ... We are told we wish to acquire the power of educating the poor man's child at the expense of the rich. I confess I am ashamed to hear such suggestions at this day and in the capitol of Virginia .... Since 1819 we have applied $45,000 a year to the education of the poor and 10,000 children are imperfectly taught for about six months in the year by its application. Except in Brooke County, where about five dollars a year suffices for the education of poor children, it takes about eight dollars a head; while in Connecticut and Scotland the cost is one fourth of that. Will the rich anywhere complain of a system which, while the children of the poor are instructed, enables them to educate their own at a cost so reduced?

Alexander Campbell was not far behind him. Repeating a remark he had made previously in *The Christian Baptist*, that "in this country ... the science of government is better understood than in any other upon earth," he left no doubt in the minds of his colleagues that he believed his adopted country should look forward to a still more glorious destiny; but he also wished to make it clear that, like Thomas Jefferson, he was convinced this destiny could be secured only by an intelligently educated, as well as moral, electorate. In his speech on suffrage, he had digressed long enough to remark:

> ... it is quite practical now to give birth to a system of education which in twenty years from this day would ren-

der it impossible for a child to be born in this Commonwealth and to live to manhood, without receiving a good education ...

And, Campbell made it plain, if the present convention would do its duty, it could evolve "such a splendid scheme" as would "carry down, for a thousand generations, the grateful admiration of our services."

But the conservative delegation had immediately made it clear that it was not the admiration of future generations it was seeking, but the solution of present needs; and among those needs it did not include free public schools. Randolph, for example, had acidly remarked that there was no necessity for free schools, as only the worthless would ever neglect education of their children anyway. He painted a graphic and pitiful picture of the industrious man slaving from dawn to dark to pay taxes for the education of the children of his good-for-nothing neighbor who could, therefore, carouse in drunkenness with the excuse that: "The government has given us a premium for our idleness, and I now spend in liquor, what I should otherwise be obliged to save to pay for their schooling." Other conservatives had expressed their fear that the poor of the West were to be educated at the expense of the East until Chapman Johnson was goaded into asking, in exasperation, "What warrant is there for supposing that the education of the poor from the public purse, is a Western interest; that their poor are more numerous or less educated than yours?" And Campbell's friend, Colonel Morgan from Monongalia, tartly pointed out that some of the opposing Eastern gentlemen had been educated at William and Mary, an institution supported in part by taxes on "the buck-skins, and the pelts of the beavers and otters taken by the Western hunters, through the medium of the surveyors' fees."

Reluctantly but finally, Campbell and the other advocates of free schools had to admit defeat on their plan to gain constitutional sanction for even a temporary tax to establish a state system of education on a firm basis. The antagonism of the conservatives, inspired by their fear of the leveling tendencies of the West, were too deeply engrained to be dislodged. Once again the republican immigrant from North Ireland saw it proved that, though the political ideals of democracy might be accepted in theory, aristocratic notions and institutions were still all too often retained in practice. Nor, Campbell would be fair enough to realize, was this the peculiar fault of Virginia, for it was human nature to place first the safeguarding of economic interests "whether these were slavery in the South or infant industries in the North; and, especially in America where the people were faced with the daily exigencies attendant on carving a new nation from a vast continent," there was "among the rank and file … a national faith in training for immediate needs and a corresponding reluctance to accept the more remote values of a 'literary' education." But more, perhaps, than the Ireland-bred delegate from Brooke County could realize, there lay at the root of the matter the American dread of taxation and the tyranny it could exercise. For revolt against taxation had been too large a factor in bringing on the War of Independence to make popular the idea of public support for a novel institution like free public schools, which, neither in Virginia nor anywhere else, had yet been fully appraised. In all the states along the seaboard, a great many of the citizens were inclined to think that "to be taxed for the support of one's neighbor's children without one's individual consent" was "an abridgment of the rights of democracy."

When the realization that no adequate system of state education could be passed through the convention, the other advocates of free schools were ready to dismiss the question altogether; but not so for the pugnacious "Reverend gentleman from Brooke." As he had been thwarted in even introducing the subject of the emancipation of slaves, it was doubly hard for him to admit rout on the other point that he considered so vital to the preservation of a republican government. Anyway, retreat never came easy for the master of Bethany. So, when all else had failed, he proposed a resolution in very general terms that he thought the convention could not fail to endorse and have inserted in the revised constitution; it read:

> Whereas, republican institutions and the blessings of free Government originated in, and must always depend upon, the intelligence, virtue, and patriotism of the community; and whereas neither intelligence nor virtue can be maintained or promoted in any community without education, it shall always be the duty of the Legislature of this Commonwealth to patronize and encourage such a system of education, or such common schools and seminaries of learning, as will in wisdom be deemed to be most conducive to secure to the youth of this Commonwealth, such an education as may most promote the public good.

This resolution was ordered to be printed. But several days later when Campbell again presented it, "the question being put on considering the resolution, the House refused to consider it." The Constitution of 1829 would carry no recognition of the duty of a state to encourage the education of its citizens. Campbell might have found some small grain of comfort in his defeat had he known that nearly a century later an historian of *The Free School Idea in Virginia* would write that Campbell had fought a good fight and would write of him" "The great common school champion of the western delegates in the Constitutional convention was Alexander Campbell .... He proposed the only resolution made during the convention, to give constitutional sanction to public education."

✠

Meanwhile, the weary weeks were passing. Fall gave way to winter. The Christmas season came. Fourteen long weeks Campbell had been absent from his beloved Bethany and Selina. Yet, there was no chance that he might be home to sit at the head of his table and carve the Christmas goose for his household. On December twenty-third, he wrote his "dear sister and wife" a long letter, and this time, there was no humor or teasing playfulness as he filled the pages with his weariness and homesickness and with tender expression of his desire and understanding that must have increased tenfold Selina's longing for her husband at her side:

> ... I am worn out with fatigue in sitting—now going to meeting as it were and sitting in a large assembly 80 days. I have not been a free man since I came here. It puts me in mind of going to school. I am under tutors and governors and I do not like it—I need not tell you that I am homesick ... I have however done all I could consistently with duty and circumstances to promote the welfare of my country and my fellowman—But our success has not been equal to our exertions. In the good cause I have been more successful and I hope that my journey here will be long remembered ...

Saturday the twenty-sixth found the gentlemen back in their seats. No decision had yet been reached on that major question with which they had begun their discussions almost three months before—the basis of representation. All by now being weary and anxious for home, they started to talk various means of compromise.

Compromise meant mutual concession, and in Campbell's opinion, all the concession was being demanded of the reformers. Since the West, in a fair fight and without any concession from the East, had defeated Green's amendment and so carried the white basis of representation for the House of Delegates, Campbell saw no reason why the West should concede to the East the basis of federal numbers for the Senate. To yield the white basis of representation in either House would place the reformers, he declared, "in awkward circumstances, because we would be called upon to compromise a principle, which, as republicans we can never, without apostasy from our faith, and a enunciation of our principles, yield." Now, "in the true spirit of conciliation and compromise," Campbell offered a proposal:

> The whole States shall be divided into one hundred Delegate districts, and twenty-four Senatorial districts, after each and every census, according to the white population; so that the House of Delegates and the Senate shall never exceed together, more than one-hundred-and-twenty-four members.

The scheme included four other resolutions providing for what Campbell considered an equitable distribution of taxation, revenue, and expenditure for internal improvements.

Campbell had barely seated himself when John Marshall was on his feet with a sharp retort for the man who could make so radical a proposal:

> One gentleman differs in the whole outline of his plan. He seems to imagine that we claim nothing of republican principles, when we claim a representation for property. Permit me to set him right. I do not say that I can hope to satisfy him or others, who say that Republican Government depends on adopting the naked principle of numbers, that we are right; but I think I can satisfy him that we do entertain a different opinion. I think the soundest principles of republicanism do sanction some relation between taxation and representation.

Marshall also would set the delegate from Brooke County straight on another point. In his remarks, Campbell had assumed

that the defeat of Judge Green's amendment had already determined the basis representation for the House of Delegates. Now,
Marshall assured the convention: "The gentleman assumed too
much when he said that question was settled."

And so it proved. Though Campbell was insisting on the
white basis for both Houses of the Legislature, a majority of the
reformers were not so radical as he. What they most desired was
the white basis for the House of Delegates; to secure this, they
were willing to yield the federal numbers in the Senate, with a
reapportionment on that basis every ten years. Yet, the conservatives were by no means ready to accept even this compromise.
Randolph, with a temper unyielding as Campbell's, expressed
their views:

> I will accept no Constitution that has the monstrous,
> the tyrannous, the preposterous, and abominable princi-
> ple, that *numbers* alone are to be regarded as a fit basis of
> Representation in the House of Delegates. You may com-
> promise until the Day of Judgment ... give us any form of
> the Senate you like with a Governor elected by that
> Senate: while this principle is retained, I will reject the
> whole — I nail my colours to the mast.

Randolph retorted that "From the days of Aristotle till that
day, no such Government had ever been heard of — it was a monster.

The drama in Richmond, it seemed, was rapidly moving to a
tragic climax; and to many, the battle here presaged a greater and
more general disaster. Leigh declared that the question of representation, "if pressed to its extremes, threatened to divide the
state." Morris professed to believe that adoption of the white basis
made inevitable an interference between masters and slaves that
"would cause a sword to be unsheathed which would be red with
blood before it found the scabbard." If Virginia were dismem-

bered, Monroe thought the dismemberment of both Georgia and South Carolina would follow; and Governor Giles said, "The forceful separation of Virginia must and will lead to the separation of the United States, come when it will." The West was even more emphatic. The reformers considered retiring from the convention in a body to make a constitution of their own, and they were apprised that their constituents at Wheeling had held a mass meeting to adopt resolutions calling upon them to secede in case the white basis was rejected.

In the end, a plan presented by Gordon of Albermarle County was the substance of that agreed upon; and its adoption sounded the death-knell to the white basis of representation. Though he was presumably a white-basis man, Gordon's plan ignored the question entirely and simply attempted an equitable distribution of representation according to counties. The West had lost its cause. And chiefly because of "the disloyalty, approaching treason, which manifested itself in the ranks of the reformers." The large and populous counties of the Piedmont foothills and the Valley led in the movement for reform, and Gordon's scheme was very attractive to their delegates; for, while few counties in other sections received more than one member to the House of Delegates by his plan, it gave most of the counties in these sections two representatives, and Shenandoah, Frederick, and Loudoun counties received three each. Since these counties profited so largely by this compromise, Cooke of Frederick County and Henderson of Loudoun County secretly agreed to support Gordon's plan—and then went into caucus with their colleagues favorable to the white basis. By this ruse, Cook, on the nomination of Henderson, was the man chosen by the reformers to represent the white basis in conferences with the conservatives, when, obviously, only someone like Campbell or Doddridge would have pushed their claims.

So, the Trans-Allegheny, deserted by its allies in the Valley and the Piedmont foothills, had been delivered into the hands of the opposition. Not only had it lost the white basis fight, but

Gordon's plan contained no principle for a reapportionment of representation in the future—and the West had come to Richmond to fight for principles. As the reformers denounced the plan as "a mere makeshift, a temporary expedient," which could not allay sectional strife and would merely lead to the calling of a second convention, the delegates turned their attention to this question of the adoption of some constitutional basis for future reapportionment. Campbell made a motion "that when the amended Constitution shall be submitted to the people the following question, by way of amendment shall be propounded to the people: Shall the basis of Representation in both branches of the Legislature be white population exclusively?" Such a radical proposal, of course was promptly defeated, thirty-nine voting in favor.

Various other schemes were suggested, but the delegate from Brooke took no further part in the discussions until January 8. John R. Cooke presented a plan for reapportionment, which, it seemed to Campbell, would retain the relative inequalities between the sections of the state unchangeable and forever. Then, with his ire over Cook's recent desertion of the reformers' cause doubtless lending acid to his tone, Campbell rose to dissent—declaring:

> ... that if he had been put to the torture to devise a mode of perpetuating the injustice done by the present scheme of apportionment between the Eastern and Western portions of the state, he could not have invented a more effectual one than that which had been proposed by the gentleman from Frederick [Mr. Cooke].

There was no doubt that the uncompromising radicalism of the Reverend gentleman from the Trans-Allegheny had long been a thorn in the flesh of the gentleman from the Tidewater; and there was a story that on one occasion John Randolph, angered at Campbell's recalcitrance, shook his long, bony finger in

Campbell's direction and cried, "That man is never satisfied! God Almighty could not satisfy him with the Bible which He gave, and Mr. Campbell went and wrote a Bible of his own." Mr. Stansbury did not report the incident in his *Debates and Proceedings;* but the remark sounds characteristic of Randolph, and there was obviously no man in the assembly more likely to irritate the wit of Roanoke than the iconoclast of Bethany.

But all the day's bickering and strife—Cooke's disaffection and Stanard's denunciation—were banished from thought when, on January eighth, Campbell sought out a quiet hour alone to write Selina another letter, the last, he hoped, from Richmond. He allowed himself a word or two of complaint on his long enslavement to political duty:

> I am in Richmond and cannot get away for a few days yet ...I feel myself in bondage and shall hail it [adjournment] jubilee when it arrives ... I had no idea of being confined half the time on this unknown business.

And he informed Selina briefly of some financial matters, anxious always that she learn and share knowledge of his affairs. But, as usual, he filled the pages chiefly with those warm pledges of love and longing which he knew would most delight the eyes and heart of his young wife:

> I have received no news from you for a long time—I suppose you have expected me to be home by this time ... But my dear, I hope it will be the longest separation which during our pilgrimage we shall ever have—I want the solace of your company very much and of my dear children ...

With the opening of next morning's convention session, thoughts of love and Bethany once more had to be sternly put aside while he returned to the fight over that dull but important question of providing for future reapportionment of representation. In the end, the plan adopted—over the biter protest of the reformers—was one proposed by James Madison, providing that a two-thirds majority of each House of the General Assembly should have authority to make the reapportionment at intervals of not less than ten years. Campbell proposed an amendment which would give the General Assembly authority to apportion representation "so that the number of Delegates in each of the four grand districts, shall bear the same proportion to the whole population of each district, as shall be ascertained by the next census"—a plan which would give a county more representation as it increased in size. But, though Campbell asked the full attention of the House for this plan, and another delegate declared it "the only proposition which had yet been brought forward, which proposed an equal and just rule for future apportionment." This amendment was defeated fifty-three to forty-five, and Madison's plan was accepted. Campbell's last proposal in the convention was on a minor matter—and likewise unsuccessful: "Mr. Campbell of Brooke now suggested various grammatical amendments in the draught of the Constitution—all of which were successively rejected."

With the main issues between the East and West thus unsatisfactorily settled and with no provision made for future amendments—the question was put, on January 14, "Shall this constitution pass?" The vote was: aye, fifty-five; no, forty—a majority that would have been reduced by one if Doddridge had not been "seriously indisposed" and confined to bed. The only member from west of the Blue Ridge who voted aye was Cooke of Frederick County.

After fourteen weeks, Campbell was free to go home to Bethany. He felt that he had made many friends in Richmond,

Winter scene at the Campbell mansion, much as it would have appeared upon his return from the Virginia Constitutional Convention in the winter months early in 1830.

and some of his most interesting evenings had been spent in conversation with the ruler of the Jewish synagogue, Rabbi Judah. Many, also, had come from a distance to hear, and see, and talk with him on religious subjects. One young man, a physician, who had become converted by reading *The Christian Baptist*, traveled more than a hundred miles to the capital city to be baptized by him. But Campbell was anxious to be at Bethany, both to see his family and to be again at his editor's desk, for he had found time at Richmond to prepare only one article for *The Christian Baptist*—some thoughts on "The Happy New Year" written on December 14 for the January issue. On the return journey, it seems, he stopped to fill only one appointment, at Upper Essex meeting-house, where he spent a very pleasant evening at the house of a friend, talking with the venerable Bishop Semple, who had come to hear him preach, hoping, perhaps, that the young man of whose talents he had thought so highly had grown more orthodox with the passing years. Alexander reached home on the first of February, having been absent since the twenty-second of September.

Immediately he plunged into his editorial work. Correspondence had piled high on his desk; and then, too, for the next few months he had on his hands the publication of two magazines at one and the same time. He had promised to issue the first number of *The Millennial Harbinger* on January 1st, 1830. Already it was February, and his new paper was not on the press. Also, to round out the seventh volume of *The Christian Baptist*, he would have to continue its publication through the July 1830 issue. Hence, for six issues the two magazines would overlap. To speed up the process, Campbell promised the readers of *The Christian Baptist* that "there will appear two numbers at a time until the seventh volume is closed."

Barring one exception, Alexander was quite satisfied by the manner in which his father Thomas had conducted the paper during his stay in Richmond: "With the selections made for this work during my absence," he remarked in the February issue, "I am generally well pleased. One item, the POSTSCRIPT to the letter from Ireland, I would have suppressed had I seen it before it was printed. I saw it for the first time in Fredricksburg, on my way home—and regretted to see it." The letter referred to was the one written to him by William Tener of Londonderry on November 5, and which had arrived when he was at the convention. The postscript read:

P.S.—I am well pleased with your New Testament, and generally with your Preface and Appendix. We are very anxious to see your Debate with Mr. Owen. He has got a great hackling in the Irish prints. All parties in Ireland rejoice in your triumph over him, and that the *Emerald Isle* produced a Sampson to combat the great Goliath of Deism and Atheism. Truly, you are an honor to the country which gave you birth. Your fame has spread over all Ireland, and I hope your Debate with Mr. Owen will be the means of extending the circulation of your other works here.

The editor of the *Northern Whig,* of Belfast, says concerning *The Christian Baptist,* 'It might do good, provided it were written with less bitterness. It is a mixture of pepper, salt, and vinegar, served up with a dish of genuine Irish wit—but a *great deal of instruction.*'

Another friend whom in the pressing affairs he had neglected writing for several months was Philip Fall of Nashville. So, on February 25th, about three weeks after he returned to Bethany, Alexander wrote Fall a long letter giving him the religious news of his sojourn in Richmond. It read, in part:

> ... Since my debate with Mr. Owen, it has been a constant race without a breathing spell. While in Richmond it was politics by day and religion by night. I preached, lectured, talked, almost every day—and for three weeks at one time I was only one evening in my own room and could not find time to write a letter home. If I did not much good to my country as one of her representatives, I hope I did some good in the Kingdom ... We have many warm friends in that section and I think the foundation is laid for a thorough reformation. I found the people inquisitive and pretty open to conviction. They offered to build me a large meeting house in Richmond and bantered me much to remain thither. But I cannot yet be persuaded to leave the western hills. I need a

Patmos; for if in a city I could not find time to write ...
The Debate has not been well managed and I fear that
much loss will ensue to me and disappointment to the
public. But so many irons in the fire some of them must
burn. My health is just middling .... I have to write or
rather scrawl out some 20 pages per day such as these
besides my other attentions .... You have got two of my
daughters in your vicinity.

I had much difficulty in writing the 1st No. of the
Harbinger as I was out of practice, but my hand will come
in by the time I get through the second.

Campbell's failure to accomplish any real good for the people
at the convention had disillusioned him with politics, and in
March he wrote a rather plaintive letter to Col. Morgan of
Morgantown:

Bethany Va. March 12, 1830
My Dear Friend:
I thankfully recd your package from Richmond with
all the documents which you had the goodness to forward
me.... I have been exceedingly pressed for time—having
found my business quite in arrears—Since my return the
citizens of Wheeling and Wellsburg and the country generally have requested me to oppose the Amended
Constitution—I have had to furnish an essay per week for
the last four, they published in the Wellsburg and
Wheeling papers—
At all events the West would, as they ought, universally
vote to reject it....
I am conscious that many are infatuated with the
charms of political life—They never had any for me and

never will have any—I view mankind in a higher relation than as a subject of *taxation*, or a defender of the Country on the Muster-roll—I view him as one who may be *immortal*, a citizen of heaven and a king and priest to God—Men are in pursuit of shadows...I have more pleasure in thinking one hour upon man's eternal destinies or in reading one section in the Oracles of God than in all the splendid schemes of earthly ambition, and political grandeur.

Please give my kind respects to your brother who proclaims the gospel. Tell him that is lot in this life, if he acquit himself well is, in my judgment much more honorable than thine, more happy and a thousand times more useful—In the mean time excuse my great haste and accept the assurance of my personal friendship.

In all benevolence
A. Campbell

Can you obtain a few subscribers for the Mil. Harbinger?

In the campaign preceding the convention, Campbell and Philip Doddridge had been at odds, but now they were fighting side by side; for Doddridge agreed with "the Reverend gentleman from Brooke" that the last hope of the West lay in defeating the ratification of the constitution. Doddridge, though in Washington serving the northwestern part of the state as a member of Congress, wrote a circular letter, which was destined to become famous in the sectional quarrel. It gave his version of how the West had been betrayed into the hands of the seaboard aristocracy by Cooke and Henderson and did not even spare the venerable Madison a share of the blame. Narrating the part the Trans-Allegheny had played in having the convention called, he concluded that the price she must now pay "is unconditional surrender of ourselves and our posterity to political vassalage, under the yoke of that Eastern Oligarchy which we have so long been endeavoring to shake off."

This letter, added to the fact that he was the only delegate from west of the Blue Ridge who had voted in favor of the constitution at Richmond, was giving Cooke of Frederick County quite a bit of explaining to do to his home district, and he wrote a series of letters justifying his position. Evidently he had discovered that the stand taken by Alexander Campbell was the one which the western citizens found to their liking, for in his "Fourth Letter to His Constituents," the "gentleman from Frederick" seemed anxious to point out that he had given his vote at least once in the convention to a proposal of "the Reverend gentleman from Brooke."

Judging from the articles in the *Richmond Enquirer*, the brunt of this campaign, if indeed not all of it, was being borne by Campbell and Doddridge. In one of its first notices of the fight over ratification, the *Enquirer* said, "we infer … not only from the language of Messrs. Campbell and Doddridge, from the resolutions of Ohio and Wythe, from the tone of some of the Western papers, but from the private information which we have received," that the opponents of ratification, "actuated as many of them are, by the best motives, will make a strong effort to discard this Constitution." The vote on ratification of the constitution was taken sometime in April. Campbell, of course, was present at the polls in Brooke County, and, according to Robert Richardson, "by request of the citizens, [he] gave a brief exposition of its main features." This brief address produced a marked effect. When the final tabulations were in, the hopes of the western democrats—and the fears of the *Richmond Enquirer* and the seaboard conservatives—were not realized. The people of Virginia ratified the new constitution by a ten thousand majority, though only two of the twenty-six counties in the Trans-Allegheny returned a majority, and most of them gave insignificant minorities, for ratification.

Campbell, disappointed and disgusted though he was with the results, had especial reason to be proud of the action of his own county. For alone of all the counties in Virginia, Brooke cast not one single vote in favor of ratification of the new Constitution. One observer at the convention may have considered the Bethany editor "too much a citizen of the world to be a perfectly safe counselor for Virginia." The very Constitution he had helped revise may have proved that he, as a minister, could never sit in the legislative halls of his state. But, both for his attitude and his efforts on behalf of the Western cause, the "Reverend gentleman from Brooke," stood justified in the eyes of his constituents.

The duty accomplished, Alexander Campbell turned his eyes resolutely and with relief toward the work at Bethany. Having discovered no "charms" in political life, he would henceforth tend the plants of liberty and toleration by cultivating his own garden in the Kingdom of the Lord.

INDEX

ALEXANDER CAMPBELL

VOLUME TWO

text set in 11 / 15 Electra

title set in Castellar and Bernhard Tango

book and jacket design by

Barbara M. Whitehead